PERCY SHELLEY FOR OUR TIMES

Two centuries after Percy Shelley's death, his writings continue to resonate in remarkable ways. Shelley addressed climate change, women's liberation, nonbinary gender, and political protest, while speaking to Indigenous, queer/trans, disabled, displaced, and working-class communities. He still inspires artists and social justice movements around the world today. Yet *Percy Shelley for Our Times* reveals an even more farsighted writer, one whose poetic methodology went beyond the didactic powers of prophetic art. Not historicist, presentist, or transhistorical, Shelley "for our times" conceives worlds outside himself, his poetry, and his era, envisioning how audiences connect and collaborate across space and time. This collection revitalizes a writer once considered an adolescent of idealist protest, showing how his interwoven poetics of relationality continually revisits the meaning of community and the contemporary. This title is part of the Flip it Open programme and may also be available Open Access. Check our website Cambridge Core for details.

OMAR F. MIRANDA is Associate Professor of English and Comparative Literature at the University of San Francisco. He is the editor and author of several scholarly works on eighteenth- and nineteenth-century literatures. His article "The Global Romantic Lyric" (*The Wordsworth Circle*, 2021) won the Bigger 6 Article of the Year award (2021). He is currently Vice President of the Keats-Shelley Association of America and is on The Byron Society of America's board of directors.

KATE SINGER is Mary Lyon Professor of Humanities at Mount Holyoke College. She is the author of *Romantic Vacancy: The Poetics of Gender, Affect, and Radical Speculation* (State University of New York Press, 2019); coeditor, with Ashley Cross and Suzanne L. Barnett, of *Material Transgressions: Beyond Romantic Bodies, Genders, Things* (Liverpool University Press, 2020); and founding coeditor of the Keats Letters Project (https://keatslettersproject.com/). She currently serves as President of the Keats-Shelley Association of America.

"A fresh, spirited collection that roundly demonstrates the contemporaneity and diversity of 'Shelley' – not by asserting that the master Poet contains multitudes, but by centering the unforeseen readers and writers who did, still, and will bend his restless verses to unforeseeable ends. 'Indianized,' disabled, unsexed, bewitched, rewilded, exiled, and intra-active, the Shelleyan corpus emerges anew, 'for our times,' even as the volume's many voices never cease to ask for whom it remains 'a book sealed.'"

Amanda Jo Goldstein, Associate Professor of English,
University of California, Berkeley

"This timely collection offers readers a Shelley who resists in both form and philosophy any easy political assignations, provoking instead a reimagining of our own assumptions about what Romantic poetry, and its criticism, can do in the world."

Jonathan Mulrooney, Professor of English,
College of the Holy Cross

"This uniformly stimulating collection of essays, expertly curated by Omar F. Miranda and Kate Singer, offers a rigorous assessment of Percy Shelley's work and influence 200 years after the first posthumous edition of his poems was published. Brave, self-aware, and critically engaged, the contributors address the spectrum of Shelley's writings, reflecting richly and refreshingly on how their complexity may be read today."

Michael Rossington, Professor of Romantic Literature,
Newcastle University, UK

"This illuminating volume takes up the question of what Shelley is, not 'to' us, but, more dynamically, 'for' us. How might Shelley's relational poetics provide us with methods and strategies for engaging the challenges of our own historical moment? The path-breaking, wide-ranging essays included here tease out the ways in which Shelley's work – especially, its limning of alternative modes of bodily and collective being – can propel, direct, and respond to our own efforts to think through the crises of 'our times.'"

Karen Swann, Professor of English, Emerita,
Williams College

PERCY SHELLEY FOR OUR TIMES

EDITED BY

OMAR F. MIRANDA
University of San Francisco

KATE SINGER
Mount Holyoke College

Shaftesbury Road, Cambridge CB2 8EA, United Kingdom

One Liberty Plaza, 20th Floor, New York, NY 10006, USA

477 Williamstown Road, Port Melbourne, VIC 3207, Australia

314–321, 3rd Floor, Plot 3, Splendor Forum, Jasola District Centre, New Delhi – 110025, India

103 Penang Road, #05–06/07, Visioncrest Commercial, Singapore 238467

Cambridge University Press is part of Cambridge University Press & Assessment, a department of the University of Cambridge.

We share the University's mission to contribute to society through the pursuit of education, learning and research at the highest international levels of excellence.

www.cambridge.org
Information on this title: www.cambridge.org/9781009206495

DOI: 10.1017/9781009206549

© Cambridge University Press & Assessment 2024

This work is in copyright. It is subject to statutory exceptions and to the provisions of relevant licensing agreements; with the exception of the Creative Commons version the link for which is provided below, no reproduction of any part of this work may take place without the written permission of Cambridge University Press.

An online version of this work is published at http://dx.doi.org/10.1017/9781009206549 under a Creative Commons Open Access license CC-BY-NC-ND 4.0 which permits re-use, distribution and reproduction in any medium for non-commercial purposes providing appropriate credit to the original work is given. You may not distribute derivative works without permission. To view this license, visit https://creativecommons.org/licenses/by-nc-nd/4.0

All versions of this work may contain content reproduced under license from third parties. Permission to reproduce this third-party content must be obtained from these third-parties directly. When citing this work, please include a reference to the
DOI: 10.1017/9781009206549

First published 2024
First paperback edition 2026

A catalogue record for this publication is available from the British Library

Library of Congress Cataloging-in-Publication data
NAMES: Miranda, Omar F., editor. | Singer, Kate, 1977– editor.
TITLE: Percy Shelley for our times / edited by Omar F. Miranda, Kate Singer.
DESCRIPTION: Cambridge ; New York, NY : Cambridge University Press, 2024.|
Includes bibliographical references and index.
IDENTIFIERS: LCCN 2023041836 (print) | LCCN 2023041837 (ebook) |
ISBN 9781009206532 (hardback) | ISBN 9781009206549 (ebook)
SUBJECTS: LCSH: Shelley, Percy Bysshe, 1792–1822 – Criticism and interpretation. |
Shelley, Percy Bysshe, 1792–1822 – Influences.
CLASSIFICATION: LCC PR5438 .P4355 2024 (print) | LCC PR5438 (ebook) |
DDC 821/.7–dc23/eng/20231122
LC record available at https://lccn.loc.gov/2023041836
LC ebook record available at https://lccn.loc.gov/2023041837

ISBN   978-1-009-20653-2   Hardback
ISBN   978-1-009-20649-5   Paperback

Cambridge University Press & Assessment has no responsibility for the persistence or accuracy of URLs for external or third-party internet websites referred to in this publication and does not guarantee that any content on such websites is, or will remain, accurate or appropriate.

Contents

Notes on Contributors	*page* vii
Acknowledgments	xii
List of Abbreviations	xiv

	Introduction: Percy Shelley's Involving Poetics of Relationality Omar F. Miranda and Kate Singer	1
1	Shelley, Treaty-Making, and Indigenous Poetry Nikki Hessell	23
2	Waiting for the Revolution: Age, Debility, and Disability in *The Triumph of Life* Fuson Wang	43
3	"A Chamæleonic Race": Shelley and the Discourses of Slavery Mathelinda Nabugodi	63
4	Dream Defenders and the Inside Songs Julie A. Carlson	85
5	Radical Suffering: Shelley's Legacy in Nonviolent Revolution James Chandler	108
6	Loathsome Sympathy: Shelley's *The Cenci* and the Problem of Empathy Alan Richardson	133
7	Hopeless Romanticism Gerard Cohen-Vrignaud	156
8	Percy Shelley's Sad Exile Omar F. Miranda	176

9	Shelley in the Overgrowth Ross Wilson	195
10	Creatrix Witches, Nonbinary Creatures, and Shelleyan Transmedia Kate Singer	214
11	Action at a Distance: Communication and Material Entanglement in *Queen Mab* and *The Mask of Anarchy* Mary Fairclough	238
12	Educating the Imagination/Defending Shelley Defending Joel Faflak	260

Further Reading   276
Index   286

Notes on Contributors

JULIE A. CARLSON is Professor of English and Associate Dean-Faculty Equity Advisor in the Division of Humanities and Fine Arts at the University of California, Santa Barbara. She is the author of *In the Theatre of Romanticism: Coleridge, Nationalism, Women* (Cambridge University Press, 1994), *England's First Family of Writers: Mary Wollstonecraft, William Godwin, Mary Shelley* (Johns Hopkins University Press, 2007), and coeditor, with Elisabeth Weber, of *Speaking about Torture* (Fordham University Press, 2012). Her articles focus on the cultural, sexual, and racial politics of British Romantic-era writing and mind studies. She is the coeditor, with Aranye Fradenburg Joy, of Brainstorm Books, an imprint of punctum books. Her current work argues that the interconnection among friendship, creativity, and social justice is a crucial legacy of British Romanticism.

JAMES CHANDLER is William K. Ogden Distinguished Service Professor in the Department of English and Department of Cinema and Media Studies at the University of Chicago. His books include *England in 1819: The Politics of Literary Culture and the Case of Romantic Historicism* (University of Chicago Press, 1998), *An Archaeology of Sympathy: The Sentimental Mode in Literature and Cinema* (University of Chicago Press, 2013), and *Doing Criticism: Across Literary and Screen Arts* (Wiley-Blackwell, 2022). In 2022 he held the Avery Distinguished Fellowship at the Huntington Library to work on his current book project: "Figures in a Field: Wordsworth and Edgeworth." Since 1989 he has served as General Editor of the monograph series Cambridge Studies in Romanticism. In 2014 he was elected to the American Academy of Arts and Sciences.

GERARD COHEN-VRIGNAUD teaches at the University of Tennessee and is the author of *Radical Orientalism: Rights, Reform, and Romanticism* (Cambridge University Press, 2015). His essays have appeared in *English Literary History*, the *Modern Language Quarterly*, *Nineteenth-Century Literature*, *differences*, and *Studies in Romanticism*, among others. His most recent article, "Love Actually: On Affect Theory and Romantic Studies" (2020), came out in *The Wordsworth Circle*.

JOEL FAFLAK is Robert and Ruth Lumsden Professor of English at Western University. He is the author of *Romantic Psychoanalysis* (State University of New York Press, 2007), coauthor of *Revelation and Knowledge* (University of Toronto Press, 2011), the editor of Thomas De Quincey's *Confessions of an English Opium-Eater* (Broadview Press, 2009), and the coeditor (with Richard Sha) of the book series Palgrave Studies in Affect Theory and Literary Criticism (2016 to present). He has edited or coedited numerous collections, including *A Handbook of Romanticism Studies* (with Julia M. Wright; Wiley-Blackwell, 2012), *Marking Time: Romanticism and Evolution* (University of Toronto Press, 2017), *William Blake: Modernity and Disaster* (University of Toronto Press, 2020), and *Romanticism and the Emotions* (with Richard Sha; Cambridge University Press, 2014), and, most recently, *Romanticism and Consciousness Revisited* (Edinburgh University Press, 2022). He is recipient of the Polanyi Prize for Literature (2021) and the Edward J. Pleva (2016) and Ontario Confederation of University Faculty Associations (2019) awards for teaching excellence. His current projects are two monographs "Romantic Psychiatry: The Psychopathology of Happiness" and "Get Happy! Utopianism and the American Film Musical."

MARY FAIRCLOUGH is Professor of Eighteenth-Century and Romantic Literature at the University of York. She is the author of *The Romantic Crowd: Sympathy, Controversy and Print Culture* (Cambridge University Press, 2013) and *Literature, Electricity and Politics 1740–1840: "Electrick Communication Every Where"* (Palgrave, 2017), and of essays and articles which investigate the intersection of literature, technology, religion, and politics in the eighteenth century and Romantic period. These include studies of Percy Shelley's *The Mask of Anarchy*, Mary Shelley's *Frankenstein*, and the work of Thomas Beddoes, Mary Wollstonecraft, Erasmus Darwin, and John Thelwall. She is currently completing a monograph on Romantic-period women's writing and devotional feeling, and editing Mary Wollstonecraft's *The Female Reader* for a forthcoming edition of Wollstonecraft's complete works from Oxford University Press.

NIKKI HESSELL is a settler scholar and Professor of English Literatures at Te Herenga Waka–Victoria University of Wellington. Her work focuses on the intersection of Romantic studies, settler colonialism, and Indigenous studies. She is the author of *Romantic Literature and the Colonised World: Lessons from Indigenous Translations* (Palgrave, 2018) and *Sensitive Negotiations: Indigenous Diplomacy and British Romantic Poetry* (State University of New York Press, 2021).

OMAR F. MIRANDA is Associate Professor of English at the University of San Francisco. He is the editor of *On the 200th Anniversary of Lord Byron's* Manfred (*Romantic Circles* Praxis Series, 2019) and the abridged teaching edition of Mary Shelley's *The Last Man* (*Romantic Circles*, 2022). His published essays have appeared in *European Romantic Review*, *Symbiosis*, *Keats-Shelley Journal*, *Studies in Romanticism*, and *Global Nineteenth-Century Studies*. His article, "The Global Romantic Lyric" (*The Wordsworth Circle*, 2021), won the Bigger 6 Article of the Year award (2021). He is currently at work on a book project that tracks the rise of global celebrity culture in the Romantic period. He is Vice President of the Keats-Shelley Association of America and is on The Byron Society of America's board of directors.

MATHELINDA NABUGODI is a lecturer in Comparative Literature at University College London. She is the author of *Shelley with Benjamin: A Critical Mosaic* (UCL Press, 2023) and one of the editors of the Longman edition of *The Poems of Shelley*. She has published articles on Shelley's translations, creative critical methods, and the racist history of hair. Her current research explores the connections between British Romanticism and the Black Atlantic while investigating the period's legacy in our own time. It is due to be published as *The Trembling Hand: Reflections of a Black Woman in the Romantic Archive* by Hamish Hamilton (UK) and Alfred A. Knopf (US).

ALAN RICHARDSON is Professor of English at Boston College. His books include *Literature, Education, and Romanticism: Reading as Social Practice* (Cambridge University Press, 1994), *British Romanticism and the Science of the Mind* (Cambridge University Press, 2001), and *The Neural Sublime: Cognitive Theories and Romantic Texts* (Johns Hopkins

University Press, 2011). He is editor or coeditor of *Romanticism, Race, and Imperial Culture* (Indiana University Press, 1996), *Three Oriental Tales* (Wadsworth Publishing, 2002), and *Early Black British Writing* (New Riverside Editions, 2004). Major awards include a National Endowment for the Humanities (NEH) Fellowship, a Guggenheim Fellowship, and the Keats-Shelley Association of America Distinguished Scholar Award. His most recent book, *Breakfast with Salamanders: Seasons on the Appalachian Trail* (Daiyu Peak Press, 2021) concerns walking, nature, Zen, and section-hiking the "AT."

KATE SINGER is Mary Lyon Professor of Humanities in the English Department and affiliated faculty in the Critical Race and Political Economy Department at Mount Holyoke College. She is the author of *Romantic Vacancy: The Poetics of Gender, Affect, and Radical Speculation* (State University of New York Press, 2019) and coeditor, with Ashley Cross and Suzanne L. Barnett, of *Material Transgressions: Beyond Romantic Bodies, Genders, Things* (Liverpool University Press, 2020). She has published essays on Percy Shelley, Mary Shelley, Maria Jane Jewsbury, Letitia Elizabeth Landon, Mary Robinson, Jane Austen, Mary Wollstonecraft, and Mary Prince. She is working on a second book that explores tropes of shapeshifting in the Romantic period and beyond and currently serves as the President of the Keats-Shelley Association of America.

FUSON WANG is Associate Professor of English at the University of California, Riverside, where he specializes in British Romantic literature, disability studies, and the medical and health humanities. He is the author of two monographs. First, *The Smallpox Report: Vaccination and the Romantic Illness Narrative* (University of Toronto Press, 2023) rewinds our own pandemic moment of vaccine hesitancy back to the Romantic-era discovery of smallpox vaccination to relearn the value of the medico-literary genre of the illness narrative. Second, *A Brief Literary History of Disability* (Routledge, 2022) offers perhaps surprising pairings of contemporary disability theory with some of the most enduring stories in the cultural imagination to illustrate the centrality of the figure of disability in literature, from the early modern period to our contemporary moment.

ROSS WILSON is Associate Professor of Criticism in the Faculty of English, University of Cambridge, and a Fellow of Emmanuel College. He has written books on Kant's aesthetics and on the work of Theodor Adorno and is the author of *Shelley and the Apprehension of Life* (Cambridge University Press, 2013) and *Critical Forms* (Oxford University Press, 2023), his book on the forms of literary criticism since 1750. He is the editor of *The Meaning of "Life" in Romantic Poetry and Poetics* (Routledge, 2009) and of *Percy Shelley in Context*, forthcoming from Cambridge University Press, and a member of the editorial collective for *Romantic Circles Reviews and Receptions*.

Acknowledgments

Percy Shelley for Our Times adopts the spirit of our volume's main argument: it is a product of connections and collaborations across times and places. First and foremost, we must thank all our authors for engaging in the many conversations, presentations, and revisions that have yielded a collection of essays that we hope will steer Percy Shelley studies forward in the years to come. We are indebted to several collegial and nurturing spaces that allowed us to test out many of our ideas, including a Shelley200 Online Event (June 2022) and the Shelley Conference (Keats House, Hampstead, London, July 2022), both expertly organized by Anna Mercer, Bysshe Coffey, Amanda Blake Davis, and Paul Stephens, with the assistance of Laura Blunsden and Ana Romanelli; a Modern Language Association 2020 roundtable on the 200th anniversary of *Prometheus Unbound* (Seattle, Washington, January 2020); a North American Society for the Study of Romanticism (NASSR)/British Association for Romantic Studies (BARS) 2022 panel (Edge Hill University, Ormskirk, UK, August 2022) that included some epic technical difficulties (we prevailed); a NASSR 2023 seminar (Sam Houston State University, Texas, March 2023); Columbia University's Nineteenth-Century British Literature Colloquium (organized by Johanna King-Slutzky and Conor Bruce MacVarish); and an Interdisciplinary Nineteenth-Century Studies (INCS) panel on "The Shelleys" (Knoxville, Tennessee, April 2023). Thank you to Emma Watkins, our sagacious, patient, and talented copy editor, for your adept skill at helping to bring the language in these pages into their stylistic and coherent elegance. We are appreciative of the financial support generously extended by Mount Holyoke College and University of San Francisco, which included grants for research assistantships, travel funding to conferences, and indexing services. With gratitude, as well, to Bethany Thomas, George Laver, and Sunantha Ramamoorthy from Cambridge University Press for your flexibility, openness, guidance, and enthusiasm. We are thankful for the socially, environmentally, and Shelleyan-conscious artwork of Janet

Allsebrook as well as for the generosity of the artist herself for permitting us to mark this collection visually with the interwoven Shelleyan concepts at its core. Of course, there were also many individuals who read pieces of this volume and listened to late-night and far-flung interpretations and dreams of new worlds: Suzanne Barnett, Madeleine Callaghan, Bysshe Coffey, Julie A. Carlson, Gerard Cohen-Vrignaud, Stuart Curran, Neil Fraistat, Anna Mercer, Alan Richardson, Sharon Ruston, Ross Wilson, Fuson Wang, and Amy Wong.

This journey would have been neither possible nor meaningful without our mutually enriching and invigorating editorial collective of two. Our work together included "several" texting exchanges and phone conversations as well as many virtual and in-person presentations and teaching sessions, including a literature seminar, "Percy Shelley's Life, Works, and Afterlives," taught at the Department of English, University of San Francisco (Spring 2022).

> … For joining me on this adventure filled with your encouraging and edifying conversations and insights. For your humanity, kindness, and generosity as a scholar, a teacher, a person, and a friend. For all your lyrical passions, your humor, and the many laughs: thank you, Kate! Rereading Percy Shelley alongside you and thinking carefully with you about why we need to continue engaging his ideas and writings have made "our times" truly dear and unforgettable …

> … For my Virgo-Leo cusp conspirator, thank you for giving all the space and time to revolve through so many attempts in expressing the queerness of Shelley orbishness. For pushing me to polish and unjargon and make accessible, for engaging in jokes and confidences and ideas that comingle and listen without prejudice, for offering care and true friendship and hope to my skepticism, for continuing to dream in exile and to recite the poems that might decolonize us even as they find room for us all …

And, of course, to Joey, Chris, Bue, Dolores, and Norman (as well as our sustaining plants), we give you back all our Shelleyan zeal for the privilege of the best kind of involvements.

Abbreviations

CP   *The Complete Poetry of Percy Bysshe Shelley*, eds. Donald H. Reiman, Neil Fraistat, Nora Crook, et al. 4 volumes to date. Baltimore: Johns Hopkins University Press, 2000–.

Letters   *The Letters of Percy Bysshe Shelley*, ed. Frederick L. Jones. 2 volumes. Oxford: Clarendon Press, 1964.

Poems   *The Poems of Shelley*, eds. Geoffrey Matthews, Kelvin Everest, Cian Duffy, Michael Rossington, et al. 4 volumes to date. London: Routledge, 1989–.

Prose   *The Prose Works of Percy Bysshe Shelley*, ed. E. B. Murray. Oxford: Clarendon Press, 1993.

SPP   *Shelley's Poetry and Prose*, 2nd Edition, eds. Donald H. Reiman and Neil Fraistat. New York: W. W. Norton and Company, 2002.

Introduction
Percy Shelley's Involving Poetics of Relationality
Omar F. Miranda and Kate Singer

The title of this collection, *Percy Shelley for Our Times*, might hardly surprise readers already acquainted with Percy Shelley's ideas and works. Even after two hundred years since his passing, Shelley's name still evokes the enduring power of art and artists, the commitment to justice and equality, and the tireless uprising against oppressive systems. He imagined, for instance, an ethical environmental relation between humans and our planet, becoming the "first celebrity vegan" and a source of inspiration for the creature's diet in Mary Shelley's *Frankenstein*.[1] Through his precocious consideration of women's rights and gender equality, he composed what has been called the "first feminist epic."[2] Even more influential was his commitment to nonviolent protest as a vehicle for political and social change, which culminated in the composition of *The Mask of Anarchy*, one of the first modern and memorable expressions of peaceful mass resistance.[3] The poem notably influenced the English social reformer and animal rights activist Henry Salt, whose own teachings on Shelley would make a significant impact on Mahatma Gandhi and Martin Luther King, Jr.[4] Furthermore, Shelley's writings have continually galvanized readers, thinkers, authors, activists, and translators throughout the Americas, Africa, Asia, and the Middle East.[5] *The Mask of Anarchy*, for example, has aided Shelley's global popularity as an anthem used in the Tiananmen Square protests (Beijing, 1989), the Arab Spring protests (Tahrir Square in Cairo, 2011), and, more recently, a British Labour Party rally (Glastonbury, UK, 2017).[6] Several workers' movements, including the Chartists and American labor union activists in the early 1900s, turned to Shelley's early poem, *Queen Mab*, as a primer for working-class education and uprising.[7] The German anti-fascists Bertolt Brecht, Theodor Adorno, and Walter Benjamin all took cues from their Shelley-inspired philosophical mentors, Karl Marx and Friedrich Engels, in looking to the transformative social and political potential of Shelley's lyrics. In popular culture, moreover, poems such as "Ozymandias" and

Adonais have inspired multiple band titles and song lyrics; references and allusions to Shelley in recent TV and film series have appeared in AMC's *Breaking Bad*, Apple TV+'s *Dickinson*, and HBO's *Succession*.[8] Given his influence on prominent individuals, audiences, and social justice movements around the globe, including the poetry that continues to rouse and speak out against state violence, fascism, and hatred, Shelley is no doubt an artist and thinker for our times. He will remain "contemporary" because he repeatedly and indefatigably interrogated, however imperfectly, many of the structural injustices that manifested in his own age, which continue in many ways more than two hundred years later in ours.

Yet, perhaps unexpectedly, *Percy Shelley for Our Times* does not center its argument on the importance of Shelley's writings for our specific moment in time. It does not contend, through a strategic presentism, that Shelley imagined a future like ours or anticipated the political, social, and philosophical questions of our own age. Had we framed our argument using such a proleptic model, we should have done no more than to occlude the fact that, in the past two centuries, Shelley has been emphatically pilloried as much as praised. Placing the poet on such a pedestal would have further intensified Shelley's divided reception history, overlooking, for example, the multiple scandals that surrounded his personal life as well as the harsh, if hasty, dismissals he has received as an idealist (William Hazlitt), an "ineffectual angel" (Matthew Arnold), and an "adolescent" (T. S. Eliot) in no small part for his politics and religious beliefs.[9] More recently, his privilege as a white, affluent, and European-born author has been central to criticisms regarding his inability to grasp the actual, everyday struggles of racial, gender, and class inequities.[10] Furthermore, basing this book on a "contemporary" Shelley tied to the bicentenary of his passing could not possibly predict or address the needs of ages and audiences to come. How would this "bicentenary Shelley," that is, anticipate his future tercentennial or quadricentennial counterparts?

Rather than focusing on Shelley's sense of foresightedness, *Percy Shelley for Our Times* explores an author who thought and wrote in even more farsighted ways. The volume discusses the relevance of Shelley's ideas to such topics as the aims of Black protest, Indigenous resistance to broken treaties, versions of nonbinary sex-gender, the possibilities of environmental rewilding, and the ethics of disability and ageism, to name only a few. In doing so, the book points to a greater vision of Shelley's – one in which intergenerational and intercultural audiences connect and speak with one another. Through our assemblage of authors and chapters, we argue that Shelley conceived a model of relationality that conjoined and collapsed notions of time and space. As an arch poet of relation, Shelley honed a methodology that repeatedly draws from the interconnections and relationships among peoples, times, places, and fields of knowledge. Our contributors think variously about these relations: as unconventional models of kinship, the difficulties of collective exile, alternative forms of posthuman and nonbinary being, lyrical and hymnic ensemble, intergenerational and intercultural caretaking, genealogies of intellectual influence, political expressions of artful mediation, and global networks of intimacy and communication.

Shelley illustrated this model of relationality most powerfully in his rendering of interwoven spheres in Act IV of *Prometheus Unbound*, a passage that reworks Miltonic cosmology and Shelley's own earlier thoughts on spatial and temporal crisscrossings in *Queen Mab*, not to mention "Mont Blanc" and its image of the "everlasting universe of things / [that] Flows through the mind" (1–2 [*SPP* 97]).[11] The second part of a sequence of "two visions," which begins with Ione's description of the chariot of light, Panthea visualizes a picture of the cosmos with mighty allegorical import (IV.202 [275]). What seems like a single, elite "sphere" is really, as Panthea dreams it,

> A sphere, which is as many thousand spheres;
> Solid as crystal, yet through all its mass
> Flow, as through empty space, music and light;
> Ten thousand orbs involving and involved,
> Purple and azure, white, green and golden,
> Sphere within sphere; and every space between
> Peopled with unimaginable shapes,
> Such as ghosts dream dwell in the lampless deep;
> Yet each inter-transpicuous; and they whirl
> Over each other with a thousand motions,
> Upon a thousand sightless axles spinning,
> And with the force of self-destroying swiftness,
> Intensely, slowly, solemnly, roll on,
> Kindling with mingled sounds, and many tones,
> Intelligible words and music wild.   (IV.239–252 [*SPP* 276–277])

We could, on the most literal level, read Panthea's "sphere" as a universe or galaxy of heavenly bodies, "ten thousand" globes of multiple colors and sizes. But such a reading quickly "collides" with other interpretations because what appear to be orbs as "[s]olid as crystal" are also porous enough to allow sound and light to flow through them. The image of cosmic physicality, for example, might also presuppose the motions at atomic and molecular levels, as Panthea imagines a continuum of matter exhibiting simultaneous micro and macro dimensions.[12] Yet these physical gradations are further complicated by layers of Shelleyan metaphoricity: spheres that embody individuals or independent communities of readers, families, audiences, cultures, nations, and even nonhumans, including animals and environments. Meanwhile, as the orbs flow in "a thousand motions" with "a thousand sightless axles spinning," they not only spin forward, evolving or progressing, but also move in multiple speeds and directions. These changing distances and varied motions among different figurations and scales of physical matter also belie models of temporality that could be linear, nonlinear, cyclical, diachronic, synchronic, triadic, or otherwise entirely.

Yet this kaleidoscopic image – of scales, persons, ideas, symbols, spaces, times, identities, and even versions of ourselves – is especially consequential because the worlds put into motion are "involving and involved." Not independent or homogenized systems, the orbs are "involving," actively partaking of interdependent motions alongside and in tandem with others, while also already "involved," belonging to this complex operation of difference. They become entangled, enveloping, associating, and divorcing through an agency not directed by human autocrats but rather through an "inter-transpicuous" network of clarity and translucence. What might appear as a single and giant concentric sphere is quickly undermined by a vision of multiple interrelated centers or "axles" through a system that eliminates hierarchies altogether. Each "peopled" orb is enmeshed with the next, each allowing light – like Asia's – to pass and illuminate others with an unordered rainbow of colors. Like the music of the Platonic spheres, they create tones, words, and wild music together, intoned by individuals, communities, material movements, and myriad trilling relations, offering the potential for a choric roundelay of verse, Shelley's and many others', sounded and resounded, addressed and redressed, recited and re-cited across geographies and eras.

Such interconnectedness does not, however, promise one ongoing harmonious chorus; this is not a naive universalist picture of interlinked agreement. The spheres move, after all, with a "self-destroying swiftness," which anticipates the discordance brought about by collisions, erosions, and disagreements. They roll "intensely, slowly, solemnly" in multiple directions and "whirl over" each other through varied levels of force and affect. Here the tensions, discomforts, and impositions of being together might lead to the possibilities of non-relations, as each orb might change its attachments by opting out or engaging with others. As our authors show, the troubles of sociality include the potential of harmful complicity, "loathsome sympathy," "sad exile," "radical suffering," hopeful despair, and other ambivalences. The orbs model theorizes those relations yet to be – those found in the "lampless deep" of motions, ideas, peoples, and poetries, the phenomena that we cannot yet see or comprehend, with whom and with what we are nevertheless already connected. Even if we cannot see or know those others within the intricate system, the orbs are necessarily "peopled with unimaginable shapes." With quintessential Shelleyan irony, they already involve those unfamiliar entities that might be emergent readers such as Ianthe (from *Queen Mab*), communities such as the kindred of *Prometheus Unbound*'s cave, or alternative beings such as the Witch of Atlas's "sexless" creation or Shelley's "pod people."[13] By virtue of these associations, then, we become Shelley's collaborators in these ever-changing mutual relations and non-relations – that is, your involvement in my own, which ties "us" together in all the orbish senses. He thinks of us as those who will not finish but continue a mutual project by reading and writing, speaking, listening, and "hearing," as Julie A. Carlson writes in her chapter on Shelleyan Black poetics, "differences in common."

Percy Shelley for Our Times defamiliarizes the idea of "our times" by seeing any one moment in time (including this volume's year of publication) within this intricate system of interlocking physical, metaphysical, ontological, metaphorical, and temporal registers. This means that we must open up any historicist, presentist, or even Romantic transhistorical approach to a much wider purview.[14] Of course, Shelley scholarship is no stranger to contemplating the poet's temporal creativity, from notions of deep time in *Queen Mab* to the anticipation and prophecy within *Prometheus Unbound* to the lyrical ruptures of modernity and "no futures" in *The Triumph of Life*.[15] Scholars have elsewhere made use of historicism's thick research on historical difference to understand Shelley's engagement with post-Peterloo politics and on transhistorical continuities of "mutability" and "eternity" to broach romantic *topos* as they persist and vary through time.[16] As Will Bowers and Mathelinda Nabugodi have recently asserted in their bicentenary collection of essays on Shelley in *European Romantic Review*, "[t]he transhistorical conversation in Shelley's verse reflects a poet who grew obsessed with the interplay of different historical epochs."[17] Other approaches, such as those that consider modernity's revolutionary ruptures, examine the lyric's ability to stop time and to create abrupt social and cognitive change.[18] Our own Romantic-era bicentenary moment has intertwined a deep historicism with a presentist flare: to commemorate what we must remember about Romantic-era poetry while conjuring its authors to speak to young, contemporary audiences.[19] Romantics 200, a joint effort of the Keats-Shelley Association of America and the Byron Society of America, along with other ventures by the Keats-Shelley Memorial Association, the Keats-Shelley House in Rome, and Keats House in Hampstead exemplify some of those events, alongside public journalism touting the necessity of the arts and humanities.

Yet, despite the importance of these memorializations, such dialectical schemes fall short of capturing the expansive Shelleyan web of temporal and spatial layerings.[20] Shelley's own historicist methods, which have been discussed by a variety of critics, moved beyond a diachronic coupling of historical moments to engage in an iterative practice of accumulating and intersecting flows of time.[21] To recall *A Defence of Poetry*, Shelley writes, "Poets are the hierophants of unapprehended inspiration; the mirrors of the gigantic shadows which futurity casts upon the present" (*SPP* 535). Although he might seem to draw the future and the present into a bipartite relation, however fractured or reversed, the entire passage is framed by the figure of the poet as mirror. This priest already refracts many presents and futures into a manifold hall of mirrors with other images and shadows of time. A poet does not merely illuminate these refractions but is already located as a medium within a network of unordered, unexpected creations of time and space. This understanding of relations ever unfolding reverberates elsewhere in *A Defence*:

> All high poetry is infinite; it is as the first acorn, which contained all oaks potentially. Veil after veil may be undrawn, and the inmost naked beauty of the meaning never exposed. A great Poem is a fountain for ever overflowing within the waters of wisdom and delight; and after one person and one age has exhausted all its divine effluence which these particular relations enable them to share, another and yet another succeeds, and new relations are ever developed, the source of an unforeseen and an unconceived delight. (*SPP* 528)

Despite beginning the passage with the metaphor of the acorn, whose growth projects a future of oaks, Shelley quickly overwrites that organic, linear metaphor when he shifts to two other vehicles: a series of veils, then a body of water with all manner of material outpouring. Poetry itself becomes a relational process that is never-ending, which always unveils fresh readings of itself, placing ideas, audiences, and their environments into association. Not simply ever in "pursuit," as Richard Holmes would have it, of the one perfect poem, Shelley's poetry may fade or transform, but, as a "fountain" of "divine effluence" that ever develops "new relations," it swims alongside other currents of its readings and interpretations.[22] Similar to the poet ushering in temporality as a hall of mirrors, here the process of unveiling new readings allows all sorts of temporal flows to reconfigure the spaces and communities that populate them.

Even with his notions of interlinked being across epochs and places, some might still wish that Shelley's thinking would have enabled him to recognize more of the oppressions of his own age, to see his own role in hierarchical relations. However precocious he was, Shelley was certainly "involved" with the deleterious complicities and harmful habits of his own times. For one, his seemingly idealistic comment in *A Defence*, that "[h]igh poetry is infinite," carries the traces of hierarchical aesthetics, such as his address to "the highly refined imagination of the more select classes of poetical readers" in the "Preface" of *Prometheus Unbound* (*SPP* 209). As Nabugodi argues in this volume, his repeated use of the metaphor of "slavery" evades mention of real, racialized bodies and the Atlantic slave trade.[23] His exhortations for working-class protests often seem to substitute for his own direct political action. His neglect of real women in his life often conflicted with his visions of gender equality; his seemingly equitable views on sexuality were compromised by his ostensible homophobia.[24] How, Nabugodi asks, could Shelley have pursued freedom for the Greeks so intensely while largely ignoring the ravages of racial capitalism and settler colonialism? How do we read Shelley and not replicate, in the very voicing of his lines, the abstractions of "tyranny" and "slavery," those violences of erasure? Can Shelley the iconoclast challenge Shelley the nineteenth-century conspirator by allowing us to give voice to these silences, make timely revisions, and take necessary actions?

However we might believe Shelley addressed, or failed to address, these problems, his model of orbs offers a potential method for working through them. He recognized the significance of his – and our – partial perspectives included among myriad connections between ideas, bodies, or even contradictory parts of ourselves. According to orbish logic, we may still encounter the "Cencis" and "Jupiters" of the world, since we are brought into association, and perhaps even face to face, with all things pernicious as much as beneficent. Nevertheless, though any single orb must necessarily belong within the greater system, it still possesses the power to "roll on" however "intensely, slowly, [or] solemnly" – to move around, to realign, and to change. As we see it, this means that it is possible to reckon with problematic associations through a nonlinear process of understanding and identification, which can then lead to choice, action, and interaction. The intricate layers of these encounters allow us to imagine, reimagine, and, if possible, enact alternative means of coexisting.

On a more meta-poetic level, Shelley's body of work, with its experimental practices of rereading and revising systems, traditions, plots, characters, and figures, likewise draws on this discerning process of relational assemblage. The iterations of Beatrice, Asia, the Witch of Atlas, the "shape all light," and even Demogorgon, for example, offer a "contexture" of beings who, while attempting to overthrow gendered oppressive systems, are nevertheless enmeshed within them.[25] Through the study of these characters, we can identify various positionalities within harmful social structures. Those differences, small and large, then enable us not only to understand and confront our own positionalities and complicities but also, hopefully, to embody alternative forms of being and becoming. Beyond showing us the complex entanglements of things as they are, the orbs provoke the speculative imagination, the opportunity of learning the art of moving forward, toward, or away, as well as revising and repositioning relations as they are both carried through history and reborn.

At its core, Shelley's work elicits multidisciplinary, multimodal ways of reading, seeing, and listening. Perhaps the most direct example would be to reconsider Shelley's famed syncretism as a pointed cross-temporal and cross-spatial mash-up, layering multiple legends, cultures, and religious stories from polychronic and polyvocal spaces and times.[26] If we look back at the many linguistic and national cultures Shelley read from as well as the many artists across the globe influenced by his work, we foresee many more branches and fruit that such cross-pollination might yield. We might continue to identify the most basic and important practice within Shelley scholarship as placing disparate forms of knowledge in his writing into conversation. For instance, work by Colin Carman on the queer ecology of the Shelleys posits a necessary but fraught relation not between human subject and Romantic natural object but amid an intimacy with the nonhuman world that speaks to queer forms of love.[27] Carlson's paradigmatic essay on Shelleyan simile offers a grammar of relation for both sympathetic affect and new political friendships.[28] More recently, Bysshe Inigo Coffey has examined the gaps, fractures, and limit-points within Shelley's poetics as arising from his philosophical and scientific understanding of materiality's own brokenness.[29] Both Richard Sha and Mark Lussier work through Shelley's interdisciplinary erudition to reveal a poet with the heart of a scientist, imagining a biochemical physics of waves and dynamism at the heart of a materiality that might inspire new thoughts and new ways of peaceful living, a politics of health and ontology Timothy Morton has likewise investigated.³⁰ Shelley's interest in polyamory arose through his reading of comparative sexualities in the classical world and religions across Europe, intertexts that refracted the strictures of monogamy through diverse affective and familial relationships. Indeed, the tradition of Shelley the "skeptical idealist," or the empiricist turned Platonist, only begins to intimate a thinker working in comparative religion, language, and philosophies at once.³¹ As textual scholars have long claimed, Shelley's own representation has been remediated by the public press of his day, booksellers, friends, biographers, artists, and editors, including Mary Shelley, in myriad and conflicting ways, with much new work to come on Shelley's publication practice, manuscripts, and affiliations that shaped the circulation and suppression of his work.³²

Moreover, rather than narrating Shelley scholarship through any theoretical *agon*, as Arthur Bradley's has done between deconstructionists and new historicist scholars, we might approach it instead as iconoclastically transiting fields.³³ For poststructuralist critics remind us that non-relation is also a form of relation that Shelley considers in poems about withdrawal and antisociality. Similarly, the "deconstructionist Shelley" really constitutes a connection between disruptive poetry and revolutionary politics, such as Forest Pyle's "kindling and ash" of an aesthetics that burns through ideology's coercive power.³⁴ From Paul de Man's contingent violence of language in Shelley's *The Triumph of Life* to Orrin N. C. Wang's disfigurement as the revolutionary politics of modernity, linguistic deconstruction that resists the monumentalization of meaning or history does not simply reveal a politics to deconstruction but ironically convenes a community around those very ruptures, or non-relations, of sovereignty, history, and language.³⁵

Other cross-temporal or cross-epistemological nodes of Shelley scholarship can be found within the denizens of "Red Shelley," who resituate different echelons of class-based wealth as systemic forms of power necessarily tied to sympathy and community affect. Marxist Shelleyans such as Terence Hoagwood find in Shelley's protest a resistance to stadial histories and to all forms of totality that would prevent other forms of economic, existential, and phenomenological living.³⁶ More recently, Greg Ellerman has revived "Red Shelley" through a "serious rethinking of [the] relations among work, wealth, and nature."³⁷ Other scholars preoccupied with questions of hierarchy and equity in Shelley's work likewise draw from the varied knowledge systems embedded in his poems. Andrew Warren considers Shelley's aristocratic class position and the psychological and affective dynamics of Romantic egotism as a means to critique the imperial and racial dynamics within his works, while Kai Pyle's Ojibwe translations and analysis of the canonical "Ode to the West Wind" recontextualize the poem's received meanings in order to reveal the power and flexibility of the Ojibwe language.[38] Work on populist Shelley by Graham Henderson's website similarly draws our attention to the networks of people and social movements created by Shelley's most pointed public resonances outside the academy.[39] Likewise, Camila Oliveira elaborates how musical reverberations of "Ozymandias" upend progressivist, ruling-class histories through the circulation of the poem's popular resistance to history written by tyrants.[40] In reminding ourselves of this scholarly work, we must continue placing this "academic Shelley" into the other public orbs that concern him.

As we see our reading and writing as part of Shelley's great connection-making conversation, we have organized *Percy Shelley for Our Times* around the shapes that our relations, and others like them, might take. This framework also includes holding space for those subjects yet to be acknowledged and written. Our first set of essays considers forms of kinship that connect Shelley to intergenerational Indigenous and disabled communities. The next group tackles Shelley's views on abolition, slavery, and racialized Blackness from three different perspectives. The importance of affect to social change launches our next set of essays on the ambivalences of empathy, hope, and exile. As exile often happens in Shelley's writings within alternative landscapes, caves, or wilderness, our next two essays reconsider Shelley's thinking about the associations between humans and nonhuman ecologies as well as his understanding of interrelation between forms of nonhuman being and nonbinary gender. Our final selections meditate on art's role as the ultimate agent and medium of change across the strata of relational being.

The volume begins with a chapter that brings Shelley in relation to First Peoples through Nikki Hessell's searing and beautiful meditation on the forsaken promises of England's sovereign in 1819 and the broken treaties in Canada and the United States during the early nineteenth century. Arguing that "Shelley's poems are [...] actually *about* Indigenous autonomy and honoring the treaties of 1819 and beyond," Hessell reveals that an "Indianized Shelley" has inspired North American Indigenous authors and peoples across generations. With incisive readings of authors such as Too-qua-stee (Cherokee), James Roane Gregory (Yuchi and Mvskoke Creek), John Rollin Ridge (Cherokee), and Joy Harjo (Mvskoke Creek), she shows how they have drawn on the language of Shelley's works as a lexicon for the legal, affective, and performative failures of England's monarchy and of the incipient US republic. Hessell finds "resolute, patient, and community-minded" orientations toward alternative models of kinship and community – and the dream of building them despite the insistence of patriarchal property and inheritance.

The subsequent chapter by Fuson Wang pays attention to a neglected population within Shelley studies, the aging and disabled, by revealing a Shelley who likewise builds kinships across all living beings. Through a trenchant rereading of Shelley's final poem, *The Triumph of Life* (and with a brief and equally powerful nod to Shelley's neglected prose fragment, "The Coliseum"), Wang challenges the enduring notion that Shelley primarily championed the season of budding spring, of youthful idealists and hopeful optimists, proposing instead that Shelley crafts an "intergenerational theory of disability" as well as a hitherto unrecognized "ethic of constant care." According to Wang's claims, "the youthful speaker (in *The Triumph of Life*) deliberately chooses a partner in the old, disabled ruins of what was once Rousseau," thereby grounding the chapter's broader claim that "the coming [Shelleyan] revolution must be at once young and old, firm and infirm, able-bodied and disabled."

Yet, for all his sensitivities and allyships, Shelley's work is nonetheless haunted by his failure to address racial politics directly – namely, the Atlantic slave trade – and his complicity with the Eurocentric and "Enlightened" civilization that underwrote such a system of racial tyranny. Three essays in this volume each differently reckon with Shelley's complicated attitudes regarding slavery and race. Nabugodi's chapter lays bare the tensions between racial politics and Shelley's liberatory poetics, including his philhellenic bias, his abstractions of "slavery," and his missed opportunity to condemn the Atlantic slave trade. As Nabugodi helps readers comprehend the complexities of Shelley's embeddedness in his own moment, she shows how the work of criticism is also always bound up in one's own time by relating the personal account of her experiences as a Black woman scholar working on Shelley. In the end, Nabugodi shows us firsthand the inherent dangers and exclusions of Shelleyan relation-making. Yet re-visionary ends are not altogether foreclosed once we truly understand that "'our laws, our literature, our religion, our arts' [Shelley's phrase] have developed in symbiosis with centuries of racialized slavery and colonial exploitation."

As we acknowledge Shelley's silence on Atlantic slavery, we then consider the possibilities of reading Shelley to work toward an anti-racist future. In their chapters, both Carlson and James Chandler reflect on these opportunities by turning mainly to philosophers, activists, and artists of color who have been inspired by Shelley's own ideas and poetics. Carlson, in particular, looks to those "poet-legislators [who] work the streets as well as universities in efforts to better realize and manifest social justice." Turning to Fred Moten's poem "barbara lee," which Carlson reads as "the most explicit engagement with Shelleyan poetic legislation by a Black radical US poet-philosopher that [she] know[s]," she meditates on Moten's concepts of ensemble and relays to imagine a diverse future of "generativity" where Shelleyan notions of relationality, or "associationism" in Carlson's phrasing, are "a key method for tying unlearning to pro-Blackness." This imperative implicates all scholars in the ivory tower; it involves all the difficulties of turning out the insiders and "inside songs" onto "choric" and "collective" expressions. The call for turning "insiders outward," as Carlson voices it, "entails substantial revisions to career, success, scholarship, activism, classrooms, interpersonal relations, and perceptions of self." In Chandler's subsequent meditation on "Radical Suffering," he lays out another significant "ensemble" by tracking a genealogy of Shelleyan thinkers from Gandhi through King via Salt, connecting Shelley to the Indian freedom and American civil rights movements. Through a reading of *Prometheus Unbound*, Chandler argues that what appealed to these thinkers and activists was Shelley's "ambitious staging of the radical love that subtends nonviolent revolution," which also necessitates radical suffering. The revolutionary subject, in his reading, absorbs pain and suffering in an act that deconstructs the binary between direct action and passive suffering. Chandler connects this type of affective political activism to Shelley's varying uses of genre and form, as each "rhetorical variation" acts differently but in relation to Shelley's "signature practice of producing a literature of immanent critique."

These accounts of Shelley's use for pro-Blackness as well as his silences in confronting Atlantic slavery are followed by three essays that consider the problems as much as the possibilities of Shelleyan dispositions to change: empathy, hope, and exile. As Chandler's essay contemplates Shelley's model of taking on the suffering of colonial violence, Alan Richardson's piece conversely considers Shelley's staging of dark empathy in *The Cenci* as he discusses what happens when empaths use their sensitivities for harm and control, including securing tyrannical family and state power. Reading Shelley through an analogical view of contemporary ideas about mirror neurons – those neurons that help us imitate the behaviors we observe in others – Richardson traces Shelley's sophisticated understanding of sympathy, revealing how fellow feeling works in pernicious ways, while also teasing out of the darkness of Shelley's tragedy "unconstrained, selfless compassion." As a counterpoint to these explorations of suffering and dark empathy, Gerard Cohen-Vrignaud revisits the tensions between hope and hopelessness in Shelley by giving us a new understanding of the aims of his "ineffectual" idealism. With provocative readings of "England in 1819," *The Mask of Anarchy*, and *The Revolt of Islam*, Cohen-Vrignaud probes the dyadic ties between "hope and despair." He tracks the wavering between these two affective states as a powerful back-and-forth movement to keep us going, literally and figuratively. For, to despair, in his reading, means to spare some hope in the toggling between a wished-for future and an undesirable present. All the while, Cohen-Vrignaud attends to the prospects of inter-relational times and spaces, which are created by "the sublime power of language to produce effects beyond the intentions of an author and the possibilities of one moment."

Omar F. Miranda's chapter treats another affective paradox related to political and social change: the "sad exile" of being at once sorrowful yet steadfast in the struggle "through and beyond the traumas of displacement and dispossession." Reading *Prometheus Unbound*, he tracks the multiple representations of Prometheus, Asia, and Demogorgon, who all survive their physical and figurative exiles individually and mutually as both a mode of dislocation, on one hand, and a form of resistance and recalibration, on the other. Miranda argues that exile and revolution in the drama are inextricably tied together not as a single or one-time event but rather as a protracted and enduring set of experiences. By newly understanding the play's action as the ongoing withdrawal from Jupiter's system, Miranda reveals "sad exile" to harbor the ambivalent yet re-visionary possibility of seeing things from afar and anew – through "everyday self-inquiry and critical distancing [...] that will continue to ensure the redeemed society's mutually determined rewards and livelihood." As Miranda argues that remaining in exile demands an exile from oneself and inured environments, Ross Wilson focuses on the necessary distances and differences between humans and the natural world in a refreshing reading of Shelleyan eco-social poetics. Closely studying Shelley's thoughts on rewilding, including how the natural world regrows and "overgrows" the remains of human civilization, Wilson shows how Shelley's environmentalism challenges recent cultural theories that give exclusive priority to the nonhuman. With readings of current ecological rewilding movements in the public press alongside incisive analyses of *Epipsychidion* and *Adonais*, he contends that Shelley's poetry repeatedly exposes the intertwining relations of the human and natural worlds, namely that nature's resurgence and rewilding grow alongside the traces of humanity.

Examining another relation between the human and the nonhuman, Kate Singer's essay considers Shelley's attempt to think before the "Error and Truth" of Enlightenment humanity, and before the binaristic split between the white male bourgeois Human and those not included in that definition of humanity. She traces his iconoclastic resistance to and exile from normative categories of gender, race, and the human in a reading of

The Witch of Atlas, with its double creation of Witch and the Witch's "sexless" creature. Singer points to Shelley's radical understanding of gender and sex beyond the male-female binary, as she considers the poet's commentary and critique on the dimorphic gender-sex systems circulating in the discourses of his day. Positioning the poem as his reply and reconception of Mary Shelley's queer creature in *Frankenstein*, Singer makes the argument that Shelley conceived of a continuum of gender and sex, one in which the gendered and racialized alterity of the Witch's creature is embraced and prioritized, even though it may be imperfectly imagined.

The last two essays consider the vast Shelleyan sense of poetry as a medium of communication and as a support for the humanities. Drawing on the feminist materialist philosopher Karen Barad, Mary Fairclough's chapter discusses Shelley's farsighted views of poetry as a medium that can operate without the necessary interventions of mediation. In her incisive argument, "Shelley abandons the opposition we see in his early sonnets between material medium and evanescent subject and instead produces an account of dynamic matter that reconstitutes models of time and space and promises to do away with mediation altogether." In laying the case for what she calls Shelley's poetic cutting, where poetic sounds and materiality might rework the mediation of textual medium into closer relations between poetry and the bodies its words touches, Fairclough contends that Shelleyan poetics collapse the distance created by both time and space, tracing the poetical possibilities of "solidarity and fellow feeling" in the construction of new audiences and new worlds. In her argument, "Shelley is for our times because he is of our time."

The volume concludes with Joel Faflak's meditation on Shelley's resounding belief in poetry as an antidote to the ongoing diminishment of the humanities within the academy. Reminding readers just how the "humanities" was born through the rhetoric of crisis (in the mid-twentieth century), Faflak argues that poetry's unique empathies, neologisms, and ever-emergent concepts can easily perpetuate uncertainty in the academy's investment in the arts and critical thought even when it asserts its primacy over systems of institutional power. In part because poetry, according to Shelley's *Defence*, will always instigate more poetry and in part because poetry creates aesthetic "happenings," Faflak doubles down on the resources we might find in lyrical breaks, new language, and new associations for words bequeathed to us. For Faflak, the Shelleyan poem "itself as a mode of consciousness, apostrophe, however painful, is able to sing, maybe even to redeem and silence the pain."

While each of the following chapters stands impressively in its own right, they all propose so much more as an assemblage of twelve essays, especially in light of the framework within which this collection is already involved. *Percy Shelley for Our Times* only begins to adumbrate Shelley's poetics and praxis of relationality: Shelley imagining his predecessors, imagining us, imagining him, envisioning the future orbs that speak back to and repeatedly redraw their own spinning and changing systems. As Martin Luther King, Jr. later affirmed in drawing on the "interrelatedness of all communities and states": "we are caught in an inescapable network of mutuality."[41] All the while, these essays also point to that lampless deep of non-declarations and non-relations, which betrays how much is yet to be shared, related, created, or resisted. We thus bequeath this collection to what will necessarily exceed and extend us: the ever-emergent, ever-evolving, ever-revolving receptions that will continue to refuse reification by any one individual or group, historical environment, or scholarly predisposition. How, we wonder, will poetry's languages, forms, and materialities continue to unveil and refract across times and spaces? And how might generations to come further interrogate Shelley's, and our own, making of meaning through language, ideas, art, kinships, conversations, and more? For, in the vastness of orbish intricacy and gradation, we are more than bystanders of circumstance: we set the multitudinous possibilities into motion, awaiting as much as activating what carries on in the immeasurable beyond of being in, of, and for our times.

Notes

1 John Davis, "Shelley: The First Celebrity Vegan," *International Vegan Union*, January 5, 2011. https://ivu.org/index.php/blogs/john-davis/141-shelley-the-first-celebrity-vegan. For more on Shelley's ecological thought and his vegetarianism, see Michael Owen Jones, "In Pursuit of Percy Shelley, 'The First Celebrity Vegan': An Essay on Meat, Sex, and Broccoli," *Journal of Folklore Research* 53.2 (2016), 1–30; Timothy Morton, *Shelley and the Revolution in Taste: The Body and the Natural World* (Cambridge: Cambridge University Press, 1994); and Chris Washington, *Romantic Revelations: Visions of Post-Apocalyptic Life and Hope in the Anthropocene* (Toronto: Toronto University Press, 2019).
2 Anahid Nersessian, "Introduction," ed. *Laon and Cythna; Or, the Revolution of the Golden City* (Peterborough, ON: Broadview Press, 2016), 23. Even as Shelley challenged contemporary understandings of monogamy at the expense of his own significant close relationships (especially Harriet Westbrook and Mary Shelley), he succeeded at building one of the first major literary relationships of "reciprocal and creative exchange" through his partnership with Mary Shelley; see Anna Mercer, *The Collaborative Literary Relationship of Percy Bysshe Shelley and Mary Wollstonecraft Shelley* (London: Routledge, 2021). This collaboration gave rise to the "radically queer ecology" of both Shelleys' many writings; see Colin Carman, *The Radical Ecology of the Shelleys: Eros and Environment* (New York: Routledge, 2019).

3 We might trace Shelley's dedication to peaceful activism back to his campaigns for Catholic emancipation during his travels to Ireland at the age of twenty. When he returned home, he argued for free speech and a free press through his own treatises and repeated offerings in Leigh Hunt's journal, *The Examiner*. This occurred during a conservative time in Britain that saw censorship and imprisonment for anti-governmental criticisms. Perhaps his refusal to recant the ideas in his early radical tract, *The Necessity of Atheism*, which got him removed from Oxford University in 1811, set his reputation as an iconoclast and contrarian that lasted the remainder of his short life. For the classic study of Shelley's early politics, see Kenneth Neill Cameron, *The Young Shelley: Genius of a Radical* (New York: Macmillan, 1950).
4 For more information about Salt's and Gandhi's interests in Shelley, see James Chandler's chapter in this volume.
5 Just a sampling of artists of color from around the globe inspired by Shelley's writings would include Gandhi (South Africa and India), Robert Sobukwe (South Africa), Mohamed Abdel-Hai (Sudan), Khalil Gibran (Lebanon), Abdülhak Hâmid Tarhan (Turkey), Aḥmad Zakī Abū Shādī (Egypt), Femi Osofisan (Nigeria), Tinashe Mushakavanhu (Zimbabwe), Kazi-Nazrul Islam (Bangladesh), Arundhati Roy (India), Rabindranath Tagore (India), Mu Dan (China), Lu Xun (China), Yang Mu (Taiwan), Shimazaki Tōson (Japan), Natsume Sōseki (Japan), Yun Dong-ju (South Korea), José María Heredia (Cuba), Rubén Darío (Nicaragua), Alejo Carpentier (Cuba/Venezuela), Leonardo Fróes (Brazil), Derek Walcott (St. Lucia), V. S. Naipaul (Trinidad), M. G. Smith (Jamaica), and Wilson Harris (Guyana). For further reading on Shelley's global reception and translation, see Omar F. Miranda's "Global Reception and Translation," in Ross Wilson, ed. *Percy Shelley in Context* (Cambridge: Cambridge University Press, in press). Moreover, understanding the "global Percy Shelley" could examine his own polyglot reading list, including his experiments in Italian verse and orientalist studies (by way of William Jones). See, for example, Timothy Webb's seminal *Violet in the Crucible* (Oxford: Clarendon Press, 1977) and Valentina Varinelli's recent *Italian Impromptus: A Study of P. B. Shelley's Writings in Italian, with an Annotated Edition* (Milan: LED Edizioni Universitarie, 2022). For studies on Shelley's orientalism, see Jallal Uddin Khan, "Shelley's Orientalia: Indian Elements in His Poetry," *Atlantis* 30.1 (2008), 35–51; Manu Samriti Chander, "Framing Difference: The Orientalist Aesthetics of David Roberts and Percy Shelley," *Keats-Shelley Journal* 60 (2011), 77–94; Gerard Cohen-Vrignaud, *Radical Orientalism: Rights, Reform, and Romanticism* (Cambridge: Cambridge University Press, 2015); and Joey S. Kim, "Disorienting 'Shapes' in Shelley's *The Revolt of Islam*," *The Keats-Shelley Review* 32.2 (2018), 134–147.
6 Matthew C. Borushko, "Violence and Nonviolence in Shelley's 'Mask of Anarchy'," *Keats-Shelley Journal* 59 (2010), 96–113; Anoosh Chakelian, "'Rise Like Lions after Slumber': Why Do Jeremy Corbyn and Co Keep Reciting a 19th Century Poem?" *The New Statesman*, June 27, 2017. www.newstatesman.com/politics/uk-politics/2017/06/rise-lions-after-slumber-why-do-jeremy-corbyn-and-co-keep-reciting-19th-century; "Another World Is Possible, Corbyn Tells Glastonbury," *The Guardian*, June 24, 2017, video, 3:04, posted

by UK Pool, June 24, 2017. www.theguardian.com/music/video/2017/jun/24/another-world-is-possible-corbyn-tells-glastonbury-video.

7   Michael Demson, "'Let a Great Assembly Be': Percy Shelley's 'The Mask of Anarchy' and the Organization of Labor in New York City, 1910–30," *European Romantic Review* 22.5 (2011), 641–655. For the classic study on radical piracy of Shelley's works, see Neil Fraistat, "Illegitimate Shelley: Radical Piracy and the Textual Edition as Cultural Performance," *PMLA* 109.3 (1994), 409–423.

8   For recent TV references to Shelley, see, for example, *Breaking Bad*, Season 5, Episode 14, "Ozymandias," directed by Rian Johnson and written by Moira Walley-Beckett, aired September 15, 2013, on AMC; *Dickinson*, Season 1, Episode 1, "Because I Could Not Stop," directed by David Gordon Green and written by Alena Smith, released November 1, 2019, on Apple TV+; *Succession*, Season 4, Episode 9, "Church and State," directed by Mark Mylod and written by Jesse Armstrong, aired May 21, 2023, on HBO. For contemporary musical references to Shelley and his works, we cite a presentation given by Dr. Camila Oliveira, "'Music When Soft Voices Live': Shelley's Reception in Contemporary Music," The Shelley Conference 2022, Keats House, Hampstead, July 8, 2022. For additional pop cultural references to Shelley, see the online resource on "Romanticism and Pop Culture" at *Romantic Circles*: https://romantic-circles.org/lab/pop-culture.

9   William Hazlitt, *The Complete Works of William Hazlitt*, ed. P. P. Howe (Tokyo: Yushodo, 1967), 16:267–270; Matthew Arnold, *The Complete Prose Works of Matthew Arnold*, ed. R. H. Super (Ann Arbor: University of Michigan Press, 1960), II: 327; T. S. Eliot, "Shelley and Keats," in *The Use of Poetry and the Use of Criticism*, 2nd ed. (London: Faber and Faber, 1964 [1933]), 89. For an overview of this criticism, see Jane Stabler, "Shelley Criticism from Romanticism to Modernism," in Michael O'Neill, Anthony Howe, and Madeleine Callaghan, eds. *The Oxford Handbook of Percy Bysshe Shelley* (Oxford: Oxford University Press, 2013), 657–672; "Shelley's Reception Before 1960," Neil Fraistat and Donald Reiman, eds. *Shelley's Poetry and Prose* (Baltimore: Johns Hopkins University Press, 2002), 539–549; and Timothy Morton, "Receptions," in Timothy Morton, ed. *The Cambridge Companion to Percy Shelley* (Cambridge: Cambridge University Press, 2006), 35–42.

10 For the argument about Shelley's radicalism instigating the censure of more conservative critics, see Fraistat and Reiman, *Shelley's Poetry and Prose*, 539–549. For critiques of Shelley's problematic liberalism, see Alex J. Dick, "'The Ghost of Gold': Forgery Trials and the Standard of Value in Shelley's *The Mask of Anarchy*," *European Romantic Review* 18.3 (2007), 381–400; Jamison Kantor, "Percy Shelley, Political Machines, and the Prehistory of the Postliberal," in Kristin M. Girten, Aaron R. Halon, and Joseph Drury, eds. *British Literature and Technology, 1600–1830* (Lewisburg: Bucknell University Press), 2023, 139–163; for gender critiques, see Anne K. Mellor, *Mary Shelley: Her Life, Her Fiction, Her Monsters* (New York: Routledge, 1988) and Teddi Chichester Bonca, *Shelley's Mirrors of Love: Narcissism, Sacrifice, and Sorority* (Albany: State University of New York Press, 1999); for critiques of empire, see Mathelinda Nabugodi, "A Triumph of Black Life?" *Keats-Shelley Journal* 70 (2021), 133–141; Jared Hickman, *Black Prometheus: Race and Radicalism in the Age of Atlantic Slavery* (Oxford:

Oxford University Press, 2017); Andrew Warren, *The Orient and the Young Romantics* (Cambridge: Cambridge University Press, 2014); Saree Makdisi, *Romantic Imperialism: Universal Empire and the Culture of Modernity* (Cambridge: Cambridge University Press, 1998); Meena Alexander, "Shelley's India: Territory and Text, Some Problems of Decolonization," in Betty T. Bennett and Stuart Curran, eds. *Shelley: Poet and Legislator of the World* (Baltimore: Johns Hopkins University Press, 1996), 169–178; Nigel Leask, *British Romantic Writers and the East: Anxieties of Empire* (Cambridge: Cambridge University Press, 1992), as well as recent and forthcoming work by Taylor Schey presented at the American Society for Eighteenth-Century Studies (ASECS) 2023 and the North American Society for the Study of Romanticism (NASSR) 2023 conferences.

11 Here is *Queen Mab*'s vision:

>   Below lay stretched the universe!
>   There, far as the remotest line
>   That bounds imagination's flight,
>   Countless and unending orbs
>   In mazy motion intermingled,
>   Yet still fulfilled immutably
>   Eternal Nature's law.
>   Above, below, around,
>   The circling systems formed
>   A wilderness of harmony;
>   Each with undeviating aim,
>   In eloquent silence, through the depths of space
>   Pursued its wondrous way. (II.70–82 [*SPP* 25])

12 See Ann Wroe, *Being Shelley: The Poet's Search for Himself* (New York: Vintage Books, 2007), 203; Heidi Scott, *Chaos and Cosmos: Literary Roots of Modern Ecology in the British Nineteenth Century* (University Park: Pennsylvania State University Press, 2014), 114–115; as well as Mark Lussier, *Romantic Dynamics: The Poetics of Physicality* (New York: Palgrave Macmillan, 2000).

13 Karen Swann, "Shelley's Pod People," in Forest Pyle, ed. *Romanticism and the Insistence of the Aesthetic*, *Romantic Circles* Praxis Series (February 2005). https://romantic-circles.org/praxis/aesthetic/swann/swann.html.

14 See the rehearsal of Arthur O. Lovejoy and Rene Wellek's debates in Jerome McGann's *Romantic Ideology* (Chicago: Chicago University Press, 1983); Frances Ferguson, "On the Number of Romanticisms," *ELH* 58.2 (1991), 471–498; and Orrin N. C. Wang's *Fantastic Modernity: Dialectical Readings in Romanticism and Theory* (Baltimore: Johns Hopkins University Press, 1996), as they play out various contentions about Romanticism as a historical response to revolutionary-era politics or a transhistorical aesthetic movement about "nature" as the scene of the imagination and the lyric.

15 Notable contemplations of Shelley and temporality include essays by Evan Gottlieb and Laura Quinney in *Romanticism and Time: Literary Temporalities* (Cambridge: Open Book Publishers, 2021); Andrew Burkett, "Deep Time: Queen Mab," *European Romantic Review* 33.5 (2022), 713–725; Lee Edelman, "The Pathology of the Future of the Endless Triumphs of Life," in Jacques Khalip and Forest Pyle, eds. *Constellations of a Contemporary Romanticism*

(New York: Fordham University Press, 2016), 35–46; Emily Rohrbach, *Modernity's Mist: British Romanticism and the Poetics of Anticipation* (New York: Fordham University Press, 2015); and Timothy Clark, "Shelley after Deconstruction: The Poet of Anachronism," in Timothy Clark and Jerrold E. Hogle, eds. *Evaluating Shelley* (Edinburgh: Edinburgh University Press, 1996), 91–108. See also Note 21.

16 See, for example, Madeleine Callaghan, *Eternity in British Romantic Poetry* (Liverpool: Liverpool University Press, 2022).

17 Will Bowers and Mathelinda Nabugodi, "Reading Shelley on the Bicentenary of His Death," *European Romantic Review* 33.5 (2022), 609–614.

18 See, for example, David Collings, *Disastrous Subjectivities: Romanticism, Modernity, and the Real* (Toronto: Toronto University Press, 2019) or Alan Richardson, *The Neural Sublime: Cognitive Theories and Romantic Texts* (Baltimore: Johns Hopkins University Press, 2010).

19 For other scholarly treatments of Shelley's futural or virtual audiences, see Stephen Behrendt, *Shelley and His Audiences* (Lincoln: University of Nebraska Press, 1989); Andrew Bennett, *Romantic Poets and the Culture of Posterity* (Cambridge: Cambridge University Press, 1999); Andrew Franta, "Shelley and the Poetics of Political Indirection," *Poetics Today* 22.4 (Winter 2001), 765–793; and Kim Wheatley, *Shelley and His Readers: Beyond Paranoid Politics* (Columbia: University of Missouri Press).

20 Some historical examples of such memorialization include Hubert Parry's musical adaptation of *Prometheus Unbound* (1880); Oxford University's memorialization of Shelley (c.1892); André Maurois's French biography of Shelley, *Ariel ou la vie de Shelley* (1923), which was popular across Europe; and the centenary celebration and staging of *The Cenci* in Prague, Italy, Germany, and France from 1919 to 1935. See also the rich reception history documented by Susanne Schmid and Michael Rossington in *The Reception of P. B. Shelley in Europe* (New York: Continuum, 2008).

21 We are, of course, deeply influenced by James Chandler's study of Shelley in *England in 1819*, where, speaking of *Peter Bell the Third*, he writes, "what the implicit time line codes is the cultural history of poetry in relation to criticism. This history extends in both directions from the present of 1819: it reaches back to the past of Homeric reception, a reception perpetually deferred by the failure of the *Iliad* and *Odyssey* to come to true 'full stops,' and it reaches forward to the future in which the merits of Shelley's work can be assessed in relation to the paradoxically unforeseeable prospect of a new 'system of criticism' of some 'transatlantic commentator.'" Chandler, *England in 1819: The Politics of Literary Culture and the Case of Romantic Historicism* (Chicago: Chicago University Press, 1998), 488. We are equally impacted by those scholars who have contemplated Shelleyan constellations and allegories akin to Walter Benjamin's methodologies, including Mathelinda Nabugodi, *Shelley with Benjamin: A Critical Mosaic* (London: UCL Press, 2023); Jacques Khalip and Forest Pyle, eds. *Constellations of a Contemporary Romanticism* (New York: Fordham University Press, 2016), as well as those thinkers who work through

impossible futures of Jacques Derrida's *l'avenir* (the future-to-come), for example, David Brookshire, ed. *P. B. Shelley and the Delimitation of the Gothic, Romantic Circles* Praxis Series (November 2015), https://romantic-circles.org/praxis/gothic_shelley; the deconstructive present of Paul de Man's irony, such as Forest Pyle, "Kindling and Ash: Radical Aestheticism in Keats and Shelley," *Studies in Romanticism* 42.4 (December 2003), 427–459; Lacanian disruptions as in David Sigler, *Fracture Feminism: The Politics of Impossible Time in British Romanticism* (Albany: State University of New York Press, 2021), and, finally, Anthropocene temporalities as in Jacques Khalip's *Last Things: Disastrous Form from Kant to Hujar* (New York: Fordham University Press, 2018).

22 Richard Holmes, *Shelley: The Pursuit* (New York: Dutton), 1975.

23 See Nabugodi's essay in this volume; Taylor Schey, "Romanticism and the Rhetoric of Racialization," *Studies in Romanticism* 61.1 (2022), 35–26; and Debbie Lee's earlier work, *Slavery and the Romantic Imagination* (Philadelphia: University of Pennsylvania Press, 2004).

24 Both Nabugodi and Singer in this volume connect Shelley's thinking about sexuality to his attitudes toward Blackness, slavery, and race; for more in-depth discussion about Shelley's views on homosexuality, see Richard Sha, "The Uses and Abuses of Historicism: Halperin and Shelley on the Otherness of Ancient Greek Sexuality," in Richard Sha, ed. *Historicizing Romantic Sexuality, Romantic Circles* Praxis Series (January 2006). https://romantic-circles.org/praxis/sexuality/sha/sha.html; Louis Crompton, *Byron and Greek Love: Homophobia in Nineteenth Century England* (Los Angeles: University of California Press, 1985); Alexander Freer, "A Genealogy of Narcissism," *Nineteenth-Century Literature* 74.1 (June 2019), 1–29; Nancy Goslee, "Shelley's Greek 'Discourse': Ancient Manners and Modern Liberty," *The Wordsworth Circle* 36.1 (Winter 2005), 2–5; and Kate Singer, "Shelley's Sexless Sexuality," in Ross Wilson, ed. *Percy Shelley in Context* (Cambridge: Cambridge University Press, in press).

25 We take the term "contexture" from Neil Fraistat, *The Poem and the Book: Interpreting Collections of Romantic Poetry* (Chapel Hill: The University of North Carolina Press, 1985), 4.

26 Albert Kuhn, "English Deism and the Development of Romantic Mythological Syncretism," *PMLA* 71.5 (December 1956), 1094–1116; Earl Wasserman, *Shelley's Prometheus Unbound: A Critical Reading* (Baltimore: Johns Hopkins University Press, 1965); Harold Bloom, *Shelley's Mythmaking* (Ithaca: Cornell University Press, 1969); Stuart Curran, *Shelley's Annus Mirabilis: The Maturing of an Epic Vision* (Pasadena: Huntington Library Press, 1975); and Jerrold Hogle, *Shelley's Process: Radical Transference and the Development of His Major Works* (Oxford: Oxford University Press, 1989).

27 Carman, *The Radical Ecology of the Shelleys*.

28 Julie A. Carlson, "Like Love: The Feel of Shelley's Similes," in Joel Faflak and Richard C. Sha, eds. *Romanticism and the Emotions* (Cambridge: Cambridge University Press, 2014), 76–97.

29 Bysshe Inigo Coffey, *Shelley's Broken World: Fractured Materiality and Intermitted Song* (Liverpool: Liverpool University Press, 2021).
30 Richard Sha, *Imagination and Science in Romanticism* (Baltimore: Johns Hopkins University Press, 2018); Lussier, *Romantic Dynamics*; and Morton, *Shelley and the Revolution in Taste*. See also Alan Bewell's chapter on Shelley in *Romanticism and Colonial Disease* (Baltimore: Johns Hopkins University Press, 2003).
31 Classic studies of Shelley's skepticism include C. E. Pulos, *The Deep Truth: A Study of Shelley's Skepticism* (Lincoln: University of Nebraska Press, 1962) and Lloyd Abbey, *Destroyer and Preserver: Shelley's Poetic Skepticism* (Lincoln: University of Nebraska Press, 1980).
32 For some of the extensive textual history around Shelley's reception and his works, see Fraistat, "Illegitimate Shelley," and the thick headnotes and commentary with the major editions of Shelley that we cite in this collection, not to mention the digital online resource of *The Shelley-Godwin Archive*, http://shelleygodwinarchive.org/. See also work on Mary Shelley's editing of Percy Shelley, including Susan Wolfson, "Editorial Privilege: Mary Shelley and Percy Shelley's Audiences," in Audrey A. Fisch, Anne K. Mellor, and Esther Schor, eds. *The Other Mary Shelley: Beyond Frankenstein* (New York: Oxford University Press, 1993), 39–72; Michael O'Neill, "'Trying to Make It as Good as I Can': Mary Shelley's Editing of P. B. Shelley's Poetry and Prose," in Betty T. Bennett and Stuart Curran, eds. *Mary Shelley in Her Times* (Baltimore: Johns Hopkins University Press), 185–197; as well as current and forthcoming work from Michael Rossington, including "Editing Shelley," in Michael O'Neill, Anthony Howe, and Madeleine Callaghan, eds. *The Oxford Handbook of Percy Bysshe Shelley* (Oxford: Oxford University Press, 2013), 646–656.
33 Arthur Bradley, "Shelley Criticism from Deconstruction to the Present," in O'Neill, Howe, and Callaghan, eds. *The Oxford Handbook of Percy Bysshe Shelley*, 673–688.
34 Forest Pyle, *The Ideology of Imagination: Subject and Society in the Discourse of Romanticism* (Stanford: Stanford University Press, 1995); Pyle, *Art's Undoing: In the Wake of a Radical Aestheticism* (New York: Fordham University Press, 2014); Joel Faflak, ed. *The Futures of Shelley's* Triumph, *Romantic Circles* Praxis Series (October 2019), https://romantic-circles.org/praxis/publication/futures-shelleys-triumph; Jacques Khalip and Forest Pyle, eds. *Constellations of a Contemporary Romanticism* (New York: Fordham University Press, 2016); Marc Redfield, *The Politics of Aesthetics: Nationalism, Gender, Romanticism* (Stanford: Stanford University Press, 2003); Pyle, *Romanticism and the Insistence of the Aesthetic*; Orrin N. C. Wang's chapters on Shelley in *Fantastic Modernity, Romantic Sobriety: Sensation, Revolution, Commodification, History* (Baltimore: Johns Hopkins University Press, 2011) and *Techno-Magism: Media, Mediation, and the Cut of Romanticism* (New York: Fordham University Press, 2022); David Collings, *Disastrous Subjectivities: Romanticism, Modernity, and the Real*; Karen Swann, *Lives of the Dead Poets: Keats, Shelley, Coleridge* (New York: Fordham University Press, 2019).

35 See chapters on Shelley in Paul de Man's *The Rhetoric of Romanticism* (New York: Columbia University Press, 1984) and in Wang's *Fantastic Modernity*.
36 Paul Foot, *Red Shelley* (New York: Bookmarks, 1995); Michael Demson, *Masks of Anarchy: The History of a Radical Poem from Percy Shelley to the Triangle Factory Fire* (Brooklyn: Verso, 2013); Michael Scrivener, *Radical Shelley: The Philosophical and Utopian Thought of Percy Bysshe Shelley* (Princeton: Princeton University Press, 1982); Terence Allan Hoagwood, *Skepticism & Ideology: Shelley's Political Prose and Its Philosophical Context from Bacon to Marx* (Iowa City: University of Iowa Press, 1988); Robert Kaufman, "Legislators of the Post-everything World: Shelley's Defence of Adorno," *ELH* 63.3 (1996), 707–733; and Robert Kaufman, "Intervention and Commitment Forever! Shelley in 1819, Shelley in Brecht, Shelley in Adorno, Shelley in Benjamin," in Michael Scrivener, ed. *Reading Shelley's Interventionist Poetry, 1819–1820*, *Romantic Circles* Praxis Series (May 2001), https://romantic-circles.org/praxis/interventionist/kaufman/kaufman.html; and William Keach, "The Political Poet," in Morton, *The Cambridge Companion to Percy Shelley*, 123–142.
37 Greg Ellerman, "Red Shelley, Once Again," *Keats-Shelley Journal* 68 (2019), 104–105, 104.
38 Warren, *The Orient and the Young Romantics* and Kai Pyle, "Ningaabii'an Negamotawag: Translating Shelley into Ojibwe," *Studies in Romanticism* 61.4 (Winter 2002), 491–502.
39 Graham Henderson, "The Real Percy Bysshe Shelley," www.grahamhenderson.ca/.
40 Camila Oliveira, "'Music When Soft Voices Live': Shelley's Reception in Contemporary Music," Thursday, May 11, 2023, Talk for Keats-Shelley Association of America.
41 Martin Luther King, Jr., "Letter from a Birmingham Jail," *Ebony*, August 1963, 23–32, 23.

CHAPTER 1

Shelley, Treaty-Making, and Indigenous Poetry
Nikki Hessell

When Mary Shelley added the posthumous title "England in 1819" to one of her husband's sonnets, she localized the terrible consequences of unjust and failing legal and political structures in a particular country in 1819. But the implications of Shelley's poem, and its diagnosis of a failing governing order, reached far beyond England, given that colonization and imperialism had created forced, negotiated, and voluntary relationships between the British and peoples all over the globe. What did it mean to be subject to Shelley's "Golden and sanguine laws which tempt and slay" if your people had been colonized by the English and were now entangled in those laws (10 [*SPP* 327])? How could your people and their descendants maintain an effective, treaty-based, nation-to-nation relationship with an "old, mad, blind, despised, and dying King" or expect long-term, kin-based, reciprocal justice from "Princes, the dregs of their dull race" (1, 2 [326])?

This chapter explores the way in which Shelley's verse speaks to, or influences, two kinds of texts: the treaties between the various Indigenous peoples of North America and British or settler governments, and Indigenous-authored poetry that interacts with these treaties. The chapter begins by conceptualizing 1819 (an iconic year in Romantic studies) as a "treaty year," one in which Shelley's "England in 1819" and *The Mask of Anarchy*, despite their apparent focus on domestic politics, can be read alongside major global diplomatic events that occurred in settler-Indigenous relationships in North America, such as Treaties 21 and 27 in British Canada and the Treaty of Saginaw in the United States. In these documents, and the negotiations around them, repeated reference was made to the status of the British monarchs, their moral standing, and their intergenerational relationships with Indigenous peoples, at exactly the moment that Shelley was suggesting that the British crown could not be trusted on these terms. I argue that while Shelley's poems and these treaty negotiations do not directly engage with each other in their moment of composition, they can be read intertextually in terms of the moral and legal failings of the British state that Shelley's poems diagnose as part of a global political culture.

The chapter then turns to late nineteenth- and early twentieth-century Native American poets who used Shelley's political poetry as a source for considering the 1819 treaties, subsequent treaty agreements, and the consequences of colonization. My focus here is on writers who were members of the southeastern Native nations referred to at the time as the "Five Civilized Tribes." These nations (the Cherokees, Chickasaws, Choctaws, Seminoles, and Mvskoke Creeks) were all subject to the genocidal policies set in motion by the 1830 Removal Act, which forced Native nations west of the Mississippi in the events now referred to in English as the Trail of Tears. Later in the nineteenth century, these peoples were further disenfranchised by the Curtis Act (1898), which breached the treaty rights established as the basis for removal, divided up and individualized land title, and dismantled tribal government. My initial focus is on Too-qua-stee (Cherokee) and James Roane Gregory (Yuchi and Mvskoke Creek). Gregory's and Too-qua-stee's different allusions to and adoptions of Shelley's 1819 poems in their own verse demonstrate, I argue, that both "England in 1819" and *The Mask of Anarchy* were interpreted by Indigenous poets as highly relevant to their contemporary concerns about broken treaties, even as they operated out of different cultural traditions and with different treaty breaches in mind. In Indigenous epistemologies and understandings of the diplomatic process, treaties had significant affective and performative dimensions as well as legal ones, and poetry was an appropriate medium through which to engage with treaty documents and discourse. The relevance of poems such as "England in 1819" and *The Mask of Anarchy* was apparent to Indigenous poets and activists precisely because Shelley had diagnosed the associated political and ethical failings that they too would explore through their poetry. The chapter also considers the ways in which Shelley's more meditative poems, such as "Mont Blanc," might be drawn into a wider conversation about colonization, treaty-making, and Indigenous peoples, when identified as influences on Indigenous expression, via the poetry of a third writer from these nations, John Rollin Ridge (Cherokee). Finally, the chapter assesses what these connections from 1819 mean for treaties and Indigenous rights today.

Since the Indigenous poets I focus on in this essay are all either Mvskoke Creek or Cherokee, I choose to take my critical and methodological guidance from scholars from those nations. Mvskoke Creek literary critic Craig Womack has noted that, in terms of literature and contact, "it is just as likely that things European are Indianized rather than the anthropological assumption that things Indian are always swallowed up by European culture."¹ My aim in this essay is to think, then, about an Indianized Shelley, one whose works were put to various uses by Indigenous authors in the name of treaty rights, sovereignty, and autonomy. Shelley's poetry, I wish to suggest, with its excoriation of corrupt power structures, its comprehension of legal orders derived from the natural world, and its visions of new and better worlds, was ideally suited to these aims. So too, in the case of *The Mask of Anarchy* in particular, were the poetic forms and allegories that Shelley expertly deployed. Before I turn to verse, however, I want to consider the significance of Indigenous treaty-making in Shelley's own historical moment.

The title "England in 1819" has provided a ready-made framework for scholars to focus intently on the events of a key year in the period we define as the Romantic era. But there is at least one aspect of the politics of 1819 that is sometimes overlooked in the field of Romantic studies: it was a boom year for treaties with Indigenous peoples. In that crucial year, having inherited some of Britain's relationships with Indigenous groups, the American government negotiated four important treaties: two with the Kickapoo, one with the Ojibwe, and one with the Cherokees. Across the border in British Canada, 1819 also marked treaties that led to two small but important land purchases, the Long Woods Treaty, now known as Treaty 21, signed with the Mississauga on March 9, 1819, and the Rideau Purchase, known as Treaty 27, also signed with the Mississauga, on May 31 the same year. It is these latter treaties, signed by the same British government that Shelley was excoriating, which I wish to focus on first in order to consider the global dimensions of Shelley's "England in 1819."

Treaty 21 and Treaty 27 were designed to give control of Indigenous land to British Canada in what is currently called Ontario. In both cases, the final documents were drawn up in 1822, several years after the initial discussions, and for that reason reflect an important change in personnel. The officials in the 1819 negotiations were, as the 1822 documents point out in identical language, acting on behalf of "his Late Majesty King George the Third, of Blessed Memory."² The final agreement, however, is signed by "the Chiefs and Principal Men of the Missisague [*sic*] Nation of Indians [and] His most Gracious Majesty George the Fourth, by the Grace of God of the United Kingdom of Great Britain and Ireland, King, Defender of the Faith." What the Mississauga are agreeing to is the relinquishment of their land "unto His said Majesty King George the Fourth, His heirs and successors, to the only proper use, benefit and behoof of His said Majesty, His heirs and successors forever," in return for "unto each man, woman and child of the said Missisagua [sic] Nation of Indians who at the time of entering into the said agreement inhabited and claimed the said tract of land, and to their descendants and posterity forever, an annuity of two pounds and ten shillings." What the documents do, in other words, is encode long-term familial relationships and lines of descent as the basis for reciprocity, legal protection, and justice, and begin those lines of descent in the particular identities of George III and George IV.

This kinship-based relationship made sense, and continues to make sense today, in terms of the legal structures that would have guided the Mississauga negotiators. As part of the wider Anishinaabe peoples, the Mississauga would have been informed by the understandings of kinship and treaties that Anishinaabe legal scholar Aaron Mills has outlined in his research, based on his work with elders:

> Nehetho elder D'Arcy Linklater offers some of the clearest statements I've encountered reflecting an understanding that treaty establishes kinship. He says […] "*Wahkotowin* (relationship) is very important to our people and at time of Treaty-making the Queen adopted us as her children to protect us and to take care of us" and that "We should talk about the Treaty and how the Queen became our relation. Relationship is sacred. She said that she would like to take care of her children." Ininiw Elder William G. Lathlin similarly states "The Elders said that we adopted the King or Queen into our family. This was not told to the King or Queen. This is the only way we were able to relate to Treaty."[3]

Shelley's poem provides a grim gloss on these ideas, not just in the opening description of the personal and political failings of the two Georges but in the wider sense that the legal and political system that sustains them is equally corrupted. Colonial treaty-making depended on the notion that the parties were entering into familial relationships with each other, both in the present and in future generations. The language used by Indigenous negotiators and replicated by settler or imperial officials reflected these kin relations: it was typical to refer to the other side of the treaty partnership as fathers, brothers, uncles, and sons. "England in 1819" serves as a reminder that the corrupt conduct of the British crown and government, conduct which had led to a "fainting country" and "a people starved and stabbed," fatally jeopardized any good-faith, kin-based relationships that Britain might wish to enter into with Indigenous peoples (5, 7 [*SPP* 326]). Shelley's "Golden and sanguine laws which tempt and slay" are woven through Treaties 21 and 27, holding out the promise of protection and fair treatment in a manner that actively seeks to influence the people signing the document before delivering violence and punitive justice, and offering the feckless leadership of the Hanovers as a deeply compromised version of the intergenerational obligations that the wider Indigenous cultures in North America adhered to and would recognize. While Shelley imagined the legal frameworks of Britain in these lines of verse, those legal frameworks no longer adhered to any kind of national boundary. A British-based legal system had, by 1819, spread across the world, and documents such as Treaties 21 and 27 did not simply reflect the "golden and sanguine laws," but were identifiable instruments *of* those laws, formed out of the language and political and cultural structures that upheld them, and entangling anyone who engaged formally with those legal instruments in that wider system of law. The familial and intergenerational relationships that treaties promised relied on the honor of the British crown to uphold its responsibilities; Shelley's 1819 poems laid out the reasons why these relationships were doomed to failure.

By 1819, the British monarchy had not controlled their American colonies for almost fifty years. But the history of nation-to-nation negotiation on the North American continent meant that, although Indigenous groups in the United States were now dealing with American federal and state governments, they continued to make reference to their long-standing connections to the nations of Europe, including Great Britain. These relationships had always been, on both sides, expressed as family relationships; the dominance of Native Americans in pre-Revolutionary times had meant that diplomacy between Indigenous nations, the British crown, and its settler representatives was conducted on their terms, making use of the discourse of fathers, uncles, and brothers that helped situate governmental actors within a web of reciprocal, hereditary, kin-based relationships. We can see some of the effects of this language in a speech given by O-ge-maw-ke-ke-to at the Treaty of Saginaw between the Ojibwe and the Americans on September 24, 1819. O-ge-maw-ke-ke-to said, via an interpreter:

> Your young men have invited us to come and light the Council fire. We are here to smoke the pipe of peace, but not to sell our lands. Our American Father wants them. Our English Father treats us better. He never asked for them.[4]

The "English Father" implies both the titular King of England, whoever might happen to occupy that role, and more specifically, George III (still technically king in 1819 and certainly the point of reference for the late eighteenth-century events to which O-ge-maw-ke-ke-to refers when he says "He never asked for them"), but also to some extent George IV, in his role as regent in 1819. We might not recognize O-ge-maw-ke-ke-to's complimentary descriptions of Georges III and IV as having much connection to the "old, mad, blind, despised and dying King" or "Princes, the dregs of their dull race," but of course they do: the flaws that Shelley so rightly points out in the British crown provide a tragic gloss on O-ge-maw-ke-ke-to's confident sense that he could refuse to negotiate with the Americans because of a strong, kin-based, diplomatic relationship with the British, personified in the royal family, an alliance that he believed could be reactivated (1–2 [*SPP* 326]). As Shelley's poem could have shown O-ge-maw-ke-ke-to, however, the leaders of Britain were deeply extractive in their conduct; "Rulers who neither see nor feel nor know, / But leechlike to their fainting country cling" were already treating their own nation in the manner they and their settler heirs intended to treat the colonies (4–5 [326]). The failures that Shelley notes in his own country's leadership are the same failures that left these prior treaty relationships in tatters, their obligations virtually meaningless, and likewise left Indigenous peoples bereft of alliances they had relied upon and cultivated over many years.

But the connections between Shelley, treaties, and Indigenous speakers and writers are not just contextual and historical questions of kinship and kingship. The language and forms of Shelley's poetry, especially his poems of 1819, became a powerful source of inspiration for Indigenous writers of later generations, who attempted to revisit the agreements made in 1819 and beyond in their poems. From the end of the War of 1812, there had been a slew of treaties between the southeastern Native nations and the United States government, as the victorious Americans looked to capitalize on their success and expand the settler-colonial state. Although some Native nations, including the Cherokees, had fought alongside the Americans against the British, the postwar treaties aimed at a ruthless land grab and the forced dismantling of Native sovereignty. Many of these treaties were organized by then-General Andrew Jackson, later, as president, to be the architect of the 1830 Removal Act, and John C. Calhoun, who would go on to be Jackson's vice president.

The poems this chapter considers are by different Indigenous authors writing at different times, but they are all composed by members of the five southeastern nations and they have a common source in the events of the watershed year of 1819. As noted by Sharon O'Brien, a settler historian who worked with members of the Muscogee Nation, the Mvskoke Creeks passed a law around 1819 "declaring that no tribal lands could be sold without approval of the national council, under penalty of death. Federal negotiators, however, ignored the nation's refusal to negotiate and concluded a series of illegal treaties," a sequence of events that eventually led to removal and then to the late nineteenth-century treaty breaches that James Roane Gregory, whose poems this chapter examines, lived through, wrote about, and fought against.[5] Meanwhile, in February 1819, the Cherokees had agreed to what they hoped would be a final treaty with the United States, sending their leaders from Georgia to Washington to negotiate. This crucial treaty document opened with a preamble about Cherokee priorities:

> Whereas a greater part of the Cherokee nation have expressed an earnest desire to remain on this side of the Mississippi, and being desirous [...] to commence those measures which they deem necessary to the civilization and preservation of their nation [...] [they] have offered to cede to the United States a tract of country.[6]

The 1819 treaty, in other words, was an attempt by the Cherokees to cede a final portion of their land in Georgia in order to see off the threat of removal to the west. This negotiation, like the Mvskoke Creek law, was part of an urgent effort by Indigenous leaders to hold on to land and sovereignty; it was designed to end the process of dispossession and disenfranchisement that had characterized the years since American independence and to be the last land cession they would make.[7] But the United States government simply failed to live up to the undertakings made in this critical treaty, leading, eventually, to the genocide of the Trail of Tears. Some key ideas discussed in Gregory's, Too-qua-stee's, and Ridge's poems thus have a particular resonance with the year 1819 and the last-ditch attempts by the Cherokee leadership to secure their homelands via treaty provisions and by the Mvskoke Creek to refuse any further treaty negotiations.

One particular term stands out as a link between Shelley's verse and some of these Indigenous-authored poems. At the conclusion of Treaty 27, the document notes: "IN WITNESS WHEREOF, the parties to these presents have hereunto set their hands and seals the day and year first above written. The Indians not knowing how to write, have made their marks against their respective seals." I want to take some liberties with Shelley's intentions here, and suggest, for the purposes of globalizing and Indigenizing his poem, that we read his phrase "a book sealed" (11 [*SPP* 327]) as referring to a sealed treaty. Both elements of Shelley's phrase overlap with treaty discourse and paraphernalia. Definitions of a "book" in Shelley's time include "a legal document, especially a charter or deed by which land is conveyed," while a "seal" described both the actual physical wax device on a document and the figurative sense of promising or authenticating one's words and undertakings.[8] The word "seal" or "sealed" appears repeatedly in the treaties of 1819 and beyond; the conclusion to

Treaty 27 describes it, in the normal legal formulation, as "signed, sealed and delivered," before the respective seals, marks, or totems of the participating signatories are recorded. Seals were the physical manifestation of sovereignty and the right to negotiate or accept terms. My point here is not that Shelley intends his readers to think of a sealed treaty – no doubt, as most commentators have pointed out, he means to refer to the Bible as a sealed book, a metaphor in which the sense of both "book" and "seal" converge around the idea of a covenant or agreement. But what might a nineteenth-century Indigenous reader have made of the word "sealed" in Shelley's poem? What would the natural associations of that word suggest to such a reader, beyond the implications of the Bible? And how might those associations then get reformulated in Indigenous poetry?

There are some Indigenous-authored poems that sit between a poem such as "England in 1819" and the treaties of 1819 and can help emphasize the importance of Shelley's promissory poetics for treaty-based relationships in the settler colonies. In 1895, the Mvskoke Creek writer James Roane Gregory, a lawyer and judge, wrote a poem called "The Promised Seal."[9]

> Monopolies greedy host, Pander,
> Claiming right, held justice to repeal,
> Truest honor to deride and slander,
> Helpless children, crushed 'neath tyrant's heel.
> Boodlers and drunken Sages, meander.
> While the pure, for just right, vain appeal.
> On their homes, land, lone outcasts, wanderers.
> Soon, heed ye well for the promised seal.
>
> That seal will equalize, the plunder
> Will be true and show each just right real.
> Least dishonor and might asunder,
> Each child shall retain humanity's weal.
> The seal of next September's thunder.
> Count each vote, vaunting haught' kneel.
> Injuns can remember—yhu'll wonder;
> They strike strong, when Injuns cast the seal.

Gregory's poetry in English often has an awkward quality, according to his editor Robert Dale Parker, and perhaps can be explained by Gregory's own comment that he thought in Mvskoke. But a reader can also hear the strong echoes of a Shelleyan syntax, meter, and vocabulary hiding behind this poem, such as the structure and sound of the opening line, "Monopolies, greedy host, Pander" compared with Shelley's "Religion, Christless, Godless" (11 [*SPP* 327]) or Gregory's "Helpless children, crushed 'neath tyrant's heel"[10] with Shelley's "A people starved and stabbed in the untill'd field" (7 [326]). It is entirely possible that the mission school-educated Gregory does have Shelley's poem in mind here (he was known to be a voracious reader) and from that foundation, we might consider the way in which Gregory interprets the hint provided by Shelley's word "sealed" (11 [326]).[11]

Parker notes he was unable to identify the titular "promised seal" mentioned in this poem, nor the event that occurred in September 1895, to which the poem refers, but I would like to suggest one possibility.[12] The relevant lines are "The seal of next September's thunder. / Count each vote."[13] Gregory was nominated for principal chief by the Progressive Party of the Creek Nation, an election that he lost in September 1895. Might the seal, then, be the seal that the principal chief used on official documents from around 1885 – the Great Seal of the Muscogee Nation? Many Indigenous groups adopted seals as a way of signaling nationhood, sovereignty, autonomy, and the paraphernalia of the state that they had seen mobilized most visibly in the seals used by European and American governments on treaty documents, alongside a host of other strategies designed to signal to their treaty partners that they had legitimate and recognizable political structures.[14] The Cherokees, Chickasaws, Mvskoke-Creeks, Seminoles, and Choctaws had all signed treaties that featured phrases such as "the parties have hereunto set their hands and seals," and the word typically implied not just a wax seal but also a mark or signature of assent.[15] Each of these groups had adopted a formal collective seal sometime in the nineteenth century after their forced removal west of the Mississippi, usually as part of a process to establish a written constitution and to regularize relationships with the federal and state governments, having seen the symbolic power of the seals used on treaties.[16] The need for this paraphernalia and material paratext had become acute by the time that Gregory was composing his poem; although the Cherokees, Chickasaws, Choctaws, Seminoles, and Mvskoke Creeks were exempted from the Dawes Act of 1887, which allotted Native land into individual titles, the 1898 Curtis Act nullified that exemption, a clear violation of the treaties of 1819 and beyond that had guaranteed control of their new tribal lands to the nations who were removed to the west.[17]

For Gregory, the idea conjured up by Shelley's "book sealed" is perhaps something more tangible than Shelley's original notion of a metaphorically sealed Bible, something instead associated with sovereignty and Indigenous autonomy, the right to make and administer laws on one's own terms and in a manner that prioritizes kinship relations. That is not necessarily what Shelley meant by "a book sealed," but it is also not outside the bounds of Shelley's political sensibilities, nor a distortion of the broader meaning of "England in 1819." Gregory's final image ("They strike strong, when Injuns cast the seal") is his own version of the phantom bursting from the grave, a darkly positive image of the hope that can arise from political despair, or as the editors of the Longman edition of Shelley's poems suggest in their interpretation of "England in 1819," a suggestion of the "way to a radically altered future" (*Poems* III: 189).

The signal importance of the word "seal" for Gregory can be ascertained from the fact that it appears in another of his Shelleyesque poems from the same year.[18] "Otheen, Okiyetos" (Mvskoke for "I really, really mean what I am saying") addresses an unnamed but hostile interlocutor, who is asked "hast thou been true,"

> Or hast thou from thy high gifted seal,
> Heaven's gift of speech, betrayed with a lie,
> Denied thy tongue, humanity's weal;
> With thy false soul, the evil one's eye?[19]

In this instance, the "seal" in question is a settler one, such as those found on treaties, which symbolizes the promises and written undertakings that state and federal governments were setting aside. The consequences of this promise-breaking are laid out in "Otheen, Okiyetos" in terms that echo Shelley's denouncement of his own government:

> Myriads of dangers compass the land,
> Each broken promise of thine, a moan
> Each link of hope, prove a chain of sand,
> Each promise, a viper of hell, sown.
>
> When did the Muskogee blood kneel low?
> Answer! (then ye will praise honor's grave).
> Never, till they fell 'neath the death blow,
> Returned glory's gift to God that gave.[20]

The images of a land in turmoil and a people struck down resonate with Shelley's ideas. Gregory's image of the Mvskogee who "fell 'neath the death blow" recalls Shelley's image of the Peterloo victims, while Gregory's sense of "honor's grave" reminds us of the "graves from which a glorious Phantom may / Burst" at the conclusion of "England in 1819" (13–14 [*SPP* 327]). These echoes in Gregory's work are not simply a shared imagery of violence and hope but also a meditation on treaties and their afterlives. The connection to the notion of broken promises and the betrayal of the meaning behind "thy high gifted seal" reimagines "England in 1819" and *The Mask of Anarchy* within Mvskoke Creek expectations of treaty relationships.

Gregory was not the only member of the Five Tribes to see potential in Shelley's verse. Too-qua-stee/De Witt Clinton Duncan (Cherokee), who had been removed from his homelands as a baby on the Trails of Tears, graduated from Dartmouth College, and became a teacher of English, Latin, and Greek, seems to have borrowed extensively from *The Mask of Anarchy* in his "The Dead Nation: An Elegy at the Tomb of the Cherokee Nation, by One of Her Own Sons" (1899).[21] Lamenting his "poor luckless nation,"[22] Too-qua-stee alludes to the Cherokee creation story and the "halcyon peace"[23] that reigned until colonization, before introducing this sequence of ideas:

> But then came Art, in rouge and ribbons dressed,
> The source of woe, borne on the winged hours,
> And, squat upon thine own salubrious west,
> Bred pestilence and rot within thy bowers.
>
> Smit by the blast of her contagious breath
> Thy children fell in armies at thy side;
> And struggling in the grip of a strange death,
> Exclaimed, 'O white man!' closed their eyes and died.
>
> Came also Might, the adjutant of Art,
> Wrenched off the hinges from the joints of truth,
> And tore its system into shreds apart—
> Repeated, in short, the moral code, forsooth.
>
> Then first it was, that on thy peaceful plains
> The roar of onset and the saber's gleam,
> Began—but hold! humanity refrains,
> And genius cannot paint a dying scream.
>
> Thus rotting Pestilence, and Art and Might,
> In moonlight orgies o'er thy children's bones,
> To honor civilization, hands unite
> And dance the music of their dying groans.[24]

Shelley's Murder, Fraud, and Hypocrisy are here reimagined as the "Pestilence, and Art, and Might" of settler-colonial violence, in a stanza form and meter which mirror that of *The Mask of Anarchy* and draw out the potential of Shelley's poem to represent a collective, plurivocal expression of anger and revolution. And this was not the only time

Too-qua-stee turned to Shelley to make a political point. His "A Vision of the End" deploys similar allegories, perhaps augmented with some of "The Rime of the Ancient Mariner."[25] In a dystopic imagining of a polluted landscape, where "government, a monstrous form"[26] is located, Too-qua-stee writes:

> It was the reign of general death,
> Wide as the sweep of eye,
> Save two vile ghosts that still draw breath
> Because they could not die.
>
> Ambition climbed above the waves,
> From wreck to wreck he strove.
> And as they sunk to watery waves
> He on to glory rode.
>
> And there was Greed—immortal Greed—
> Just from the shores of time.
> Of all hell's hosts he took the lead,
> A monarch of the slime.[27]

Like his "Pestilence, and Art, and Might" in "The Dead Nation," Too-qua-stee's Greed and Ambition here echo Shelley's allegories of political corruption and malfeasance, symbolizing the ways in which kinship and reciprocal treaty-based relationships had become perverted in Cherokee country. While Shelley's royals were "mud from a muddy spring," Too-qua-stee's allegorized settler leader is a "monarch of the slime," a vile version of the father/uncle/brother figure who was imagined in settler-Indigenous treaties.

In these poems, the grotesqueness that Shelley located in Peterloo and in the wider nation in 1819 has been localized to illustrate the failure of treaty promises in the United States. Too-qua-stee's "The Dead Nation," in particular, was a direct response to the loss of Native land and sovereignty heralded by the 1898 Curtis Act and was one of a number of poems he devoted to that subject. The immediate effect of the Curtis Act was the loss of 90 million acres of Native land, land which had been guaranteed via treaties to the Five Tribes when they relocated, some voluntarily but many under violent duress, to the west of the Mississippi. In response to these treaty violations, poets such as Gregory and Too-qua-stee saw enormous potential in the poems of liberty, resistance, and the sovereignty of the people that Shelley had produced in 1819, both as records of previous acts of resistance and as diagnostic tools for the dishonorable behavior of settler governments and officials when it came to treaty promises and the kinship relationships they encoded.

There is another strain of Shelleyan influence in nineteenth-century Native American poetry, however, one that mobilizes an alternative set of Shelley's poems and imagines an alternative kind of Indigenous relationship with settler-colonial treaty partners. John Rollin Ridge (Cheesquat-a-law-ny/Yellow Bird) belonged to a prominent Cherokee family and was a prolific poet. His life was profoundly shaped by Indigenous-settler treaties. His father and grandfather were members of the Treaty Party, a group of Cherokee men who signed an unauthorized agreement with the United States government, the 1835 Treaty of New Echota. This treaty required the Cherokees to leave their lands in the southeast and move to the western side of the Mississippi, despite consistent and vigorous opposition from Principal Chief John Ross and many other Cherokees. In 1839, most of the Treaty Party, including Ridge's father and grandfather, were assassinated as traitors for their part in the 1835 agreement, an event that is still controversial in Cherokee country today.[28] Ridge remained true to the deeply conservative values of the Treaty Party throughout his life, which included support for slavery and a strong strain of anti-Black racism, a belief in assimilation as the only path forward for Indigenous peoples but within the context of "Indian Country" becoming its own state in the Union, and a sympathetic but patronizing attitude to Native Americans who were not part of the Five Tribes. He would go on to be a treaty negotiator himself for the Cherokee Nation.

Scholars have noted that Ridge's poetry reflects the influence of Shelley, whom he had probably read at school, but on this occasion, it is not the radical political poems but the meditative works on nature and Shelley's concepts of the role of the poet that operate as intertexts.[29] A poem such as Ridge's "To a Mockingbird Singing in a Tree," for example, domesticates Shelley's skylark while retaining the address to a bird that should "Soar on, as now, abhorrent of control."[30] The poem ends, as Shelley's does, with a lesson about listening to nature:

> If living thought can never die,
> Why should thine own expire? If there is love
> Within thy heart, it must live on,
> Nor less than man's have dwelling-place above;
> Thy notes shall then be brighter far
> Than now they be! And I may listen, too,
> With finer ear, and clearer soul,
> Beneath a shade more soft, a sky more blue.[31]

This notion of the role of the poet in listening to and interpreting nature is developed further in Ridge's "Mount Shasta," the poem of which he was most proud.³² It opens with a stanza that echoes some of Shelley's language in "Mont Blanc," an obvious inspiration for Ridge's verse:

> Behold the dread Mt. Shasta, where it stands
> Imperial midst the lesser heights, and, like
> Some mighty unimpassioned mind, companionless
> And cold. The storms of Heaven may beat in wrath
> Against it, but it stands in unpolluted
> Grandeur still; and from the rolling mists upheaves
> Its tower of pride e'en purer than before.
> The wintry showers and white-winged tempests leave
> Their frozen tributes on its brow, and it
> Doth make of them an everlasting crown.
> Thus doth it, day by day and age by age,
> Defy each stroke of time: still rising highest
> Into Heaven!³³

While much of "Mount Shasta" could be excerpted to draw attention to Shelley's (and Romantic literature's) language and concerns, I want to focus on one moment in the poem, and a corresponding moment in "Mont Blanc," which brings the notion of treaties and Indigenous sovereignty into the literary framework. In the final stanza of "Mount Shasta," Ridge looks towards the future of the American West, writing:

> And well this Golden State shall thrive, if like
> Its own Mt. Shasta, Sovereign Law shall lift
> Itself in purer atmosphere—so high
> That human feeling, human passion at its base
> Shall lie subdued; e'en pity's tears shall on
> Its summit freeze; to warm it e'en the sunlight
> Of deep sympathy shall fail:
> Its pure administration shall be like
> The snow immaculate upon that mountain's brow.³⁴

Although very different in its sentiments, the poem's turn to law, government, and the administration of the land connects to a power Shelley too vests in a summit when he writes:

> Thou hast a voice, great Mountain, to repeal
> Large codes of fraud and woe; not understood
> By all, but which the wise, and great, and good
> Interpret, or make felt, or deeply feel. (80–83 [*CP* III: 85])

Ridge composed his poem in 1853–1854, after moving to California to join the gold rush, but he remained deeply involved in the affairs of what he consistently referred to as "the Cherokee Nation."[35] In these lines, he contemplates the possibility of a sovereign administration that would mirror the authority of the landscape, almost vesting legal power in the mountain. His focus here is on the "Golden State" of California, but he was also entirely committed to the idea of Native statehood, the long-held belief that the area of the United States occupied by the Five Tribes following their removal should become an autonomous state of the Union.[36] This view corresponded with Ridge's complicated political outlook; it was a position that championed Indigenous assimilation into the political structures of the United States, while at the same time carving out space for his people's sovereignty and autonomy. In the 1850s, while writing poems like "Mount Shasta," Ridge also wrote journalism advocating for a Native state, one that would, like California, be able to construct its own "Sovereign Law" grounded in the natural world, as well as articles that advocated for the role of the poet by quoting the dying words of Pushmataha, a Choctaw leader who had passed away while in Washington negotiating with the US government.[37] In Ridge's mind, the roles of statesmen, treaty negotiator, and poet were all intertwined, in a reflection of what his biographer aptly calls his "almost Shelleyan belief in the power of the pen."[38] A poet-legislator like Ridge could, he believed, translate the mountain's sovereign power into an alternative political reality in which Indigenous statehood could be realized.

Shelley's poetry operates as an intertext for the 1819 treaties and the relationships that flowed from them for different reasons on the two sides of the US-Canadian border. In the case of Treaties 21 and 27 in Canada, as discussed earlier, the relevance of Shelley's characterization of the British monarchy is clear; treaties between the British crown and the First Nations of Canada relied on the integrity of the leaders that Shelley derided in "England in 1819" and *The Mask of Anarchy*. The context in the United States was different, of course, but some of Shelley's themes of corrupt political leadership, injustice, and violence against innocent people could be easily transferred from the British to the American government, which, despite the revolutionary rhetoric about throwing off the tyranny of British rule, had reproduced that tyranny in its relationships with Indigenous peoples. The work of transferring those themes, and of binding Shelley's poetry to the broken American treaties of 1819, is undertaken in the poems of Gregory, Too-qua-stee, and Ridge, all of whom are able to intuit the power of Shelley's conceptualizations of injustice and of what Kir Kuiken has dubbed "counter-sovereignty" in his verse, although they put those conceptualizations to very different literary and political uses.[39]

As the Cherokee literary scholar Daniel Heath Justice has noted,

> Indigenous texts are by and large responsive, not reactive. They are at least as concerned with developing or articulating relationships with, among, and between Indigenous readers as they are with communicating our humanity to colonial society, if not more so. Indeed, I'd go so far as to argue that *relationship* is the driving impetus behind the vast majority of texts by Indigenous writers – relationship to the land, to human community, to self, to the other-than-human world, to the ancestors and our descendants, to our histories and our futures, as well as to colonizers and their literal and ideological heirs – and that these literary works offer us insight and sometimes helpful pathways for maintaining, rebuilding, or even simply establishing these meaningful connections.[40]

Justice's comments are useful for conceptualizing what poets like Gregory, Too-qua-stee, and Ridge were aiming to do in their utilization of Shelley. They are "responsive" to his verses, I would suggest, not "reactive," and they deploy that responsiveness in the service of relationships between peoples, lands, generations, and systems. They are similarly responsive to the treaties that guaranteed their rights and sovereignty, just as treaties themselves are, at least in theory, responsive to relationships.

So much for the Shelley of the nineteenth century, but what about the "Shelley for our times" that this collection imagines? What is the relevance of the poems, the treaties, and the subsequent Indigenous responses to Shelley for our twenty-first-century moment? On July 9, 2020, the US Supreme Court issued a landmark decision around Native title and treaty rights. The McGirt decision confirmed that an 1866 treaty between the United States and the Mvskoke Creek nation in Oklahoma guaranteed land rights and sovereignty over their territories in the state.[41] The decision was widely seen as a vindication of the treaty rights of all of the nations that had been removed to Oklahoma and other western states.

It was fitting that one of the most widely read responses to the McGirt decision was penned by the then-US poet laureate, the Mvskoke Creek poet Joy Harjo. In Harjo's *New York Times* article in response to the McGirt decision, she notes the way justice and time are linked in Mvskoke epistemology:

> The Old Ones have always reminded us that we will be here long after colonization has worn itself out. An elder explained to me once, pressing her fingers together, "See this?" I could see no light between her fingers. "This is the time since European settlement." Then, she spread her arms from horizon to horizon: "This is the whole of time."[42]

Harjo does not need Shelley's ideas to speak her truth; the structures of Mvskoke knowledge are more than enough. But, as Romantic scholars, we can see the ways in which Harjo and Shelley express a shared ideal, manifested across different timescales. "Ye are many, they are few" is a condensed, present-focused expression of the fact that real power lies not with those who currently occupy the offices of state but with those who are resolute, patient, and community-minded. Literary activism is a crucial part of this spirit of resistance, and it stretches from Shelley, across "Indian country" to Gregory, Too-qua-stee, and Ridge, and on to Harjo in a series of vital embodiments of the idea that "poets are the unacknowledged legislators of the world."

As Susan Wolfson, Stuart Curran, Timothy Webb, and others have argued, a lot hangs on that word "may" in Shelley's final couplet in "England in 1819": "graves from which a glorious Phantom may / Burst, to illumine our tempestuous day" (13–14 [*SPP* 327]).[43] It is, as Wolfson points out, either tentative or enabling, depending on how you want to read it, suggesting either "perhaps" or "is empowered to."[44] It could signify a rather tenuous possibility, something situated in an uncertain future. But it also has an enabling, empowering potential, the same kind of political potential concentrated in our phrase "not if, but when," or, as Joy Harjo put it, "Justice is sometimes seven generations away, or even more. And it is inevitable."[45] While I personally prefer the more optimistic reading of Shelley's "may," a reading that emphasizes the sovereignty and autonomy of people to reimagine their world, I think the genuine uncertainty and irresolution of that term isolates the vital point that sovereignty and autonomy can be entirely real and yet still ineffective in the face of the forces that work against them. It is that tension that makes Shelley's poems so powerful for readers well beyond their apparently localized and temporalized context. And it is that potential that means that Shelley's poems are, on some quite meaningful level, actually *about* Indigenous autonomy and honoring the treaties of 1819 and beyond.

Notes

1 Craig S. Womack, *Red on Red: Native American Literary Separatism* (Minneapolis: University of Minnesota Press, 1999), 12.
2 The text of the Long Woods Treaty and the Rideau Purchase (Treaties 21 and 27) can be found here: www.rcaanc-cirnac.gc.ca/eng/1370372152585/1581293792 285#ucls19.
3 Aaron Mills, "Miinigowiziwin: All That Has Been Given for Living Well Together: One Vision of Anishinaabe Constitutionalism," PhD diss. (University of Victoria, 2019), 237.

4 Fred Dustin, *The Saginaw Treaty of 1819 between General Lewis Cass and the Chippewa Indians* (Saginaw: Saginaw Publishing, 1919), 10–11.
5 Sharon O'Brien, *American Indian Tribal Governments* (Norman: University of Oklahoma Press, 1989), 122. While it is more usual to use the spelling "Mvskoke" today, I have here used the spelling that would have been correct in the nineteenth century and which is still used in the official name of the Muscogee Nation; see their website at www.muscogeenation.com/.
6 Treaty with the Cherokee, 1819. *Indian Affairs: Laws and Treaties*, Volume 2, ed. Charles J. Kappler (Washington: Government Printing Office, 1904), 177–181.
7 For details of the 1819 treaty negotiations, including discussion of the motivations of the Cherokee negotiators, see Robert J. Conley, *The Cherokee Nation: A History* (Albuquerque: University of New Mexico Press, 2005), 100–103; Duane Champagne, *American Indian Societies: Strategies and Conditions of Political and Cultural Survival*, Cultural Survival Report 32 (Cambridge: Cultural Survival, 1989), 46; Susan M. Abram, *Forging a Cherokee-American Alliance in the Creek War: From Creation to Betrayal* (Tuscaloosa: University of Alabama Press, 2015), 94–103; Rachel Caroline Eaton, *John Ross and the Cherokee Indians* (New York: AMS Press, 1921), 27; William G. McLoughlin, *Cherokee Renascence in the New Republic* (Princeton: Princeton University Press, 1986), 258–279.
8 See Oxford English Dictionary, definition 1d.
9 James Roane Gregory, "The Promised Seal," in Robert Dale Parker, ed. *Changing Is Not Vanishing: A Collection of American Indian Poetry to 1930* (Philadelphia: University of Pennsylvania Press, 2011), 180.
10 Gregory, "The Promised Seal," 180, l. 4.
11 "Memories of James Roane Gregory 1842–1912," *Indian Pioneer History Project for Oklahoma*, https://okgenweb.net/pioneer/ohs/gregory-james.htm.
12 Parker, *Changing Is Not Vanishing*, 180.
13 Gregory, "The Promised Seal," 180, ll. 13–14.
14 The Cherokee Nation provides perhaps the clearest example of this tactic of mirroring, with its bicameral legislature, judiciary, a constitution, and a host of other structural elements deliberately copied from settler norms, but there are other examples across North America and around the world.
15 See, for example, Treaty with the Creeks, 1827. Kappler, *Indian Affairs*, 284–285, 285.
16 For details of the five seals, see Muriel H. Wright, "Official Seals of the Five Civilized Tribes," *Chronicles of Oklahoma*, 18.4 (1940), 357–370.
17 For brief summaries of the Dawes Act and the Curtis Act, see Donald L. Fixico, ed. *Treaties with American Indians: An Encyclopedia of Rights, Conflicts, and Sovereignty*, 3 volumes, (ABC-Clio, 2008).
18 James Roane Gregory, "Otheen, Okiyetos," in Parker, *Changing Is Not Vanishing*, 181.
19 Gregory, "Otheen, Okiyetos," 181, ll. 5–8.
20 Gregory, "Otheen, Okiyetos," 181, ll. 9–16.

21 Too-qua-stee/De Witt Clinton Duncan, "The Dead Nation: An Elegy at the Tomb of the Cherokee Nation, By One of Her Sons," in Parker, *Changing Is Not Vanishing*, 202–203. For biographical information, see *Native American Writing in the Southeast: An Anthology, 1875–1935*, eds. Daniel F. Littlefield, Jr. and James Parrins (Jackson: University Press of Mississippi, 1995), 30–31.
22 Too-qua-stee, "The Dead Nation,"30, l. 1.
23 Too-qua-stee, "The Dead Nation," 30, l. 12.
24 Too-qua-stee, "The Dead Nation," 30–31, ll. 13–32.
25 Too-qua-stee/De Witt Clinton Duncan, "A Vision of the End," in Parker, *Changing Is Not Vanishing*, 204–205.
26 Too-qua-stee, "A Vision of the End," 204–205, l. 17.
27 Too-qua-stee, "A Vision of the End," 204–205, ll. 29–40.
28 John Rollin Ridge witnessed and left an account of the murder of his father; see James W. Parins, *John Rollin Ridge: His Life and Works* (Lincoln: University of Nebraska Press, 2004), 30.
29 For an overview of Ridge's poetry and its relationship to that of the British Romantic poets, including Shelley, see Parins, *John Rollin Ridge*, 76–94.
30 John Rollin Ridge, "To a Mockingbird Singing in a Tree," in Parker, *Changing Is Not Vanishing*, 94–96, l. 32.
31 Ridge, "To a Mockingbird" 94–96, ll. 41–48.
32 Ridge's tombstone epitaph read: "John Rollin Ridge – California, Author of 'Mount Shasta' and Other Poems," Parins, *John Rollin Ridge*, 221.
33 John Rollin Ridge, "Mount Shasta," in Parker, *Changing Is Not Vanishing*, 86–88, ll. 1–13. Parins, *John Rollin Ridge*, identifies further connections with Shelley's poems, 86–88.
34 Ridge, "Mount Shasta," 86–88, ll. 68–76.
35 Ridge often added the initials "C. N." to the signature or pseudonym on his works, indicating "Cherokee Nation." See Ryan Carr, "Lyric X-Marks: Genre and Self-Determination in the Harp Poems of John Rollin Ridge," *Melus: Multi-Ethnic Literature of the U.S.*, 43.3 (2018), 42–63, 53.
36 See Parins, *John Rollin Ridge*, 176–179, for Ridge's views on statehood. An excellent discussion of the literary and print culture matters around the proposed State of Sequoyah can be found in Kathryn Walkiewicz, "Pressing for Sequoyah: Print Culture and the Indian Territory Statehood Movement," *J19: The Journal of Nineteenth-Century Americanists*, 6.2 (2018), 335–364.
37 Parins, *John Rollin Ridge*, 123.
38 Parins, *John Rollin Ridge*, 123.
39 Kir Kuiken, *Imagined Sovereignties: Toward a New Political Romanticism* (New York: Fordham University Press, 2014), 172.
40 Daniel Heath Justice, *Why Indigenous Literatures Matter* (Waterloo: Wilfrid Laurier University Press, 2018), xix, emphasis in original.
41 The full Supreme Court decision in *McGirt* v. *Oklahoma* can be found at: www.supremecourt.gov/opinions/19pdf/18-9526_9okb.pdf. The text of the 1866 treaty can be found in "Treaty with the Creeks, 1866," in Kapler, *Indian Affairs*, 931–937.

42 Joy Harjo, "After a Trail of Tears, Justice for 'Indian Country,'" *The New York Times*, July 14, 2020.
43 Susan J. Wolfson, *Romantic Shades and Shadows* (Baltimore: Johns Hopkins University Press, 2018), 118–119; Stuart Curran, *Poetic Form and British Romanticism* (Oxford: Oxford University Press, 1986), 55; Timothy Webb, *Shelley: A Voice Not Understood* (Manchester: Manchester University Press, 1977), 107.
44 Wolfson, *Romantic Shades and Shadows*, 119.
45 Shelley's own sense of the inevitability of justice might also be relevant here; see his comments on the doctrine of Necessity in the notes to *Queen Mab* (*CP* II: 258–262).

CHAPTER 2

Waiting for the Revolution
Age, Debility, and Disability in The Triumph of Life

Fuson Wang

Percy Shelley has been a young man's poet. Ever since Matthew Arnold dubbed his predecessor a "beautiful and ineffectual angel, beating in the void his luminous wings in vain," Shelley's readers would pit the poet's youthful radicalism against their own grown-up politics and poetics.[1] T. S. Eliot would, for example, rhapsodize about his teenage years misspent idolizing the Romantic poet just to articulate his own newfound, mature modernism:

> The ideas of Shelley seem to me always to be ideas of adolescence – as there is every reason why they should be. And an enthusiasm for Shelley seems to me also to be an affair of adolescence: for most of us, Shelley has marked an intense period before maturity, but for how many does Shelley remain the companion of age? I confess that I never open the volume of his poems simply because I want to read poetry, but only with some special reason for reference. I find his ideas repellent; and the difficulty of separating Shelley from his ideas and beliefs is still greater than with Wordsworth.[2]

In Eliot's Harvard lecture, he insists that our "affair of adolescence" with Shelley's poetry can hardly survive to be the "companion of age." The "intense period" of unsustainable excitement and early intrigue about political anarchism in *Prometheus Unbound* and extramarital free love in *Epipsychidion* must inevitably settle down into something less "repellant" and more concretely moral, ethical, Christian, and pragmatic. In his mid-forties, Eliot, now the mature professor and poet, would find it impossible to separate Shelley's beautiful poetry from the degenerate and ineffectual philosophy. After all, how could Eliot's early twentieth century glean any actionable insight from the puerile performances of a nineteenth-century poet who died just shy of thirty?

Two hundred years after Shelley's death, we might amend the cliché to say that he is a young woman's poet (tabling for just a moment his problematic gender politics).[3] His is the social media-savvy voice of Alexandria

Ocasio-Cortez, dreaming of a Green New Deal and the systematic dismantling of institutional inequities; Arnold's the establishment voice of Nancy Pelosi, gently chastising the frenetic beat of ineffectual wings. In this view, youthful radicalism can afford to wait out the corruption of the world, but old age – Arnold's cultural pragmatics, Eliot's moral maturity, and Pelosi's political incrementalism – demands the realpolitik of short-term compromise. In some of his work, Shelley himself invites this ageist false dilemma. In his unfinished essay "On Life," he observes that "As men grow up, this power [of reverie] commonly decays, and they become mechanical and habitual agents" (*SPP* 507–508). These aging, "mechanical and habitual agents" inexorably fail to author what he calls "the poetry of life," the transformative thought that creates and legislates a regenerated and reformed world (530). Shelley mounts an impassioned case for the urgency of this "poetical faculty" for his own times: "The cultivation of poetry is never more to be desired than at periods when, from an excess of the selfish and calculating principle, the accumulation of the materials of external life exceed the quantity of the power of assimilating them to the internal laws of human nature" (531). In a passage that may as well be describing the eponymous "our times" of this volume, Shelley argues that in a time when greed, selfishness, and materialism have piled on the superficial trappings of happiness, this ostensibly youthful poetry is there to utter into existence the eventual revolution. We only await the "glorious Phantom" to "illumine our tempestuous day" in "England in 1819" or the revolutionary "Spring" in "Ode to the West Wind" (13–14 [327]; 70 [301]). And in *Prometheus Unbound*, Demogorgon's concluding speech dilates the same glorious promise into apocalyptic time: "to hope till Hope creates / From its own wreck the thing it contemplates" (IV.573–574 [286]).

What if, however, there is little time to wait? What if, like the figure of Jean-Jacques Rousseau in *The Triumph of Life*, the body grows old, deformed, and disabled in the meantime? As Shelley was writing his final major poem, he himself was about to turn thirty and had borne years of suffering due to his own chronic ailments.[4] In the decaying body of an aging revolutionary, Shelley had started to imagine more honestly embodied images of disease, debility, and disability. Mary Shelley, in her posthumous note to *Queen Mab*, documents the shift from the eager, adolescent author of the scandalous, anti-Christian poem to the man a decade later who would sue to stop the circulation of pirated copies of the same poem:

> He did not in his youth look forward to gradual improvement: nay, in those days of intolerance, now almost forgotten, it seemed as easy to look forward to the sort of millennium of freedom and brotherhood, which he thought

the proper state of mankind, as to the present reign of moderation and improvement. Ill health made him believe that his race would soon be run; that a year or two was all he had of life. He desired that these years should be useful and illustrious. He saw, in a fervent call on his fellow-creatures to share alike the blessings of the creation, to love and serve each other, the noblest work that life and time permitted him. In this spirit he composed QUEEN MAB. (*CP* II: 849)

In his youthful epigraph to *Queen Mab*, Shelley would happily chant along with Voltaire's burn-it-all-down catchphrase "*Écrasez l'infâme*," but the adult Shelley found it increasingly difficult to wait for the "millennium of freedom and brotherhood" yet to come. To be as "useful and illustrious" as "time permitted him," he would eventually temper the explosive and exuberant revolution of *Queen Mab* into the exquisitely baroque process of reform in *Prometheus Unbound*. But in *The Triumph*, Shelley's lifelong revolution against *l'infâme* – not just the Church but all systems of human oppression and intolerance – had begun to lose steam in the exhausting grind of life's mental and physical attritions and depredations.

Along Shelley's triumphal pageant of a personified Life are the energetic youths who dance ahead of the chariot and the elderly followers who try desperately to keep up, mimicking as best they can (but ultimately failing) the lively dance. Old and young alike exhaust themselves but in elementally distinct ways: "frost in these [old men and women] performs what fire [does] in those [youthful dancers]" (175 [*SPP* 488]). Corrupting nihilism pervades Shelley's maenadic Life, but it is not, however, strictly destiny. In a spot of optimism, Shelley's speaker observes those "sacred few who could not tame / Their spirits to the Conqueror [Life]" (128–129 [487]). Refusing to submit their revolutionary struggles to the triumphal pageant, "they of Athens and Jerusalem," Socrates and Jesus respectively, manage to escape the vicious cycle of Life's influence (134 [487]). Since the speaker's dream vision imagines the "sacred few" at the age of martyrdom, Jesus would have been in his early thirties and Socrates in his early seventies. In both the fallen and unfallen visions of Life, the dancing throng and the sacred few, Shelley repeatedly pairs images of youth and old age in what I argue is the poem's central binary. It persists to the end of the fragmented poem in the long encounter between the youthful fever-dreaming poet and the decaying zombie corpse of Rousseau.

Even though this meeting of the minds is unfortunately left incomplete, many critics are convinced that this conversation would have gone the way of the corrupted dancers instead of some revelatory get-together of Jesus and Socrates. John A. Hodgson argues, for example, "But so far as the essence of life on earth is in question, the vision's answer is quite explicit, and thoroughly pessimistic."⁵ In this view, the poem's three main encounters of youth and age – the dancers behind and ahead of Life's chariot, Athens and Jerusalem, Rousseau and the speaker – altogether signify the almost inevitable corruption and triumph of natural life over the revolutionary human spirit. In this essay, I suggest instead that, for Shelley, the revolution must be at once young and old, a broadly intergenerational coalition of both the Ocasio-Cortezes and Pelosis of the world. In the unwritten lines of *The Triumph*, Shelley would have struggled to articulate this revolution of generations. In his carefully staged encounters with age and debility, Shelley pieces together a prescient disability theory. As we grow old and disabled waiting for the revolution, Shelley's *The Triumph* is meant to give us an anti-ableist ethics to hold on to in the meantime.⁶

I Disabling Environments

Alan Bewell has already laid some crucial groundwork to view Shelley as this burgeoning disability theorist. "Literature has often employed epidemics as metaphors for social ills," Bewell explains, but Shelley tends to "go beyond metaphor to suggest that power *is* disease; it is the force that creates pathogenic spaces in the world."⁷ And in the conclusion to his chapter on Shelley's biosocial utopianism, Bewell reads Shelley's verse, especially *Queen Mab* and *Prometheus Unbound*, as sophisticated constructions of "one of the most important social theories of disease articulated in the nineteenth century."⁸ The colonial disease-bearing environments that Bewell so carefully documents, in other words, are not merely Shelley's decorative metaphors but an earnest and compelling theory about how socially constructed environments themselves not only facilitate contagion but generate the disease itself. Bewell boils down this revolutionary climatology into a simple axiom: "it is not people but places that are sick."⁹ It is no great leap, then, to append to Shelley's "social theories of disease" what we now call the social model of disability. In a gentle rephrasing, that axiom could even serve as the very definition of the social model: it is not people who are *disabled* but places that are *disabling*.¹⁰

The Triumph immediately begins to set the scene of these disabling environments with a forty-line framing device that exactly pits twenty lines of the sun-drenched joy and harmony of "All flowers" and "all [mortal] things" against the twenty lines of the unsettled speaker's perverse "But I" that abruptly arrives out of sync with the natural rhythms of "Continent, / Isle, Ocean" (9, 16–17, 21, 15–16 [*SPP* 483–484]). From the very beginning, the speaker finds himself jarringly out of place in a disabling environment paradoxically bathed with an *en*abling sunlight that purports to nourish all flowers and all things. The introductory frame poses an insistent question that animates almost all readers and critics of the poem: can the speaker finally awake into the harmonious natural scene, cured of doubt, skepticism, and suspicion of life's diurnal course? Or, to borrow Shelley's own language, while all else is busy greeting the arriving sun, can the somnolent speaker finally "unclose" his own "trembling eyelids to the kiss of day" (9–10 [483–484])? The surrounding environment abounds with painful oppositions that yearn for resolution but are kept frustratingly open. Bewell prefers to read with the youthful, hopeful Shelley: "Revolution is ecological reclamation, the recovery of a nature produced by human labor and love that has been destroyed by social degradation."[11] In this view, the diseased and disabling environments that surround us can be reclaimed, and the inaccessible natural scene of the first twenty lines can be recovered eventually. Paul de Man, however, takes a bleaker view and concludes that Shelley warns that "nothing, whether deed, word, thought, or text, ever happens in relation, positive or negative, to anything that precedes, follows, or exists elsewhere, but only as a random event whose power, like the power of death, is due to the randomness of its occurrence."[12] The power of the poem, in other words, is Shelley's abject resignation to the arbitrary whims of the relentless, triumphal pageant of Life and his ultimate inability to recuperate a meaningful "relation" with sun, birds, ocean, isle, and continent.[13] Unfortunately, the poem is a fragment that cuts off one word into line 548, so such conclusions are not easily won. Critics, in short, have either read *The Triumph* as the late, dark turn of Shelley's idealism or filled in the missing Italian tercets with eager projections of a revitalized political activism. In either case, as the revolution matures, the questionable sustainability of a fervent, anarchist politics begins to press upon the aging poet.

Shelley's statement of the problem, I will suggest, is neither exactly Bewell's *reclamation* of healthful environments nor de Man's critique of the naïve fantasy of historicist *recuperation*. Both analyses shape the problem into a clean opposition between the diseased, fallen world of the triumphal pageant and the poet's struggle to reclaim or recuperate an unfallen idealism. These interpretive binaries measure Shelley's success at clawing back from the brink of nihilism. In this view, Shelley is fighting to recover his Promethean idealism from Byronic cynicism. From the careening chariot, poorly driven by its blinded, four-faced Janus, Shelley is trying to call back his favorite avatars of poetic hope: "the chariot of the Fairy Queen" or the "moonlike car" of the Spirit of the

Hour (59 [*CP* II: 166]; III.iv.111 [*SPP* 267]). The commonplace of Shelley criticism seems to be the poet's desperate shuttling between opposites, forever reclaiming, recuperating, and reconciling pessimism with optimism, conflict with achievement, despair with aspiration, cynicism with idealism, negation with affirmation, tragedy with comedy, as Michael O'Neill notes a "subtle swiftness" in Shelley's "interplay between aspiration and despair."[14] Stuart Sperry invites us "to recollect how protractedly optimism and pessimism, affirmation and negation struggle throughout Shelley's verse."[15] Paul Foot argues that both violence and nonviolence coexist in his characterization of a "red Shelley": "For every quotation or reference in Shelley which proves his suspicions of the mob, his hatred of violence or his belief that political reform can only be accomplished gradually by constitutional means, there is another which proves the opposite."[16] Jerrold Hogle's influential description of Shelley's process of transference similarly articulates this ambivalence as "a rootless passage between different formations."[17] Hugh Roberts nails down "Shelley's 'two thoughts,' which have alternately dominated Shelley criticism for so long" as "a misrecognized form of his 'Lucretianism.'"[18] This brief sampling of the most influential Shelley criticism paints Shelley as a poet of oppositions, always trying to restore, with varying degrees of success, the decay and deformity of an aging revolution to the youthful energy of the first twenty lines' dawning day.

Both Bewell and Nora Crook medicalize this opposition into disease and cure: "Shelley's real fight was with *l'infâme* [the Roman Catholic Church], a belief system which saw disease as necessary, a scourge to goad mankind into righteousness, a merited chastisement which might be tempered, but never abolished."[19] Instead, in Shelley's unorthodox "belief system," *l'infâme* – the diseased social environments of imperial power (Bewell) or religious oppression (Crook) – could be and needed to be treated, cured, and "abolished." In these medical accounts, the powerfully evocative natural scene of the first twenty lines is exactly the goal of Shelley's enthusiastic citation of Voltaire's *Écrasez l'infâme*, the permanent cure for the diseased social environments that have corrupted the human spirit. Here, disease is an acute exception to health. In eradicating that exception, Shelley imagined, according to Bewell, that "for the first time perfect health might be within the grasp of human beings."[20] The symptomology of the poem, however, refuses easy diagnoses of "perfect health," and it is ultimately unclear which social environment is diseased. Even the tranquil harmony at the beginning of *The Triumph* of "the Sun their father" (18 [*SPP* 484]) could prove an *ignis fatuus*, deceiving with promises of a peaceful totality of ocean, birds, and flowers. The vision of ostensibly "perfect health" only serves, for example, to mock and disable the poet's own soporific blindness. Blinded by the paternal sun, father to all but him, the speaker must look away and seek another conception of healthful ecology by plunging himself into a different dream. The goal of curing acute disease finally comes up short in explaining Shelley's inability to settle on a stable notion of "perfect health."

Instead of *acute* disease – illness that vanishes as quickly as a cure is identified – I substitute the language of *chronic* illness, debility, and disability. In addition to curing the social environments of the diseases of imperial overreach, religious intolerance, and systemic oppression, Shelley also articulates an ethic of constant care. The idea of "perfect health" means more than quickly administering the identified social cure. As Demogorgon warns at the end of *Prometheus Unbound*, the end of Jupiter's tyrannic reign does not mean the work is done:

> Gentleness, Virtue, Wisdom, and Endurance,—
> These are the seals of that most firm assurance
> Which bars the pit over Destruction's strength;
> And if, with infirm hand, Eternity,
> Mother of many acts and hours, should free
> The serpent that would clasp her with his length,—
> These are the spells by which to reassume
> An empire o'er the disentangled Doom. (IV.562–569 [*SPP* 285])

Demogorgon warns us of a precarious utopia with a looming contingency of "doom" even if "the pit over Destruction's strength" is barred with "that most firm assurance." Even utopias eventually age, and Eternity's "infirm hand" might slip and allow the serpent to infect the world anew. The "spells by which to reassume / An empire o'er the disentangled Doom" – "Gentleness, Virtue, Wisdom, and Endurance" – signify a kind of perennial care for the chronic illness of the human condition. The "infirm hand" of age becomes much more prominent in *The Triumph*, a poem that allows no rest stop at a Promethean utopia and finally demands "that most firm assurance" of a just theory of disability.

II Eagles to Their Native Noon

Having turned away from the sun's benevolent but disabling paternalism, the dreaming speaker finds a second potential utopian cure in those that sit out the grotesque pageant of Life and prefer the quiet dignity of immortal martyrdom:

> All but the sacred few who could not tame
> Their spirits to the Conqueror, but as soon
>   As they had touched the world with living flame
>
> Fled back like eagles to their native noon,
>   Or those who put aside the diadem
> Of earthly thrones or gems, till the last one
>
>   Were there; for they of Athens and Jerusalem
> Were neither mid the mighty captives seen
>   Nor mid the ribald crowd that followed them
>
> Or fled before... (128–137 [*SPP* 487])

A raucous travesty of the late Republican Roman triumph, Life's pageant makes an elaborate show of "mighty captives" while the "ribald crowd" of old men and women lag behind, and the youth who "fled before" are dancing themselves into an orgiastic "foam after the Ocean's wrath / Is spent upon the desert shore" (163–164 [488]). Only "the sacred few" would not submit to "the Conqueror" Life; "they of Athens [Socrates] and Jerusalem [Jesus]" forgo "the maniac dance" and ensure the immortality of their lives through the enduring discourses of philosophy and religion (110 [487]). Like the biblical eagles who renewed their youth by flying into the sun, the poisoned Socrates and the crucified Jesus return to "their native noon" and continue to light the way through millennia of human history.[21] An attractive and even seductive reading of this passage has been that the *The Triumph* was Shelley's elaborate suicide note set to the infernal beat of Dante's *terza rima*. And his drowning along the way from Livorno to Lerici anointed him, at the glorious end, among the "sacred few" as he heroically martyred himself to the cause of human liberty. Here is another of Shelley's potential cures for social ills, a twisted vision of "perfect health" through immortalized self-harm.

But just as the speaker turns away from the nourishing beams of the sun in the very beginning, he quickly leaves both Socrates and Jesus behind to focus on the fascinating, debased spectacle of the triumphal pageant. Yet again, the speaker refuses to settle on what should be an ideal. Ahead are the "Maidens and youths" who "fling their wild arms in the air / As their feet twinkle" (149–150 [*SPP* 488]). And behind:

> Old men, and women foully disarrayed
>   Shake their grey hair in the insulting wind,
>
> Limp in the dance and strain with limbs decayed
>   To reach the car of light which leaves them still
>   Farther behind and deeper in the shade. (165–169 [*488*])

Socrates and Jesus can hardly compete with the relentless pace of the wild, intricate, and musical verse that follows. Shelley's speaker obliquely revisits and revises the concluding slogan of *The Mask of Anarchy*: "Ye are many— they are [the sacred] few" (372 [326]). The many are endlessly interesting while the few are swept away into forgetfulness. Even those "sacred few" who institutionalized philosophy and religion will hardly matter compared to the rushing, democratic throng of human life. This is, in short, no suicide note, no prelude to the poet's own desired martyrdom. Shelley will always be much more a poet of the clamorous crowd than an obedient partisan of "the sacred few" or the philosopher kings who would systematize the good life from the top down.

Instead, the good life must be theorized in the crush of the aging, deforming, debilitated, and disabled dancers, "mid the mighty captives" and "mid the ribald crowd." Whereas "they of Athens and Jerusalem" had the luxury of skipping out on the triumphal pageant of Life, Shelley's speaker quickly marks the uselessness of his avian simile and the seductive illusion of eternally renewed youth. When eagles stare down the sun, they are born anew, but our own eyes and bodies are mere vessels of multiplying vulnerabilities and inevitable decay. Neither the paternal sun from the first twenty lines nor the youth-renewing sun of "the sacred few" can compete with the all too human interest of the dimmer but more spectacular dance of Life. Even in death, it seems Shelley was still refusing the martyrdom of Socrates and Jesus. Found on Shelley's waterlogged and badly decomposing corpse on the shores of Viareggio, about halfway between Livorno and the intended destination of Lerici, was the last volume of John Keats's poetry, which included similarly ecstatic yet disappointing lines about the eternal youth of figures on a Grecian urn, "For ever warm and still to be enjoy'd, / For ever panting, and for ever young."[22] By the end of "Ode on a Grecian Urn," Keats's speaker, much like Shelley's, is cast out of the eternally frozen scene and chastised by the "Cold Pastoral" of immortal youth.[23] The naïve image of a revolutionary utopia, forever warm and young, cruelly excludes the aging crowd to privilege the able-bodied few. In *The Triumph*, the stable sunlight of vitality is always a lie or at least a bright red herring: the paternal sun of the introduction, the eagles and "their native noon," and, as I will discuss in Section III, the "shape all light" only shelter "the sacred few" (352 [*SPP* 494]). We can hardly all be martyrs, and Shelley's speaker consistently refuses to go the way of Socrates or Jesus. Instead, the speaker attends to the disabling environments that grind people down with the relentless pace of Life, stopping not for "they of Athens and Jerusalem" but for the miserable cripple left behind by the perpetual parade, the withered corpse of "what was once Rousseau" (204 [489]).

Rousseau's age and decay are not, then, just a quick and easy allegory of the corruption of his fiery, unorthodox, passionate, and revolutionary youth. Ultimately, there is no cure for age. An instructive adage of modern disability studies reminds us that if we live long enough, we will certainly become disabled ourselves. Shelley's complex conception of "perfect health," I contend, acknowledges this inconvenient truth and attempts to move beyond the limited language of cure. Bewell judiciously hints at this looming problem in his Shelley chapter but ultimately does not fully pursue it:

> Shelley's idea of a future world in which "Health floats amid the gentle atmosphere" (*Queen Mab* VIII.114) therefore should be seen as an early articulation of a profoundly modern stance toward the body and overall human health, one that has shaped the course of medicine. The cure has changed – from vegetarianism, to Beddoes's "pneumatics," to sanitation, to bacteriology, to antibiotics, to the mapping of genes – but the belief that disease can be completely controlled remains a deep, if frequently troubled, modern faith.[24]

In his search of the panacea that legitimized the "belief that disease can be completely controlled," Shelley himself, not just we moderns as Bewell notes, thoughtfully troubled his faith in total cures. Shelley's eager interest in the cures of vegetarianism and pneumatics was only part of his vision of "perfect health." The speaker of *The Triumph* stops for the withered Rousseau and not "the sacred few" because health is not wholly about loudly trumpeted cures but also about the low-level hum of care for and inclusion of aging, vulnerable, disabled, and debilitated bodies. The triumphal pageant, in which "Old age and youth, manhood and infancy, / Mixed in one mighty torrent did appear," demands more than a one-and-done, one-size-fits-all cure (52–53 [*SPP* 485]).

In Susan Wendell's intersectional feminist work, she speaks from both scholarly expertise and personal experience to show how uniform demands on the body and the strictly standardized pace of capitalist and industrial life have often been predicated on the normatively able-bodied subject. The idea of curing oneself into "perfect health," in other words, coercively shapes and enforces perfection from an exclusionary norm. A harmful social construction of disability assumes a kind of homogeneous temporality, and falling behind, as the old men and women of the triumphal pageant do, must be a sign of *im*perfect health, a measurable failure of productivity, value, and human flourishing. As Wendell explains, what we would now call ableist ideology emerges from these kinds of reflexive, unexamined assumptions:

The *pace of life* is a factor in the social construction of disability that particularly interests me, because it is usually taken for granted by non-disabled people, while many people with disabilities are acutely aware of how it marginalizes or threatens to marginalize us. I suspect that increases in the pace of life are important social causes of damage to people's bodies through rates of accident, drug and alcohol abuse, and illnesses that result from people's neglecting their needs for rest and good nutrition. But the pace of life also affects disability as a second form of social construction, the social construction of disability through expectations of performance.[25]

Wendell warns that even when "perfect health" is predicated on an ostensibly stable norm, standards can suddenly shift, and the pace of life can quickly hasten beyond bodily limitations, establishing "expectations of performance" that end up leaving everyone behind. Those ahead of the chariot dancing themselves into their sexual foam will eventually fall behind, and Shelleyan health eventually requires a more inclusive plan. Seth Reno has recently described this plan as Shelley's preference for "interconnectedness," what he identifies as "the predominant model (and sometimes metaphor) that Shelley uses to envision love."[26] What Reno describes as Shelley's interconnected love repeatedly redirects the speaker's dreaming eye away from the attractive *ignis fatuus* of the youth-renewing cure and toward the diligent care for disabled or contingently disabled bodies strewn along the path of Life's aging triumph. Shelley's speaker can only look to the triumph and march to Wendell's *"pace of life,"* not to the impossible and cruel pace of martyred death. At this mature stage in his poetic career, Shelley warns against the ageist privileging of eternal youth over the decrepit corruption of old age; instead, his speaker continues to turn away from easy panaceas to attend to the disabled figures left behind. In this way, the *The Triumph* finally abandons the harmful language of cure to reevaluate and reconstruct the social models of "perfect health."

III Staring at Rousseau

Biblical psalms may have been the source for Shelley's youthful image of eagles returning "to their native noon," but William Wordsworth's "Ode: Intimations of Immortality" is probably the more proximate reference. Wordsworth's speaker begins wistfully that "There was a time when" he was more attuned to the textures of natural sublimity and more capable of youthful poetic reverie.[27] In the epigraph, Wordsworth cites his earlier work to proclaim that "The Child is father of the Man"; the pure joy of childhood experience serves as a chastising reminder for the corruptions and compromises of adulthood.²⁸ By the end of Wordsworth's first stanza, the speaker laments that age has robbed him of poetic vision: "The things which I have seen I now can see no more."²⁹ In an article that was perhaps the first to consider seriously the relation of Shelley's *The Triumph* to Wordsworth's "Intimations" ode, John Hodgson spells out the structural similarity while pointing out the ideological difference: "Shelley's *The Triumph* relates to Wordsworth's *Intimations* Ode not only as a symbolic parallel but also as an eschatological inversion."³⁰ In Hodgson's view, Rousseau's tale of youthful energy sapped by the attritions of age parallels the journey of Wordsworth's speaker, but since Rousseau is telling his story posthumously, nothing can be done; the story is mere pessimistic eschatology. About a decade later, de Man pressed the connection even further and observed that Shelley's reference to the "Intimations" ode "has misled even the most attentive readers of *The Triumph of Life*."³¹ In a reading not incompatible with Hodgson's, de Man distinguishes between Wordsworth's adult forgetfulness and Shelley's Rousseau: "this is precisely what the experience of forgetting, in *The Triumph of Life*, is not."³² De Man goes on to explain that Rousseau is *not* forgetting "some previous condition" of idyllic youth; instead, "we have no assurance whatever that the forgotten ever existed."³³ In these readings of Rousseau's disfigurement, the speaker of *The Triumph* encounters the "old root" who has "fallen by the way side" of the triumphal pageant as an entirely tragic and abject figure that sets in motion Hodgson's pessimistic eschatology and de Man's quasi-nihilistic deconstruction (541 [*SPP* 500]).

When the speaker discovers Rousseau, then, the encounter would be nothing but what we would now call a gross-out scene. In the influential readings of Hodgson and de Man, the speaker stares down the void right in its frightening, disfigured, and disgusting face:

> I turned and knew
> (O Heaven have mercy on such wretchedness!)
>
> That what I thought was an old root which grew
> To strange distortion out of the hill side
> Was indeed one of that deluded crew,
>
> And that the grass which methought hung so wide
> And white, was but his thin discoloured hair,
> And that the holes it vainly sought to hide
>
> Were or had been eyes (180–188 [*SPP* 489])

What was once the Wordsworthian sublime of the natural landscape is here transformed by age into the sobering and disappointing body of

Rousseau. What was perhaps a wondrous old root heroically hanging on to the hill side is no more than a withered human frame. What was perhaps a sprawling heath of weathered grass is no more than thinning and greying human hair. Rousseau himself knew to hide his disgusting shame as he tries in vain to cover the eyeless sockets from the speaker's penetrating stare. Even the starer himself feels the shame. In a parenthetical aside, the speaker can hardly stifle his *sotto voce* prayer for the withered husk of a once great philosopher: "O Heaven have mercy on such wretchedness!" The stare, it seems, has produced bad feelings all around. Rousseau is ashamed of his appearance, and the speaker is ashamed of his own thoughts.

Rosemarie Garland-Thomson's surprising but ultimately compelling thesis in *Staring: How We Look* (2009) helps to clarify this queasy encounter with the hollowed-out corpse of Rousseau. Staring, according to Garland-Thomson, is not always about the starer's imposition of dominant social protocols upon the stigmatized staree:

> The stare is distinct from the gaze, which has been extensively defined as an oppressive act of disciplinary looking that subordinates its victim [...] At the heart of this [book's] anatomy [of staring] is the matter of appearance, of the ways we see each other and the ways we are seen. It unsettles common understandings that staring is rudeness, voyeurism, or surveillance or that starers are perpetrators and starees victims. Instead, this vivisection lays bare staring's generative potential.[34]

It is from this disability theoretical standpoint that I want to measure the "generative potential" of staring at the old, disabled body of Rousseau. This pivotal moment in *The Triumph* is neither Foucault's gaze ("an oppressive act of disciplinary looking") nor what we understand as proper or acceptable staring. "In acceptable staring," Garland-Thomson explains, "an appropriate viewer synthesizes visual apprehension into knowledge that benefits the knower in carrying out cultural requirements."[35] Acceptable staring induces a normative ethics; it is staring with a legitimate purpose.

Rather than this pragmatic lucidity of ethical didacticism, Shelley's staring speaker produces something stranger. There is little to learn from the wild gestures of shame that follow from staring and being stared at in *The Triumph*. Unlike the acceptable, ethical, political, and appropriate stare, Shelley's seems incredibly *in*appropriate. "Proper staring is decorous, selective looking, not just random gawking," Garland-Thomson explains.[36] In contrast, the speaker's encounter with Rousseau is more like what she calls "baroque staring," an uncontrollable "gawking" that is flagrantly stimulus driven, the rogue looking that refuses to be corralled into acceptable attention [...] Unconcerned with rationality, mastery, or coherence, baroque staring blatantly announces the states of being wonderstruck and confounded. It is gaping-mouthed, unapologetic staring.[37]

Even here, staring is not simply "rudeness, voyeurism, or surveillance"; the baroque stare's inappropriateness challenges notions of "rationality, mastery, or coherence." It is instead an "unrepentant abandonment to the unruly, to that which refuses to conform to the dominant order of knowledge."[38] The speaker's baroque stare willfully ignores the sublime beauty of the paternal and youth-renewing sun to stare at the "unruly" body of Rousseau (1–20 [*SPP* 483–484]; 128–137 [487]). Rather than build his revolutionary ideology from the intergenerational, superstar pair of Jesus and Socrates, the youthful speaker deliberately chooses a partner in the old, disabled ruins of what was once Rousseau.[39]

Like the speaker, Rousseau also turned away from conventionally nourishing sunlight to stare unapologetically at the dark travesties of Life. In one of the most enigmatic and frequently discussed images of *The Triumph*, Rousseau encounters "A shape all light" created from the perfect reflections that the "Sun's image radiantly intense / Burned on the waters of the well" (352, 345–346 [*SPP* 494]). Beautiful, attractive, and immortally youthful, the shape all light "forever seemed to sing / A silver music on the mossy lawn" while she gracefully enchanted the sublime natural landscape with easy forgetfulness (354–355 [494]). Just as the poem's first sun supposedly shines on "All flowers" and "all things," this shape is meant to embody "*all* light" (9 [483]; 16 [484]). That language of normative totality, however, has been this poem's consistent, disabling lie. The philosophical light of Rousseau's own mind is extinguished in favor of the universal enlightenment of the "shape all light." As he gazes upon her, he loses his own kindling light, "As if the gazer's mind was strewn beneath / Her feet like embers, and she, thought by thought, / Trampled its fires into the dust of death" (386–388 [484]). The competing fire of Rousseau's mind is snuffed out until before his sight "Burst a new Vision never seen before" (411 [496]). At the end, he becomes much more interested in the triumphal pageant of Life and stares baroquely at its cruder, wilder, and sadder action:

> From every form the beauty slowly waned,
>
> > "From every firmest limb and fairest face
> > The strength and freshness fell like dust, and left
> > The action and the shape without the grace

> "Of life; the marble brow of youth was cleft
>   With care, and in the eyes where once hope shone
> Desire like a lioness bereft
>
> "Of its last cub, glared ere it died (519–526 [499])

As the dominating light of "the fair shape waned in the coming light" (412 [496]), Rousseau could make out aging faces and weakening limbs. Eternal hope had faded into ephemeral desire. The shape all light has no answer to the speaker's final question to Rousseau – "Then, what is Life?" (544 [500]) – because she can only trample fiery thought into the embers of happy, ignorant dust. By the end of the poetic fragment, three suns have passed – the paternal sun of the introduction, the eagles' youth-renewing sun, and now the reflected sun of a shape all light – and all three times, Shelley directs us away from the deceiving light. Instead of gazing fondly at the warmly lit world of established religions and philosophies, *The Triumph* forces us to stare baroquely at age, debility, and disability to answer the speaker's final question. Together, Rousseau and the speaker, the unsacred, disabled mockery of "they of Athens and Jerusalem," would piece together in the unwritten tercets an intergenerational theory of truly embodied life.

IV OK Boomer

Recall that T. S. Eliot was much more skeptical of Shelley's enduring appeal. In Eliot's view, those unfinished lines in *The Triumph* could hardly make up for Shelley's radical, youthful verse; as a whole, Shelley's body of work was unsustainable, immoral, blasphemous, and a thoroughly inappropriate "companion of age." For Eliot, young and old are always at odds, but he may have sensed in *The Triumph* a maturing Shelley that developed more honest accounts of the embodied contingencies and disappointments of age. He predicted that had Shelley survived into artistic maturity, he would have started to take the biblical adage to heart: "When I was a child, I spoke as a child, I understood as a child, I thought as a child; but when I became a man, I put away childish things."[40] Shelley died young, however, so Eliot is left only with disapproving hypotheticals:

> It is open to us to guess whether his mind would have matured too; certainly, in his last, and to mind greatest though unfinished poem, *The Triumph of Life*, there is evidence not only of better writing than in any previous long poem, but of greater wisdom […] There is a precision of image and an economy here that is new to Shelley. But so far as we can judge, he is never quite escaped from the tutelage of Godwin, even when he saw through the humbug as a man; and the weight of Mrs. Shelley must have been pretty heavy too.[41]

The formal and technical aspects of *The Triumph* – "better writing" and "precision of image and economy" – show marked improvement, but what Eliot is really after is "greater wisdom" than unruly and unreadable long poems like *Queen Mab* and *Prometheus Unbound* could possibly allow. I disagree, of course, with this analysis of Shelley's earlier work, but this chapter's real interpretative departure from Eliot is about ideological influence: "the tutelage of Godwin" and "the weight of Mrs. Shelley." Presumably, what he means by this is what he calls the "humbug" of the radically optimistic doctrine of perfectibility and human immortality in William Godwin's *St. Leon* and Mary Shelley's *Frankenstein*.[42] With the grotesque parade of fragile human life in *The Triumph*, Eliot sees Shelley attempting but ultimately failing to get away from the puerile optimism of the Godwinian perfectibility of our mortal bodies. As I have argued, Shelley *does* dispense with his father-in-law's techno-optimistic promise of immortality – the gentle sun that eternally restores age into youth – but, in *The Triumph*, Shelley evolves Godwinian perfectibility into an intergenerational disability theory that can survive the *longue durée* of revolutionary time.

It may be tempting to imagine Shelley clapping back at Eliot's curmudgeonly analysis with an "OK boomer," but that is not quite right either. In a recent *New York Times* article, Taylor Lorenz uses the phrase to mark the end of polite and friendly conversations across generations. The phrase "has become Generation Z's endlessly repeated retort to the problem of older people who just don't get it, a rallying cry for millions of fed up kids."[43] Old age becomes inextricably tied up with climate change denial, systemic racism, casual misogyny, religious intolerance, and income inequality. What Shelley offers for this volume's "our times," then, is a path of de-escalation in this swelling generational conflict, most fully and complexly articulated in the disability theory of *The Triumph* as I have discussed but perhaps more compactly and didactically presented in his short prose fragment "The Coliseum." The scene begins with an old, blind man and his daughter Helen visiting the ruins of the Coliseum when everyone else is busy commemorating the feast of Passover. An eccentric, emaciated, and iconoclastic youth wearing an ancient chlamys – a clear portrait of Shelley himself – barges into the scene, calls him a "wretched old man,"[44] and accuses him of not being able to understand the true sublimity of the sight of ruins before him.[45] This knee-jerk charge of "OK boomer," however, results in a cringey comeuppance. Little does the brash youth know, the old man is blind and depends on his daughter's sighted descriptions to engage with the colossal ruins.[46] Kevin Binfield has read this as Shelley's expanding intergenerational vision that develops "an awareness of the life beyond the narrow circle of self"[47] and finally "permits a link between generations."[48] Cian Duffy has read it in the terms of the unresolved clash between old-fashioned reform and youthful revolution.[49] Shelley's point is that charging in with the ableist and ageist "OK boomer" on our lips short-circuits any generative discussion of human progress and perfectibility.

Like *The Triumph*, "The Coliseum" is unfinished but leaves off with the promise of mutual education between old and young, Rousseau and the dreaming poet, the blind old man and the chlamys-clad revolutionary. The young man would explain his iconoclastic dress, his budding anarchism, and his radical atheism while the old man would expand on his aesthetic theory of the nonvisual sublime. Rather than blustering into the scene with accusations of obsolete superstition and dynastic corruption, Shelley has youthful radicalism trip upon the figure of disability. The fragment is most clearly a riff on the opening scene of Sophocles's *Oedipus at Colonus*, but whereas Oedipus, accompanied by his daughter Antigone, quickly declares his blindness to the stranger to avoid misunderstanding, the young stranger in "The Coliseum" suffers an egregious blunder. Shelley strategically restages this classical scene as an awkward but instructive encounter. Shelley deliberately stops for the old, blind man in "The Coliseum" and the "cripple" Rousseau in *The Triumph*. In this way, Shelley shies away from grand, pragmatic politics of reform or revolution, recommending instead a more modest intergenerational coalition that can abide both the quake of violent revolution and the rumble of incremental reform. Much has changed in the two centuries since Shelley's death, and we are tasked in this volume with the difficult question of Shelley's place in our updated and decolonized syllabi. In many ways, we are only just learning ourselves how to take disability theory and disability history seriously, and I would argue that Shelley's work teaches us how to slow down, stop, and stare at the baroque figures of age, debility, and disability. With Shelley, we learn that the coming revolution must be at once young and old, firm and infirm, able-bodied and disabled.

Notes

1 Matthew Arnold, *The Complete Prose Works of Matthew Arnold*, ed. R. H. Super, Volume II (Ann Arbor: University of Michigan Press, 1960), 327.
2 Arnold, *The Complete Prose Works*, 80.
3 Paul Foot's "red Shelley," the revolutionary poet who strove to better the world, is, according to his celebratory account, "not even primarily a man's poet." Foot claims that, in both theory and practice, Shelley was undeniably a feminist who "was writing for women as few other male poets have written in the English

language." See Paul Foot, *Red Shelley* (London: Sidgwick & Jackson, 1980), 159. Anne K. Mellor, however, is more skeptical. In her account, Shelley's construction of the woman-as-lover merely "effaces her into a narcissistic projection of his own self," *Romanticism and Gender* (New York: Routledge, 1993), 25.

4 For a comprehensive and compelling account of Shelley's lifelong struggle with illness, especially venereal disease – either real or imagined – see Nora Crook and Derek Guiton's *Shelley's Venomed Melody* (Cambridge: Cambridge University Press, 1986). Rousseau's own experience with venereal disease was a stumbling block for his idealist philosophy of love and left him "polarised between elusive, disembodied beauty and predatory sensualism." In *Triumph*, Crook and Guiton argue that Shelley is deliberately "identifying himself with a morally flawed poet (Rousseau)." See Crook and Guiton, *Shelley's Venomed Malady*, 225, 229.

5 John A. Hodgson, "The World's Mysterious Doom: Shelley's *The Triumph of Life*," *ELH* 42.4 (1975), 595–622, 595.

6 This essay depends on the close connection between age and disability. Thanks to the pioneering work of Rosemarie Garland-Thomson, this connection is now a critical commonplace in the field of disability studies. As I explain later in the essay, the instructive adage is that if we live long enough into old age, we will all eventually become disabled.

7 Alan Bewell, *Romanticism and Colonial Disease* (Baltimore: Johns Hopkins University Press, 1999), 209.

8 Bewell, *Romanticism and Colonial Disease*, 241

9 Bewell, *Romanticism and Colonial Disease*, 209.

10 This cursory summary suffices for my reading of Shelley's *The Triumph of Life*. For a much more robust account of the social model of disability, however, including its history, its positive impacts, and its limitations, see Tom Shakespeare's *Disability: The Basics* (London: Routledge, 2018), especially the first chapter, "Understanding Disability," 1–23. Shakespeare's book provides an eminently lucid and accessible introduction to the key debates in disability studies, including the social model.

11 Bewell, *Romanticism and Colonial Disease*, 219.

12 Paul de Man, "Shelley Disfigured," in *The Rhetoric of Romanticism* (New York: Columbia University Press, 1984), 93–123, 122.

13 In Paul de Man's readings of the rhetoric of Romanticism, he frequently uses the figure of disability to signify hermeneutic ruptures in our reading practices. In his Shelley essay, reading is a form of disfiguring, and autobiography is a form of defacement. In his analysis of Wordsworth, he pays special attention to deaf and mute characters: "But the question remains how this near-obsessive concern with mutilation, often in the form of a loss of one of the senses, as blindness, deafness, or, as in the key word of the Boy of Winander, *muteness*, is to be understood and, consequently, how trustworthy the ensuing claim of compensation and restoration can be" (Paul de Man, "Autobiography As De-facement," in de Man, *The Rhetoric of Romanticism*, 73–74). He questions, in other words, how Wordsworth can possibly view disability as anything other than loss and "mutilation."

14 Michael O'Neill, *The Human Mind's Imaginings: Conflict and Achievement in Shelley's Poetry* (Oxford: Oxford University Press, 1989), 178.
15 Stuart M. Sperry, *Shelley's Major Verse: The Narrative and Dramatic Poetry* (Cambridge, MA: Harvard University Press, 1988), 200.
16 Paul Foot, *Red Shelley*, 167.
17 Jerrold E. Hogle, *Shelley's Process: Radical Transference and the Development of His Major Works* (Oxford: Oxford University Press, 1988), 15.
18 Hugh Roberts, *Shelley and the Chaos of History: A New Politics of Poetry* (University Park: Pennsylvania State University Press, 1997), 411.
19 Crook and Guiton, *Shelley's Venomed Melody*, 230.
20 Bewell, *Romanticism and Colonial Disease*, 205.
21 That eagles stare into and fly toward the sun to renew their youth is most likely a biblical reference: "[The Lord] satisfieth thy mouth with good *things; so that thy youth is renewed like the eagle's.*" Robert Carroll and Stephen Prickett, eds. Psalm 103.5, *The Bible: Authorized King James Version with Apocrypha* (Oxford: Oxford University Press, 2008), 696. What is interesting in Shelley's simile, however, is that this renewal of youth is reserved specifically for Jesus and not for the inclusive, second-person "thy" of the biblical passage. For everyone else, the swindle of immortal youth and vitality is a "maniac dance" alongside the triumphal pageant of Life (110 [*SPP* 487]).
22 In his account of Shelley's death, Edward Trelawny initially recognized his friend's attire on the washed-up body but could only confirm Shelley's identity beyond a doubt when he saw the open volume of John Keats's *Lamia, Isabella, The Eve of St. Agnes, and Other Poems* (1820). Included with the three long narrative poems explicitly named in the title were several shorter poems, including the "Ode on a Grecian Urn." John Keats, "Ode on a Grecian Urn," in Elizabeth Cook, ed. *John Keats: The Major Works* (Oxford: Oxford World's Classics, 2009), 288–289, ll. 26–27.
23 Keats, "Ode on a Grecian Urn," l. 45.
24 Bewell, *Romanticism and Colonial Disease*, 206.
25 Susan Wendell, *The Rejected Body: Feminist Philosophical Reflections on Disability* (New York: Routledge, 1996), 37, emphasis in original.
26 Seth T. Reno, *Amorous Aesthetics: Intellectual Love in Romantic Poetry and Poetics, 1788–1853* (Liverpool: Liverpool University Press, 2019), 114.
27 William Wordsworth, "Ode (There Was a Time)," in Stephen Gill, ed. *William Wordsworth: The Major Works Including The Prelude* (Oxford: Oxford University Press, 2008), 297–302, l. 1.
28 Wordsworth, William, "My Heart Leaps Up When I Behold," in *The Major Works*, 246, l. 7.
29 Wordsworth, "Ode," l. 9.
30 Hodgson, "The World's Mysterious Doom: Shelley's *The Triumph of Life*," 607.
31 De Man, "Shelley Disfigured," 104.
32 De Man, "Shelley Disfigured," 104.
33 De Man, "Shelley Disfigured," 104.

34 Rosemarie Garland-Thomson, *Staring: How We Look* (Oxford: Oxford University Press, 2009), 9–10.
35 Garland-Thomson, *Staring*, 50.
36 Garland-Thomson, *Staring*, 50.
37 Garland-Thomson, *Staring*, 50.
38 Garland-Thomson, *Staring*, 50.
39 Here, I am implying that the speaker is at least a partial stand-in for Shelley himself. At the time of their martyrdoms, Jesus was in his early thirties and Socrates in his early seventies. Similarly, Shelley/the speaker would be approaching thirty while Rousseau died a few years shy of seventy. The poem's "baroque" pairing of the speaker and Rousseau is in many ways a pale and deliberately messy imitation of Jesus and Socrates, "the sacred few."
40 T. S. Eliot, *The Use of Poetry and the Use of Criticism* (Cambridge, MA: Harvard University Press, 1933), 218.
41 Eliot, *The Use of Poetry and the Use of Criticism*, 81.
42 *Frankenstein* is a very different novel from *St. Leon*, and Eliot's conflation of Mary Shelley and William Godwin is misleading. Here, it will just suffice to say that *Frankenstein* critiques the singular quest for technological immortality while *St. Leon* is more ambivalent.
43 Taylor Lorenz, "'OK Boomer' Marks the End of Friendly Generational Relations," *New York Times*, October 29, 2019, par. 2. www.nytimes.com/2019/10/29/style/ok-boomer.html?smid=url-share.
44 Percy Bysshe Shelley, *Zastrozzi and St. Irvyne*, ed. Stephen C. Behrendt (Peterborough, ON: Broadview Press 2002), 272.
45 I defer to Stephen Behrendt's analysis here for this clarity about Shelley's self-portrait. Behrendt cites Thomas Medwin's commentary, the character's exquisite grace, his sickliness, and his androgynous features to argue for the correspondence between character and author. Stephen C. Behrendt, "'His Left Hand Held the Lyre': Shelley's Narrative Fiction Fragments," in Alan M. Weinberg and Timothy Webb, eds. *The Neglected Shelley* (Abingdon: Routledge, 2016), 95–116, 104.
46 Shelley, *Zastrozzi and St. Irvyne*, 272–273.
47 Kevin Binfield, "'May They Be Divided Never': Ethics, History, and the Rhetorical Imagination in Shelley's 'The Coliseum,'" *Keats-Shelley Journal* 46 (1997), 124–147, 129.
48 Binfield, "Ethics, History, and the Rhetorical Imagination in Shelley's 'The Coliseum'," 146.
49 Cian Duffy, *Shelley and the Revolutionary Sublime* (Cambridge: Cambridge University Press, 2005), 164–166.

CHAPTER 3

"A Chamæleonic Race"
Shelley and the Discourses of Slavery
Mathelinda Nabugodi

"Poets, the best of them – are a very chamæleonic race," Shelley observed in a letter to John and Maria Gisborne in July 1821; "they take the colour not only of what they feed on, but of the very leaves under which they pass" (*Letters* II: 308).[1] This chapter explores the ways in which Shelley's poetry is colored by contemporary practices of racial enslavement and adjacent discourses – anti-Black prejudices propagated by the pro-slavery West India Interest as well as by abolitionists and liberal thinkers. It is no coincidence that the same decades that witnessed the apex and later abolition of the transatlantic slave trade also produced Romanticism, a literary movement in so many ways centered on the celebration of individual, imaginative, and creative freedom. Yet the relations between racial politics and liberatory poetics have historically been neglected by scholars of Romanticism. In attempting to situate Shelley's poetry and poetics against a deliberately broad notion of "discourses of slavery," I do not mean to suggest that Shelley was explicitly intervening in the debates about the rights and wrongs of enslaving Africans, but rather that his valorization of liberty should not be read in isolation from the historical context of transatlantic slavery.

I begin by linking Shelley's comment on poets being chameleons to his view of the relation between the poet and his time before focusing on a number of his works: the prefaces to *Adonais* and *Laon and Cythna*, the dramas *The Cenci* and *Hellas*, as well as "A Discourse on the Manners of the Ancient Greeks Relative to the Subject of Love," written as a preface to Shelley's translation of Plato's *Symposium*.[2] Spanning a range of genres, none of these pieces is about racial slavery, yet they offer telling indications of Shelley's own complicity with this system. That being said, the point is not to accuse Shelley of being a racist. Rather, my aim is to gain purchase on what Shelley might mean *for our times*, firstly, by unpacking his own conception of the relation between poetry and history and, secondly, by analyzing how his writing is embedded in its historical present. In highlighting how Shelley's work reflects the racial prejudices of the Romantic era, I hope to call attention to how our own critical engagements with his work reflect the prejudices of ours. Critics are, after all, no less chameleonic than poets – we, too, take our colors from the materials we feed on and the time we live in. For this reason, this chapter includes some autobiographical recollections from my own early career as a critic of Romantic poetry that would normally be outside the purview of criticism. I introduce them here because it is only by foregrounding the relation between writing – be it poetic or critical – and the historical present of composition that we can begin to explore the historicity of writing as such: how texts are both of the moment in which they are written *and* of the moment in which they are being read.

Shelley's assertion that poets are "a very chamæleonic race" was an invitation to trace echoes of Goethe's *Faust* – which Shelley had been reading together with John Gisborne – in his recently completed *Adonais*. The poem is one of Shelley's most densely intertextual works: in addition to *Faust*, its allusions range across European literary history from the ancients (Bion, Moschus, Plato, Theocritus, Virgil) to the great moderns (Milton, Spenser) and to Shelley's contemporaries – first and foremost Keats who is the subject of Shelley's elegy. Shelley's suggestion that the poem's intertextuality is "chamæleonic" is the more apt because it can be associated with Keats's own poetics. It recalls a letter that Keats wrote in late October 1818 in which he describes himself as a "camelion Poet" who has "no identity" and "no self."[3] For Keats, poetic chameleonism implies a receptive fluidity, an ability to embody other subject positions. "When I am in a room with People," he continues, "then [I am] not myself home to myself: but the identity of every one in the room begins to press upon me that I am in a very little time annihilated."[4] Such receptiveness may be admirable as an aesthetic principle, yet from a political viewpoint it is problematic – a chameleonic approach to social questions threatens to collapse into a politically irresponsible or apathetic stance: the poet as turncoat parroting the most popular opinions of their day.[5]

This latter is a prospect that worries Shelley. Throughout his career, he attempted to define the relationship between poetry and the contemporary, often by seeking to extricate poetry from the political entanglements of its time. His most extended statements on this question appear in *A Defence of Poetry*, which defends the art with reference to its timeless beauty and truth. "A poet participates in the eternal, the infinite, and the one; as far as relates to his conceptions, time and place and number are not," he confidently asserts (*SPP* 513). But the *Defence* is a history as well as a theory of poetry, tracing the form's development from earliest human society. Whenever Shelley addresses the work of any specific poet, he is forced to acknowledge that even the best of them are incapable of transcending the moral prejudice of their time and place – so his favorite poets Dante and Milton, for example, are destined to "walk through eternity enveloped and disguised" in the "distorted notions" of Christianity that dominated the worldview of their time (526). In another passage, he speaks of poets being "infected" with the "gross vice or weakness" of their contemporaries (520). This means that, although Shelley considers poetry to be timeless, he also recognizes that the poets who write it are inevitably shaped by their historical moment. Poets are "chamæleonic" in an additional sense: they take on the colors of the time they live in regardless of whether they consciously agree with them or not. His solution to this double bind (between historical contingency and timelessness) is offered in the concession that "a poet considers the vices of his contemporaries as the temporary dress in which his creations must be arrayed, and which cover without concealing the eternal proportions of their beauty" (516). In other words, the poet is a moral chameleon, writing eternal poetry that is nonetheless colored by the vices of their time. Shelley speaks of poets, yet it is hard to see how any writer could be excluded from this condition: philosophers, historians or critics are no less chameleonic than poets when it comes to reflecting contemporary prejudices. This means that, if we wish to analyze Shelley's relation to his time, or his relevance for ours, we must also attend to our own chameleonism with regards to the moment that we live in. Moreover, and this is the main contention of this chapter, when it comes to anti-Black racism, critics writing in the early twenty-first century are still sharing in the vices of Shelley's contemporaries. In *The Romantic Ideology*, Jerome McGann famously indicted Romanticists for uncritically accepting the philosophical positions of the Romantic poets whom they would criticize. This chapter explores a comparable problem: the extent to which scholars of the Romantic era unwittingly accept the anti-Black discourses that were generated throughout the eighteenth century to justify the enslavement of Africans. These discourses can be found among abolitionists no less than slavery apologists, and of course also in the works of the great poets.

Shelley was already in Italy when Keats wrote the "camelion Poet" letter, and while the two poets may of course have discussed the matter, it seems more likely that Shelley's formulation echoes Godwin's flattering description of a "man of talent" in his essay "Of an Early Taste for Reading": "When I read Thomson, I become Thomson; when I read

Milton, I become Milton. I find myself a sort of intellectual camelion, assuming the colour of the substances on which I rest."[6] Godwin argues that genius manifests itself in a child's capacity for literary absorption. Shelley's suggestion that a poet is a chameleon effectively transposes the mimetic imagination of a young reader to the adult poet. For Godwin, the opposite of the man of genius is not the dull and plodding man (although such a man is outlined at the start of the essay) but the slave, as becomes clear in the warning that he issues at the close of the essay:

> But what is most to be feared, is that some adverse gale should hurry the adventurer a thousand miles athwart into the chaos of laborious slavery, removing him from the genial influence of a tranquil leisure, or transporting him to a dreary climate where the half-formed blossoms of hope shall be irremediably destroyed. That the mind may expatiate in its true element, it is necessary that it should become neither the victim of labour, nor the slave of terror, discouragement and disgust. This is the true danger[.][7]

"Of an Early Taste for Reading" was published in 1797 and has evidently absorbed the abolitionist rhetoric of its time – the transportation of a thousand miles (across the Atlantic, presumably) from freedom into slavery, from a genial to a dreary clime, from innocent leisure to hopeless toil: all these are staples of abolitionist imagery. Although Godwin makes no mention of skin color, his choice of rhetorical tropes evokes a person who has been kidnapped from Africa. The image is clearly a warning to his readers of what happens to the young person who does not cultivate their intellectual talents – but why does Godwin need to evoke the transatlantic slave trade to bring this point across? Does he really think that his readers are in "true danger" of ending up enslaved on an overseas plantation? Or does the image of an enslaved African serve another apotropaic purpose: suggesting complete intellectual denigration, everything that his readers would seek to avoid for themselves and their children? Although Godwin's statement clearly condemns slavery, its rhetorical power rests on a contrast between "man of genius" and "slave of terror" that reinscribes a racial hierarchy that places free whites and enslaved Blacks at opposite ends on the scale of intellectual refinement. In this gesture, Godwin's argument, chameleon-like, takes its color from the racial assumptions of the 1790s.

The chameleon poet metaphor allows for both conscious and unconscious use of source materials. Whereas Keats emphasizes how the poet responds to his social environment, and Godwin considers how precocious children respond to reading, for Shelley, its primary import lies in the relations that it establishes between works. The notion of poets as chameleonic dovetails with his belief that all poets are collaborating on a single work, which he in the *Defence* describes as "that great poem, which all poets, like the co-operating thoughts of one great mind, have built up since the beginning of the world" (*SPP* 522). And yet *Adonais* is very firmly anchored in a specific historical circumstance: it is an elegy for Keats that takes vengeance on hostile reviewers. "I have dipped my pen in consuming fire to chastise his destroyers," he informs Claire Clairmont in a letter announcing the poem's completion (*Letters* II: 302).[8] The poem grows out of the squabbles taking place in the literary magazines of Shelley's day. The preface contrasts the timeless value of Keats's poetry with the inferior compositions lauded by his critics, taking particular aim at the *Quarterly Review* and one of its associates, whom he calls "a most base and unprincipled calumniator."[9] This could be a reference to Henry Hart Milman (on June 11, 1821, he wrote to Charles Ollier that he had "discovered that my calumniator in the Quarterly Review was the Rev^d. Mr. Milman") or to Robert Southey, whom he considered to be behind attacks on his own and Keats's work (*Letters* II: 298–299).[10] Between poem and preface, *Adonais* embodies the poet's split temporality: at once enmeshed in the parochial concerns of his time and contributing to a great poem that transcends any given historical present. A poet may participate in "the eternal, the infinite, and the one," but he also engages in bickering and petty point-scoring with his contemporaries (*SPP* 513).

*

The archive is the material interface in which past and present are conjoined. Timeless poems are embodied in aging manuscripts and books. Several of Shelley's poems are explicitly rooted in archival documents: *Prometheus Unbound*, for instance, rewrites a lost drama of the same name by Aeschylus (and his copy of Aeschylus, allegedly found in his pocket after he drowned, is now archived in the Bodleian Library, Oxford); the plot of *The Cenci* is taken from a "manuscript copied from the archives of the Cenci Palace at Rome"; "Julian and Maddalo" is an oral history record of a conversation with Byron; *Hellas* takes another Aeschylean drama, *The Persians*, alongside Shelley's reading of newspaper reporting on the Greek War of Independence as its sources. *Queen Mab*, with its copious notes citing an eclectic mix of authorities – Bacon and the Bible, Rousseau and Lucretius, Holbach and Hume, Pliny and Spinoza, to name a few – is another kind of archive, capturing young Shelley's reading habits. Drawing on archival materials in the composition of a work serves to tether that work to history in a particular way. It is an assertive gesture, symbolizing not merely a lack of better inspiration but an appropriation of the past in the service of one's own creative project. It also reveals the proximity between poetic creation and critical interpretation: Shelley's rewriting of *Prometheus Unbound* is also an analysis of what bondage meant for the Greeks and for Shelley's own post-Napoleonic generation.

In *No Archive Will Restore You*, Julietta Singh offers a personal meditation on the relation between a writer and their archive. The following passage describes the experience of budding critics trying to gain a foothold in the academic marketplace.

> We were graduate students in a small cultural theory program, plummeting deeper and deeper into debt, which is in a sense its own hellish kind of archive. We were hoping to be one of the rare exceptions that would be plucked into that almost mythical land of tenure-track work. [...] Why *did* we stay on, with the odds so stacked against us? I don't blame the archive per se, but it undoubtedly held out a kind of promise for each of us that kept us tethered to academia. The archive was an elusive hope of our individual salvation. If we could find the right archive, the right stash of materials that was sexy enough to sell ourselves, we could be spared the depression, the anxiety attacks, the pre-mid-life crises that would come when, one by one, we realized we were not going to be chosen. When, in the face of that brutal rejection, we had no idea what the fuck to do with ourselves. If only we could stumble upon the right archive, the secrets that no one else had yet discovered, we might still be one of the chosen ones.[11]

To me it seems possible that Shelley, who spent much of his career fussing over the lack of popular acclaim, would recognize himself in Singh's recollection. If *Queen Mab* displays his youthful ambitions, signaling philosophical erudition and political credentials, later works like *Adonais* or *Hellas* demonstrate Shelley's mastery of the literary canon, his right to a place among the timeless poets. "It is absurd in any review to criticize Adonais, & still more to pretend that the verses are bad," he wrote highmindedly when the poem failed to attract the praise he had anticipated (*Letters* II: 388).[12] From the start to the finish of his *oeuvre*, Shelley's citations and intertextual allusions reveal his "archive" (in Singh's sense): the source materials that he gathers in the hope of being plucked into the mythical land of eternal poets.

For us, coming to his works as critics, Shelley's own work is the archive. I encountered it subject to that precarious condition outlined by Singh, hoping for it to be sexy enough to allow me to secure a foothold in the academy. At first, in my student days, I defined "sexy" as canonical: dead white poet, philosophical complexity, revolutionary politics, proto-feminism, cosmopolitan lifestyle, and an epic death story to boot (that shipwreck: an accident? a suicide?). Working with Shelley would give me the gravitas to compensate for being a young woman of color from a migrant background with little social or cultural capital. But today, more than a decade later and in light of the various crises and reckonings that shake our present, the definition of academic "sex appeal" is shifting, becoming more attuned to questions of social and racial justice. Sadly, this attunement has come at the cost of human lives: most dramatically the murder of George Floyd in May 2020 that sparked global Black Lives Matter protests and focused attention on legacies of enslavement and colonialism and how they determine structural inequalities in our own time. Suddenly, confessional books on everyday racism by Black authors were topping the bestseller charts while universities and subject associations hurried to proclaim their solidarity. Saidiya Hartman summed up the mood perfectly in the following observation:

> What we see now is a translation of Black suffering into white pedagogy. In this extreme moment, the casual violence that can result in a loss of life – a police officer literally killing a Black man with the weight of his knees on the other's neck – becomes a flash point for a certain kind of white liberal conscience, like: "Oh my god! We're living in a racist order! How can I find out more about this?"[13]

For me, in a deeply problematic way, the translation of Black suffering into white pedagogy has entailed a translation of structural disadvantage into a career opportunity. In the English department of our time, as a living Black woman, I am suddenly more sexy than dead, white Shelley. Although academia has long operated under the "color-blind" pretense that critical labor is objective and impersonal, it has never *not* mattered that I am a Black woman working on Romanticism – often the only Black person in the room. Here are some examples from my experience at university:

The first supervision for my undergraduate dissertation:
    ME. I am interested in British and German Romanticism.
    DISSERTATION SUPERVISOR. Have you considered writing about Toni Morrison?

As a PhD student making small talk over conference coffee with other PhD students:
    RANDOM PHD STUDENT. So what do you work on?
    ME. Shelley.
    PHD STUDENT. Oh, how interesting! I didn't realize that Shelley wrote on slavery.

At a formal dinner in a Cambridge college:
    ME. My postdoctoral project is about Shelley.
    PROFESSOR EMERITA. How curious for someone of your complexion to work on such a canonical poet.

It is embarrassing to bring this up, yet it is perhaps more absurd to pretend that the color of my skin and my "most peculiar" name (that's a quote from another encounter with an established academic) do not affect my professional life. "Your silence will not protect you," as Audre Lorde famously put it.[14] So perhaps it is not surprising that my search for "the right archive, the right stash of materials that [is] sexy enough to sell" increasingly brings me to myself, my own "authentic" voice and experience. This is one reason why my answer to the question of what Shelley might mean *for our times* is as much about my own historical situation as it is about Shelley: critical interpretation cannot be abstracted from the person who offers it and the time in which they live.

Introducing my lived experience of academia into an academic text is a form of resistance against the unconscious (white supremacist) biases of the academy: an environment historically developed for privileged white men to prosper. Allied modes of resistance come from all possible directions: Black, feminist, queer, Indigenous, decolonial and other anti-normative theories and practices have served to challenge how knowledge is produced and circulates in the academy. "Where do you know from?" Eugenia Zuroski asks in an exercise for graduate students that calls attention to the contingent nature of knowledge production.[15] In part, the interest in personal experience reflects the state of identity politics in an age of influencers, selfies, and 24/7 social media performance, but, equally importantly in this context, it is rooted in Romantic notions of subjectivity. In the *Defence*, Shelley celebrated poetry's ability to dispel "the dull vapours of the little world of self," but in private correspondence he acknowledged the impossibility of escaping its microcosm: "So much for self – *self*, that burr that will stick to one" (*SPP* 525; *Letters* II: 108–109).[16] Indeed, being preoccupied with the self is something of a Romantic malaise, from Wordsworth's fourteen-book epic on the growth of his own mind to Byron's self-mythologizing Oriental tales or Coleridge's *Biographia Literaria* that purports to settle "the true nature of poetic diction: and at the same time to define with the utmost impartiality the real *poetic* character of a poet" through an autobiographical narrative.[17] For the Romantics, a reflective engagement with the specificity of their own experience unlocks the truth of poetry as such – yet the very notion that such a transition from individual self to universal truth is possible rests on a set of beliefs about personhood that is, in and of itself, premised on the historically specific philosophical context of Romanticism. So how do I, as a Black woman of the twenty-first century, even begin to approach this allegedly timeless and impartial truth when the experience through which it is formulated differs so much from my own?

*

Shelley did not have much to say about racial slavery. When I state this to experts in the field, they tend to be quick to point out that he did not take sugar in his tea, as if this biographical anecdote is enough to counterbalance the fact that his lifelong engagement with the politics and poetics of freedom is completely silent on the subject of the plantation. For him, the political problem of emancipation crystallized in the bloody Terror that followed the French Revolution, including how to avoid its repetition. In the preface to *Laon and Cythna*, a poem that processes this history, he places the blame for the Terror squarely on the shoulders of the oppressed masses:

> Could they listen to the plea of reason who had groaned under the calamities of a social state, according to the provisions of which, one man riots in luxury whilst another famishes for want of bread? Can he who the day before was *a trampled slave*, suddenly become liberal-minded, forbearing, and independent? This is the consequence of the habits of a state of society to be produced by resolute perseverance and indefatigable hope, and long-suffering and long-believing courage, and the systematic efforts of generations of men of intellect and virtue. (*Poems* II: 36–37, emphasis mine)

In short, the French were not ready for the liberty they suddenly gained during the revolution. The implication is that men should bear their chains with "resolute perseverance and indefatigable hope" – in other words, nonviolent resistance – until they are ready to be freed. But let's pause to consider Shelley's choice of the phrase "trampled slave." Taking its color from the discursive landscape of the 1790s, the phrase evokes abolitionist sentimentality: the poor slave is to be pitied, but he may by no means take his emancipation into his own hands. This figure is a rhetorical construct with little relation to actual enslaved people, people whose legal status was that of chattel, which is to say personal property with no more right to self-determination than possessed by a chair or a brick. In other words, Shelley uses the concept of slavery as an abstract political metaphor – comparable to the neo-Lockean sense in which the American revolutionaries of the 1760s and 1770s argued that "taxation without representation is slavery"[18] or Mary Wollstonecraft compared the lot of white middle-class British women to that of enslaved Africans. "Is one half of the human species, like the poor African slaves, to be subject to prejudices that brutalize them," she demands, surely intending to startle her reader into feeling the outrage of reducing white women to the abjection of Black slaves.[19]

The ethical shortcoming of the preface to *Laon and Cythna* is not just that it draws on the language of slavery that suffused the political discourse of its time but that it offers the very same argumentative strategies that the West India Interest mobilized to defend slavery: slavery cannot be abolished because the enslaved are not ready for freedom. If they were to be emancipated, they would at once pursue violent and barbaric revenge against their former masters. Even William Wilberforce, whose twenty-year-long parliamentary campaign for abolishing the slave trade has made him the poster boy of abolition in mainstream historiography, was *against* emancipation of the slaves themselves. Speaking in the Commons in 1805, Wilberforce referred to enslaved Black people in the Caribbean as "a degraded race of beings, actuated only by a brutal impulse" and clarified that, while he might ultimately hope for their eventual emancipation, it could not possibly take place until "a period, the distance of which ha [*sic*] had never attempted to calculate" – a future so distant that it may never come.[20] Hansard records the continuation of Wilberforce's speech as follows:

> [H]e felt that the immediate emancipation of the n----es in the West Indies could not be expected, for that before they could be fit to receive freedom it would be madness to attempt to give it to them yet he owned he looked forwards, and so he hoped did many others, to the time when the n----es in the West Indies should have the full enjoyment of a free, moral, industrious, and happy peasantry.[21]

Leading abolitionists subscribed to the same racist stereotypes about Black people lacking in aptitude for self-governance that slavers used to defend the institution.

Shelley's analysis of the French Revolution therefore takes its colors from the contemporary elite's patronizing attitude towards the rights of the laboring classes. He employs the same modes of reasoning in outlining why the workers of pre-revolutionary France were not ready for freedom as contemporary pro-slavery advocates used to justify the continued enslavement of Black people. This is why pro-slavery sentiments can be so seamlessly parsed in Shelley's terms: enslaved Africans cannot "suddenly become liberal-minded, forbearing, and independent," and emancipation must be postponed until such a date when "the systematic efforts of generations of men of intellect and virtue" – this could be read as a reference to the English missionaries and clergymen who were responsible for Christianizing the slaves – have rendered them sufficiently civilized to deserve freedom. What is even more troubling is the stance that Shelley takes in this conflict. When he writes of "men of intellect and virtue" whose task it is to civilize the masses, he is referring to himself and other progressives like himself (an arc that potentially includes twenty-first-century "woke" academics), whose writings will prepare oppressed people to be able to handle freedom – as if all people do not have an inborn right to freedom and self-determination without such efforts at civilization.

As the proximity between Shelley's explanation of the Terror and pro-slavery rhetoric shows, the disturbing thing about this mode of reasoning is that it is essentially about excluding certain groups of people from what Hannah Arendt has termed "the right to have rights" unless they comply with certain conditions: being "liberal-minded," "forbearing," "independent" – and above all not demanding reparations or retribution for past wrongs.[22] Yet, as Arendt makes clear, denying someone's right to have rights amounts to their "expulsion from humanity altogether."[23] While Arendt is concerned with the Holocaust, Orlando Patterson identifies a comparable mode of excluding people from the concept of the human in chattel slavery. He terms the condition of the enslaved a "social death."[24] Along similar lines, Hartman has noted that "the slave is neither civic man nor free worker but excluded from the narrative of 'we the people' that effects the linkage of the modern individual and the state," and so it follows that the "everyday practices of the enslaved occur in default of the political, in the absence of the rights of man."[25]

*

Shelley returns to the question of who is entitled to and who is excluded from the domain of rights more directly in his representation of Beatrice Cenci, for which reason we can read Beatrice as a proxy for the enslaved. Most critics begin their reading by noting Beatrice's entrapment in a society governed by a patriarchal "triple entente" of Father, Pope, and God in which, as a woman, Beatrice has no legal avenue to seek redress for the crime she has suffered – being raped by her father.[26] "What have I done?" Beatrice demands after the act,

> Am I not innocent? Is it my crime
> That one with white hair, and imperious brow,
> Who tortured me from my forgotten years,
> As parents only dare, should call himself
> My father, yet should be! (III.i.70–74 [*Poems* II: 781])

Beatrice interprets the rape as punishment, although her only crime is the tautological fact of having been born her father's daughter. A person kidnapped or born into slavery faces a similar predicament: their life is one long punishment though their only crime is having been born of a certain skin color. Furthermore, Shelley repeatedly emphasizes Beatrice's exclusion from the law: "is it that I sue not in some form / Of scrupulous law, that ye deny my suit?" she asks the noblemen of Rome during the banquet scene at the end of Act I (I.iii.135–136 [*Poems* II: 757]). The gendered violence propels her insight into her position outside the patriarchal law of Papal Rome: "in this mortal world / There is no vindication and no law / Which can adjudge and execute the doom / Of that through which I suffer" (III.i.134–137 [*Poems* II: 783]). She exists outside of the sphere of rights. This is also true of enslaved persons who were subject to violations that remained expressionless within the legal code of the British Empire, which defined them as chattel devoid of legal personhood. Even in the rare cases when a Black – free or enslaved – person's testimony was admitted in court, a fine-grained calculus governed how much it was worth compared to that of a white man.

Being excluded from the domain of rights, Beatrice cannot expect retribution through the usual legal means. "I pray / That you put off, as garments overworn, / Forbearance and respect, remorse and fear, / And all the fit restraints of daily life," she says to her lover Orsino and stepmother Lucretia in a scene after the rape (III.i.207–210 [*Poems* II: 788]). Her words in effect conjure a space outside the law where the conventions of social interactions do not apply – this can be understood as the domain of chattel slavery, a life lived in the absence of the right to have rights. Beatrice goes on to explain why her being wronged in this space necessitates an extrajudicial justice: "I have endured a wrong, / Which, though it be expressionless, is such / As asks atonement" (III.i.213–215 [*Poems* II: 788]). When Beatrice takes the atonement into her own hands, the action can be read as an instruction to the oppressed masses. After having "prayed / To God, and [...] talked with [her] own heart," Beatrice sentences her father to death – "Mighty death! / Thou double-visaged shadow! Only judge! / Rightfullest arbiter!" (III.i.218–219, 177–179 [*Poems* II: 788, 786]). Read as an allegory on slavery, Beatrice's actions advocate a summary execution of all slave traders and plantation owners. However, if the play suggests analogies between Beatrice's parricide and a people's regicide or armed self-emancipation, Shelley's preface condemns the thought: "Revenge, retaliation, atonement, are pernicious mistakes," he unequivocally states (*Poems* II: 730). Such pernicious mistakes may make good tragedy, but Shelley clearly does not recommend violence as political principle. Instead, he prescribes forgiveness, "the fit return to make to the most enormous injuries is kindness and forbearance" (*Poems* II: 730). This is emancipation on the model of the Wedgwood medallion; "Am I not a man and a brother?" the kneeling man demands. The image has such a hold on the white imagination that, over time, it has congealed into the mainstream view of abolition according to which the heroic Wilberforce liberated the poor, pitiful Blacks. This is a history that erases the repeated uprisings, revolts, and rebellions by enslaved Caribbeans that made the fear of successful Black self-emancipation into one of the most potent forces in eighteenth-century colonial politics.

Shelley's preface to *The Cenci* reveals the naiveté of his political imagination: ultimately, to practice forbearance is to acquiesce in your own oppression. A more fruitful way of reading *The Cenci* as an allegory on chattel slavery emerges if the drama is placed in constellation with M. NourbeSe Philip's *Zong!*, which is one of our time's most haunting confrontations with the afterlife of the Middle Passage. Like *The Cenci*, *Zong!* is based on an archival record of true historical events. The poem is named after a slave ship whose captain, Luke Collingwood, decided to throw circa 150 Africans overboard so as to claim compensation for lost "cargo." A large part of the tension in both works arises from the fact that they deal with a crime too horrible for words: in Beatrice's words, this is "a wrong so great and strange [...] / Ask me not what it is, for there are deeds / Which have no form, sufferings which have no tongue" (III.i.139–142 [*Poems* II: 784]). Such crimes exceed representation and can only be manifested negatively, as a reticence, the failure of speech. Early critics remarked on Shelley's foolhardiness in centering a drama on an act that could not have been performed, and barely even openly talked about, on a London stage in 1819, but this is precisely the point. Paul Endo sees this as an example of the Shelleyan sublime:

> Shelley often *stages* silence, choosing not to mediate. The namelessness of *The Cenci* is just such an instance: it is not symptomatic of a daemonic, pathological "incapacity," but must be regarded as a calculated attempt [...] to *postpone* naming and the propagating of a high sublime meaning or "moral purpose."[27]

The very namelessness names a region of justice that exists in default of the judicial system of its time. Philip uses a comparable technique to delimit a notion of justice that is in default of the legal code in which the court case of the *Zong* was conducted. The case was brought because the insurers refused to pay compensation for the murdered Africans and solely hinged on this destruction of property being willful. "There is no telling this story," Philip repeatedly insists in the "Notanda" accompanying her elegy: words are not able to convey the magnitude of the crime. Yet the story must be told and *Zong!* does the telling, or "un-telling."[28] It starts from a report on the court case: every single word in *Zong!* originates in that archival document. Philip unmoors the words of the report, loosens them from the grotesque formality of that courtroom, and lets them spill over the page as fragments of sentences, further fragmenting into pure sound before, finally, they sink into the page – the final section is printed in fading grey ink so as to reinforce visually "the un-telling of what cannot, yet must, be told."[29] Philip's "un-telling" helps us read Beatrice's repeated insistence on the nameless, wordless, expressionless nature of the wrong that she suffers. Where Philip decomposes language, Shelley repeatedly spells out language's inability to bear witness or achieve redress. Which is to say that, despite their differences, *Zong!* and *The Cenci* are related because they thematize the failure of language to represent certain forms of violence: both Philip and Shelley take an archival record describing an unspeakable crime and turn it into poetry. These historical documents are most palpable in the silences and absences at the core of each respective work, a speechlessness that places a demand on any critic seeking to interpret these works – a demand to face the ethical implications of writing about imaginative works that deal with real historical atrocity. How do we speak about past injustices without appropriating them for our professional archive? Without converting someone else's suffering into an opportunity for professional advancement? Without speaking over when we try to give voice to the dead?

*

With *Hellas*, Shelley faces a new revolution – the Greek War of Independence – and another challenge with combining the eternal value of poetry with contemporary politics. In the drama's preface, Shelley proudly informs his readers that the "*Persae* of Aeschylus afforded me the first model of my conception" but also that "Common fame is the only authority which I can allege for the details which form the basis of the poem, and I must trespass upon the forgiveness of my readers for the display of newspaper erudition to which I have been reduced" (*SPP* 430–431). The work is thus an amalgam of the daily news and timeless tragedy. In addition, *Hellas* is a piece of propaganda writing, intended to stir his fellow Englishmen to intervene in the Greek War. "What little interest this poem may ever excite, depends on its *immediate* publication," he wrote to his publisher Charles Ollier shortly after completing it, a statement quite at odds with the timelessness that Shelley usually ascribes to poetry (*Letters* II: 365).[30] "If *Hellas* is filled with atemporal ideals," Mark Kipperman comments on this letter, "they had timely urgency for Shelley."[31] Aligning Shelley's treatment of the Greek War to his comments on the French

Revolution, Michael Erkelenz reads the drama's ending in pragmatic terms: what "begins as a celebration of Greek battle victories ends as a call for mercy and a warning of the consequences of revenge. *Hellas* [...] everywhere addresses the dangers that the modern Greeks may only repeat the mistakes of other revolutionaries before them."[32] Timothy Webb has similarly suggested that the play's "revolutionary optimism is tempered by the recognition that revolutions which are based on blood will, in their turn, give rise to other revolutions and further bloodshed."[33]

Despite these cautionary caveats about potential violence, Shelley's preface is assured in its representation of the Greek War of Independence as one of the great political events of its time: Shelley links it to revolutionary upheavals in Spain, France, and Italy and closes with an assertion that the "world waits only the news of a revolution of Germany to see the Tyrants who have pinnacled themselves on its supineness precipitated into the ruin from which they shall never arise" (*SPP* 432). In other words, *Hellas* is the herald of a liberated Europe and, as so often in this period, Europe stands for the world at large – so Shelley does not pause to consider how the upheavals in Spain, France, and Italy interacted with anti-imperial unrest in their overseas colonies. This Eurocentrism explains why the small-scale guerrilla warfare of the Greeks has world-historical ramifications. As much as dramatizing a particular conflict, Shelley conceives of the drama as a series of "lyric pictures" in which he has "wrought upon the curtain of futurity which falls upon the unfinished scene such figures of indistinct and visionary delineation as suggest the final triumph of the Greek cause as a portion of the cause of civilization and social improvement" (430). The drama has a complex relation to its own historical moment. It creates its archive – creates itself *as* an archive – by assembling ancient materials (Aeschylus's *The Persians*) and contemporary newspaper sources in order to write a future in which the Greeks are free and Shelley's present is past. While, in the *Defence*, Shelley described drama as "a prismatic and many-sided mirror" reflecting its own present, *Hellas* anticipates a *future* moment in which Shelley's readers will be able to see their own time reflected in Shelley's drama (520).

Yet as I read the drama in the present of Shelley's future, his ambitions for *Hellas* seem to have misfired. At the time of my reading, the most urgent political development in the Romantic period is neither the conflict in Greece nor the power plays between European monarchies but rather imperial expansion fueled by an ascendant white supremacism. The period witnessed the growth and consolidation of a racial capitalism that helped finance an industrial revolution in Europe even as it fed into further colonial extraction and expansion across the globe. *Hellas*'s entanglement in British empire-building comes into view more clearly when the vision of Greece presented in one of its choral passages is read alongside a poem that has become a centerpiece in the culture wars of the early 2020s: "Rule, Britannia!" Both James Thomson's poem and Shelley's chorus begin with an account of how the two states emerge out of the sea: "When Britain first, at Heaven's command, / Arose from out the azure main," are the opening lines of Thomson's poem.[34] Shelley's Greece arises with a similar command: "'Let there be light!' said Liberty, / And like sunrise from the sea, / Athens arose!" (682–684 [*Poems* V]).[35] Although Shelley substitutes Liberty for God, his adoption of the phrasing "Let there be light!" from Genesis 1:3 indicates the divine nature of this decree. This also makes Britannia/Athens indominable. "If Greece must be / wreck," Shelley writes, "yet shall its fragments reassemble / And build themselves again impregnably [...] above the idle foam of Time" (1002–1006 [*Poems* V]). Thomson expresses the same confidence in his Britannia: "Thee haughty tyrants ne'er shall tame; / All their attempts to bend thee down / Will but arouse thy generous flame."[36] Both nations are like those roly-poly dolls that always get up again: any attempt to subdue them will inevitably result in a reassertion of their glory.

A more disturbing feature that *Hellas* shares with "Rule, Britannia!" is the assumption that enslavement is a moral failing of the enslaved: their nation is not so blest by God, their hearts not "manly" enough to guard it from invaders.[37] The victim-blaming attitude permeates *Hellas*. As one of the choral interludes puts it:

> O Slavery! thou frost of the world's prime,
> Killing its flowers and leaving its thorns bare!
> Thy touch has stamped these limbs with crime,
> These brows thy branding garland bear,
> But the free heart, the impassive soul,
> Scorn thy control! (676–681 [*Poems* V])

As with the many references to enslavement that punctuate the drama, this passage does not refer to real enslaved bodies – this "branding garland" has no relation to the actual marks with which Europeans stamped Africans to claim ownership over their bodies – but drifts into allegory. Its real purpose is to show how physical bondage does not make slaves of those who carry freedom in their heart. Rather than attacking the logics of enslavement, Shelley introduces the concept as a foil to the freeman whose heart and soul scorn its debasement, much like contemporary portrait artists would introduce a Black page to highlight the whiteness of their aristocratic sitter. Outwardly branded but inwardly free, the Greeks may be defeated, but they shall never be slaves. This sentiment is captured in a description of the battle at Wallachia offered by Hassan. In the preface, Shelley asserts that the Greek "defeat in Wallachia was signalized by circumstances of heroism, more glorious even than victory"; in the drama, this heroism is manifested as rejection of enslavement (*SPP* 431). Here is Hassan's account of the Pacha's offer to the defeated Greeks at Wallachia:

> then said the Pacha, "Slaves,
> Render yourselves—they have abandoned you,
> What hope of refuge, or retreat or aid?—
> We grant your lives"—"Grant that which is thine own!"
> Cried one, and fell upon his sword and died!
> Another—"God, and man, and hope abandon me;
> But I to them and to myself remain
> Constant"—he bowed his head and his heart burst.
> A third exclaimed—"There is a refuge, tyrant,
> Where thou darest not pursue and canst not harm
> Should'st thou pursue; there we shall meet again."
> Then held his breath and after a brief spasm
> The indignant spirit cast its mortal garment
> Among the slain;—dead earth upon the earth!
> So these survivors, each by different ways,
> Some strange, all sudden, none dishonourable,
> Met in triumphant death (385–401 [*Poems* V])

This increasingly fantastical series of suicides – spontaneous combustion of the heart, a brief spasm of held breath – breaks with the visceral violence characteristic of the drama's battle scenes. The Greeks at Wallachia do not die from physical as much as moral wounds: their free deaths symbolizing their triumph over enslaved life. *Hellas*'s repeated representations of slavery all roundly condemn the enslaved. Like Thomson's Britons, Shelley's Greeks "never will be slaves!"

*

Shelley's idealization of ancient Greece is another way in which his work, chameleon-like, takes on the colors of its time. David Ferris argues that the Romantics defined their own modernity in a differential relation to ancient Greece – Athens becomes the standard against which modern times have to measure themselves and invariably come up short. In other words, Romanticism constructs Athens as an ideal that it cannot achieve.[38] And yet there is one respect in which Shelley considers the moderns to have advanced on antiquity. In "A Discourse on the Manners of the Ancient

Greeks Relative to the Subject of Love," intended as an introduction to his translation of Plato's *Symposium* (the first complete English translation that did not censor the discussion of sex between men), Shelley seeks to explain Greek sexual practices by contextualizing them in the society of their time. "One of the chief distinctions between the manners of ancient Greece and modern Europe, consisted in the regulations and the sentiments respecting sexual intercourse," he writes. "The fact is, that the modern Europeans have in this circumstance, and in the abolition of slavery, made an improvement the most decisive in the regulation of human society."[39] And yet, far from having abolished slavery, Europeans of Shelley's time were simply practicing it offshore, in their colonies; if this counts as an "improvement" in "the regulation of human society," the improvement seems to consist primarily in the geographical separation between production and consumption, the exploitation of labor and enjoying the fruits of that labor. In other words: the advent of global capitalism.

In either case, the question of slavery occupies a marginal position in Shelley's "Discourse": the thrust of his argument is to explain why Greek men preferred to have sex with other men. He does so with reference to the subjugation of women:

> Among the ancient Greeks the male sex, one half of the human race, received the highest cultivation and refinement: whilst the other, as far as intellect is concerned, were educated as slaves, and were raised but few degrees in all that related to moral and intellectual excellence above the condition of savages.[40]

The "slaves" referred to here are of course not the kidnapped Africans of his own time but the victims of the domestic slavery that existed in ancient Athens. Nonetheless, the premise of Shelley's reasoning is clear: uncultivated and unrefined women, slaves and savages are all equally undesirable. This explains why Greek men had to turn to other men for erotic satisfaction – a practice that Shelley here describes as a "gross violation in the established nature of man."[41] Whatever we make of Shelley's homophobia, it is curious to note how readily he dismisses what he perceives as violations practiced in Athens. While he acknowledges that "personal slavery and the inferiority of women" caused a "diminution" in "the delicacy, the strength, the comprehensiveness, and the accuracy of their conceptions, in moral, political, and metaphysical science, and perhaps in every other art and science," he does not hesitate to proclaim the overall superiority of the ancient Greeks.[42]

The best part of modernity still carries traces of this ancient superiority. In the preface to *Hellas*, Shelley proclaims that "We are all Greeks – our laws, our literature, our religion, our arts have their root in Greece" (*SPP* 431). For Shelley, modern Europeans are Greek by virtue of our participation in the afterlife of Greek culture, but the statement implies that – like the Greeks – we can also let our civilizational virtues cohabitate with the oppression of women and "savages." That is, we need not be troubled by the existence of slavery when celebrating ancient Greek liberty: the fact that the philosophers could spend their days chatting in the agora because they had slaves to do the work for them. Such a cavalier attitude towards the victims of slavery has survived from Shelley's time into our present – and, like chameleons, we take our colors from it, for instance, when we create curricula that cordon off Black History from British History; the poetry of Romanticism from the historic records of the transatlantic slave trade. "Still today," Achille Mbembe has noted, "it is not obvious to the eyes of all that the enslaving of the Negroes and colonial atrocities are part of our world memory; even less that this memory, as common, is not the property of the sole peoples that suffered these events, but of humanity as a whole."[43] This ensures that the history of Britain's involvement in the trafficking and ownership of Africans, rather than being the common heritage of all Britons, remains the purview of the descendants of the formerly enslaved – hence the easy assumption, in the small chat over conference coffee, that, being Black, I must work on slavery. Because, indeed, is it not much more pleasant to agree that we are all Greeks than to assert that we are all slavers because "our laws, our literature, our religion, our arts" have developed in symbiosis with centuries of racialized slavery and colonial exploitation?

To assert how the legacies of enslavement affect our life is not about generating guilt, an emotive response that is not productive to critical engagement. Christina Sharpe offers an alternative way of relating to history in her remark that, in engaging with eighteenth- and nineteenth-century materials from around the Atlantic rim, we are working with "the archives of a past that is not yet past."[44] Such an acknowledgment does not provoke guilt; rather, it underlines the continuities between historic and present-day manifestations of racial injustice: the vices of Shelley's contemporaries are also our own. "That history and that destruction – both of which, it bears repeating, are ongoing – are very much at the center of our thinking," Jared Sexton has noted, "as are the questions regarding how one might inhabit that history and that destruction."[45] Placing something at the center of one's thinking is not the same as offering an answer: how to inhabit the history we have inherited will remain an open question so long as that history remains an open wound. This is why it is imperative to resist the tidiness of a conclusion, a satisfactory sense of closure that encourages you to turn the page and read the next chapter. Instead, I would like to finish with an invitation, borrowed from Dionne Brand, to close the book and take a moment to reflect, observe, feel, sit in the room with history:

> One enters a room and history follows; one enters a room and history precedes. History is already seated in the chair in the empty room when one arrives. Where one stands in a society seems always related to this historical experience. [...] How do I know this? Only by self-observation, only by looking. Only by feeling. Only by being a part, sitting in the room with history.[46]

Notes

1 Percy Bysshe Shelley to John and Maria Gisborne, July 16, 1821.
2 The sections on *Hellas* and "A Discourse on the Manners of the Ancient Greeks Relative to the Subject of Love" have previously been published in Mathelinda Nabugodi, "Old Anew: Hellas," *European Romantic Review* 33.5 (2022), 639–652.
3 John Keats to Richard Woodhouse, October 27, 1818, *Selected Letters of John Keats: Based on the Texts of Hyder Edward Rollins, Revised Edition*, ed. Grant F. Scott (Cambridge, MA: Harvard University Press, 2005), 195.
4 To Richard Woodhouse, October 27, 1818, *Selected Letters*, 195. In this regard, the "camelion Poet" exercises what Keats elsewhere calls "negative capability." Critics have taken various approaches to squaring Keats's renunciation of individuality with his own highly individual style. See Julie Camarda, "Keats's Chameleon Poetics, Or, the Natural History of 'Ode to a Nightingale'," *Keats-Shelley Journal* 68 (2019), 40–71, for a recent overview of scholarship on Keats's chameleonism as well as a reading that anchors Keats's comments on the "camelion Poet" in contemporary literary and scientific understandings of the chameleon.
5 William D. Brewer provides a useful survey of how the "chameleon" metaphor operates in the Romantic period in the introduction to his *Staging Romantic Chameleons and Imposters* (New York: Palgrave Macmillan, 2015).
6 William Godwin, "Essay V: Of an Early Taste for Reading," in *The Enquirer: Reflections on Education, Manners, and Literature* (London: Robinson, 1797), 29–35, 32, 33. Nicholas Roe has suggested that Keats's "camelion Poet" letter alludes to this passage of Godwin's essay in *John Keats and the Culture of Dissent* (Oxford: Clarendon, 1997), 247.
7 Godwin, "Of an Early Taste for Reading," 35.
8 Percy Bysshe Shelley to Claire Clairmont, June 16, 1821.
9 Preface to *Adonais*, in Michael Rossington and Jack Donovan, eds. *The Poems of Shelley*, 4 volumes to date (London: Routledge, 1989–), IV: 235–330, 260–261. Unless otherwise indicated, Shelley's prefaces, poetry, and dramas are quoted from this edition, hereafter abbreviated *Poems*.

10 Percy Bysshe Shelley to Charles Ollier, June 11, 1821.
11 Julietta Singh, *No Archive Will Restore You* (Santa Barbara: punctum books, 2018), 21–22.
12 Percy Bysshe Shelley to John Gisborne, January 26, 1822.
13 Saidiya Hartman, interview by Catherine Damman, *Artforum*, July 14, 2020, www.artforum.com/interviews/saidiya-hartman-83579.
14 Audre Lorde, *Your Silence Will Not Protect You* (London: Silver Books, 2017).
15 Eugenia Zuroski, "Where Do You Know From? An Exercise in Placing Ourselves Together in the Classroom," *MAI Feminism*, January 27, 2020, https://maifeminism.com/where-do-you-know-from-an-exercise-in-placing-ourselves-together-in-the-classroom/.
16 Percy Bysshe Shelley to Leigh Hunt, August 15, 1819.
17 Samuel Taylor Coleridge, *Biographia Literaria; or Biographical Sketches of my Literary Life and Opinions*, in *Samuel Taylor Coleridge*, ed. H. D. Jackson (Oxford: Oxford University Press, 1985), 157.
18 For the use of "slavery" as political metaphor in pre-revolutionary America, see Zachary Mcleod Hutchins, "The Slave Narrative and the Stamp Act, or Letters from Two American Farmers in Pennsylvania," *Early American Literature* 50.3 (2015), 645–680.
19 Mary Wollstonecraft, *A Vindication of the Rights of Woman with Strictures on Political and Moral Subjects* (Cambridge: Cambridge University Press, 2012 [1792]), 330.
20 Hansard, House of Commons, February 28, 1805, 1st series, Volume III, col. 672–673.
21 Hansard, House of Commons, February 28, 1805, 1st series, Volume III, col. 673.
22 Hannah Arendt, *The Origins of Totalitarianism* (Cleveland: Meridian Books, 1962 [1951]), 296.
23 Arendt, *Totalitarianism*, 297.
24 Orlando Patterson, *Slavery and Social Death: A Comparative Study* (Cambridge, MA: Harvard University Press, 1982).
25 Saidiya V. Hartman, *Scenes of Subjection: Terror, Slavery, and Self-Making in Nineteenth-Century America* (Oxford: Oxford University Press, 1997), 65.
26 The formulation "triple entente" is from James Rieger, *The Mutiny Within: The Heresies of Percy Bysshe Shelley* (New York: George Braziller, 1967), 114, but the analogy appears in various guises throughout criticism on the play. For example, Michael Scrivener, *Radical Shelley: The Philosophical Anarchism and Utopian Thought of Percy Bysshe Shelley* (Princeton: Princeton University Press, 1982), 193–194; Young-Ok An, "Beatrice's Gaze Revisited: Anatomizing 'The Cenci,'" *Criticism*, 38.1 (1996), 27–68, 55; Stuart Curran, *Shelley's Cenci: Scorpions Ringed with Fire* (Princeton: Princeton University Press, 1970), 134. See, however, Michael Kohler for a refutation of this argument, "Shelley in Chancery: The Reimagination of the Paternalist State in 'The Cenci'," *Studies in Romanticism*, 37.1 (1998), 545–589.
27 Paul Endo, "The Cenci: Recognizing the Shelleyan Sublime," *Texas Studies in Literature and Language*, 38.3–4 (1996), 379–397, 393.

28 M. NourbeSe Philip, *Zong! As Told to the Author by Sataey Adamu Boateng* (Middletown: Wesleyan University Press, 2008), 189.
29 Philip, *Zong!*, 199.
30 Percy Bysshe Shelley to Charles Ollier, November 11, 1821.
31 Mark Kipperman, "History and Ideality: The Politics of Shelley's *Hellas*," *Studies in Romanticism* 30.2 (1991), 147–168, 151.
32 Michael Erkelenz, "Inspecting the Tragedy of Empire: Shelley's *Hellas* and Aeschylus' *Persians*," *Philological Quarterly* 76.3 (1997), 313–337, 330.
33 Timothy Webb, *Shelley: A Voice Not Understood* (Manchester: Manchester University Press, 1977), 200.
34 James Thomson, "Rule Britannia!," in *The Complete Poetical Works of James Thomson*, ed. J. Logie Robertson (Oxford: Oxford University Press, 1908), 422–423, ll. 1–2.
35 Volume 5 of *Poems* is in press.
36 Thomson, "Rule Britannia!," ll. 19–21.
37 Thomson, "Rule Britannia!," l. 30.
38 David Ferris, *Silent Urns: Romanticism, Hellenism, Modernity* (Stanford: Stanford University Press, 2000), 54.
39 Percy Bysshe Shelley, "A Discourse on the Manners of the Ancient Greeks Relative to the Subject of Love," in Richard Holmes, ed. *Shelley on Love: An Anthology* (London: Anvil Press Poetry, 1980), 101–112, 105.
40 Shelley, "Discourse," 107.
41 Shelley, "Discourse,"108.
42 Shelley, "Discourse," 106.
43 Achille Mbembe, *Necropolitics,* trans. Steven Corcoran (Durham, NC: Duke University Press, 2019), 126.
44 Christina Sharpe, *In the Wake: On Blackness and Being* (Durham, NC: Duke University Press, 2016), 73. The formulation describes Philip's *Zong!*.
45 Jared Sexton, "Afro-Pessimism: The Unclear Word," *Rhizomes: Cultural Studies in Emerging Knowledge* 29 (2016), §17.
46 Dionne Brand, *A Map to the Door of No Return: Notes to Belonging* (Toronto: Vintage, 2011), 25.

CHAPTER 4

Dream Defenders and the Inside Songs

Julie A. Carlson

> I am a lover of humanity, a democrat and an atheist
> —Percy Bysshe Shelley, Guest registry at the
> Hôtel de Villes de Londres, Chamonix[1]

The "our times" that structure my reflections on Percy Shelley are highly cognizant of structural racism, white privilege, and racial divisiveness. They are less woke than distrustful of proclamations and practices of anti-racism. Consequently, my focus is on the relevance of Shelleyan poet-legislators to these times, by which I mean poet-scholar-activists of all shades (including the Dream Defenders, who were born in the wake of Trayvon Martin's murder) who affirm the transformational powers of imagination – "artivists" in today's parlance.[2] As the "dream defenders" and "inside songs" of my title suggest, these poet-legislators work the streets as well as universities in efforts to better realize and manifest social justice, interchanges that are simultaneously affirmed and challenged by "Percy Shelley." They are affirmed by "Red Shelley," long championed by the Left for his street credibility and uptake by numerous labor and suffrage causes, and challenged by the whiteness and Eurocentrism of "Shelley." My essay dwells at this crossroads by asking whether the rationales for championing Red Shelley are applicable to a "Black" Shelley understood as not only anti-racist but also anti-antiBlack.[3] For reasons that I hope become clear even while their outcomes are necessarily blurry, my way into this inquiry is via the "inside songs" referenced in and opened out by Fred Moten's Shelleyan poem "barbara lee."[4]

I Shel*lee*

Moten's "barbara lee," whose third section begins with the statement, "According to Shelley, poets are the unacknowledged legislators of the world," is the most explicit engagement with Shelleyan poetic legislation by a Black radical US poet-philosopher that I know.[5] Published in the volume *B Jenkins* in 2010, the poem commemorates US Representative for California's Thirteenth Congressional District Barbara Lee, the second Black woman ever to serve in Congress when she was elected in 1996 and the only representative in either body of Congress to vote against President Bush's military authorization act in the immediate aftermath of the attack on the World Trade Center on September 11, 2001. This extraordinary act is what "barbara lee," a poem composed in three sections, elucidates and seeks to perpetuate. Sections one and three are written in prose and describe the disruptive workings of poetry in an updated (ante-) defense of poetry (as their section titles "[The Poetics of Political Form]" and "[The Unacknowledged Legislator]" suggest). These sections flank section two, "[Statement in Opposition]," that ventriloquates Lee's congressional speech in a twenty-one-line ballad: "speaker, members / heavy, but risen / against muted, / I had to rely on / the inside songs. / welcome to the same / new world."[6] Thus, even the form of "barbara lee," that encircles her poetic speech within prose descriptions of poetry's political efficacy, enacts what the ballad states when lee credits inside songs with her capacity to resist the groupthink of xenophobic discourse. The signal difference from *A Defence of Poetry* is the concluding line specifying "The unacknowledged legislator is Barbara Lee." This apparent tautology does not annul the Shelleyan circuitry of poet and legislator. For what makes Representative Lee an unacknowledged legislator is her poetry that, according to section three, bespeaks an ante-representational and therefore "ante-American" as well as anti-racist ethos.[7]

This assertion of poetry's anti-racism addresses two topics posed by the poetic legislation affirmed in "barbara lee." The broad topic concerns mechanics or *how* poetry upends the status quo, which section three presents as formal properties: "busting out of the sentence or cutting being-sentenced," singing "the form of [an] endless running," operating "on the edge of things," turning "what is turned against into a vestibule, an ante-room," taking "this turn in a cramped, cracked stanza, homelessly acting like she at home by taking flight, held still in forced movement."[8] In effect, an organized disruptor, "the unacknowledged legislator" is "compel[led]"

> to love (the way to get to) what hasn't happened yet, to care for the way what hasn't happened yet is in the midst and on the edge of its negation,

to turn in and on negation's language until it comes out, if not comes out right, as ante-nation language.⁹

Such a poetic legislator "speaks the ethics that attend" a "history of displacement" by way of

> tones and fragments that get under the skin of the standard, words and phrases that slip or seep into the underground of the *patria*, that re-emerge as a set of broken claims to patriotism or a set of claims breaking patriotism, depending on how you hear.¹⁰

In other words, her schooling in "bent poetics" prepares Representative Lee to oppose policies that promote us-versus-them mentalities that sanction bellicosity and identity-categorical thinking. Ears inclined to poetry pick up on seepage, outbursts, enjambed states, and jam sessions, even in the rare instances when they inhabit halls of power.

The specific topic is how Lee is able to stand alone in opposing the military authorization act at a time when to deliberate, let alone call for deliberation, was deemed equivalent to treason. For this, she says, "I had to rely on / the inside songs." Inside songs sustain her because they in-form her, a "runaway" whose history of displacement knows firsthand the false promises of patriotism. Thus, they situate 9/11 in a context that is traumatic but unexceptional, the appropriate response to which is "suffering with" rather than causing more suffering through more killing[11]:

> I, the
> runaway, say don't go
> off. somebody blew
> us up. welcome
> to the state of
> mourning. come
> look at the difficult
> broken flesh. stay
> a little while.¹²

Both modes of poetic in-formation are what keep lee "unmade," not on the make, and unseduced by the "glaring hyper-visibility" periodically accorded by media politics to difference.¹³ In effect, she stands alone knowing that she is not standing alone by virtue of being backed by "the inside songs" of her constituents and that are constituents of her. In turn, electoral constituents hear in her "musicked speech" a "general responsibility of advance" that they take to the streets "where the poetics of political form lives" as "displaced social life, that outer space structured by inner sound."¹⁴

This is a remarkable blurring of Lee, lee, and Shelley by a poet-philosopher-activist of the Black radical tradition. Like *The Mask of Anarchy*, "barbara lee" responds to an intra-international emergency by disseminating the mechanics and indirect directives of song. Shadowing forth, veiling, secreting open secrets of love via airborne underground sounds and balladic passages: such are the formal devices supporting Shel*lee*an political transformation. Equally important, motivation and ability to act are reliant on inside songs that are choric, collective, and pitched toward futurity in loving the way to get to what hasn't happened yet. But these commonalities are limited, perhaps even a limit case.[15] After all, "barbara lee" is exceptional in Moten's *oeuvre* for attending to a US elected official and a canonical British Romantic poet – each a rare occurrence. Then there is the emphasis on "black poetry" in the poem's opening lines: "Ever since Plato, some poets remain surprised that they don't run shit, that they ain't even citizens. But black poetry suffers its politics of non-exclusion. Abide with this distress."[16] Reference to "black poetry" complicates any implied inherence of Shelley in Lee and in "barbara lee," even granting Moten's repeated insistence that "black" does not signify a racial identity but instead a racialized perspective that foregrounds those who are "under-privileged" and originarily displaced.[17] Both facts about "barbara lee" raise the larger question of Shelley's applicability to our racially divisive times. If the revolutionary aspects of even Red Shelley are suspect to non-white radical poet-scholar-activists, what value inheres in Shelley's writings for anti-racist Romanticists? From inside the field, the question is whether the ethos undergirding the #Bigger Six Collective, "formed in 2017 to challenge structural racism in the academic study of Romanticism" by building "from it rather than within it," can be extended to a canonical offender.[18] Or, as the (virtual 2021) conference "Black Studies & Romanticism" asks, does Black Studies have anything to gain from studying the revolutionary praxis of British Romanticism?[19] As embodied in "barbara lee," the question concerns bodies. Are "the inside songs" perceptibly anti-racist and ante-American because their poet-Speaker is Black?

A roundabout answer exists in the ways that inside songs are mobilized in and via "barbara lee." For "the inside songs" is a direct reference to free jazz composer and bassist William Parker's *I Plan to Stay a Believer: The Inside Songs of Curtis Mayfield* (Aum Fidelity, 2010), a compilation of eleven Curtis Mayfield songs arranged by Parker that he and his eight-piece band performed and taped in various venues between 2001 and 2008.[20] Combining free jazz, soul, and gospel styles, it features Leena

Conquest singing Mayfield lyrics, Amiri Baraka rapping his poems, a ninety-strong children's choir from the suburbs of Paris (tracks 5, 11), and the New Life Tabernacle Generation of Praise Choir of Brooklyn (tracks 6, 7). The album disseminates "Curtis Mayfield" as the "soundtrack" of the 1960s that, in Parker's words (cited in Aldon Nielsen's), "brought all musical modes together into a circle marked 'People's Music,' with lyrics mapping demands for 'reclamation of land, self-determination, and right to change existing structure rather than assimilation into a quagmire called progress'."[21] Parker's liner notes gloss the subtitle: "Every song written or improvised has an inside song which lives in the shadows, in-between the sounds and silences and behind the words, pulsating, waiting to be reborn as a new song."[22] The core track of this lyric potentiality is "People Get Ready / The Inside Song" (track 6), with "The Inside Song" being one of only two original compositions by Parker in *Believer* (the other being "Ya He Yey Ya" affixed to "I'm So Proud").

In "barbara lee," then, the efficacy of "inside songs" resides in the referrals that they set in motion. The phrase refers to a prior text that embodies an ongoing history of improvisational activism that ties reading to hearing and poetry to protest songs. It links "plan[s] to stay a believer" to the "People's Music" of the 1960s to the rhythms and the blues that comprise freedom songs of an enslaved and believing people – songs that have kept those struggles other than a struggle and that link "meaning" to responsiveness. When "inside" a poetic legislator, these songs address constituents and conditions that officially Lee/lee does not represent, whether as a legislator or a Black cis woman – in this instance, Arab, Muslim, and Brown people living in and outside of the United States. They move her "out" from what "occurs inside, in the name of that other, outer interiority," and they make that inside-outside opening bearable and sustainable over the long haul.[23] Encountered in the poem, however, "properly" apprehending "the inside songs" requires insider knowledge for their relaying capacity between word and sound, reading and believing, inside and outside, to occur. We have to begin somewhere.

Are Shelley's "people" ready or readied by "Shelley" for this?

II Shelley Outside

The closest analogue to Black poetry's inside songs is the "little volume of popular songs wholly political" that Shelley announces to Leigh Hunt as "destined to awaken and direct the imagination of the reformers."[24] Red Shelleyans have prized this collection ever since for containing some of "the most famous protest poems in the English language," especially *The Mask of Anarchy*, "England in 1819," and "Song to the Men of England."[25] Extensive documentation exists of their uptake by a host of nineteenth- and twentieth-century labor, suffrage, and freedom movements, including by Chartists, Owenites, Wobblies, union movements, suffragettes, and nonviolent independence campaigns in India, Africa, South Korea, and the United States.[26] More recent engagements are documented on Graham Henderson's The Real Percy Bysshe Shelley website. We learn, for example, that English e-learning specialist and improv musician Mark Summers read "England in 1819," *The Mask of Anarchy*, and "Poetical Essay on the Existing State of Things" at #TakeBack Brum, a street protest in Birmingham in the UK organized by the People's Assembly against austerity in early October 2016, and that the English fashion designer John Alexander Skelton, outraged over the authorities' failure to memorialize the Peterloo Massacre adequately, produced a clothing line referencing the massacre and had runway models recite the entire ninety-one stanzas of *The Mask of Anarchy*.[27] In other words, these songs continue to arouse assembled comrades at various conclaves, and they are the chief – though by no means only – focus of scholarly commemorations of revolutionary Shelley. A series of recent Shelleyan bicentennials – of Mary Shelley's *Frankenstein* (2018), of the Peterloo Massacre and *The Mask of Anarchy* (2019), of Percy Shelley's death (2022) – attest to the world-transforming output of both Shelleys and the passageways that their works forge between (so-called) popular and academic audiences. At commemorative moments like these, "Shelley" becomes almost a household word, especially in the UK.

Radical claims made by Shelley for his little volume rest on solid, but also unsettled, grounds that become far shakier when claiming a white Red Shelley as Black. On the one hand, real accord exists between bent and Shelleyan poetics, starting with the street cred that preceded and ultimately eventuated in publication of his songs. As has been well-rehearsed, only two of the "destined" poems were published in his lifetime ("Ode to the West Wind" and "Ode to Liberty"), because even radical printers, some who were his friends, were unwilling to face the likely charges of seditious libel in printing them.[28] Delayed far longer was publication of them as a volume, not occurring until 1990 by Redwords, a socialist press that in 2019 reissued *Shelley's Revolutionary Year* to coincide with the bicentennial of Peterloo, once again under the super-vision of Paul Foot.[29] Originally, however, these seditious poems were passed underground, where they became a groundswell that gradually began to operate as a political one. This history of censorship attests more broadly to

Shelley's outlier status as "atheist, republican, revolutionary, philosophical anarchist, leveler, feminist and vegetarian," also exile, who was dismissed in his first year from Oxford for publishing with Thomas Jefferson Hogg *The Necessity of Atheism* and was one of only two men in the entire nineteenth century in Britain to be denied custody of his children.[30] Nor did the harshness of these sentences deter him from continuing to speak out or call out precisely those officials with the power to silence him. The Irish Marxist poet Ciarán O'Rourke states in a review of the reissued *Shelley's Revolutionary Year* that Shelley's "instinct in life was to resist all forms of entrenched authority (religious and political)"; his "concern was always to unmask the structures of power that dominated his society."[31]

Yet tensions discernible in the texts and reception of Red Shelley expose an insider privilege that dogs his revolutionary vision and reputation. I mean less the obvious fact that he is a white cis-male born into an aristocratic family than how these qualities complicate two differing features of his reception as red. One relates to the disproportionate emphasis given to poems in this volume when affirming his radicalism – both their disproportion relative to his entire body of works and the generic emphasis placed on "songs" as manifesting populist sympathies. A related tension concerns acknowledged and unacknowledged oscillations between the "many" and the "few" as intended audiences for his works. Prefaces and letters written by Shelley to secure a publisher or readership for a particular work spell out the correlations he assumes among class position, textual competence, and comprehension of a figurative and allusive versus a straightforward or popular style. As William Keach pointed out long ago, these documents are startlingly blunt about how few of his texts are written for the many; virtually all of them, except for those in the little volume, are written "to the *Sunetoi*," roughly equivalent to "cognoscenti" or "initiated," though often claimed to speak on behalf of the many.[32] As Keach goes on to say in "Rise Like Lions?" Shelley's tactics are radically suspect. Why browbeat an audience if the aim is to encourage their uprising; why imply that they are to blame for the endurability of structures that they did not devise and have no investment in preserving?[33] As concerns Red Shelleyans, class and audience get even more entangled depending on which auditory arena is being envisioned and privileged: street or university; rising or waning poet-activists; potential converts or diehard professors. Perceived splits between and within these arenas highlight epistemological conflicts over the kinds of anti-racist appeal that songs make. A matter of word or sound? Which mode of sound system? Appeals to body or mind? Ear, pulse, or cortex? Manifested via deliberate indirection or direct action?

Fault lines are even easier to discover in claims for Black Shelley. As mentioned, Shelley is a rarity in Moten's *oeuvre*. Few, if any, grassroots anti-racist projects in the United States acknowledge him as a major inspiration, despite remarkable resonances. The absence is hardly surprising, given growing impatience over hearing exclusively from or about white models and their presumed leadership capabilities. Still, the absence suggests that characterizing Shelley as an ally only adds fuel to the fire unless Shelleyans devise new ways of disseminating him. For the weak spot in Shelley's lifelong efforts to "unmask the structures of power that dominated his society" is the priority he grants to the West as source, model, renovator, and amplifier of creativity, freedom, and inspiration. The avowed Occidentalism undergirding his "philosophical view of reform," the ethos of the prose text meant to accompany the "little volume of popular songs wholly political," positions him on the inside of an antiBlack conceptual system that keeps white-body privilege blowing through his texts, regardless of his intentions or cultural syncretism.[34] It buoys "his" imagination even in times of darkest despair because the concept of imagination is an endless source of renewable energy for those West-bound and identified.

Put bluntly, this critique leaves Shelley out in the cold and leaves many Shelleyans cold. Neither outcome invalidates the critique, but recognizing the reality of structural racisms should work to strengthen, not occlude, fugitive efforts to dismantle it. A less schematic line of questioning might ask what in Shelley sounds anti-antiBlack to non-white poet-auditors, and what besides dreaming ensures that attacks on "the system" by white poet-auditors are actually minority-serving? The works of Benjamin Obadiah Iqbal Zephaniah provide one such mixed-mediated diasporic approach to inside songs.[35] Self-described "poet, writer, lyricist, musician, and naughty boy," Zephaniah calls Shelley "the original dub poet" and declares unabashedly that "I love the guy." He works to "spread the word" about Shelley's revolutionary energy by pairing Red Shelley and Bob Marley, reading his own poems along with Shelley's poems at youth clubs and Rastafarian gatherings, and selecting as the one book he would bring to a desert island Edward Moxon's 1853 edition of *The Poetical Works of Percy Bysshe Shelley*.[36] "There was never any guarantee that I would love this guy because our backgrounds are so different. He was the son of a baronet," Zephaniah the son of Caribbean immigrants to the Handsworth district in Birmingham, the "Jamaican capital of Europe." In fact, Zephaniah's first encounter in school with *The Mask of Anarchy* went so poorly that he wrote off Shelley as "one of those dead white poets who write difficult poetry for difficult people" until he later happened upon Paul Foot's *Red

Shelley, whose detailed contextualization of *The Mask of Anarchy* not only changed his view on Shelley but also forged an alliance between them on the activism of song. The "music" he heard in Shelley's "lines" compelled him "to put my fist down and take up my pen" on behalf of folks "on the streets," the place from where poets "write our legislation."[37]

Hugely influential in the UK and around the globe, and affiliating his poems with multiple causes (refugee crises, global human rights, anti-racism, veganism, prison abolition), Zephaniah's "Black" encompasses "Romany, Iraqi, Indians, Kurds, Palestinians, all those that are treated Black by the united white states," including "the battered White woman, the tree dwellers, and the Irish," as he explains in the introduction to *Too Black, Too Strong*, the title of his third collection of poems.[38] Moreover, his incredible impact and popularity have not gone to his head. *The Guardian* published this reply to the notification in late November 2003 that his name was being submitted to the Queen for appointment to the Order of the British Empire. "OBE me? Up yours, I thought. I get angry when I hear that word 'empire'; it reminds me of slavery [...] and thousands of years of brutality."[39] The reply also reprints the poem "Bought and Sold" that opens *Too Black, Too Strong* and whose opening lines specify how "Smart big awards and prize money / Is killing off black poetry [...] The lure of meeting royalty / And touching high society / Is damping creativity and eating at our heart." It concludes: "It's sick and self-defeating if our dispossessed keep weeping / And we give these awards meaning / But we end up with no voice."[40] Like "barbara lee," then, which locates Black poetry "next to the buried market, at the club underneath the quay," "planning to refuse until the next jam, at a time to be determined and fled," Zephaniah takes poetry "everywhere," especially to those who "do not read books" but appreciate a good performance. "barbara lee" is more and less categorical: "Poetry investigates new ways for people to get together and do stuff in the open, in secret." "Getting together and doing stuff is a technical term that means X. Something going on at the sight and sound center of sweet political form."[41]

Both Zephaniah and Moten, then, work to counter the "dead image that academia and the establishment" often convey of poetry but from differing stances, neither of which is wholly outside or within either sphere.[42] Zephaniah stopped formal schooling at age thirteen, his struggles with dyslexia contributing to disaffection fanned by a hostile system. "If my teacher had taken time to explain the context [of *The Mask of Anarchy*], that would have turned me on to poetry then and there."[43] Moten is a highly accomplished cultural theorist at the university, who cultivates "black study" through undercommons methodologies that at times instrumentalize, at times disinter, the values of higher ed. Zephaniah's conviction that Shelley "would have been with us in the climate fight, Black Lives Matter, Me Too [movement]" is based on his extrapolating from the "so many" who "have looked to [Shelley's] lines" for support confirmation that they also are pro-Black. Moreover, that conviction is generated out of Zephaniah's near-exclusive focus on Shelley's "popular songs wholly political" and how they disperse Shelley's message in both senses of dispersal. Moten's stake in Black-identifying Shelley is far less assured for reasons relating to pitched battles between "black study" and university training that he and Stefano Harney repeatedly wage.[44] AntiBlack manifestations are structurally endemic to university core values: meritocracy, textual literacy, privilege and tenure, publish or perish.

> How do we keep the job from taking play out of work and work out of play? How do we keep work from rising to the status of "the work" or, higher still, "my work"? [...] It's a real problem, in conditions of "freedom," to work for the institution you work against. But that's a better problem than not working against the institution that works against us and our needs, and desires, and calling.[45]

How Moten handles this problem is similar to his ante-oppositional approach to "the inside songs." As mentioned, "/ the inside songs /" is Parker's phrase which Moten identifies in the poem "william parker/fred mcdowell" that precedes "barbara lee" in *B Jenkins*. In "william parker/fred mcdowell," "the inside / songs of curtis mayfield" are placed in an "inner ear" that achieves an "inside / outside opening" via "the ear's folds, its courses / in the open space."[46] In "barbara lee," they perform these openings through the relays they set in motion: back toward freedom songs repeatedly readying people and toward potential songs looming "in the shadows, in-between the sounds and silences and behind the words, pulsating" of existing songs. Outside of "barbara lee," Moten's wording avoids "inside" more or less completely, preferring "interinanimation" and other veerings off "in the name of that other, outer interiority," an outer interiority at once demarcated and invaded by the "surround" that de/composes it.[47] On a basic level, avoidance of the inside expresses Moten's affiliation with outliers, fugitives, diasporic peoples, and outlaws as well as rejection of insider/outsider logics that theoretically have long been deconstructed but that keep showing up everywhere. More complexly, Moten's avoidance bespeaks the composition of "black" song as ante-scriptorial and ante-individuated that reclaims (something like) political agency by disarticulating Blackness and objecthood while still affirming the materiality of both. "Knowledge of Freedom," the opening chapter of *Stolen Life*, book two of Moten's trilogy on how to "consent not to be a single being," recasts this racist conceptual history via "black chant," "wherein a terrible reality is lent to song and word in their interinanimation" that sonically disrupts the critical philosophy of Immanuel Kant.[48] Because this enlightened knowledge system bases its freedom on the denial of freedom to persons cast as things, no one should want it until what freedom signifies is remade from the ground up.

It can sound as if this remaking is exactly what Shelleyan song is doing in its fugitive planning. Breaking up power structures by breaking through entrenched terminology, patterns, affects, and associations is Shelley's style of subversion, the ethereality and abstractness of which techniques escaped detection by print censors, many critics, and allegedly most of his "popular" readership. At the same time, they are pronounced in scholarly accounts of his radicalism, where Shelley has served as a posterchild of deconstruction from the early '80s onward and, lately, of posthuman-environmental entanglements. However, for all the potential that is unleashed via deconstruction, posthuman reconstructions in and of Shelley are not necessarily anti-antiBlack. White-body supremacy dwells readily in a subject restored to sheer potentiality, and the atmospheres and environments into which Shelleyan personae are often diffused are themselves suffused in racist histories and conceptualizations.[49] Thus, something more and less tangible is required of Shelleyan song in order for the futurity for which it is readying people to actually qualify as anti-racist and pro-Black. "Knowledge of Freedom" specifies two such in/tangibles: "ensemble" as a non-individualist and non-subordinating mode of agency, "commonality" or "the general" as the means and outcome of doing things. Both formulations work to reclaim the "honor of the whole" from universalisms or public universities by proceeding from a "Blackness" re-cognized as a "general theory of the generative."[50] Again, this Blackness does not have to be one's ontological or experiential reality, but it is claimable only by those who attend "to its paraontology, whose most prominent feature is [...] 'originary displacement.'"[51] Good thing that "generativity," one of Moten's approximates for imagination, already exists in many: "the most important thing we have to imagine about the black tradition" is that "it is common. Blackness is (in) common."[52] But common is not the same thing as the "same" "thing," especially when claimed by entitled poet-legislators whose dissatisfactions with the status quo, and pronounced outrage over feeling displaced, run roughshod over the needs of historically and economically displaced persons. With the entitled, the commonness associated with Blackness has to be lived manifestly. Evidence of this occurs "when we act like we can hear difference in common."[53]

III Inside Outside Opening

Manifesting through daily actions that poet-legislators hear difference in common is a good litmus test of anti-racism. Exercising differences in common is at the core of the Radical Imagination Gymnasium in Portland, Oregon, cofounded in the belief (a) that "radical imagination" is "not a 'thing' that we, as individuals, 'have'" but instead "a commons of possibility" worked out "between people" and (b) that it is a "group of muscles," currently "weak and underused," that through "sustained routine" and regular workouts might "build enough muscle memory to reverse the dominant tendencies of the imagination dictated by market logic."[54] Abilities to *hear* difference in common are strengthened through techniques of street activism and para-academic approaches to Shelley. Street protests amplify Black chant and innovate on calls and responses, as when Angela Davis asked crowd members in Occupy gatherings to repeat each sentence of her speech to ensure that everyone in the crowd could hear what was being said and have the experience of voicing it for themselves.[55] Chanting Shelley's protest songs was how they first made themselves known; setting others to music broadcast Shelley in concert halls throughout nineteenth-century Europe.[56] Present-day para-academics like Zephaniah accentuate performance over reading in spreading Shelley's words across the globe. Others, like John Webster, combine both into *Shelley Songs: A Folk-Rock Song Cycle with Lyrics from Italy 1818–1822*, released with Brindaband in 2021.[57] Many more launch songs of protest from a Shelleyan phrase or title – some fifty-three albums named "Ozymandias," for example, according to Camila Oliveira.[58]

Performative approaches to Shelley's soundscapes are less practiced in university settings for understandable but increasingly counterproductive reasons. It is as if the unparalleled musicality of his verse and the involutions of its semantic upheavals have made Shelley scholars such expert readers that we fail to recognize their sonic features other than in print.[59] Such textual high fidelity hampers opportunities to *hear* difference in common and to encounter *difference* in common via exposure to Shelley. Imagine an entire class chanting *The Mask of Anarchy* on student picket lines and as preparation for them. Imagine common causes that might be forged through comparing one song-tradition of protest to another.[60] Restricting the use of either approach reduces Shelley's appeal to the generation that radical pedagogues are hoping through his verses to inspire to rise up. Comparative indifference to audio formats bypasses students' visual-sonic competencies. Comparative indifference to teaching non-Eurocentric texts limits student familiarity with the most unimaginable actual revolutionary event occurring in Shelley's day in Saint Domingue/Haiti – an event that, as Michel-Rolph Trouillot has argued, was conceptually inaccessible to that age and, to a large degree, remains so to ours owing to literary-historical preconceptions.[61]

These realities need ears that can hear what they are and are not demanding. The demand is not that we jettison or denigrate the richness of Shelley's textual legacy or the competencies that they cultivate. It is that we contextualize them as partial, situationally invested, hardly the whole story and that we explore their meaningfulness via less exclusively text-bound values and protocols. As Moten puts it, "textualism is never disconnected from the impulse to confirm the knowledge" being conveyed.[62] For some knowledge traditions, the primary knowledge conveyed in texts is of the knowledges erased by textualism but that reside in flesh "tempered by experiences of profound depravation" and passed on through word of mouth and DNA.[63] Efforts to transcribe this knowledge have given rise to critical fabulation, theory in the flesh, treating the body as archive, methodologies that give words to somatic memories and facts that are recoverable only through imagination.[64] Recourse to these methods is less demanded by textually rich traditions such as British Romanticism, but they are hardly irrelevant to them. Indeed, they contextualize *text* as one medium among many that foregrounds some messages and silences others. Plus, they are integral to the special meaningfulness of poetry – both its materials (rhythm, breath, sound, pace, pattern, resonances) and purposes. "We want the creative faculty to imagine that which we know; we want the generous impulse to act that which we imagine; we want the poetry of life: our calculations have outrun conception; we have eaten more than we can digest" (*SPP* 530).

Actively approaching Shelley in these ways is more likely to activate Shel*lee*an inside songs. This route takes account of physical dimensions of "approach" – that diverse bodies and minds are coming at "Shelley" with different reasons and abilities to engage or disengage. The fantasy that we are on the same page in reading the same poem is an affront to the (neuro-) diversities assembled in any classroom. At the same time, inquiring into the affects and associations evoked by the same poem in different individuals is a fruitful way to share an experience of experiencing a poem. I hear something like this in Moten's call to produce a "performance of a text in the face of its unintelligibility" rather than "a reading" or "even an interpretation."[65] The latter activities, however valuable and difficult to pull off, suggest a one-way flow of communication from one disembodied mind to another. Moreover, they presume intelligibility and the desirability of making intelligible very difficult textual realities, worthy goals that deliver a somewhat one-sided message about reality. By contrast, performance, especially as elucidated in Black performance studies, starts from embodiments of difference in affect, personage, thought, and society.[66] Its measure of success is not consensus but rather how much and how far a performance moves people.

This has implications for teaching Shelley's poems so that they effect what his "poetry" envisions as "the generous impulse to act that which we imagine." One could even claim that "performance of a text" allows us to get beyond the troubling words that Shelley often uses in imagining social transformation – like oneness, eternal, the beautiful, empire of love – to the plurality, entanglement, gender fluidity, and antiBlackness that radical Shelleyans perceive "in-between the sounds and silences and behind the words, pulsating, waiting to be reborn as a new song" in his songs.[67] But these perceptions have to be made and received in common and as common in order for their reality to begin to have an effect on reality. In my view, their salience is best apprehended by accentuating and combining the embodied and associational features fundamental to Shelley's poetry. Embodied dimensions appeal to the body and aid in synchronizing a diverse assembly of bodies. Associational "logics" highlight dynamic interconnections between word and thought as well as language and community. The material for both exists in classrooms *in potentia* and as our future.

Learning to live with difference and to accommodate dissensus, then, is a "learning outcome" that anti-racist Shelleyans might get behind. The problem is that it provokes major anxiety in minds grounded in Western concepts of community and harmony, anxiety that is doubly triggered (so to speak) when confronting "race," in Shelley and in the classroom. Here the somatic techniques at which Shelley's poems excel in modulating breathing patterns, lulling through sound, regulating heartbeats and pulses are good places to start inquiry.[68] Exercised at the start of class, they can clear space for thought by regulating student agitation and by acknowledging how traumatic retention activates fight, flight, and freeze mechanisms that profoundly reduce the ability to learn or take risks.[69] Moreover, the contradictory affects triggered in interracial group discussions of race (fear, exhaustion, denial, anger, impatience) impede hopes of proceeding, let alone proceeding together.⁷⁰ The situation is equally fraught for teachers fearful of confronting angry reactions to their (perceived) lack of engaging actual classroom material – in this case, live bidirectional encounters between texts and people and what emerges, or can emerge, if those interactions are valued and orchestrated.⁷¹

Thus, class participants might "get together to decide how to get together to decide how to read [a particularly challenging text]. The implication of a collective enterprise is now explicit – I don't think anybody can do it by themselves."⁷² For one thing, the unintelligibility that is heightened by poetry is not unintelligible in the same way or for the same reasons for each auditor-reader. Exploring those differences pluralizes associational resonances – transport? Chains like dew? Asia? Hermaphroditus? – and establishes common ground through a shared process of unlearning different habits and traditions. For another, certain unintelligibilities heightened in poetry make manifest histories silenced by dominant textual regimes. The text that Moten's students had to get themselves together in order to decide how to get together to read is M. NourbeSe Philip's virtually incomprehensible *Zong!* It is so because of what it cannot and must not tell. Owing to the absence of first-person evidence, Philip resorts to "the text of the legal decision [*Gregson* v. *Gilbert*] as a word store" for the story of 150 "African men, women, and children thrown overboard in an attempt to collect insurance monies." Being true to this material requires "a variety of techniques." "I separate subject from verb, verb from object—create semantic mayhem, until my hands bloodied, [...] reach into the stinking, eviscerated innards," like "some seer, sangoma, or prophet who [...] reads the untold story that tells itself by not telling."⁷³ Such differences in the motivations for syntactic deconstruction have to be apprehensible even when teaching material from only one literary-historical tradition, especially one whose slippery signifiers stabilize racial hierarchies. This knowledge cannot be acquired in any one class, but its truth should inform the space and be open for exploration.

There is no simple way for established Shelleyans to unlearn the cultural-textual privileges that accompany Shelley studies or to demonstrate successful unlearning. Nor is there any definitive reason to encourage aspiring poet-legislators of all backgrounds to become Shelleyans. In our times, leftist Shelleyans have less concern to swell "our" ranks than develop passageways between us and rank-and-file activists. In fact, pursuing the latter is a surer way of achieving the former than declaring that these passageways exist. Such a defence of poetry combines the twin senses and arenas of performing: doing and professional acting. This "poetry" loosens defensiveness about the "self" and "Percy Shelley" but without leaving individuals or canonical authors wholly defenseless. Rather, it invites these entities to become ensemblic and find "new ways for people to get together and do stuff, in the open, in secret."

Shelley's associationism is a key method for tying unlearning to pro-Blackness. It not only revises concepts by improvising new terms but also links semantic associations to interpersonal associations and vice versa. More, it links expansion of the one to expansion of the other, widening the circumference of imagination in its joint exercising of aesthetic and moral outcomes. The deep connection between what we know and who we know either keeps us inside a self-fulfilling cognitive cycle or relays us onward and outward via encounters with difference. On a daily level, knowing people from different cultural-educational backgrounds broadens our familiarity with differing wants, tastes, and reasons to protest, a knowing that does not guarantee understanding or affection but whose lesser abstractness is pitched that way. Professionally, scholars tend to downplay the interconnection between what we know and who we know, but denying it hardly erases it. In fact, endnotes and acknowledgments broadcast the company we keep as a way of authorizing the validity of our research.[74] These acknowledgments no longer ratify our scholarship as good or a public good if the company they prize is monocultural and egocentric – qualities of "pint-pot" imaginations, the effects (but not causes) of which Shelley correctly assessed. "All things that Peter saw and felt / [...] seemed to melt / Like cloud to cloud, into him. / And so the outward world uniting / To that within him, he became / Considerably uninviting / To those who, meditation slighting / Were moulded in a different frame" (273–282 [*SPP* 350]).

Here too, re-cognizing through diversifying the interplay between disciplinary logics and circles of friends gives scholar-poet-activists something more and less arduous to do. Blurring boundaries between work and play, research and socializing, this intersectional diversifying activates a full array of embodied exchanges – even in professional associations. Having a diverse circle of friends naturally amplifies what we are encouraged to read, watch, play, perform, or imbibe. Having a multiracial media library cultivates cultural competence that may lead to interracial solidarities and friendships. Intersecting the two has the added benefit that conscious choices of what and who to know begin to function on unconscious levels, unlinking habitual pathways of association, altering vectors of attraction and repulsion, forging new procedural memories that elicit new habits of acting. This is way easier said than done. But perhaps the relative ease of saying is why professors are more comfortable sticking to reading and writing, and why others have grown suspicious of talk.

"barbara lee" performs this updating, multi-mediating and relaying of Shelley's (ante-) defense of poetry. Through "musicked speech" that renders audible this legislator's backing and unmaking by the inside songs of her constituents, "barbara lee" enacts associational logic as "a general responsibility of advance." And it credits Shelley with launching the performance. The rarity of Moten's engagement does not diminish the terrible beauty of lodging Shelley in "barbara lee." Instead, it contextualizes Shelley and temporary versus permanent dwelling. Moreover, reference to Shelley comes after rather than before the poem's detailed description of "black poetry," implying that bent poetic traits are more conducive than straight ones to achieving justice legislation in our times. As leaderless leaders, bent traits accentuate sound over semantics, fugitivity over stability, fleshiness over uplift, improvisation over heritage or legacy. Also, while "[The Unacknowledged Legislator]" singles out "Shelley" and "Barbara Lee," lee's ballad "[Statement in Opposition]" credits unnamed, collective, generative songs. This reduces Shelley's impact, whose "popular songs wholly political" link achievement of greater freedom to "*unwritten* songs" rather than songs conceived for other voicings and instrumentation. Yet lee relies on these songs when venturing into hostile territory as invincible intangible fortifications. Loving the inside songs is not a problem but clinging to them obstructs their associational promise. The capacity to perform songs that turn insiders outward entails substantial revisions to career, success, scholarship, activism, classrooms, interpersonal relations, and perceptions of self, the massiveness of which changes cannot be minimized. Whether they seem worth the strain depends on what associational worlds Shelleyans are after.

"look at the difficult / broken flesh. stay / a little while."

Notes

1 This epigraph is the translation of Percy Shelley's infamous signature in Greek in the guest registry at the Hôtel de Villes de Londres in Chamonix (the actual page of which was found and given in 2016 to the University of Cambridge). I thank Jim Chandler for launching this train of thinking, Kate Singer, Omar F. Miranda, Jacques Khalip, and Marc Redfield for providing opportunities to present it, and William Keach and Jacqueline Mullen for reshaping its claims. My experiences performing in two ensembles undergird its central convictions, the soul music group *Shelter* (Ron Paris, Wendy Sims-Moten,

Antoine Richardson) and the Salonistas (Felice Blake, Nadège Clitandre, Laila Sakr, Sherene Seikaly, and Jenn Tyburczy). I thank them for backing and moving me.

2 Like many scholars, I follow Kenneth Neil Cameron's expansive definition of "legislator" to mean public-opinion shaper more than officials who make laws. See his *The Young Shelley: Genesis of a Radical* (New York: Macmillan, 1950). For information about the Dream Defenders, see www.dreamdefenders.org.

3 For alternatives to co-optation by the anti-racism industry, see Felice Blake, Paula Ionides, and Alison Reed, *Antiracism, Inc.: Why the Way We Talk about Racial Justice Matters* (Brooklyn: punctum books, 2019).

4 On "blur" in distinction to "opposition" and "not-in-betweenness" as it pertains to Blackness, see Fred Moten, *Black and Blur* (Durham, NC: Duke University Press, 2017), 239–269.

5 Fred Moten, "barbara lee," in *B Jenkins* (Durham, NC: Duke University Press, 2010), 86, ll. 84, 87.

6 Moten, "barbara lee," ll. 1–6.

7 Moten, "barbara lee," 87.

8 Moten, "barbara lee," 86–87.

9 Moten, "barbara lee," 87.

10 Moten, "barbara lee," 87.

11 On "suffering with" and the "action" of *Prometheus Unbound* as "partly defined by the conceptual movement between" the "distinction between undergoing rather than undertaking" suffering, see James Chandler's chapter in this volume.

12 Moten, "barbara lee," 85, ll. 7–15.

13 Moten, "barbara lee," 86.

14 Moten, "barbara lee," 86, 87.

15 However, I do emphasize Shelley's and Moten's shared critiques of pessimism. For Moten's skepticism about Afropessimism, see "Blackness and Nothingness (Mysticism in the Flesh)," *South Atlantic Quarterly* 112.4 (2013), 737–780.

16 Moten, "barbara lee," 84.

17 "[B]lackness and black people are not the same, however much it is without doubt the case that black people have a privileged relation to blackness, that black cultures are (under)privileged fields for the transformational expression and enactment of blackness," Fred Moten, *Stolen Life* (Durham, NC: Duke University Press, 2018), 18, also 9–10.

18 See the Bigger 6 Collective website, http://Bigger6.com. See Bakary Diaby and Deanna Koretsky's review of Moten's *Stolen Life* and Ryan Hanley's *Beyond Slavery and Abolition: Black British Writing, c. 1770–1830*, where they raise the question of whether "black studies need[s] eighteenth- and nineteenth-century studies." "Beyond Slavery, Knowledge of Freedom: Bakary Diaby and Deanna Koretsky Review *Stolen Life* and *Beyond Slavery and Abolition*," *Romantic Circles Reviews* (January 6, 2022), https://romantic-circles.org/reviews-blog/beyond-slavery-knowledge-freedom-bakary-diaby-and-deanna-koretsky-review-stolen-life.

19 "Black Studies and Romanticism: A Virtual Conference," https://commons.mtholyoke.edu/blsandr/. See also the special issue of *Studies in Romanticism*, ed. Patricia A. Matthews, on "Race, Blackness and Romanticism" (Spring 2022).
20 The eleven tracks were recorded live during concerts in Paris (March 2001), Amherst (April 2002), Chiasso, Switzerland (February 2007), New York (June 2008), Commons and Botticino, Italy (October 2008). They are "I Plan to Stay a Believer," "If There's a Hell Below," "We the People Who Are Darker Than Blue," "I'm So Proud," "This Is My Country" (Paris), "People Get Ready / The Inside Song," "This Is My Country" (New York), "It's Alright," "Move On Up," "Freddie's Dead," and "New World Order."
21 Aldon Nielsen, "Belief in Lyric," *American Studies* 52.4 (2013), 171–179, 176.
22 Cited in Nielsen, "Belief in Lyric," 175.
23 Moten, "barbara lee," 86. For a more factual speculation about what Lee might have been listening to on the night before she made her speech as well as which songs Clear Channel immediately banned from the airwaves after the attack (among others, "Disco Inferno," "I Feel the Earth Move," "Bennie and the Jets"), see Mary Anthony Neal, *Songs in the Key of Black Life: Rhythm and Blues Nation* (New York: Routledge, 2003), xiv–xvi.
24 Percy Bysshe Shelley to Leigh Hunt, May 1, 1820. *The Complete Works of Percy Bysshe Shelley*, ed. Roger Igpen and Walter E. Peck, Volume X, 1818 to 1822 (New York: Charles Scribner, 1926), 164.
25 Quoted as the introduction to Percy Shelley, *Popular Songs: The Political Poems of 1819–1820* (Seattle: Entre Ríos Books, 2016). The heyday of this position was the early 1980s with the publication of Paul Foot, *Red Shelley* (London: Sidgwick and Jackson, 1980); P. M. S. Dawson, *The Unacknowledged Legislator: Shelley and Politics* (Oxford: Clarendon Press, 1980); and Michael Scrivener, *Radical Shelley: The Philosophical Anarchism and Utopian Thought of Percy Bysshe Shelley* (Princeton: Princeton University Press, 1982). The headnotes and annotations in *The Poems of Shelley: 1819–1820*, eds. Jack Donovan, Cian Duffy, Kelvin Everest, and Michael Rossington (London: Routledge, 2011), Volume 3, give very useful composition and publication histories of these poems. For the best contemporary synthesis and articulation of this tradition, see Jacqueline Mulhallen, *Percy Bysshe Shelley: Poet and Revolutionary* (London: Pluto Press, 2015).
26 For a sampling, see Bouthaina Shaaban, "Shelley in the Chartist Press," *Keats-Shelley Memorial Bulletin* 34 (1983), 41–60; M. Siddiq Kalim, *The Social Orpheus: Shelley and the Owenites* (Lahore: Government College, 1983); Benjamin Schacht, "Freedom Songs: Socialist Multiculturalism and the Protest Lyric from Percy Shelley to Chaim Zhitlovsky," *The Gotham Center for New York City History* (2021), www.gothamcenter.org/blog/freedom-songs-socialist-multiculturalism-and-the-protest-lyric-from-percy-shelley-to-chaim-zhitlovsky; Timothy Morton, "Receptions," in Morton, ed. *The Cambridge Companion to Shelley* (Cambridge: Cambridge University Press, 2006), 35–42; Michael Demson, *Masks of Anarchy: The History of a Radical Poem from Percy Shelley to the Triangle Factory Fire* (Brooklyn: Verso, 2013); Art Young,

Shelley and Nonviolence (The Hague: Mouton, 1975); Greg Ellermann, "Red Shelley, Once Again," *Keats-Shelley Journal* 68 (2019), 104–105; Graham Henderson's The Real Percy Shelley website, www.grahamhenderson.ca/percy-bysshe-shelley.

27 "Shelley Lives: Taking the Revolutionary Poet Shelley to the Streets," The Real Percy Bysshe Shelley website, April 18, 2017, www.grahamhenderson.ca/guest-contribution/Day/1/Year/smy98spfpcn6tnqjreivvugioyhtl9, and "Shelley Storms the Fashion World with *Mask of Anarchy*," The Real Percy Bysshe Shelley website, March 31, 2017, www.grahamhenderson.ca/blog/category/John+Alexander+Skelton.

28 Susan J. Wolfson, "Popular Songs and Ballads: Writing the 'Unwritten Story' in 1819," in Michael O'Neill, Anthony Howe, and Madeleine Callaghan, eds. *The Oxford Handbook of Percy Bysshe Shelley* (2012; online Edition, 2013), https://doi.org/10.1093/oxfordhb/9780199558360.001.0001.

29 As Paul Foot writes, "[t]his is the first edition of a book which was proposed for publication 170 years ago by one of England's most famous writers" (Shelley, *Shelley's Revolutionary Year*, intro. by Foot [London: Redwords, 1990], 13). In 1979, The Journeyman Press issued as a chapbook a reprinting of a lecture given in 1888 and printed then for private circulation (twenty-five copies) by Edward Aveling and Eleanor Marx Aveling on *Shelley's Socialism* and "for the first time" printed together seven poems and two fragments entitled *Popular Songs Wholly Political* (London: Journeyman Press, 1979).

30 Graham Henderson, "Shelley in the 21st Century," The Real Percy Bysshe Shelley website; May 27, 2016, www.grahamhenderson.ca/blog/shelley-in-the-21st-century, and Michelle Levy, "Byron, Shelley, and Deviant Fatherhood," paper presented at the North American Society for the Study of Romanticism, Montreal, August 13–16, 2005; on exile, see Omar F. Miranda's chapter in this volume.

31 Ciarán O'Rourke, "*Shelley's Revolutionary Year*: A Review," The Real Percy Bysshe Shelley website, January 21, 2020, www.grahamhenderson.ca/book-reviews-blog/ciaran-orourke-paul-obrien-shelleys-revolutionary-year.

32 The quoted phrase is Shelley's in a letter written to John Gisborne about the intended audience of *Epipsychidion*, the implications of which Keach pursues in "Knowing Readers: Shelley and the Sunetoi," a lecture first delivered at the Modern Language Association (MLA) Convention, December 29, 1985.

33 William Keach, "Rise like Lions? Shelley and the Revolutionary Left," *International Socialism* 2.75 (1997), www.marxists.org/history/etol/newspape/isj2/1997/isj2-075/keach.htm. See also Jen Morgan, "Uses of Shelley in Working-Class Culture: Approximations and Substitutions," *Key Words: A Journal of Cultural Materialism* 13 (2015), 117–137 and Scrivener, *Radical Shelley*.

34 On "white-body supremacy" as circumventing issues of intention and experience, see Resmaa Menakem, *My Grandmother's Hands: Racialized Trauma and the Pathways to Healing Our Hearts and Bodies* (Las Vegas: Central Recovery Press, 2017), xix, 10–12.

35 Huge thanks to Jacqueline Mulhallen for bringing the work of Zephaniah to my attention at the #Shelley at 200 conference and to Madeleine Callaghan for sending links to the interviews.

36 The first quote is the tagline to Zephaniah's website: https://benjaminzephaniah.com/?doing_wp_cron=1660839314.5112290382385253906250. The subtitle to his autobiography, *The Life and Rhymes of Benjamin Zephaniah: An Autobiography* (New York: Simon and Schuster, 2018), adds "activist." Other quotations are found on the website or in two conversations with British Shelleyan scholars taped by BBC4 in preparation for celebrations of #Shelley at 200. "Percy Shelley: Reformer and Radical" (1) (July 3, 2022) and (2) (July 10, 2022), www.bbc.co.uk/programmes/m0018wy2. See also Sue Lawley's podcast with him on *Desert Island Discs* on June 8, 1997, www.bbc.co.uk/programmes/p0094495.
37 Listen to Zephaniah, "The Original Dub Poet," www.bbc.co.uk/sounds/play/m0018wy2.
38 Benjamin Zephaniah, *Too Black, Too Strong* (Hexham: Bloodaxe Books, 2001), 13.
39 Benjamin Zephaniah, "Me? I Thought, OBE Me? Up Yours, I Thought," *The Guardian*, November 27, 2003. www.theguardian.com/books/2003/nov/27/poetry.monarchy.
40 Zephaniah, *Too Black, Too Strong*, 15, 16.
41 Quotes from Moten are from "barbara lee," *B Jenkins*, 84; from Zephaniah, the 2022 BBC podcasts.
42 Benjamin Zephaniah, "Biography," https://benjaminzephaniah.com/biography/?doing_wp_cron=1662229217.6135818958282470703125.
43 On the "withdrawn" offer of a position in poetry at Trinity College Cambridge and his losing out to Seamus Heaney in the 1989 competition to be Oxford Professor of Poetry, see podcast with Sue Lawley on *Desert Island Discs*.
44 Fred Moten and Stefano Harney, *The Undercommons: Fugitive Planning and Black Study* (Wivenhoe: Minor Compositions, 2013); also Stefano Harney and Fred Moten, "the university (last words)," www.academia.edu/43580248/The_university_last_words_by_stefano_harney_and_fred_moten.
45 "the university (last words)," 2, 5.
46 Moten, "william parker/fred mcdowell," *B Jenkins*, 26.
47 Harney and Moten, "Politics Surrounded, *The Undercommons*, 14–21.
48 Moten, "Knowledge of Freedom," in *Stolen Life*, 1–95, 29. For a compatible investigation of Kantian philosophy and racial logic, see Rei Terada, "The Racial Grammar of Kantian Time," *European Romantic Review* 28.3 (2017), 267–278.
49 For the insufficiencies of space clearing, see "Romanticism and Its Discontents," eds. Anne-Lise François, Celeste Langan, and Alexander Walton, *European Romantic Review*, Special Issue, 28.3 (2017).
50 Moten, "Knowledge of Freedom," 44, 8.
51 Moten, "Knowledge of Freedom," 20–21, 19. "Knowledge of the invaluable is prior to the experience of being-(de)valued. It's just that the experience of being-(de)valued helps us not to forget what we already know." Moten, "Approximity," (foreword to) *21/19: Contemporary Poets in the Nineteenth Century Archive*, eds. Alexandra Manglis and Kristen Case (Minneapolis: Milkwood Editions, 2019), 1–4.
52 Moten, "Knowledge of Freedom," 21.
53 Moten, "Knowledge of Freedom," 94.

54 Radical Imagination Gymnasium, http://psusocialpractice.org/the-radical-imagination-gymnasium%EF%BB%BF/. Founders Patricia Vazquez Gomez, Erin Charpentier, Travis Neel, and Zachary Gough took their inspiration from Max Haiven's book, *Crises of Imagination, Crises of Power: Capitalism, Creativity, and the Commons* (London: Zed Books, 2014).

55 See Charles Howard, "Angela Davis: Power to the Imagination," November 1, 2011, *The Huffington Post*, www.huffpost.com/entry/angela-davis-occupy-philly_b_1067740.

56 Shelley sent Edward Fergus Graham lines of his to be set to music as early as April 1810; see Jessica K. Quillin, *Shelley and the Musico-Poetics of Romanticism* (Burlington: Ashgate, 2012), 5.

57 John Webster with Brindaband, https://music.apple.com/us/artist/john-webster/30456321; described in his talk, "On Setting Shelley to Music," given at the Shelley Conference (#Shelley200), Keats House, Hampstead, July 8–9, 2022.

58 Camila Oliveira, "Music When Soft Voices Live: Shelley's Reception in Contemporary Music," talk given at the Shelley Conference (#Shelley200), Keats House, Hampstead, July 8–9, 2022.

59 See, for example, the papers delivered at the 2006 MLA session and published in Susan J. Wolfson, ed. *"Sounding of Things Done": The Poetry and Poetics of Sound in the Romantic Ear and Era*, *Romantic Circles* Praxis Series (April 2008), https://romantic-circles.org/praxis/soundings/index.html.

60 See "Music That Moves: Sonic Narratives in Modern Korea," eds. Dafna Zur and Susan Hwang, Special Section of *Korean Studies* 46 (2022), 1–194.

61 Michel-Rolph Trouillot, *Silencing the Past: Power and the Production of History*, 2nd rev. ed. (Boston: Beacon Press, 2015).

62 "Knowledge of Freedom," 93.

63 "Knowledge of Freedom," 91. For a discussion of epigenetics and race, see Josie Gill, *Biofictions: Race, Genetics and the Contemporary Novel* (London: Bloomsbury, 2020), 121–127.

64 On critical fabulation, see Saidiya Hartman, "Venus in Two Acts," *Small Axe* 12.2 (2008), 1–14; on theory in the flesh, see Cherríe Moraga and Gloria Anzaldúa, eds. *This Bridge Called My Back, Fortieth Anniversary Edition* (Albany: State University of New York Press, 2021); on body as archive, see Deborah A. Miranda, *Bad Indians: A Tribal Memoir* (Berkeley: Heyday, 2013) and Dian Million, "Felt Theory: An Indigenous Feminist Approach to Affect and History," *Wicazo Sa Review* 24.2 (2009), 53–76.

65 Moten, *Stolen Life*, "The Touring Machine (Flesh Thought Inside Out)," 167.

66 See Stephanie Leigh Batiste, "Performance," in Erica R. Edwards, Roderick A. Ferguson, and Jeffrey O. G. Ogbar, eds. *Keywords for African American Studies* (New York: New York University Press, 2018), 136.

67 See Eric Lindstrom, "Poetry Is Not a Luxury: Audre Lorde and Shelleyan Poetics," *Romantic Circle* Praxis Series (December 2021), http://romantic-circles.org/node/226721; Kate Singer, "The Witch of Atlas," https://theshelleyconference.com/2022/06/09/shelley200-roundtable-shelley-for-our-times/; Julie A. Carlson, "Like Love: The Feel of Shelley's Similes," in Joel Faflak and Richard Sha, eds. *Romanticism and the Emotions* (Cambridge: Cambridge University

Press, 2014), 76–97; Mathelinda Nabugodi, "A Triumph of Black Life?" *Keats-Shelley Journal* 70 (2021), 133–141.

68 See Bysshe Inigo Coffey, *Shelley's Broken World: Fractured Materiality and Intermitted Song* (Liverpool: Liverpool University Press, 2021), 13–15, 87–89 (also how the breathing patterns manipulated in *Rosalind and Helen* exhort us to *"read this aloud"* [88, emphasis in original]).

69 See Bessel Van Der Kolk, *The Body Keeps the Score: Brain, Mind, and Body in the Healing of Trauma* (New York: Penguin Books, 2014), 53–58.

70 Resmaa Menakem, *My Grandmother's Hands: Racialized Trauma*, 37–52; also Menakem, *The Quaking of America: An Embodied Guide to Navigating Our Nation's Upheaval and Racial Reckoning* (Las Vegas: Central Recovery Press, 2022), 101–128, 133–139.

71 On devising writing classes that embrace dissensus, see Asao B. Inoue, *Antiracist Writing Assessment Ecologies: Teaching and Assessing Writing for a Socially Just Future* (WAC Clearing House, 2015).

72 Moten, *Stolen Life*, "The Touring Machine (Flesh Thought Inside Out)," 167.

73 M. NourbeSe Philip, *Zong!* (Middletown: Wesleyan University Press, 2008), 191, 193–194.

74 See Sara Ahmed, *Living a Feminist Life* (Durham, NC: Duke University Press, 2017), 7–10. Cherríe Moraga's Latinx Public Writers lecture series "In Good Company" is grounded in this conviction, www.lasmaestrascenter.ucsb.edu/current-events/in-good-company-the-latinx-public-voice.

CHAPTER 5

Radical Suffering
Shelley's Legacy in Nonviolent Revolution
James Chandler

I

In 1960, in the midst of the lunch counter sit-ins protesting racial discrimination across the American South, the Student Nonviolent Coordinating Committee (SNCC) was established in Raleigh, North Carolina to support the ongoing struggle for civil rights.[1] In June of that year, SNCC circulated the first issue of a newsletter, *The Student Voice*, which included a history of its founding, a program of events, and a brief statement of purpose by the Reverend James Lawson, whom Martin Luther King, Jr. would later call "the mind of the movement" and "the leading strategist of non-violence in the world."[2] Lawson's influential statement reads in part:

> We affirm the philosophical and religious ideal of nonviolence as the foundation of our purpose, the pre-supposition of our faith, and the manner of our action. Non-violence as it grows from the Judaic-Christian tradition seeks a social order of justice permeated by love [...]
>
> Through nonviolence, courage displaces fear; love transforms hate; hope ends despair. Peace dominates war; faith reconciles doubt. Mutual regards cancel enmity. Justice for all overthrows injustice [...]
>
> Love is the central motif of nonviolence. Love is the force by which God binds man to himself and man to man. Such love goes to the extreme; it remains loving and forgiving even in the midst of hostility. It matches the capacity of evil to inflict suffering with an even more enduring capacity to absorb evil, all the while persisting in love. [See Figure 1]

As Congressman John Lewis (then a member of SNCC and already a disciple of Lawson) would later recall, Lawson's statement provided a set of principles for the conduct of American protests going forward. Their reach soon extended to nonviolent political movements in Northern Ireland and

WHAT IS SNCC?

The Student Nonviolent Coordinating Committee was established on April 17, 1960, at the close of the Raleigh Conference held at Shaw University, Raleigh, N. C. The Raleigh Conference, a meeting of Southern student protest leaders and Northern supporters, was sponsored by the Southern Christian Leadership Conference.

The Coordinating Committee is composed of representatives from the Southern states and the District of Columbia. Its purpose is to coordinate activities, analyze the status of the movement and map plans for the future. It is self-directing, but welcomes the participation and assistance of supporting observer groups.

To date, the Committee has held two meetings. All Southern states have not secured an official delegate yet. The present voting membership is as follows:

Alabama------------Mr. Bernard Lee
                  Mr. Jesse Walker
Florida------Mr. Lorenzo J. Brown
Georgia--------Miss Marian Wright
                  Mr. Julian Bond
                  Mr. Lonnie C. King
Kentucky--Mr. Edward B. King, Jr.
MarylandMr.Clarence Mitchell, III
N. C.------------Mr. David Forbes
S. C.--------Mr. Charles F. McDew
Tennessee---Mr. Marion Barry, Jr.
VirginiaMr. Virginius B. Thornton
D. C.------Mr. Henry James Thomas

Mr. Marion S. Barry, Jr. is chairman; Mr. Henry James Thomas, committee secretary; Miss Jane Stembridge, Office secretary. Each state is entitled to one vote.

PICTURES: PAGE 1

The photographs reproduced on the front page of "The Student Voice" were taken at the Raleigh Conference.

The top photograph, taken in the main auditorium, reveals the students at a planning session.

Lower left- attack victim in a downtown Raleigh incident which occurred during leaflet distribution. Lower right - Richard Counts of Benedict College, who was jailed in Columbia, S. C. for sitting-in. Annie Hackett, student of Benedict.

PHILOSOPHY

The following is taken from the Report of the Student Nonviolent Coordinating Committee, compiled following the May 13-14 meeting:

STATEMENT OF PURPOSE

"Carrying out the mandate of the Raleigh Conference to write a statement of purpose for the movement, the Temporary Student Nonviolent Coordinating Committee submits for careful consideration the following draft. We urge all local state or regional groups to examine it closely. Each member of our movement must work diligently to understand the depths of nonviolence.

We affirm the philosophical or religious ideal of nonviolence as the foundation of our purpose, the pre-supposition of our faith, and the manner of our action. Non violence as it grows from Judaic-Christian traditions seeks a social order of justice permeated by love. Integration of human endeavor represents the crucial first step towards such a society.

Through nonviolence, courage displaces fear; love transforms hate. Acceptance dissipates prejudice; hope ends despair. Peace dominates war; faith reconciles doubt. Mutual regards cancel enmity. Justice for all overthrows injustice. The redemptive community supercedes systems of gross social immorality.

Love is the central motif of nonviolence. Love is the force by which God binds man to himself and man to man. Such love goes to the extreme; it remains loving and forgiving even in the midst of hostility. It matches the capacity of evil to inflict suffering with an even more enduring capacity to absorb evil, all the while persisting in love.

By appealing to conscience and standing on the moral nature of human existence, nonviolence nurtures the atmosphere in which reconciliation and justice become actual possibilities."

Prepared by - Rev. J.M. Lawson, Jr. Saturday, May 14, 1960

PRESENT STATUS of SNCC

Resume of the May meeting of The Student Nonviolent Coordinating Comm:

This, the first meeting of the Committee, was held on the campus of Atlanta University, Atlanta, Georgia on May 13-14, 1960. Mr. Marion S. Barry, Jr. of Fisk University was elected to serve as chairman and

Figure 1 *Student Voice* (Student Nonviolent Coordinating Committee, SNCC), Vol. 1, No. 1 (June 1960). Civil Rights Movement Archive (www.crmvet.org/)

South Africa that emulated the American civil rights movement. In diverse national and international conflicts, Lawson's words became words to live by, even to die by.

Beyond the New Testament theology cited by Lawson, the writings and actions of Mahatma Gandhi are rightly seen as a crucial point of origin for the American civil rights movement. Students of Percy Shelley, however, might be forgiven for hearing in Lawson's document certain resonances of the poet's writings from almost a century and a half earlier, especially his responses to the 1819 Peterloo Massacre, when a peaceful public assembly in Manchester was attacked by the local Yeomanry with support from the Fifteenth Regiment of British Hussars, themselves veterans of Waterloo. Indeed, Shelley's writings responded to conditions and events that seem, in retrospect, to have established a kind of template for such fatal encounters between peaceful social-justice protesters and armed forces of the state as took place in Selma and Derry.

The most famous of Shelley's writings about Peterloo, *The Mask of Anarchy*, probably offers his best-known slogan for the politics of nonviolence – "Ye are many, they are few" – a line later echoed by activists around the world.[3] Yet his most explicit and detailed treatment of the subject appears in a very different piece of writing composed in the aftermath of Peterloo, *A Philosophical View of Reform*, the unfinished pamphlet in three parts that would not be published until 1920. In section three of the *View*, Shelley sketches out a scenario for the work of the "true patriot" in bringing about a more just society in a moment of crisis.[4] As part of his effort "to enlighten and to unite the nation and animate it with enthusiasm and confidence [...] [h]e will promote [...] open confederation" and "discourage all secret confederations" (*PVR* 48). And to this end, "[he] will urge the necessity of exciting the people frequently to exercise their right of assembling, in such limited numbers as that all present may be actual parties to the proceedings of the day" (*PVR* 48). To this point, Shelley echoes the teachings of William Godwin, who had advocated open assembly and discouraged cabals a quarter of a century earlier in *Political Justice*. But the ghastly case of Peterloo leads Shelley to a final piece of advice for this true patriot:

> Lastly, if circumstances had collected a considerable number as at Manchester on the memorable 16th of August, if the tyrants command the troops to fire upon them or cut them down unless they disperse, he will exhort them peaceably to defy the danger, and to expect without resistance the onset of the cavalry, and wait with folded arms the event of the fire of the artillery and receive with unshrinking bosoms the bayonets of the charging battalions. (*PVR* 48)

Coming almost a century and half before SNCC (and seventy-five years before Gandhi's passive resistance campaign for Indian rights in South Africa), this passage stands as the earliest such statement that I know of. Yet it does not seem to be well known to activists in or even scholars of these movements. There is no mention of Shelley in, for example, any of the essays collected in *Revolutionary Nonviolence: Concepts, Cases and Controversies* (2020) or, say, in Judith Butler's philosophical investigations in *The Force of Nonviolence: An Ethico-Political Bind*, published in the same year.[5]

A number of questions thus urge themselves on our attention. There is a historical question about the relation of Gandhi's views to Shelley's, a question complicated by the fact that the *Philosophical View of Reform* was not published until long after Gandhi's South African campaigns: the first edition of the *View* appears in 1920 from Oxford University Press. There is the biographical question as to how Shelley was able to come to the views he so precociously held on this matter. There is the literary critical question about how Shelley's tendency to write in different genres matters to his expression of these views: to see the point of this question, one need only consider the difference between the stanza of the *Mask* and the paragraph of the *Philosophical View of Reform*. There is the question of how Shelley's views developed in relation to those of *his* own contemporaries. And then there is that question of why Shelley's writings on nonviolence have had relatively little acknowledged uptake in our own moment.

II

To take up that last question first (though I return to it in closing), it is important to recognize that none of the three civil rights leaders I have mentioned acknowledge Shelley as part of their canon of thinkers and writers. There is no evidence, for example, that Shelley's writings formed any part of Lawson's curriculum in the Divinity School at Vanderbilt, where he mentored Lewis and others in the late 1950s. Among English-language writers in the nineteenth century it is Henry David Thoreau, not Shelley, who tends – under the slightly different rubric of "civil disobedience" – to be included in the canon the movement developed from Lawson's curriculum. Lawson's 1960 "Statement of Purpose" does refer more broadly to the "Judaic-Christian tradition," however, and it seems fair to say that the New Testament injunction to "turn the other cheek" seems to capture something crucial about Lawson's teachings. This emphasis turns out to be important for the Shelley connection in a number of ways.

Like John Keats, Shelley was no friend to ecclesiastical Christianity, but unlike Keats Shelley did reserve a special place in his thinking for Christ himself. There are moments in his mature work where the trope of the "imitation of Christ" seems to be in play, and occasionally the figure of Christ himself – as distinct from Christianity – becomes explicit in Shelley's thinking. Writing in May of 1820 to Leigh Hunt about Charles Ollier, the publisher of *Prometheus Unbound*, Shelley waxed expansive:

> [I]n fact they are all rogues. It is less the character of the individual than the situation in which he is placed which determines him to be honest or dishonest[;] perhaps we ought to regard an honest bookseller, or an honest seller of anything else in the present state of human affairs as a kind of Jesus Christ. The present system of society as it exists at present must be overthrown from the foundations with all its superstructure of maxims & of forms before we shall find anything but disappointment in our intercourse with any but a few select spirits. (*Letters* II: 191)

There are reasons, as we shall see, to think of Shelley's greatest hero, Prometheus himself, as typifying such Christ-like virtue in Shelley's syncretistic understanding of how the human imagination expresses itself across cultures.

The comment about Ollier, however, also indicates Shelley's sense of the depth and scale of the issues he was confronting: if the passage I cited from the *Philosophical View of Reform* shows Shelley's commitment to nonviolence, the comment about Ollier shows his commitment to revolution. It is all the more surprising, then, that there should be no recognition of Shelley's precocious writings among the nonviolent revolutionaries of the American civil rights movement, not even in Lawson's aptly titled recent volume, *Revolutionary Nonviolence*. By contrast, scores of references can be found in that book to the teachings of Gandhi, another figure who generally falls *outside* the Judeo-Christian tradition – though, like Shelley, Gandhi was open to the teachings of Christ (for a time, he actually sought to bridge the gap between Hinduism and Christianity). The figure of Gandhi, as it turns out, offers a path for connecting Shelley and the American civil rights movement. The path is circuitous but not altogether without signposting.

Lawson's intellectual debt to Gandhi, for example, amounts to more than a recognition that the latter's teachings were "in the air" after his successful campaign for Indian independence. Lawson's life experience in fact supplies specific links between the Christian-led American civil rights movement and the earlier movement that resulted in the decolonization of India in 1947. Ten years John Lewis's senior, Lawson was of age to be drafted for military service in the Korean War. At Oberlin College, he was introduced to Gandhi's life and thought by two of his teachers, A. J. Muste and Bayard Rustin. Though he qualified for a college deferment, he instead became a conscientious objector and spent thirteen months in prison as a result in the early 1950s. Thereafter, he went to India, specifically to study the ways and means of Gandhian nonviolence, and then undertook a tour of African countries involved in the struggle to liberate themselves from European imperialism. His writings on nonviolence show the extent to which he had taken on the Gandhian concept of *satyagraha* – or "soul force" – which Lawson has recently re-urged as "both a philosophy and a methodology" for the movement identified with Black Lives Matter.[6] But Lawson also makes it clear that Gandhism was already central to his mentoring of Lewis's cohort in the late 1950s.

It might not seem that Gandhi's teachings on nonviolence bring us any closer to Shelley, especially if we focus narrowly on *A Philosophical View of Reform*. Since the *View* wasn't published until 1920, and since Gandhi had already published his own fully developed account of passive resistance in his first book, *Hind Swaraj* (1909) – it appeared in English translation that same year as *Indian Home Rule* – there seems to be a gap in transmission. There are nonetheless some broad lines of connection between Shelley and the young Gandhi. Like Shelley, Gandhi had a syncretistic view of religion, which he acquired in part from his mentor in the 1890s, the Jain savant Raychandbhai. He was well-versed in Hindu doctrines pertaining both to vegetarianism and to passive resistance. Such resemblances do not, however, count as evidence for a line of transmission, not of the sort that is widely claimed for Leo Tolstoy, whom Gandhi cited often and is known to have read before writing *Hind Swaraj*.

I want to suggest that while Shelley's importance to Gandhi is more mediated, it arises earlier and may prove no less important. The mediation comes in the person of one Henry Salt, a London intellectual in the Fabian circle of writers like George Bernard Shaw. Gandhi made Salt's acquaintance early on during his sojourn in London to obtain his law degree (1888–1891). Gandhi himself writes in his autobiography that the initial connection was on the basis of their shared practice of vegetarianism.[7] Leela Gandhi has beautifully shown how Gandhi's encounter with Salt would have led him to Shelley on the question of vegetarianism, but I want to suggest that Shelley's importance to Salt, and thus potentially to Gandhi, far exceeded their common interest in what Shelley called "the vegetable system of diet."[8] Salt's keen interest in Shelley extended to a range of moral and political issues, and we have it on Salt's own authority that one of these issues is revolutionary nonviolence.⁹ Salt, the Fabian socialist, recognized that Shelley's goal was nothing less than the overthrow of "the present system of society as it exists at present [...] with all its superstructure of maxims & of forms" – *and* the achievement of this outcome without resort to physical force. Salt understood that Shelley believed that the great cause was to be won, in Salt's words, by "a passive and constitutional process": "[i]t was because [Shelley] aimed at a complete but bloodless revolution that he distrusted and deprecated much of the teaching of Cobbett and his followers, in whose speeches he detected too many traces of the spirit of revenge."¹⁰

In reconstructing Shelley's articulation of nonviolent revolution, Salt was of course working with an archive missing certain pieces that are available to us today. He probably would not have known Shelley's letter to Hunt about Ollier, for example, nor would he have had access to the full surviving text of *A Philosophical View of Reform*: Salt acknowledges that it exists but notes that it "is to this day known only by excerpts and paraphrases."¹¹ He seems to have read all the rousing poems that Shelley wrote in the wake of Peterloo, like *The Mask of Anarchy*, and even quotes at some length from Shelley's "Song to the Men of England." Much of Salt's sense of Shelley's politics of revolutionary nonviolence, however, comes from Shelley's pre-Peterloo compositions. And he singles out *Prometheus Unbound* for his highest praise. A "trumpet blast of universal freedom," he writes, "may be said to ring through every passage of 'Prometheus Unbound'."¹² For Salt, *Prometheus Unbound* is "that splendid vision of the ultimate emancipation of humanity from the oppression of custom."¹³ He saw it as the crowning achievement of the poems Shelley composed over the previous half-decade or so, a series of compositions "perfected by the solemn idealistic harmonies of 'Prometheus Unbound.'" These were all poems, Salt declared, that "Shelley devoted to the purpose of showing how the world may be regenerated by the power of love."¹⁴

Salt published these words in *Percy Bysshe Shelley: A Monograph* in 1888, the very year of Gandhi's arrival in London. He had already published an earlier book on Shelley (*A Shelley Primer*) just the year before, and he would go on to publish subsequent books on Shelley in 1896 and 1913. In light of the intensity of Gandhi's involvement with Salt and his circle, and his interest in the vegetarianism that Salt himself traced back to Shelley's writings, it seems reasonable to assume that Gandhi had some exposure – in these London years that were so formative for his future thinking – to Shelley's wider political views about nonviolent revolution. It is true that Thoreau is another figure on whom Salt published in these years: his biography of the American pioneer of civil disobedience appeared in 1889. And it is also true that Gandhi and Salt would correspond about Thoreau decades later.[15] The Gandhi-Thoreau connection, accordingly, has had its share of critical attention.

Yet there are aspects of Salt's appreciation of Shelley that make him a figure even more apposite than Thoreau for understanding the sources of Gandhi's revolutionary nonviolence. One of these is that Gandhi became a more committed vegetarian than Thoreau and one more dedicated to integrating a vegetarian sensibility into an understanding of politics. Another is suggested by Salt's comment that Shelley was put off by any teachings, like Cobbett's, that he thought betrayed "traces of the spirit of revenge." In both the advocacy of the vegetarian sensibility and the opposition to the spirit of revenge, therefore, we might say that Salt sees Shelley as resisting on principle what we might call *bloodthirst*. Gandhi's own principled resistance to bloodthirst would be enshrined in the doctrine and discipline of *satyagraha* and eventually bequeathed to early leaders of the American civil rights movement like Lawson, Lewis, and of course King himself.

In one respect, these three Black leaders might even be seen as hewing closer to Shelley's version of this principle than to Gandhi's, for, like Shelley, they readily and explicitly name it "love." "The great secret of morals is Love," Shelley famously wrote in his 1821 *A Defence of Poetry* (published in 1841), in part a rewriting of *A Philosophical View of Reform* (*SPP* 517). We recall that Lawson, translating *satyagraha* into his own terms for the young civil rights movement in 1960, positioned love at the heart of his philosophy, "the central motif of nonviolence": "Love is the force by which God binds man to himself and man to man." Lawson's way of framing his understanding of the Gandhian movement as centered on love, after all, is why contemporary students of Shelley might read his 1960 "statement of purpose" with that shock of recognition that is my starting point in this essay.

III

Not all thinkers about revolutionary nonviolence in our time follow Lawson in framing the issues – or in describing the kind of "force" or *graha* they involve – in such Shelleyan terms. Judith Butler, for example, in her recent meditation on nonviolence, argues that it "is less a failure of action than a physical assertion of the claims of life."[16] In Shelley's moral and political vocabulary, "life" proves to be a far more equivocal word than "love," a point not lost on readers of his dismaying and unfinished final poem, *The Triumph of Life*. In what remains his greatest achievement, *Prometheus Unbound*, Shelley showed that love – not life – was the answer, as Salt clearly understood. And yet Shelley himself was not always obviously consistent in framing such issues from one work to another, and it is worth considering how and why this might be so. It has to do with Shelley's complex understanding of genre.

I noted earlier that Shelley's most explicit treatment of the question of nonviolence was his discussion of passive resistance in giving advice to those who, like the protesters at Peterloo, find themselves participating in a peaceful assembly that comes under physical attack. But the advice he gives in this case, when one looks closely, seems to center more on temperance and courage than on love. The "true patriot," writes Shelley, "will exhort them peaceably to defy the danger, and to expect without resistance the onset of the cavalry, and wait with folded arms the event of the fire of the artillery and receive with unshrinking bosoms the bayonets of the charging battalions" (*PVR* 48). To complicate matters further, Shelley goes on in the *View* to suggest that even the virtues of temperance and courage involve something more like a *calculation* than an act of moral or political virtue. His larger overview of the situation in which nonviolent resistance is called for, indeed, is decidedly cast in terms of risks and benefits:

> Men are every day persuaded to incur greater perils for a less manifest advantage. And this, not because active resistance is not justifiable when all other means shall have failed, but because in this instance temperance and courage would produce greater advantages than the most decisive victory. (*PVR* 48)

Removing the issue even further from the domain of morals, and thus from that of love, Shelley goes on to buttress this explicit risk-benefit analysis with a detailed (and remarkably prescient) psychological analysis of the likely conduct of an armed authority in the confrontation. Although, by "the instinct of his trade," the soldier will chase down "those who fly" or beat down those who resist, nonetheless, "if he should observe neither resistance nor flight he would be reduced to confusion and indecision" (*PVR* 49). The soldier thus faced with "an unresisting multitude of their countrymen drawn up in unarmed array before them, and bearing in their looks the calm, deliberate resolution to perish rather than abandon the assertion of their rights," may be induced to recollect "the true nature of the measures of which he was made the instrument, and the enemy might be converted into the ally." This is, I think, a striking analysis of the social-psychological forces at work in the new kind of confrontation represented by Peterloo. But what, one might well ask, has love got to do with it?

In the terms of *A Philosophical View of Reform*, the answer seems to be: not much. So what then to make of Shelley's apparent departure here from his own foundational commitment to the principle of love? The answer to this further question can be found in the larger argument of the *View* itself, and ultimately in a larger understanding of genre in Shelley's body of work. The *View* was written, as I have already suggested, under the pressure of certain immediate historical circumstances centering on Peterloo and the repressive legislation rushed through Parliament before the end of the year: the notorious Six Acts. We have seen that its third section provides Shelley's way of engaging directly with the political crisis of this moment. Section one, by contrast, offers a compressed and schematic history of the relationship between liberty and intellectual production from the time of the ancient Greeks to the present day. Paradoxically, and crucially, this history has implications that seriously delimit the *View* itself – the very text in which it appears. It is a remarkably subtle rhetorical feat, and one not as fully appreciated as it should be.

The key passage in section one's sweeping history narrates the modern phase of the story, a phase that for Shelley occurs roughly in the seventeenth century. Shelley identifies in that epoch a momentous breakthrough in literature and thought that corresponds to what he would later call his nation's "last struggle for liberty" (*PVR* 8). To the poetry of Milton, and the revolution in which he participated, Shelley juxtaposes a new level of philosophical investigation: "deeper enquiries into the point of human nature than are compatible with an unreserved belief in any of those popular mistakes upon which popular systems of faith with respect to the cause and agencies of the universe, with all their superstructure of political and religious tyranny, are built" (*PVR* 8). Shelley has a roster of key thinkers who effected this great transformation, loosely associated with what we sometimes still call the Scientific Revolution: "Lord Bacon, Spinoza, Hobbes, Boyle, Montaigne, regulated the reasoning powers, criticized the history, exposed the past errors by illustrating their causes and their connexion, and anatomized the inmost nature of social man" (*PVR* 8).

Problematically, these great breakthroughs give way to the phase we now call "the Enlightenment," though for Shelley it was less about intellectual light than about pragmatic application. The philosophes and other political thinkers of the eighteenth century, he argues, resorted too quickly to cashing out the philosophical advances of the previous century in the service of schemes of social improvement. They did so for understandable reasons: society was in desperate need of change. In taking this pragmatic turn, however, they proved themselves short-sighted:

> Considered as philosophers their error seems to have consisted chiefly in a limitation of view; they told the truth, but not the whole truth. This might have arisen from the terrible sufferings of their countrymen inviting them rather to apply a portion of what had already been discovered to their immediate relief, than to pursue one interest, the abstractions of thought, as the great philosophers who preceded them had done, for the sake of a future and more universal advantage. (*PVR* 9)

The eighteenth-century compromise, according to Shelley, involved delimiting the horizon of inquiry and settling on a repertoire of terms and concepts that frame even the most advanced discourses of the current moment:

> The result of the labours of the political philosophers has been the establishment of the principle of Utility as the substance, and liberty and equality as the forms according to which the concerns of human life ought to be administered. By this test the various institutions regulating political society have been tried, and as the undigested growth of the private passions, errors, and interests of barbarians and oppressors have been condemned. And many new theories, more or less perfect, but all superior to the mass of evil which they would supplant, have been given to the world. (*PVR* 10)

Thus, as Shelley saw it, was born the utilitarianism of an enlightened thinker like Jeremy Bentham. And thus was established the United States of America, whose "system of government [...] was the first practical illustration of the new philosophy" (*PVR* 10). Shelley praises the US constitutional experiment, but he makes it clear that its limits are those of the utilitarianism that subtends it. What the United States lacks is what Shelley calls most simply "poetry," and this, for Shelley, turns out to be the strong suit of contemporary Britain.

Seen in this light, the great irony of *A Philosophical View of Reform* is that some of its most salient terms, such as the terms of its particular account of revolutionary nonviolence, are precisely those of the limited philosophical outlook whose etiology Shelley carefully traces in section one. In a sense, moreover, the reasons for his resort to the utilitarian outlook in the *View* are the same as of the pragmatic enlightenment philosophes: that is, the pressures of the historical moment. In other words, section three, with its detailed advice for protesters, should be recognized as Shelley's detailed pragmatic engagement with a present political and social crisis. That is why his analysis is carried out in the language of cost-benefit calculations. And that is why, in writing to his friend Leigh Hunt about what he was doing, he said that he was working on a pamphlet "like Bentham's something," that could serve as a kind of handbook for the movement. Bentham is himself named in section one of the *View* as a figure associated with "the principle of utility" (*Letters* II: 201). No thinker of that moment, after all, was more thoroughly associated with this principle than Bentham.

At the same time, however, the *View* is a piece of writing *not* altogether "like Bentham's," since it also contains a meta-view, a radically "philosophical view" of the practical advice it offers in the current circumstances. Like so many of Shelley's relentless literary experiments, that is, the *View* stages an immanent critique of the genre in which it is cast. One need only think of the immanent critique of satire with the satirical *Peter Bell the Third*, the immanent critique of the sublime Romantic landscape poem with "Mont Blanc" (and the picturesque one with "Stanzas Written in Dejection Near Naples"), the immanent critique of English tragic drama with *The Cenci*, or the immanent critique of Athenian tragedy with *Prometheus Unbound*.[17]

IV

If the enlightened pragmatism of Shelley's approach to nonviolent resistance in *A Philosophical View of Reform* amounts to a utilitarian response to an immediate crisis, then one must look elsewhere in his writings for the "deeper inquiries" we saw described in the *View* as incompatible with "systems of faith with respect to the cause and agencies of the universe, with all their superstructure of political and religious tyranny." The masterpiece singled out by Salt, *Prometheus Unbound*, probably answers to that purpose as well as any work in Shelley's *oeuvre*. True, it is not without its own sense of address and historical context: like *The Revolt of Islam* before it, Shelley's idealized drama vaguely shadows the historical situation of Europe after the Napoleonic Wars. At the same time, explicitly cast as a revision of the plot of Aeschylus's ancient tragedy, its "action" takes place on a level well beyond the historical particulars of its moment. Indeed, historical particulars are generally registered in *Prometheus Unbound* only by way of artfully indirect representations.

Consider the moment in Act III, when the Spirit of the Hour returns from his tour of reawakened earth to report to Prometheus and Asia on the new order of things that accompanies their own transformation. The Spirit-messenger delivers an account, in Salt's words, of a "world [...] regenerated by the power of love."

> There was a change ... the impalpable thin air
> And the all-circling sunlight were transformed
> As if the sense of love dissolved in them
> Had folded itself round the sphered world. (III.iv.100–103 [SPP 267])

It is when the Spirit reports on the details of the change that the poem produces its indirect representation of the actual state of the world in 1818–1819 by dint of reporting what love has overcome:

> None fawned, none trampled; hate, disdain, or fear,
> Self-love or self-contempt on human brows
> No more inscribed [...]
> None with firm sneer trod out in his own heart
> The sparks of love and hope, till there remained
> Those bitter ashes, a soul self-consumed,
> And the wretch crept, a vampire among men,
> Infecting all with his own hideous ill.
> None talked that common, false, cold, hollow talk
> Which makes the heart deny the *yes* it breathes
> Yet question that unmeant hypocrisy
> With such a self-mistrust as has no name. (III.iv.133–152 [267–268])

Shelley's dismaying representation of the state of society becomes a catalogue of contemporary ills worthy of the most somber realist – a Defoe or Balzac. Yet its "realism" is presented not only in fictional retrospect but also in the perspective of a "philosophical view" even more markedly than in *A Philosophical View of Reform*.[18] Shelley here depicts the ills of the society "as it is" (to use the idiom of the moment), with all its superstructure of maxims and forms, but only from the point of view of their having already been overcome in the nonviolent revolution for which he is advocating.

Begun in September 1818, *Prometheus Unbound* was largely composed well before the state of emergency that would lead Shelley to resort to the quasi-utilitarian compromise he brokered in the *View*, with its pragmatic advice for dealing with armed forces on the street. It is a work thus freed to aspire to the kind of transformative breakthrough achieved by the likes of Milton and Spinoza in the seventeenth century. The central issue it addresses on that aspirational level, accordingly, is none other than the revolutionary power of love and its implications. Moreover, what lends *Prometheus* far greater relevance for such shadows of futurity as Gandhi and Lawson is the way in which it explicitly connects love with *suffering* – here understood as the condition in which the realms of the ideal and actual can come together.

When John Lewis wrote in his memoir about his discipleship with James Lawson in the late 1950s, the nexus of love and "redemptive suffering," which Lewis called "a holy and *affective* thing," was very much the heart of the lessons he learned from Lawson: "It opens us and those around us to a force beyond ourselves, a force that is right and moral, the force of righteous truth that is the basis of human conscience."[19] Lewis cautions, however, that this suffering is only redemptive if it is accompanied with "a graceful heart":

> This is a very difficult concept to understand, and it is even more difficult to internalize, but it has everything to do with the way of nonviolence. We are talking about *love*, here [...] a love that accepts the hateful and even the hurtful.[20]

When Shelley set to work on *Prometheus Unbound* in pursuit of such "deeper inquiries" that he felt utilitarianism unfortunately left behind – inquiries best pursued through poetry in his expanded understanding of the term – something like the "difficult concept" that Lewis learned from Lawson was exactly what he sought to explore.

Though its temporality is not straightforward, *Prometheus Unbound* is rightly seen as a drama whose decisive moment occurs soon after it begins, with Prometheus's Act I "recalling" of his curse on Jupiter. The choreography of this episode is staged in such a way, however, as to raise a question about how it counts as an "action" in the first place, perhaps even *whether* it counts as an action. For when Prometheus speaks the paronomasia – "the Curse / Once breathed on thee I would recall" (58–59, remember / retract, *SPP* 211) – it is an open question whether we should consider his disposition in this key episode as active rather than passive. At stake is a further paronomasia in Act I about two senses of suffering, as when, for example, Prometheus is called "Awful Sufferer" (I.352 [*SPP* 220]). On the one hand, to suffer is to endure pain. Adam Smith explained that the core sense of "sympathy" is "our fellow feeling with the sufferings, not that with the enjoyments, of others."[21] Such enjoyments can be a comfort to suffering, though not for Prometheus, who acknowledges to Earth that he may not share her fleeting comforts – "flowers and fruits and happy sounds" – as do "all else who live and suffer" (I.187–188 [215]).

And yet, on hearing his own curse spoken back to him, Prometheus announces, pivotally, "I wish no living thing to suffer pain" (I.305 [*SPP* 218]). This introduces a second sense of suffering as *undergoing* rather than *undertaking*. This sense is reinforced by Panthea, who reports that the fearsome Phantom looks "Like one who does, not suffers wrong"

(I.239 [*SPP* 216]). The "action" of Shelley's drama is in part defined in the movement between these two understandings of what it means to suffer. Thus, the very form of Prometheus's "recalling" of the curse involves, in effect, his suffering of his own curse, now spoken to him by the Phantasm of Jupiter. The act of the curse, in other words, is undone by another act in which an undertaking becomes an undergoing, when the one who issues the curse is made to suffer the effect of his own words. What is clarified in the reversal of position so carefully staged in this pivotal moment is not only the initially unacknowledged revanchism of Prometheus's starting point in the drama but also the degree to which that revanchism establishes the power of Jupiter in the first place. To forgive Jupiter, in the vision of this drama, is to eliminate him.

Prometheus Unbound's poetic exploration of pain in relation to the grammatical categories of active and passive is fundamental to its "deeper inquiries" into those issues of causality and human nature that Shelley praised in early modern writers. Indeed, its crucial reversal of perspective on the curse, in which one suffers what one does, quite specifically dramatizes his idea of love in action. Shelley's most ambitious staging of the radical love that subtends nonviolent revolution, in short, thus plays out as an act of radical suffering.

What is at stake here for Shelley, finally, is the politics of a certain understanding of sensibility, an understanding especially prominent within a tradition of British empiricism where, as William Empson once noted, "The word [*sense*] considers sensations not as means of knowledge, but of suffering."[22] Prometheus is a figure traditionally associated with both knowledge and suffering, and Shelley's intervention in the politics of sensibility is perhaps best grasped in contrast to one of the most important accounts of poetic sensibility – of the relation of knowledge and suffering – in his own moment. I mean the account offered in an important 1815 apologia by Wordsworth, unquestionably the poet with whom Shelley engaged most strenuously in the last years of his abbreviated career. As with so many of the issues that mattered to him, it was with and against Wordsworth that Shelley developed his mature understanding of suffering.

Shelley dramatically altered his view of Wordsworth soon after the publication of the 1815 *Poems*, which included not only a preface but also an "Essay Supplementary" that defended his poetry in the face of what he took to be popular neglect and critical abuse. The essay, in particular, would prove negatively pivotal for Shelley's future writing and provoke the immanent critique he undertook in two crucial poems of 1816: "To Wordsworth" and *Alastor, or The Spirit of Solitude*. Yet because of

Wordsworth's circuitousness, what Shelley found so objectionable in the poet's 1815 self-defense, and in its implications for love and suffering, is not immediately obvious. Wordsworth launches the essay inauspiciously with a brief history of English poetry that explains the failure of his readers fully to appreciate his poetry on the principle that, with few exceptions, no truly great and original poet has ever been properly appreciated in his own time. The second phase of the essay enters more deeply into this explanation with a second principle: that truly great and original poets, among whom Wordsworth unabashedly numbers himself, all face "the task of *creating* the taste by which he is to be enjoyed."[23]

Why, Wordsworth asks, should this task be so challenging? And then he answers his own question with a series of cagey questions:

> Is it in breaking the bonds of custom, in overcoming the prejudices of false refinement, and displacing the aversions of inexperience? Or, [...] does it consist in [...] making [the reader] ashamed of the vanity that renders him insensible of the appropriate excellence which civil arrangements, less unjust than might appear, and Nature illimitable in her bounty, had conferred on men who may stand below him in the scale of society? Finally, does it lie in establishing that dominion over the spirits of readers by which they are to be humbled and humanized, in order that they may be purified and exalted?[24]

I call these questions cagey because after answering "No," Wordsworth pivots to declare not that they are the wrong questions but rather that they are asked with a mistaken assumption in mind: "If these ends are to be attained by the mere communication of *knowledge*, it does *not* lie here."[25] The critique of this assumption about the role of knowledge in these matters in turn leads directly to a critique of contemporary ideas about the term "TASTE," as involving "a metaphor, taken from a *passive* sense of the human body, and transferred to things which are in their essence *not* passive, – to intellectual *acts* and *operations*."[26]

Once the question of suffering surfaces out of this mistaken understanding of taste as "passive," it elicits an analysis by which Shelley must have been struck:

> Passion, it must be observed, is derived from a word which signifies *suffering*; but the connexion which suffering has with effort, with exertion, and *action*, is immediate and inseparable. [...] To be moved, then, by a passion is to be excited, often to external, and always to internal, effort; whether for the continuance and strengthening of the passion, or for its suppression, accordingly as the course which it takes may be painful or pleasurable.[27]

For Wordsworth, the argument about knowledge and suffering sets the stage for an account of genius (modeled on his own) in which the relationship of original poet and active/passive reader is recast in the roles of inspiring leader and energized follower.

> Genius is the introduction of a new element into the intellectual universe [...]. What is all this but an advance, or a conquest, made by the soul of the poet? Is it to be supposed that the reader can make progress of this kind, like an Indian prince or general – stretched on his palanquin, and borne by his slaves? No; he is invigorated and inspired by his leader, in order that he may exert himself; for he cannot proceed in quiescence, he cannot be carried like a dead weight.[28]

The QED of this circuitous line of reasoning is the poet's striking formulation of what Thomas De Quincey calls the distinction between the literature of knowledge and the literature of power: "Therefore to create taste is to call forth and bestow power, of which knowledge is the effect; and *there* lies the true difficulty."[29]

There would have been much to provoke Shelley in Wordsworth's mid-career reframing suffering and sensibility within a broader ideological framework. If the poet-reader relationship is cast hierarchically, as a form of dominion of a leader over a follower, the larger picture of society here emerges as likewise hierarchical. It is structured as a "scale" of positions each with its "appropriate excellence." Most especially, Shelley would not have failed to notice that, for Wordsworth, what "vanity" makes us "insensible" to is not the *suffering* of those below us on the scale but rather the appropriate *excellence* of their position there, conferred as it is not only by the great bounty of "Nature" but also by civil arrangements that prove to be, in the poet's words, "less unjust than might appear." Shelley may well have recognized that Wordsworth here openly, if indirectly, espouses a central principle in Edmund Burke's social theory – the idea of a "true moral equality" (as Burke put it) that outweighs the abstract inequality pursued both by contemporary reform movements and by the nonviolent revolutionary movements to which they gave rise.[30]

But is there in fact evidence that Shelley read Wordsworth this way, that he saw Wordsworth's argument about suffering in light of some such form of acquiescence in the political status quo? In Act I of *Prometheus Unbound*, the "Awful Sufferer" at the center of the drama, having "recalled" his curse on Jupiter by having it spoken to his own face by the Phantasm of Jupiter, is subjected to a further series of trials and temptations. He is shown the image of another sufferer, "a youth / With patient looks, nailed to a crucifix"

(I.584–585 [*SPP* 228]). One of the Furies who torments Prometheus with this "emblem" taunts him with the suggestion that such suffering is the opposite of redemptive: "those who do endure / Deep wrongs for man" achieve nothing more than to "heap / Thousand-fold torment on themselves and him" (I.594–596 [228]). The problem is that what the Furies call the "slaves" of the Church that bears Christ's name – a name that Prometheus will not speak for it has "become a curse" – have inverted Christ's own values (I.604 [228]). The "wise, the mild, the lofty, and the just" have become the victims of the system run by these "slaves," which has not only brought terror into their lives but also ensured insensibility to the spectacle of suffering created by inquisition and oppression (I.605, 606 [228]).[31]

Beneath this spectacle lie yet darker facts of the contemporary world, since, as the Fury reveals this hidden order of things, "In each human heart terror survives / The ruin it has gorged" (I.618–619 [*SPP* 229]). Those who are "strong and rich—and would be just" cannot maintain their openness to suffering in this milieu: they "live among their suffering fellow men / As if none felt" (I.630–631 [229]). These lines, about an insensibility that rationalizes a social hierarchy by projecting insensibility onto its victims ("as if none felt"), are meant to be the Fury's final trump card, the last best effort to lead Prometheus to despair. Yet Prometheus responds in a fashion that marks his own ultimate moral triumph in the play (though we are still in Act I):

> PROM: Thy words are like a cloud of winged snakes
>   And yet, I pity those they torture not.
> FURY: Thou pitiest them? I speak no more! [Vanishes] (I.632–634 [229])

Shelley here stages one of the most complex acts of human sympathy imaginable. Prometheus expresses pity for a specific but complex category of fellow humans, namely those who do not suffer pain at the thought that many human beings who "would be just" do not themselves suffer pain at the spectacle of injustice. Such persons avoid suffering sympathetically with the victims of injustice on the grounds that those others do not suffer pain in the first place. They thereby abjure the power of love.

By 1816, Shelley had determined that Wordsworth had, in effect, taken the lead in this rarefied but unfortunate group, having compromised his extraordinary powers of imagination by turning to opinions unworthy of those powers. It was precisely the capacity for sympathetic imagination – for love – that Shelley's *Peter Bell the Third*, a satire of Wordsworth in the Byronic mode, would find lacking in Wordsworth:

> He had as much imagination
> As a pint-pot—he never could
> Fancy another situation
> From which to dart his contemplation,
> Than that wherein he stood. (298–302 [*SPP* 351])

At the same time, *Peter Bell the Third* would also complicate the picture, for in staging this censure of Wordsworth in Lord Byron's satiric mode, Shelley also suggests that Byron – like Shelley in his Byronic mode – is incapable of putting himself in *Wordsworth's* place. Though himself a celebrated contemporary Promethean, the author of a famous poem on the subject the year before Shelley's, Byron could not bring himself to pity Wordsworth, as Shelley ultimately could, and, more to the point, as Shelley's Prometheus could pity all those who "would be good" but had ceased to be sensible to the suffering generated by an unjust society.

Wordsworth's insensibility, carried out as it is precisely in the name of "widening the sphere of human sensibility," is something for which Byron had no patience: he could not, as it were, suffer it. He could not even feel, as Shelley did, what Wordsworth suffered in having his genius so neglected and misunderstood by the critical establishment of his moment. The mode of satire in which Byron was so deeply invested, in other words, was itself for Shelley a performance of insensibility. Indeed, it was nothing other than a modern iteration of older ecclesiastical modes of retribution, ways of inflicting pain and suffering on those judged to be sinners – as Shelley made explicit in his fragment of a satire on satire.[32]

Notwithstanding Shelley's meta-critique of Byronic satire, he saw in Wordsworth's late theory of poetry and suffering a terrible falling away from what Wordsworth might have been. Wordsworth's disappointments and resulting capitulations had perverted his great powers of imagination and feeling, and they did so, tragically, at the expense of a larger vision of radical suffering that could have been put in the service of political and social transformation.[33] The result was a skewed model of the poet's relation to his readers, who, on his 1815 accounting, needed to feel what *he* felt, and suffer what *he* suffered, even as he required their active collaboration in this process by "the exertion of a co-operating *power*" in their minds. It is a model that came to dominate theories of reading through Matthew Arnold and into the massively influential program in "practical criticism" launched by I. A. Richards at Cambridge in the 1920s. In breaking with it, decades later, Raymond Williams critiqued it explicitly as Richards's "Passsive-Active theory of reading," though he never explicitly connected it with Wordsworth's

1815 polemic.³⁴ Shelley may have been the first to offer such a critique, and in doing so he worked out a poetics of suffering in the context of nonviolent revolution.

V

In tracing the formation of this poetics, in its cultural and political contexts, I have implicitly been answering some lingering questions about why Shelley's views have not had the recognition they might deserve in twentieth-century discussions and beyond. One answer surely has to do with a fact that the Shelley of these mature writings, unlike the Shelley who had distributed pamphlets in Dublin and organized workers in Wales, was no longer himself an on-the-ground activist. His prescribing dangerous courses of action from an Italian villa a thousand miles away from the scenes of lethal confrontation might well not have led activist leaders like Gandhi and Lewis to acknowledge his example. Shelley was an engaged writer, in a sense, but he was also sensitive to the limits of *poésie engagée*: "Didactic poetry is my abhorrence," he wrote in the preface to *Prometheus Unbound* (*SPP* 209). I have also argued that Shelley's concern with any such engagement tends to be mediated by his sophisticated work with genre. Northrop Frye long ago pointed out that "the basis of generic criticism is [...] rhetorical, in the sense that the genre is determined by the conditions established between the poet and the public."³⁵ Shelley's experiments with genre gauge that relationship at various distances to a variety of occasions. His play with various genres thus enables rhetorical variations on his signature practice of producing a literature of immanent critique. And to compound the difficulty, the immanent critique often has a specific target in his own moment: a Wordsworth, a Byron, or a Bentham. To appreciate what he is doing requires some understanding of how, as he warns in the preface to *Prometheus Unbound*, "the study of contemporary writings might have tinged [his] composition" (*SPP* 207).

For all these reasons, it is not always easy to lift Shelley's writings out of context, and such challenges, compounded by the difficulty of his style, may have set limits for his recognition in the subsequent line of revolutionary nonviolence. Any follower of Gandhi or Lawson who did read Shelley carefully, moreover, might have encountered a further problem, for Shelley did not, in some of his writings, rule out the resort to violence in defense of the revolutionary cause. Henry Salt himself noticed this feature of Shelley's writings in some of its incarnations, especially the popular idiom of the "political songs" he composed after Peterloo. Salt pointed to one, "Song to the Men of England," and particularly to the following two quatrains:

> The seed ye sow, another reaps;
> The wealth ye find, another keeps;
> The robes ye weave, another wears;
> The arms ye forge, another bears.
>
> Sow seed—but let no tyrant reap:
> Find wealth—let no imposter heap:
> Weave robes—let not the idle wear:
> Forge arms—in your defence to bear.[36]

Salt acknowledges that there are moments when Shelley seems to suggest that, in the face of intransigence, "a forcible reformation would become both necessary and justifiable."[37] Over the course of the 1960s and beyond, the nonviolent movement for US civil rights would come to share the field of struggle with the Black Power movement. Over the course of the 1970s and beyond, the nonviolent movement for civil rights in Ireland would come to share the field of struggle with the Irish Republican Army. Shelley's prophetic justification of such "necessities" might not have endeared him to those who were trying to keep the nonviolent faith.

This question of faith brings us to perhaps the most significant limitation on Shelley's recognition among the leaders of the twentieth-century's nonviolent revolutions: his entrenched anti-clericalism. The great leaders with whom we began, Lawson and King, were both men of the cloth. Lewis, their disciple, was a devout Christian. Desmond Tutu was an Anglican bishop when he supported the movement in South Africa. Even a leader of the civil rights march in Derry that ended with Bloody Sunday, Ivan Cooper, remained throughout his nonviolent activism a loyal member of the Church of Ireland. Gandhi's orientation may have been syncretistic, but he was no enemy of established religions. For Shelley, by contrast, the interconnection between what he called "political and religious tyranny" is deep and strong from his early pamphlet on atheism until his death. His Prometheus is a Christ-figure scrubbed clean of institutional Christianity.

At the same time, as I have suggested throughout, it is important to acknowledge the work of those scholars who have shown how far Shelley's political imagination – precisely in its atheistic syncretism – was itself shaped by his readings in cultures beyond Europe.[38] Europe's industrial revolution may have set the conditions for Shelley to articulate his developed understanding of revolutionary nonviolence, but the expansive imagination that conceived that understanding in the first place was informed by the non-European texts and contexts to which he began to turn in earnest from as early as 1811–1812. Such exposure, of course, guarantees nothing in itself. Robert Southey read many of the same non-European materials Shelley did and made widely circulated poetry out of them. But while Shelley admired Southey's epic, *The Curse of Kehama*, he was unhappy with the poem's handling of the issue Shelley explicitly named "faith." Shelley's disappointing meeting with Southey in 1811, when he is reported to have fallen asleep during Southey's reading of that poem for his benefit, may well have clarified the young poet's early commitment to the *skeptical* mode of syncretist imaginings that informed his later work, the writings that Gandhi would have encountered through Henry Salt decades later.

Shelley's skeptical syncretism rhymes with his dark view of history, and his well-nigh Voltairean recognition of the worldwide atrocities committed in the name of religion. At the end of that same year, 1812, on the advice of Godwin, the young Shelley wrote to a friend that he was "determined to apply [himself] to a study that is hateful and disgusting to [my] very soul […] I mean that record of crimes and miseries, History" (*Letters* I: 340). His words echo Voltaire – "l'histoire n'est que le tableau des crimes et des malheurs" – but they do so by way of Southey himself, who, in his 1798 poem "History," apostrophizes his subject as "Thou chronicle of crimes" – as his admirer Shelley would have known.[39] But as against the piety of Southey in 1812, the young Shelley was already clear that the point of facing history's crimes and miseries was about overcoming them. The study of history, he explained, is not for the sake of the past. Rather, it is "above all studies necessary for him who would be listened to as a mender of antiquated abuses" (*Letters* I: 340). This "mending" required a kind of "optimism" that the anti-clerical Voltaire, for his part, famously proscribed at the conclusion of that relentless record of crimes and miseries that is *Candide*. If we still listen to Shelley today, surely it is partly because, while fully acknowledging historical atrocity and categorically refusing religious consolation, he somehow managed to find some grounds for hope – hope in the prospect of nonviolent revolution, hope in the mending of vice by way of imaginative love and in the mending of misery by way of radical suffering.

Notes

1 I wish to thank the two editors of this volume for excellent suggestions to improve and sharpen this essay, and both Amanda Jo Goldstein and Julie A. Carlson for their keen reading and penetrating comments. By no means least, I thank my research assistant Eric Powell, himself a Shelleyan, for his invaluable help in researching and revising it.

2 King spoke these words of Lawson on the eve of his assassination, the same night he praised him in his "Mountaintop" speech in Memphis, where he had come to support Lawson's efforts in the sanitation workers' strike: Martin Luther King, Jr., *I Have a Dream: Writings and Speeches that Changed the World* (New York: HarperCollins, 1992), 198. For a recent assessment of the inherent limitations and subsequent distortions of King's nonviolent movement, see Dara T. Mathis, "King's Message of Nonviolence Has Been Distorted," *Atlantic Monthly*, April 3, 2018, www.theatlantic.com/politics/archive/2018/04/kings-message-of-nonviolence-has-been-distorted/557021/.
3 See Timothy Morton, "Receptions," in Timothy Morton, ed. *The Cambridge Companion to Shelley* (Cambridge: Cambridge University Press, 2007), 43–44. Gandhi is known to have quoted the poem in his later decades.
4 Percy Bysshe Shelley, *A Philosophical View of Reform*, in Roger Ingpen and Walter E. Peck, eds. *The Complete Works of Percy Bysshe Shelley*, Volume 7 (London: Ernest Benn, 1926–30), 3–55, 48. Hereafter cited as *PVR* by page number in the text.
5 Richard Jackson, Joseph Llewellyn, Griffin Leonard, Aidan Groth, and Tonga Karena, eds. *Revolutionary Nonviolence: Concepts, Cases and Controversies* (London: Zed Books, 2020) and Judith Butler, *The Force of Nonviolence: An Ethico-Political Bind* (London: Verso, 2020).
6 James M. Lawson, Jr., "The Power of Nonviolence in the Fight for Racial Justice," in *Revolutionary Nonviolence: Organizing for Freedom* (Oakland: University of California Press, 2022), 20.
7 In his autobiography, Gandhi wrote: "I read Salt's book [on the history of vegetarianism] from cover to cover and was very much impressed by it. From the date of reading this book, I may claim to have become a vegetarian by choice. […] My faith in vegetarianism grew on me from day to day. Salt's book whetted my appetite for dietetic studies." M. K. Gandhi, *An Autobiography: The Story of My Experiments with Truth*, trans. Mahadev Desai (Ahmedabad: Navajivan Publishing House, 1927), 48.
8 See Leela Gandhi, *Affective Communities: Anticolonial Thought, Fin-de-Siècle Radicalism, and the Politics of Friendship* (Durham, NC: Duke University Press, 2006), 70ff. Meena Alexander briefly notes that what Gandhi learned from Salt about Shelley extended beyond vegetarianism, but her account is somewhat skewed by its misdating of Gandhi's encounter with Salt to a decade later than its actual occurrence in the late 1880s, prior to Gandhi's inaugural nonviolent activism in South Africa. See her "Shelley's India: Territory and Text, Some Problems of Decolonization," in Betty T. Bennett and Stuart Curran, eds. *Shelley: Poet and Legislator of the World* (Baltimore: Johns Hopkins University Press, 1996), 172–173. See also John Drew, *India and the Romantic Imagination* (Delhi: Oxford University Press, 1987), 229–284.
9 Salt's biographer notes that "Shelley's prose and poetry clearly helped introduce Salt to free thought, socialism, vegetarianism, and unconventional views on sex and marriage." See George Hendrick, *Henry Salt: Humanitarian and Man of Letters* (Urbana: University of Illinois Press, 1977), 89. Henrick also

notes that George Bernard Shaw, a fellow Fabian, also declared his affiliation with Shelley on multiple related grounds: "Like Shelley, I am a Socialist, an Atheist, and a Vegetarian," 95. This declaration was made in 1887, the year before Gandhi's arrival in London.

10 Henry S. Salt, *Percy Bysshe Shelley: A Monograph* (London: Swan, Sonneschein, Lawrey & Co., 1888), 152.
11 Salt, *Percy Bysshe Shelley*, 150.
12 Salt, *Percy Bysshe Shelley*, 148–149.
13 Salt, *Percy Bysshe Shelley*, 147.
14 Salt, *Percy Bysshe Shelley*, 147.
15 For a discussion on Gandhi's interest in Salt's take on Thoreau, see Hendrick, *Henry Salt*, 110–112.
16 Butler, *Force of Nonviolence*, 24.
17 I have adapted the Frankfurt School notion of "immanent critique" from the explication of the concept by my late colleague, Moishe Postone, in *Time, Labor, and Social Domination* (Cambridge: Cambridge University Press), 87–88, especially as that notion was extended to literary analysis in Neil Larsen, "Literature, Critique, and the Problem of Standpoint," *Mediations* 24.2 (Spring 2009), https://mediationsjournal.org/articles/literature-immanent-critique-and-the-problem-of-standpoint. I make no direct connection between immanent critique and nonviolent revolution, though it is instructive to contrast Shelley's approach to Wordsworth's "Passive-Active theory of reading." I return to this later in the chapter. One might speculate that immanent critique registers Shelley's take on Wordsworth's genius in *A Defence of Poetry* as caught between bogus conscious opinion and genuine, though unconscious, inspiration from the zeitgeist.
18 For a similar strategy to the one in the speech of the Spirit of the Hour, see the catalogue of ills in the sonnet "England in 1819," all to be overcome in the moment when they are called the "graves" from which an illuminating "glorious phantom" may burst (*SPP* 326). For Shelley's discussion of realism, see the preface to his play *The Cenci* (*SPP* 140–45).
19 John Lewis (with Michael D'Orso), *Walking with the Wind: A Memoir of the Movement* (New York: Simon and Schuster, 1998), 76–77.
20 Lewis, *Walking*, 77.
21 Adam Smith, *Theory of Moral Sentiments* (Indianapolis: Liberty Classics, 1976), 103.
22 William Empson, "Sense and Sensibility," *The Structure of Complex Words* (Cambridge, MA: Harvard University Press, 1989), 250–269.
23 W. B. J. Owen and Jane Worthington Smyser, eds. *Prose Works of William Wordsworth*, Volume 3 (Oxford: Oxford University Press, 1974), 80.
24 Owen and Smyser, *Prose Works of William Wordsworth*, 80.
25 Owen and Smyser, *Prose Works of William Wordsworth*, 81, emphasis in original.
26 Owen and Smyser, *Prose Works of William Wordsworth*, 81, emphasis in original.
27 Owen and Smyser, *Prose Works of William Wordsworth*, 81–82.
28 Owen and Smyser, *Prose Works of William Wordsworth*, 81–82.

29 Owen and Smyser, *Prose Works of William Wordsworth*, 82, emphasis in original.
30 Edmund Burke, *Reflections on the Revolution in France* (London: Penguin, 1986), 124.
31 By the time Shelley wrote *Prometheus Unbound*, Wordsworth had already begun to affiliate himself more openly with the Christian church in *The Excursion*. The Shelleys read it together on its appearance, and after they did Mary Shelley summarized their response to it in a crisp four-word review featuring exactly the word that Percy used for churchgoing Christians in Act I of *Prometheus Unbound*: "He is a slave." See *The Journals of Mary Shelley: 1814–44*, eds. Paula R. Feldman and Diana Scott-Kilvert, 2 volumes (Oxford: Clarendon Press, 1987), I: 25. Note that to be a slave, in the Shelleys' pejorative sense, is to refuse suffering, not to be inflicted by it – an obvious point of *mis*alignment between the discursive contexts of post-Waterloo British struggles for "liberty" and post-1960 American struggles for racial justice.
32 Shelley develops at length this trope of satire as a neo-medieval form of punishment in his fragmentary poem "A Satire upon Satire."
33 In contrast to this charge of renegadism, Wordsworth was insistent in ways both explicit and inexplicit, on the *continuity* between his positions in 1800 and 1815 at every turn. See my "'Wordsworth' after Waterloo," in Kenneth Johnston and Gene W. Ruoff, eds. *The Age of William Wordsworth* (New Brunswick: Rutgers University Press, 1988), 84–111.
34 See my "I. A. Richards and Raymond Williams: Reading Poetry, Reading Society," *Critical Inquiry* 46.2 (2020), 325–352.
35 Frye, *Anatomy of Criticism*, 247.
36 Salt, *Percy Bysshe Shelley*, 151.
37 Salt, *Percy Bysshe Shelley*, 153.
38 On the "paganism" of Shelley and his generation, see, for example, Martin Priestman, *Romantic Atheism: Poetry and Freethought, 1780–1830* (Cambridge: Cambridge University Press, 1999), 219–252. See also Alexander, "Shelley's India," 169–173.
39 The echoes were first pointed out by R. W. King, "A Note on Shelley, Gibbon, Voltaire and Southey," *The Modern Language Review*, 51.2 (April 1956), 225–227.

CHAPTER 6

Loathsome Sympathy
Shelley's The Cenci *and the Problem of Empathy*

Alan Richardson

I begin by placing this essay in relation, first, to my earlier work on Percy Shelley's *The Cenci* and then to my current critical approach, cognitive historicism. After a revisionary look, partly inspired by recent mirror neuron research and its relation to empathy, at eighteenth-century and Romantic-era sympathy theory, I offer some critical remarks on what Shelley called (in *Prometheus Unbound*) "loathsome sympathy" as it functions in *The Cenci*. Finally, I question the current, almost cult-like, vogue for empathy in light of its problematic aspects and significant limitations.

My interest in *The Cenci* goes back over three decades, and I devoted a chapter of my first book to Shelley's verse tragedy.[1] I thought then, as now, that Shelley's conception of sympathy plays a key role both in *The Cenci* and in *Prometheus Unbound*: the latter expresses the redemptive and transformative power of sympathy, while the former delineates a perverse and perverting version of the same human faculty that one might call, after Shelley, "loathsome sympathy" (I.451 [*SPP* 223]). Less clear, however, was how Shelley thought sympathy, especially its loathsome aspect, functioned, because I then understood sympathy largely in mentalistic and idealist terms. No surprise, given that my model for analyzing character interaction in Romantic drama followed Hegel's *Phenomenology*, and that model's idealist bias revealed itself in the very title of my 1988 study, *A Mental Theater*. By the time my second book, a historicist study of education, literacy, and Romantic discourse, appeared, I was happy to leave my early work behind me and this essay marks the first time I have revisited *The Cenci* in print.[2]

The mode of criticism I practice now (and have helped to develop), cognitive historicism, might sound as though it retains the very mentalistic bias that I now feel limited my youthful approach. However, the term "cognitive" in such compounds as cognitive science and cognitive neuroscience no longer excludes apparent antonyms like "emotive," nor does it imply a disembodied, decontextualized view of the human mind and mental behaviors. To the contrary, cognitive historicism as practiced by Ellen Spolsky and myself among others, along with overlapping approaches such as Lisa Zunshine's cognitive cultural criticism, programmatically assumes an embodied, emotive, and sociohistorically situated "mind-brain."[3] Let me insist on this last point. Although cognitive historicists, like cognitive literary critics generally, take a keen interest in presumably invariant features of the brain, mind, cognition, and behavior, such "human universals" are always developed, displayed, understood, and represented in relation to specific physical, social, and cultural environments.[4] In addition, although cognitive literary critics accept a basic scientific worldview and respect the power of sophisticated empirical investigation, they also appreciate the provisional nature of even the most widely accepted empirical findings and remain aware of the contentious status of much current work in the mind and brain sciences.

Mirror neuron theory provides a good case in point. Initially discovered in macaque monkeys, mirror neurons, quite surprisingly, become active both when the monkey performs a given action and when it observes another monkey doing the same thing. In this way, mirror neurons trouble the distinction between motor and sensory areas in the brain and, more intriguingly, seem to soften the divide between self and other. As such, mirror neurons have been described as providing the "foundation for empathy" and, more broadly, the first "plausible neurophysiological explanation for complex forms of social cognition and interaction."[5] Some neuroscientists and philosophers of mind have cast doubt on such claims, noting, to begin with, that most human studies involve indirect evidence and extrapolation from what has been learned about monkeys (single brain cell recordings can rarely be made in human subjects for ethical reasons).[6] Such skepticism has not prevented other brain scientists from making still larger claims for mirror neurons, however, as with V. S. Ramachandran's well-known contention that mirror neurons provide the key to a scientific understanding not solely of empathy but of imitation, language, and culture itself.[7]

Congenial as I find Ramachandran's assertion that mirror neurons "liberated our brain from its Darwinian shackles" by enabling cultural evolution to take over from genetic adaptation, I am neither motivated nor qualified to pronounce on whether mirror neurons are indeed the "neurons that shaped civilization" or instead the "most hyped concept in neuroscience," to quote rival essay titles.[8] Yet when I first encountered mirror neuron theory, I could not help being intrigued by a twenty-first-century materialist account of empathy that seemed to provide much of what was missing from my understanding of eighteenth-century and Romantic-era accounts of sympathy. (What these accounts centrally mean by *sympathy* overlaps significantly with what we now mean by *empathy*, a term introduced into English only in 1909 [*OED* def. 2a].) More than that, mirror neuron research has developed in ways that speak suggestively to the function of sympathy in Romantic-era texts such as *The Cenci*, as I now understand them. As summarized, for example, in Marco Iacoboni's *Mirroring People: The Science of Empathy and How We Connect with Others*, the discovery of mirror neurons has enabled an embodied, emotive, and intersubjective approach to empathy that gives special attention to nonverbal communication (especially by means of gestures and facial expressions) and to unconscious and involuntary responses.[9] I believe that sympathy and its "loathsome" double exhibit virtually the same features in *The Cenci*, and perhaps in many other Romantic-era works as well.

Mirror neuron theory, then, can provide a springboard for a novel appreciation of the workings of sympathy in Romantic-era texts. But only a springboard: the question remains, how did *Shelley* understand and represent sympathy in his early nineteenth-century moment? It simply won't do to claim that Shelley "anticipated" anything like a mirror neuron approach to sympathy, since we have no way of theorizing what such anticipation would mean. Authorial "intuition" might work for Shelley himself, who did grant poets a certain kind of prophetic insight, but it does not work for us, as we have no credible model for how literary prophecy might function. One could always claim that research on mirror neurons has given us insight into a universal propensity and that Shelley, as a great writer, could have observed this propensity in action and then described it. Although considerably less mystical, this claim still raises questions, beginning with the problem that the mirror neuron account of empathy remains more a series of persuasive hypotheses than a body of established facts. Even if we could confidently assert that mirror neuron research had revealed stable and universal features of human nature, we would still need to ask how Shelley, in his own sociohistorical environment, found these features observable, representable, and important enough to be worth representing. In other words, the account of empathy arising out of research on mirror neurons provides a suggestive analogy to Shelley's understanding and representation of sympathy, and nothing more.

Suggestive analogies, however, have their uses. In this case, the analogy between mirror neuron approaches to empathy and eighteenth-century sympathy theory proves salient enough to have struck neuroscientific researchers themselves. Iacoboni, for example, quotes these words from

Adam Smith's *Theory of Moral Sentiments* (1759) as the epigraph to a chapter on mirror neurons and empathy: "When we see a stroke aimed, and just ready to fall on the leg or arm of another person, we naturally shrink and draw back our own leg or our own arm; and when it does fall, we feel it in some measure, and are hurt by it as well as the sufferer."[10] Here, Iacoboni comments, Smith "nicely" describes the phenomenon of an unconscious, involuntary, visceral empathic reaction "well over two hundred years" before anyone had dreamed of mirror neurons.[11] And the mention of Smith reminds us that the key mirror metaphor itself goes back to the eighteenth century – both Smith and David Hume deploy it in relation to sympathy – and figures prominently in Shelley's *The Cenci* as well.

The question now becomes whether, looking back through the lens provided by recent mirror neuron theory, one can discover elements of a comparably embodied, intersubjective, irrational, and physically immediate account of sympathy that Shelley, for reasons of his own, might have extrapolated from the variants of sympathy theory then current. Shelley's interest in medical and scientific models of mind and mental behavior has by now been well established, as has his early enthusiasm for materialist and "corporealist" approaches to mind.[12] In addition, as I have pointed out elsewhere, Shelley uses "brain" to stand for mind – then still an avant-garde tendency in poetry – more often than any of his fellow high Romantic poets.[13] A number of salient instances occur in *The Cenci*, including Count Cenci's outcry "my brain is swimming round" in the banquet scene of the first act, when Beatrice alone has dared to challenge him, and Beatrice's parallel lament, "My brain is hurt," in the aftermath of her rape by her father (I.iii.164 [*SPP* 155]; III.i.1 [164]). How, for Shelley, does an act of such calculated and horrific violence damage, and perhaps alter, the victim's brain? To what extent did available accounts of sympathy help Shelley to imagine and give poetic expression to such a process?

The question becomes the more pressing given that leading eighteenth-century models of sympathy, not to mention Shelley's own remarks in the *A Defence of Poetry*, can sound quite unabashedly mentalistic if not altogether idealist. For Shelley in the *Defence*, sympathy can be defined as a "going out of our own nature and an identification with the beautiful which exists in thought, action, or person not our own"; because such sympathy depends on imaginative identification, the imagination is the "great instrument of moral good."[14] Shelley here seems to be elaborating on Jean-Jacques Rousseau, who writes in *Émile* (1762) that "it is only imagination which makes us feel the ills of others."[15] Smith's understanding of sympathy involves a famously complex mental process, including a moment of judgment that in turn depends on recourse to an "impartial spectator" or idealized self within the self.[16] And Hume's influential definition of the "principle of sympathy" at least sounds quite abstract and mentalistic: "the conversion of an idea into an impression by the force of imagination."[17] These pronouncements seem to render sympathy an altogether mentalistic process, leaving the body notably out of account.

And yet Hume's theory, at least, has been described as relying fundamentally on embodied forms of communication and display: "language, tone of voice, body language, and facial expression."[18] This characterization points us in an important direction, one worth following especially because Hume's discussion of sympathy in the *Treatise of Human Nature* (1739–1740) proved so influential for the theories to come. Most literary scholars have brought their interest in fictional and dramatic representation to their reading of Hume and have often emphasized, for that reason, the ways in which sympathy for Hume can act at a distance, as to be sure it can.[19] Yet the prototypical instances of sympathetic identification in Hume involve irrational thought processes, embodied communication, and physical proximity. This last feature is easy to miss as Hume describes it with the abstract term "contiguity," and contiguity can of course take many forms. But, primarily though not exclusively, contiguity in this context implies a close if not intimate physical connection. Thus compassion "depends, in a great measure, on the contiguity, and even the sight of the object," which shows, Hume adds, that "'tis derived from the imagination," that is, from the faculty of visual imaging.[20] Sympathy requires the "relation of contiguity," which usually entails our ability to perceive "external signs in the countenance and conversation" of the other.[21] Citing his own experience, Hume notes that a "cheerful countenance infuses a sensible complacency and serenity into my mind; as an angry or sorrowful one throws a sudden damp upon me."[22] This paradigmatic example requires only nonverbal communication and registers as feeling; it attests to our intuitive, irrational understanding of human universals, since "nature has preserved a great resemblance among all human creatures," both in the "fabric of the mind" and in "that of the body."[23]

This basic "propensity" to "sympathize with others" and "receive by communication their inclinations and sentiments" does not depend on moral development or education and is already "conspicuous in children."[24] Indeed, "*sympathy*, or the communication of passions, takes place among animals, no less than among men."[25] Hume goes so far as to hint at what sounds like an explanation at the neural level: "As in strings equally wound up, the motion of one communicates itself to the rest; so all the affections readily pass from one person to another, and beget correspondent movements in every human creature."[26] Although sympathetic reactions centrally involve the body and (perhaps) its nervous system, and paradigmatically feature close physical proximity and nonverbal displays such as gesture and expression, Hume does allow for sympathetic communication by means of language alone, or we could not be moved by letters, by novel reading, or by verbal reports. Yet physical "contiguity" seems for Hume to inspire the most direct, automatic, and unconscious instances of sympathy: "no sooner any person approaches me, than he diffuses on me all his opinions, and draws along my judgment in a greater or lesser degree."[27]

Smith also describes the workings of sympathy in ways that suggest neural transmission and an embodied understanding of human psychology. "Persons of delicate fibres," for example, prove especially liable to spontaneous sympathetic reactions, and the sympathetic imagination allows for physiological as well as psychological identification: "By the imagination [...] we enter as it were into his body."[28] Smith, however, usually insists on a fairly elaborate process involving mental simulation (by means of the imagination, a more robust faculty for Smith than for Hume), judgment, and ultimately an appeal to an idealized "impartial spectator," a "judge within" the mind that enables us to evaluate our own behavior as well as to empathize with other people.[29] In theory, then, sympathy for Smith is highly mediated and inevitably delayed. Even seeing "our brother [...] upon the rack," we cannot refer to our immediate sense experience but rather to the "imagination only," which, by "representing to us what would be our own" sensations in such case, can "at last" begin to affect us with compassion for his "agonies," such that we can "even feel something which, though weaker in degree, is not altogether unlike them."[30] We could hardly be further here from the immediacy attested to by Hume.

Yet people with delicate nerves are not alone in at least seeming to react instantly, emotionally, and irrationally to the emotional displays of others. "The passions, upon some occasions, may seem to be transfused from one man to another, instantaneously, and antecedent to any knowledge of what excited them," and hence of any rational or impartial judgment.[31] So with both grief and joy, which "strongly" (and nonverbally) "expressed in the look and gestures of any one," may "at once affect the spectator with some degree" of the same emotion.[32] Those watching the contortions of a rope dancer will unconsciously "writhe and twist and balance their own bodies, as they see him do, and as they feel that they themselves must do if in his situation."[33] Here one can readily see the appeal of Smith to mirror neuron researchers as a philosophical forerunner providing them with an eighteenth-century pedigree. And in terms of the argument I am making here, Shelley could readily have extrapolated from Smith's rhetoric, as opposed to his fully developed model, support for a view of sympathy as embodied, involuntary, relying primarily on nonverbal sensory cues, and "instantaneous" in its effects.

We should not lose sight, however, of the features of Smith's theory that distance it from mirror neuron theory in the present. In fact, in its interest in representation, judgment, and a comparatively robust exercise of imagination or (in today's terms) simulation, Smith's theory can point up some of the limitations of mirror neuron accounts of empathy. Smith, for example, can account for empathic reactions in the *absence* of any emotional display, or even of the appropriate emotion, on the part of the object of one's compassion. We may feel acute embarrassment on behalf of a foolish person's rudeness, though "he himself appears to have no sense" of his social impropriety; we blush for him "because we cannot help feeling" our own sense of humiliation in such a case.[34] (The relevance of this example to a whole range of theatrical situations, from bedroom farce to tragic irony, should be obvious.) We empathize with the "dreadful [...] wretchedness" of insanity, though the sufferer "perhaps laughs and sings."[35] We can even feel sympathy, Smith claims, for the dead, "shut out from life and conversation," a "prey to corruption and the reptiles of the earth," though the dead themselves remained unmoved in the "profound security of their repose."[36] These examples point up the capacity of imaginative identification to function independently of the direct bodily or verbal cues insisted upon by mirror neuron theory. As I will argue, Shelley in *The Cenci* both highlights the immediate and unconscious effects of sympathy and retains a place for the more elaborate workings of the sympathetic imagination in his conception of "self-anatomy."

Edmund Burke's relatively brief remarks on sympathy in the *Philosophical Enquiry* (1757) also make "imagination" key to sympathetic identification, yet Burke's notion of imagination most resembles Hume's in the directness of its operations and its close relationship to the senses and to what would now be called "feeling." Reasoning as he generally does on what Immanuel Kant termed "physiological" principles, Burke holds that "by the force of natural sympathy" physical displays of such passions as love, fear, anger, grief, and joy affect "every mind" in the same manner, acting upon "certain, natural and uniform principles."[37] Itself a "passion" rather than a chain of mental procedures, sympathy arises independently of the "reasoning faculty," showing the automatic and involuntary character it frequently assumes in Hume (and in mirror neuron accounts of empathy). We are moved as others "are moved, and are never suffered to be indifferent spectators of almost anything" that others do or "suffer." Sympathy involves "a sort of substitution, by which we are put in the place of another man, and affected in many respects as he is affected," a spontaneous reaction that depends not on reason and judgment but on the "mechanical structure of our bodies," presumably including the nervous system.[38] Burke, that is, advocates not only a "physiological sublime" but a physiological approach to sympathy as well.[39]

Burke's discussion of imitation follows closely upon that of imagination, and the transition makes clear that these two human propensities are as tightly linked for Burke as they are for mirror neuron theorists today. Imitation "arises from much the same cause as sympathy," Burke writes, because just as "sympathy makes us take a concern in whatever men feel," so imitation "prompts us to copy whatever they do [...] without any intervention from the reasoning faculty, but solely from our natural constitution."[40] Like sympathy, imitation begins at a physiological, nonverbal level and sympathy can in fact be facilitated through bodily imitation. Burke gives a striking example of this phenomenon late in the *Enquiry*, citing the "curious story" of the "great physiognomist Campanella." According to Burke's source, Campanella could empathically "penetrate into the inclinations" of other people by composing "his face, his gesture, and his whole body, as nearly as he could into the exact similitude of the person he intended to examine." Investigating the resulting changes in his own mental and emotional state, Campanella could then "enter into the dispositions and thoughts of people" as accurately as if he had been "changed into" them.[41] This passage of the *Enquiry* proved memorable enough to take on a literary afterlife: James Hogg, for example, gives his devil figure Gil-Martin the same method and uncanny degree of success in the *Private Memoirs and Confessions of a Justified Sinner*, and Edgar Allan Poe attributes the same ability to his detective Dupin in "The Purloined Letter."[42]

Fantastic as the Campanella anecdote sounds, recent neuroscientific experiments inspired by mirror neuron theory have zeroed in on the basic mechanism behind Burke's claim. Looking specifically (in a functional magnetic resonance imaging [fMRI] study) for links between the supposed human mirror neuron system and the limbic areas, well associated with basic emotions, Iacoboni and his group found that emotion areas duly became activated when test subjects observed faces displaying "fear, sadness, anger, happiness, surprise, and disgust," as did the insula (which connects the limbic area to sites associated with mirror neurons). More to the point, such activation increased when the experimental subjects "were also imitating what they saw."[43] Imitating other people's gestures and facial expressions may indeed augment our ability to empathically reproduce and thus intimately comprehend the emotions they are feeling.

Rousseau's account of sympathy stands out for the comparatively late emergence of the sympathetic faculty, at least in the admittedly artificial case of Émile. Brought up in relative social isolation, Émile remains predominantly concerned with his own needs and emotions until around the age of puberty. At that point, however, his sympathetic feelings break out with the kind of immediacy and automaticity seen in Hume and at times in Smith. "He will begin to have gut reactions at the sounds of complaints and cries, the sight of blood flowing will make him avert his eyes; the convulsions of a dying animal will cause him an ineffable distress before he knows whence come these new movements within him."[44] The emergence of sympathy depends on the prior development of a capacity for imaginative identification, resulting in an emphasis on imagination comparable to that of Smith. No one begins to enter into the pains and pleasures of others "until his imagination is animated and begins to transport him out of himself."[45] Yet sympathetic identification seems rapidly to become second nature, operating with the force and speed of instinct. Émile "suffers when he sees suffering"; "it is a natural sentiment."[46] As the phrase "when he sees" suggests, although it depends on a process of imaginative "transport," sympathy remains first and foremost tied to immediate sensory experience, as "all men are affected sooner and more generally by wounds, cries, groans, the apparatus of painful operations," in short, "all that brings objects of suffering to the senses."[47] Although such reactions may be found variously modified in particular individuals due to their differing histories, "they are universal, and no one is completely exempt from them."[48]

We can no longer doubt that prominent eighteenth-century theorists of sympathy, even those who developed highly mediated accounts that stressed representation, imaginative simulation, and internal reflection, also made room for an approach that, in its sensory immediacy and cognitive automaticity, not to mention its "natural" and "universal" status, approximates the neuroscientific understanding of empathy emerging out of mirror neuron research today. In other words, my brief survey of influential writers on sympathy both confirms and extends Ildiko Csengei's identification of the "co-existence of disparate yet interconnected notions of sympathy" in the long eighteenth century, "some mechanistic" – that is, "automatic and immediate" – and others "based on imaginary processes of identification."[49] If indeed (as many neuroscientific studies have by now suggested) the mirror neuron approach to empathy turns out to have some degree of empirical validity, the less surprising that earlier theorists of sympathy found themselves at times articulating a comparably automatic, embodied process, even in the face of their own more complex models.

All questions of truth value aside, however, we can safely postulate the availability to Shelley and other Romantic-era writers of an embodied and emotive understanding of sympathy, transmitted rapidly and unconsciously by means of facial expressions, gestures, and vocal tonalities, bypassing judgment and volition, and conveyed, as Csengei discusses, by such metaphors as "contagion" and "magnetism."[50] Understood in this manner, sympathetic reactions resemble more the mechanical process of mirroring than the highly mediated, staged connotations of the theater that informs David Marshall's influential reading of Smith's *Theory of Moral Sentiments*.[51] Again, I am not arguing that one understanding is preferable to the other but rather that both models of sympathy could be found in various eighteenth-century discourses, at times inhabiting (however uneasily) the works of the same author or even within the same text. Shelley's "official" understanding of sympathy, as set forth in *A Defence of Poetry*, clearly assumes the "imaginary processes of identification" characteristic of sympathy theory at its most mentalistic. In *The Cenci*, however, where Shelley set out to depict the workings of a corrupting, "loathsome" version of sympathy, he found an embodied, unconscious, and (I would add) neural model of sympathetic communication ready to hand.

In an important essay on Shelley and "animal magnetism," Nigel Leask argues that, throughout the later poetry, Shelley remains torn between a Platonizing idealism and a "materialistic naturalism positing the self-sufficiency of sensibility," an embodied sensibility transmitted through the nervous system – even across individuals.[52] Yet in writing *The Cenci*, by his own account, Shelley temporarily abandoned his Neoplatonic "metaphysics" altogether and turned instead to the remorseless delineation of a "sad reality" (*SPP* 140). Seeking to represent "all the feelings of those who once acted it," their "various interests, passions, and opinions, acting upon and with each other," Shelley drew extensively upon sympathy theory at its most mechanistic and magnetic (141). In fact, he portrays his principal characters as compulsively driven to engage in sympathetic or (in current terms) "theory of mind" activities. As Beatrice's former suitor (and would-be betrayer) Orsino puts it: "'tis a trick of this same family / To analyse their own and other minds" (II.ii.108–109 [162]). Orsino goes on to label such activity, at once introspective and other-directed, "self-anatomy," as though in reading one another's minds the Cencis simultaneously attempt to anatomize, to dissect, one another's brains and nervous systems. What this feels like has already been described by Orsino himself, following an interview with Beatrice early in the play.

> I fear
> Her subtle mind, her awe-inspiring gaze,
> Whose beams anatomize me nerve by nerve
> And lay me bare, and make me blush to see
> My hidden thoughts. (I.ii.83–87 [150–151])

Beatrice's father also seeks, in his mental anatomizing, to penetrate to the material level of "every nerve of you," to trace out and deform the very "foldings of the brain" (II.i.155 [159]; IV.i.179 [179]).[53]

Cenci, in other words, seeks ultimately to torture Beatrice from the inside out, and in the process he makes use of the very psychic mechanisms that underlie empathy (or, in Shelley's terms, sympathy). Mirror neuron researchers have pointed out the lack of any firm and reliable connection between empathic understanding and ethical or "prosocial" behavior: "if we see that someone is in pain, we are not automatically induced to feel compassion for him."[54] Some cognitive psychologists go further, suggesting that empathy may even be recruited in the service of positively inducing pain. "Empathy can have a dark side," according to Grit Hein and Tania Singer, such as "when it is used to find the weakest spot of a person to make him or her suffer."[55] The psychologist Paul Bloom, in his recent book *Against Empathy*, concurs, calling the empathic understanding of others an "amoral tool," used by successful "con men, seducers, and torturers."[56] This represents a decidedly minority view, as most cognitive accounts of torture and other antisocial behaviors speak instead of an empathy deficit. Yet whether or not the notion of "dark empathy" proves psychologically plausible, it certainly plays a notable role in the spectatorial culture of our own time: Hannibal Lecter and Tony Soprano, for example, both show an uncanny ability to understand their victims from the inside precisely in order to manipulate, torment, or destroy them with greater success.[57] Bloom gives a fictional example of his own, referring readers to the monstrous yet empathic torturer O'Brien in George Orwell's *1984*.[58] We can see Shelley's Count Cenci, if not as the single great progenitor of such figures, at least as an early and notable ancestor. (Whether the sadistic empath can be found *only* in fictional works, and not in real life, remains an open question.)

In keeping with Hume's emphasis on the role of visual experience and "contiguity" in arousing sympathy, Shelley offers a number of quite detailed descriptions of his characters' facial expressions. As I have argued elsewhere, facial descriptions of this sort in many Romantic-era texts should be understood less in terms of physiognomy than of physiology.[59] That is, Shelley represents faces in motion, often adding in accompanying changes in gesture or complexion or vocal tonality. Consider two examples from Act I: first, Beatrice's description of her father's expression. "I fear that wicked laughter round his eye / Which wrinkles up the skin even to the hair" (I.iii.37–38 [*SPP* 152]) – indeed, this particular example reads almost like a passage from the pioneering neurologist Charles Bell's *Anatomy and Philosophy of Expression*.[60] It also represents a moment of intersubjective communication – Count Cenci fully intends Beatrice to react anxiously – as does this attempt, again by Beatrice, to read the expression of her dubious ally Orsino.

> Even now you look on me
> As you were not my friend, and as if you
> Discovered that I thought so, with false smiles
> Making my true suspicion seem your wrong. (I.ii.30–33 [149])

We can appreciate not only what Lisa Zunshine would term the multiple levels of "embedment" in this brief speech – Beatrice sees that Orsino affects not to know that he in fact knows that Beatrice suspects that Orsino is deceiving her – but also the rapidity with which Beatrice registers all this, the wordless, physiological communication by means of glances and smiles, and the role that emotion or "passion" plays in such exchanges.[61]

The first scene of Act II, in which Cenci begins to torment Beatrice with intimations of his intent to rape her, moves from one such description to the next, again emphasizing facial expressions while evincing the multimodal and intersubjective character of what Hume calls "*sympathy*, or the communication of passions."[62] Here is one example of how the entire body becomes involved in an expressive act:

> How pale you look; you tremble, and you stand
> Wrapped in some fixed and fearful meditation,
> As if one thought were over strong for you:
> Your eyes have a chill glare. (II.i.29–32 [*SPP* 156]; Lucretia on Beatrice)

And here is one that stresses the intersubjective character of sympathetic communication, the way that one knows one's own mind in part by reading the expressions of others: "And every one looked in his neighbour's face / To see if others were as white as he." Lucretia, narrating this moment, adds that she herself "felt the blood / Rush to [her] heart," elucidating the sudden pallor that propagates itself as if by rapid contagion (II.i.38–41 [156]). Contagion becomes an explicit theme in the play, or rather, to use Shelley's terminology, contamination.

Cenci's ultimate design concerns nothing short of transforming Beatrice into a mirror version of himself, and thus at once destroying her and living on through her. I argued much the same long ago, but this time around I can better appreciate the physicality of Cenci's strategy and its relation to an embodied version of sympathy theory.[63] Cenci's description of how his own facial, gestural, tonal, and physiological confusion becomes transferred to Beatrice brings this out quite starkly, and I will here quote only the key lines of that speech, which brings to a culmination the series of such descriptions in Act I, Scene ii:

> Then it was I whose inarticulate words
> Fell from my lips, and who with tottering steps
> Fled from your presence, as you now from mine. (II.i.112–114 [*SPP* 158])

This psychophysiological mirroring is intensified rhetorically, here, in the figure of parallel (heightened further by elision) and structurally, later in the play, by the corollary relation between Orsino and Giacomo, Beatrice's brother, in the play's subplot.

Finding Giacomo an easier mark than his formidable sister, Orsino goes to work on him as well, eliciting Giacomo's sympathetic responses to his skillful deployment of gestures, glances, tones, and facial expressions. Mistrustful of the workings of his own "unwilling brain," Giacomo begs Orsino to back off: "My heart denies itself / To think what you demand" (II.ii.87–88 [*SPP* 162]). But Orsino represents himself as Giacomo's secret mirror – "a friend's bosom / Is as the inmost cave of our own mind" – and claims to read his true intentions: "You look what I suspected" (II.ii.87–92 [162]). Weakening under the assault of Orsino's seemingly mesmeric influence, Giacomo again pleads with him to leave off: "Spare me now!" (II.ii.92 [162]). All too late. As he will bitterly lament after being accused of Cenci's murder:

> O, had I never
> Found in thy smooth and ready countenance
> The mirror of my darkest thoughts; hadst thou
> Never with hints and questions made me look
> Upon the monster of my thought, until
> It grew familiar to desire (V.i.19–24 [188])

Orsino can correctly claim, "You cannot say / I urged you to the deed," but claims this knowing that verbal directness would only have counteracted his deployment of manipulative mirroring (V.ii.18–19 [188]). This is the same distorting or "monstrous" mirroring that Prometheus must resist in *Prometheus Unbound* – "Methinks I grow like what I contemplate / And laugh and stare in loathsome sympathy" (I.451–452 [223]) – and what some in the present have called "dark" empathy.[64]

Wishing to convey the sheer power and emotional intensity that the sympathetic relation can take, Hume describes moments when his own individual agency gives way, at least partially, to the desires and passion of the other: "no sooner any person approaches me, than he diffuses on me all his own opinions, and draws along my judgment in a greater or lesser degree."[65] Cenci's relentless program of verbal, physical, and finally sexual abuse of Beatrice seeks to prolong and greatly intensify such moments of other-identification, and the play attests to his success in doing so in a number of ways. One concerns the rhetoric of contamination. Cenci boasts to Lucretia, Beatrice's stepmother, that his daughter will soon "grope through a bewildering mist / Of horror" (II.i.184–185 [*SPP* 159]); in the aftermath of the rape, Beatrice tells Lucretia that a "clinging, black, contaminating mist" surrounds her, unconsciously deploying Cenci's own imagery to describe the contagious effect of his assault (III.i.17 [164]). Later in the same scene, she speaks of Cenci's blood circulating in her "contaminated veins" (III.i.96 [166]). Another textual manifestation of Cenci's successful infiltration of his daughter's subjectivity has Beatrice unknowingly adopting Cenci's rhetoric. In the play's opening scene, Cenci declares that he has "no remorse and little fear" (I.i.84 [147]); after agreeing to Cenci's murder, Beatrice tells Lucretia to put off "remorse and fear" (III.i.208–209 [168–169]).

If Beatrice comes most to resemble her father through planning and helping to execute his murder, one could argue that Count Cenci, foreseeing this very possibility, in fact plans the murder himself. Though rarely noted, Cenci seems to plant the seeds of his own murder in haranguing Lucretia over her alleged disloyalty. "You were not here conspiring?" he asks Lucretia as Beatrice and her younger brother Bernardo exit the stage (II.i.137 [*SPP* 158]). Were they not discussing:

> How just it were to hire assassins, or
> Put sudden poison in my evening drink?
> Or smother me when overcome by wine? (II.i.141–143 [158])

Not long afterward, Cenci will be strangled to death by hired assassins after Lucretia has put, not poison, but an opiate in his evening goblet of wine (IV.ii.30 [181]; IV.iii.45 [182–183]). If Cenci, who has tired of life, plans his own murder as part of his program of turning Beatrice into his mirror image, he seems to claim as much in hinting at an "act" that "shall soon extinguish all / For me" (II.i.188–189 [159]). All indeed.

Beatrice claims that the murder will have a mirror-like, homologous relation to the rape that it avenges – "something which will make / The thing that I have suffered but a shadow / In the dread lightning which avenges it" (III.i.87–89 [*SPP* 166]). One could also mention the ironic use of "atonement" – at once conveying revenge and a collapsing together of identities, at-one-ment – that occurs not once but three times in relation to the murder (III.i.215 [169]; III.i.333 [171]; IV.iv.92 [185]). And Cenci intimates the perverse mirroring – the loathsome sympathy – at the heart of his program when, during his extended curse on Beatrice, he hopes that she will bear a child, "a hideous likeness of herself, that as / From a distorting mirror, she may see / Her image mixed with what she most abhors" (IV.i.146–148 [179]). Her incestuous child, in other words, will both literalize and prolong the program of loathsome sympathy that Cenci's torment and rape of Beatrice have set in motion and that his murder has sealed.

"The minds of men are mirrors to one another," Hume writes of sympathy.[66] Smith suggests that without sympathy – without the ability to reflect on one's own actions and passions as we imagine others would regard them – one could have no sense of personal identity at all. So, a person growing up "solitary" from birth would have no way to regard his own "character" because "he is provided with no mirror" in which to consider himself: "Bring him into society, and he is immediately provided with the mirror which he wanted before."[67] If sympathy ultimately forms character, can a perverse kind of sympathy deform it? So Giacomo wonders in Act V, in his final interview with Orsino, "O, had I never / Found in thy smooth and ready countenance / The mirror of my darkest thoughts" (V.i.19–21 [*SPP* 188]). So, by Act V, the spectator or reader is forced to wonder of Beatrice, as Shelley certainly intended. "It is in the restless and anatomizing casuistry with which men seek the justification of Beatrice, yet feel that she has done what needs justification [...] that the dramatic character of what she did and suffered, consists" (142).

Mary Shelley considered Act V "a masterpiece," and one can imagine why she singled it out for special praise.[68] Primarily, the powerful emotional effect of this act relies on the splitting of our sympathetic response that Shelley seems to have aimed for all along, and the resulting "anatomizing" that links our own overcharged sympathetic faculties to those of the characters. Two features of the act seem designed to intensify such audience engagement: first, the way in which onstage sympathetic communication fails or malfunctions, particularly in relation to the Pope's reported responses (or rather, lack of responsiveness) when twice asked for a compassionate act of clemency. When even Barnardo, despite his guileless naivety, fails to move the Pope, his metaphor for losing Beatrice says more than he perhaps intends:

> To see
> That perfect mirror of pure innocence
> Wherein I gazed, and grew happy and good,
> Shivered to dust! (V.iv.129–132 [*SPP* 201])

The mirror of empathy, grown increasingly distorted throughout the play, altogether shatters at its end.

A second remarkable feature concerns the metatheatrical aspects of this final act, which not only stages a show trial of sorts (inquisition might be a better term) but regularly announces its own theatrical status. Orsino reports (in soliloquy) that he tried to "act a solemn comedy" (V.i.77 [*SPP* 190]); Beatrice denounces the trial as a "wicked farce" (V.ii.38 [191]). Later she worries that the inevitable public execution will constitute a "spectacle" compelling enough to empty the "theatres" (V.iii.38–39 [196]) – a claim that strikingly echoes Burke's contention that a notable public execution would result in the "emptiness of the theatre," such is the power of "real sympathy."[69]

These instances of metatheater underscore how eager Shelley was to have this play performed: in stark contrast to *Prometheus Unbound*, *The Cenci* certainly cannot be regarded as a closet drama. Rather, Shelley hoped that his dramatic verse would provoke sympathetic reactions in live audiences through its embodied performance by theatrically trained and charismatic actors. The role of Beatrice, in particular, he hoped would be played by Eliza O'Neill, an actress whose performances, according to Mary Shelley, had "deeply moved" him through the "intense pathos, and the sublime vehemence of passion she displayed."[70] Apparently for Shelley, an actress of O'Neill's caliber could provoke sympathetic reactions in the audience in spite of the considerable disadvantages of the London theaters of the day.[71]

Having begun by referring to empirical psychological studies of empathy and its possible relation to brain activity, I want to emphasize, before concluding, that I would not claim anything like psychological realism or even plausibility for Shelley's *The Cenci*. Shelley certainly attempted to endow his characters with something like real psychological mechanisms, drawing on the sympathy theory available to him and which I have reexamined in light of the current neuroscience of empathy. I find the correspondences between sympathy theory then and empathy research now of great interest, and at least some of the psychic mechanisms that both forms of inquiry attempt, however imperfectly, to describe may well prove real ones. Whether or not mirror neurons in humans turn out to have the importance recently ascribed to them, too much convincing empirical evidence for what one might term "mirror neuron *effects*" has mounted up to dismiss altogether – *some* kind of neural system, or combination of systems, must be functioning in more or less the ways that the mirror system is thought to function by researchers like Iacoboni and Ramachandran. But while Shelley based his main characters on historical originals, they remain literary constructs, and whatever Shelley himself thought, they do not seem to behave or react very much like real people might. Sadists and torturers like the historical Count Cenci tend to manifest marked deficits in empathy, not perverse or "dark" versions of empathy, in contrast to such fictional counterparts as Orwell's O'Brien, Harris's Hannibal Lecter, or Shelley's Cenci himself.

Still, the critical accounts of Bloom, Breithaupt, and others have brought out, at the very least, crucial limitations to human empathy, at a time when empathy has attained both a cult-like status and a significant market niche within our current twenty-first-century American moment. Writing in 2016, Bloom surveyed the Amazon.com book site and found "over fifteen hundred books" displaying the term "*empathy* in their title or subtitle."[72] He notes in particular books aimed at parents and teachers, self-help books, and guides to boost marketing and sales. This trend has shown no signs of diminishing over the five years since: a quick internet search today yields sites with titles like "8 Genius Examples of Empathic Content Marketing in Action" and a *Forbes* "council post" entitled "Empathy is the Key to Great Marketing." Empathy has itself become commoditized, as the *New York Times Magazine* acidly noted in reviewing a celebrity-studded and "seriously weird" Pharrell Williams "MasterClass" on empathy, one that apparently involves more self-promotion than genuine fellow-feeling: a "compilation of commodified theory of mind."[73]

If sheer overselling has begun to inspire widespread skepticism regarding empathy as social panacea, this may help to underscore its limitations, particularly in regard to some of the most vexing and potentially cataclysmic problems facing human beings at this time: climate change, habitat destruction, species extinction, and environmental degradation generally, not to mention global pandemics. Bloom cites climate change as a particularly glaring problem for which "empathy favors doing nothing."[74]

Empathy works at the level of individuals rather than populations and inevitably favors the local (on Hume's contiguity principle) over the global. The philosopher Jesse Prinz, in his own brief "Against Empathy," defines it as an "essentially dyadic emotion" arising "between two individuals," powerless to address large-scale problems: "Environmental destruction and widespread diseases cannot be combated by addressing the plight of a few individuals."[75] Faced with issues like global warming and the COVID-19 pandemic, our best hope may lie, Prinz declares, in the "extirpation of empathy."[76]

New developments in both the life sciences and the humanities may be converging toward a new consensus, not simply on the shortcomings of empathy but on the limitations of thinking in terms of individuals at all. In *Entangled Life*, for example, the biologist Merlin Sheldrake gestures toward both the massive and intricate web of interconnections in what we call "nature" and the (overlapping) web of interconnected species informing the "human" as well. "We are ecosystems, composed of – and decomposed by – an ecology of microbes [...] ecosystems that span boundaries and transgress categories": not least the category of the "individual."[77] The historian Dipesh Chakrabarty, in *The Climate of History in a Planetary Age*, similarly defines the planet as a "dynamic ensemble of relationships" among and across species, advocating a radically "new form of cosmopolitanism" that is "larger than the human" and capable of extending "ideas of politics and justice to the nonhuman, including both the living and the nonliving."[78] Mind-bending as they are, such proposals both adhere to the empirical findings and sophisticated models emerging out of fields like biology, neuroscience, and ecology and address the novel requirements of ethics and politics in a time of planetary crisis and the looming threat of extinction.

This does not mean preferring a utilitarian ethics of cool calculation over the human warmth associated with empathy. As Bloom notes, empathy can and should be distinguished from compassion, a feeling for rather than with suffering beings, one that can be broadly extended as in Buddhist teachings on "great compassion": "Less empathy," Bloom summarizes, "more kindness."[79] The Bodhisattva ideal of great compassion in Mahayana Buddhism, which Bloom cites, depends on practices that erode one's conviction in a separate, individual self; *karuna* (compassion), *anatman* ("no-self"), and *pratityasamutpada* (the mutual co-arising and interweaving of self and other) all name different facets of the Bodhisattva way.[80] We may seem to have strayed quite far here from Shelley. Yet the same poet who memorably embodied, in *The Cenci*, the figure of the perverse empath also offered, in *Prometheus Unbound*, an alternative highly resonant with the ideal of "great" or universal compassion pointed to by Bloom and central to the Mahayana schools of Buddhism (about which Shelley could have known virtually nothing).[81] Repeatedly assailed by the Furies' attempts to entrap him in a mirror relation of "loathsome sympathy," Prometheus prevails through taking up the universalizing compassion he simply, and powerfully, announces in retracting his curse on Jupiter: "I wish no living thing to suffer pain" (I.305 [*SPP* 218]). As the drama unfolds – or, rather, as dramatic tension gives way to lyric, choric, and hymnic modes – the borders between Prometheus and humankind increasingly blur and humankind as a whole emerges "Sceptreless, free, uncircumscribed" (III.iv.194 [269]).[82] In a word, unbound. The design of *The Cenci* and *Prometheus Unbound* taken together implies that the dyadic relation between individuals undergirding tragedy – as well as what we now call empathy – must at last give way to an unconstrained, selfless compassion if we are to join with other beings, living and nonliving, in repairing a damaged and afflicted world.

Notes

1 Alan Richardson, *A Mental Theater: Poetic Drama and Consciousness in the Romantic Age* (University Park: Penn State University Press, 1988), 100–123.
2 Richardson, *Literature, Education, and Romanticism: Reading as Social Practice* (Cambridge: Cambridge University Press, 1994).
3 See Ellen Spolsky, "Cognitive Literary Historicism: A Response to Adler and Gross," *Poetics Today* 24.2 (2003), 161–183; Richardson, *The Neural Sublime: Cognitive Theories and Romantic Texts* (Baltimore: Johns Hopkins University Press, 2010), 1–16; and Lisa Zunshine, "Introduction," in Zunshine, ed. *Introduction to Cognitive Cultural Studies* (Baltimore: Johns Hopkins University Press, 2015), 1–33.
4 For an early and influential statement on this point, see Patrick Colm Hogan, "Literary Universals," *Poetics Today* 18.2 (1997), 223–249.
5 Marco Iacoboni, *Mirroring People: The Science of Empathy and How We Connect with Others* (New York: Farrar, Straus and Giroux, 2009), 5.
6 See especially Gregory Hickok, *The Myth of Mirror Neurons: The Real Neuroscience of Communication and Cognition* (New York: Norton, 2014).
7 V. S. Ramachandran, "The Neurons That Shaped Civilization," in *The Tell-Tale Brain: A Neuroscientist's Quest for What Makes Us Human* (London: Norton, 2011), 117–135.
8 Ramachandran, "Neurons," 117, 133; Christian Jarrett, "Mirror Neurons: The Most Hyped Concept in Neuroscience?," *Psychology Today* (online), December 10, 2012.

9 See, for example, Iacoboni, *Mirroring People*, 106–129.
10 Iacoboni, *Mirroring People*, 106.
11 Iacoboni, *Mirroring People*, 107. For a more extended examination of connections between Smith's sympathy and mirror neuron research in the present, see L. Lynne Kiesling, "Mirror Neuron Research and Adam Smith's Concept of Sympathy: Three Points of Correspondence," *Review of Austrian Economics* 25.4 (December 2012), 299–313.
12 Sharon Ruston, *Shelley and Vitality* (Houndmills: Palgrave Macmillan, 2005), 74–101.
13 Richardson, *Neural Sublime*, 30–33.
14 Shelley, "A Defence of Poetry," in David Lee Clark, ed. *Shelley's Prose, or, The Trumpet of a Prophecy* (Albuquerque: University of New Mexico Press, 1954), 275–297, 282–283.
15 Jean-Jacques Rousseau, *Émile or Education*, trans. Allan Bloom (New York: Basic Books, 1979), 231.
16 Adam Smith, *The Theory of Moral Sentiments*, eds. D. D. Raphael and A. L. Macfie (Indianapolis: Liberty Press, 1982), 26.
17 David Hume, *A Treatise of Human Nature*, eds. David Fate Norton and Mary J. Norton (Oxford: Oxford University Press, 2000), 273.
18 Wendy S. Jones, "Emma, Gender, and the Mind-Brain," *ELH* 75.2 (2008), 327.
19 See, for example, Adela Pinch's influential reading of Hume in *Strange Fits of Passion: Epistemologies of Emotion, Hume to Austen* (Stanford: Stanford University Press, 1996), 17–50.
20 Hume, *Treatise*, 239–240.
21 Hume, *Treatise*, 206–207.
22 Hume, *Treatise*, 206.
23 Hume, *Treatise*, 207.
24 Hume, *Treatise*, 2.
25 Hume, *Treatise*, 225.
26 Hume, *Treatise*, 368.
27 Hume, *Treatise*, 378.
28 Smith, *Moral Sentiments*, 10, 9.
29 Smith, *Moral Sentiments*, 134.
30 Smith, *Moral Sentiments*, 9.
31 Smith, *Moral Sentiments*, 11.
32 Smith, *Moral Sentiments*, 11.
33 Smith, *Moral Sentiments*, 10.
34 Smith, *Moral Sentiments*, 12.
35 Smith, *Moral Sentiments*, 12.
36 Smith, *Moral Sentiments*, 12–13.
37 Edmund Burke, *A Philosophical Enquiry into the Origin of Our Idea of the Sublime and Beautiful and Other Pre-revolutionary Writings*, ed. David Womersley (London: Penguin, 1998), 49–199, 73.
38 Burke, *A Philosophical Enquiry*, 91.

39 Vanessa L. Ryan, "The Physiological Sublime: Burke's Critique of Reason," *Journal of the History of Ideas* 62.1 (April 2001), 265–279.
40 Burke, *A Philosophical Enquiry*, 94–95.
41 Burke, *A Philosophical Enquiry*, 162.
42 James Hogg, *The Private Memoirs and Confessions of a Justified Sinner*, ed. John Wain (Harmondsworth: Penguin, 1986), 127, 132; Edgar Allan Poe, "The Purloined Letter," W. H. Auden, ed. *Selected Poetry, Prose, and Eureka* (New York: Holt, Rinehart, and Winston, 1950), 106. The Poe example is discussed in Iacoboni, 119–120.
43 Iacoboni, *Mirroring People*, 118–119.
44 Rousseau, *Émile*, 222.
45 Rousseau, *Émile*, 223.
46 Rousseau, *Émile*, 251.
47 Rousseau, *Émile*, 226.
48 Rousseau, *Émile*, 227.
49 Ildiko Csengei, *Sympathy, Sensibility, and the Language of Feeling in the Eighteenth Century* (New York: Palgrave Macmillan, 2012), 31, 54.
50 Csengei, *Language of Feeling*, 44.
51 David Marshall, *The Figure of Theater: Shaftesbury, Defoe, Adam Smith, and George Eliot* (New York: Columbia University Press, 1986), 167–192; see also Marshall, *The Surprising Effects of Sympathy: Marivaux, Diderot, Rousseau, and Mary Shelley* (Chicago: University of Chicago Press, 1988), 3–5.
52 Nigel Leask, "Shelley's 'Magnetic Ladies': Romantic Mesmerism and the Politics of the Body," in Stephen Copley and John Whale, eds. *Beyond Romanticism: New Approaches to Texts and Contexts 1780–1832* (London: Routledge, 2016), 65–67.
53 For a suggestive reading of *The Cenci* in terms of "nervous action" and in relation to Romantic-era neurology, see Matthew Wilson Smith, *The Nervous Stage: Nineteenth-Century Neuroscience and the Birth of Modern Theatre* (New York: Oxford University Press, 2018), 37–44.
54 Giacomo Rizzolatti and Corrado Sinigaglia, *Mirrors in the Brain: How Our Minds Share Actions and Emotions*, trans. Frances Anderson (Oxford: Oxford University Press, 2008), 190–191.
55 Grit Hein and Tania Singer, "I See How You Feel but Not Always: The Empathic Brain and Its Modulation," *Current Opinion in Neurobiology* 18 (2008), 153–158, 154.
56 Paul Bloom, *Against Empathy: The Case for Rational Compassion* (New York: HarperCollins, 2016), 37.
57 Fritz Breithaupt cites the fictional character Hannibal Lecter (best known from the 1991 Jonathan Demme film *The Silence of the Lambs*) as a prime example of "empathetic sadism" in *The Dark Sides of Empathy*, trans. Andrew B. B. Hamilton (Ithaca: Cornell University Press, 2019), 173–174. The Hannibal Lecter character was created by the novelist Thomas Harris, initially in *The Red Dragon* (New York: Putnam, 1981).
58 Bloom, *Against Empathy*, 37–38.

59 Richardson, "Facial Expression Theory from Romanticism to the Present," *Introduction to Cognitive Cultural Studies*, ed. Lisa Zunshine (Baltimore: Johns Hopkins University Press, 2010), 65–83.
60 Charles Bell, *Essays on the Anatomy of Expression in Painting* (London: Longman, Hurst, Rees, and Orme, 1806); rev. as *The Anatomy and Philosophy of Expression as Connected with the Fine Arts*, 7th ed. (London: George Bell, 1877).
61 For representative discussions of levels of embedment see Lisa Zunshine, "Theory of Mind and Experimental Representations of Fictional Consciousness," *Narrative* 11.3 (October 2003), 270–291 and Zunshine, "Why Jane Austen Was Different, and Why We May Need Cognitive Science to See It," *Style* 41.3 (Fall 2007), 273–297.
62 Hume, *Treatise*, 255.
63 Richardson, *A Mental Theater*, 106–113.
64 In addition to Hein and Singer, "I See How You Feel but Not Always," see especially Breithaupt, *The Dark Sides of Empathy*.
65 Hume, *Treatise*, 378.
66 Hume, *Treatise*, 236.
67 Smith, *Moral Sentiments*, 110.
68 Mary Shelley, "Note on The Cenci," in Roland A. Duerkson, ed. *Appendix I to The Cenci* (Indianapolis: Bobbs-Merrill, 1970), 113.
69 Burke, *A Philosophical Enquiry*, 93.
70 Shelley, "Note on *The Cenci*," 111.
71 Joanna Baillie's "Introductory Discourse" to her *Plays on the Passions* emphasizes these limitations, advocating a smaller, more intimate theatrical space so that audience members can see (and respond to) the actors' facial expressions and minute gestures. As does Shelley in *The Cenci*, Baillie also includes careful description of gestures and facial expressions in her tragedies. See my essay "A Neural Theater: Joanna Baillie's Plays on the Passions," in Thomas Crochunis, ed. *Joanna Baillie, Romantic Dramatist: Critical Essays* (New York: Routledge, 2004), 130–145.
72 Bloom, *Against Empathy*, 19.
73 Mireille Silcoff, "What Can You Learn from a Celebrity Masterclass on Empathy?" *The New York Times Magazine*, December 14, 2021, online. www.nytimes.com/2021/12/14/magazine/celebrity-empathy.html#:~:text=But%20mainly%2C%20what%20this%20Masterclass,ones%20that%20actually%20need%20filling.&text=Mireille%20Silcoff%20is%20a%20writer%20based%20in%20Montreal.
74 Bloom, *Against Empathy*, 126–127.
75 Jesse Prinz, "Against Empathy," *The Southern Journal of Philosophy* 49.s1, Special supplement (2011), 228–229.
76 Prinz, "Against Empathy," 228.
77 Merlin Sheldrake, *Entangled Life: How Fungi Make Our Worlds, Change Our Minds and Shape Our Futures* (New York: Random House, 2020), 337, 360.

78 Dipesh Chakrabarty, *The Climate of History in a Planetary Age* (Chicago: University of Chicago Press, 2021), 13, 47, 70.
79 Bloom, *Against Empathy*, 138.
80 For an introduction to Mahayana Buddhist teachings in relation to our current moment of ecological crisis, see John Daido Loori, *Teachings of the Earth: Zen and the Environment* (Boston: Shambhala Press, 2007).
81 Mark S. Lussier notes Shelley's lack of any "special knowledge" of Buddhist traditions, while relating the passage of Shelley's Prometheus "beyond suffering and selfhood" to the Mahayana ideal of "great compassion" in *Romantic Dharma: The Emergence of Buddhism into Nineteenth-Century Europe* (New York: Palgrave Macmillan, 2011), 91.
82 See Lussier's reading of *Prometheus Unbound* in relation to Mahayana Buddhist teachings in *Romantic Dharma*, 88–112, which parallels (as Lussier notes) my reading in *A Mental Theater*, 124–153.

CHAPTER 7

Hopeless Romanticism

Gerard Cohen-Vrignaud

In an 1810 issue of *The Examiner*, Leigh Hunt defended himself and his fellow reformers from "the charge of being *romantic*, that is, of indulging in fanciful speculations inconsistent with the nature of politics and mankind [...] he is said to be *romantic*, – a well-meaning man, but too lively in his imagination, – a man of good natural sense, but utterly unacquainted, poor fellow, with the world." Hunt counted himself among these romantics against whom *they*, wizened skeptics of change, offered only "affected ridicule" and disdain:

> [W]e differ [...] in having reasonable expectations of political honesty, in thinking that it is *possible* for the present system of things to be considerably *purified*, and in endeavouring to bring about so desirable and so necessary an event. They may, if they please, think it romantic to hope for political virtue [...] to look for a better state of affairs, to attempt the purity of elections and the responsibility of rulers, and to endeavour at freeing ourselves from the perpetual waste of treasure and blood.[1]

Though Hunt is keen to portray as "reasonable" the hopes some of his contemporaries mocked, this essay dwells upon this political attunement generically coded as "being *romantic*," articulated through a "we" that "differ[s]" from the status quo and "look[s]" forward to "a better state."

Heading into a decade of domestic activism in Britain, Hunt's lead article highlights the everyday, often pejorative use of the word "romantic," which predates and postdates its periodizing sense, derived etymologically from "romance," the genre that most caters to the "too lively [...] imagination" memorably satirized by *Don Quixote* and many imitators since.[2] Scholars don't usually appreciate when their specialist vocabulary is promiscuously applied by the general public. As Raymond Williams put it in his account of modern tragedy, "it is very common" for those "trained in [...] the academic tradition to be impatient and even contemptuous of what they regard as loose and vulgar uses of 'tragedy' in ordinary speech and in the newspapers."[3] But Williams goes on to argue for the relevance of heartrending events commonly labeled "tragic" to the mechanics of theatrical tragedy. Likewise, I am drawn to the "loose" and popular understanding of romantics, though my focus here is on what this style reveals about their aestheticized stance toward political reality rather than the literary genre itself. The ubiquitous epithet of "romantic" betrays undeniable ambivalence as to the "hope for political virtue" that characterizes fervent reformers. Through the case of Shelley and the sometimes-dismissive reactions he has provoked, this chapter explores what it means – politically and aesthetically – when a genre (romance) becomes a personality type (the romantic).

As our period's scholars have long emphasized, one cannot disentangle Romanticism from its association with the "romantic" tropes of the medieval genre, from the "internalized quest" of the era's lyrics to the reworking of romance tropes by second-generation Romantics.[4] But this chapter is less interested in the conventions of romance than its generic tendency to leap imaginatively past probability's limitations. The genre's commonplaces certainly conform to this inclination: the impossible quest, the unconsummated, idealized love, the supernatural obstacles and miraculous escapes, the high-flown sentiments, all these features characterize romance enthusiasts as favoring a dreamscape of "fanciful speculations." As Hunt's words reveal, there are two vectors to this stigma. On the one hand, calling out a romantic amounts to "affected ridicule" on the "well-meaning" by those who claim to be better "acquainted" with "the nature of politics and mankind." On the other hand, the defiant embrace of romance by the political reformer telegraphs a willingness to appear a "beautiful and ineffectual angel, beating in the void his luminous wings in vain," as Matthew Arnold unforgettably damned Shelley.[5]

What this state of affairs for the romantic reveals is that everywhere realism prevails over romance as the social style of maturity. A sober Charlotte Lucas thus answers Elizabeth Bennet's shock at her marriage with Mr. Collins by saying, "I am not romantic you know."[6] This norm makes the historical emergence of Romanticism all the more surprising. How to account for an aesthetic movement whose very name rests on the embarrassing reality-avoidance of romance, rendered notorious by the enduring joke of that "poor fellow," Don Quixote? Romanticism certainly deepens the philosophical, aesthetic, and political gravitas of romance, moving beyond the genre's frivolous fabulation and toward the grandeur of faith and commitment.[7] In deifying the imagination, Romanticism erects a civic religion of the human spirit in which preferring the potential over the actual becomes program rather than pathology. Nonetheless, Romanticism's generic lineage indelibly locates its roots in our lowly taste for visions often derided as escapist: as David Duff puts it, romance's "imaginative force was recognized, but its legitimacy not generally accepted."[8] The same may be said for Romanticism insofar as popular parlance, which opposes the "romantic" to the "realist," reveals ours to be a school for fantasists.

This common-sense take on romantic illegitimacy has been grounded less in the genre itself than in the deluded characters ensnared by it (from Don Quixote to Emma Bovary and on). A young David Hume thus rehearses his precocious skepticism by witheringly indicting the type of "human Mind [...] smit with any Idea of Merit or Perfection beyond what its Faculties can attain," which therefore "runs in a moment quite wide of Nature," "indulges its devout Fervors," and "raises up to itself a new set of Passions, Affections, Desires, and Objects, & in short a perfectly new World of its own, inhabited by different Beings, & regulated by different Laws, from this of ours."[9] Enlightened realism derives its identity from its temperate opposition to romantic excesses (perfectionism, emotivity, exciting visions unfettered from natural laws, the aesthetic equivalent to religious devotion). By contrast, Romanticism emerged in consonance with this generic inclination, in Hunt's words, for engineering "a better state of affairs" by "freeing ourselves" from "the present system of things." Political struggles for equality and justice have benefited greatly from a steady stream of such romantics "born for opposition" because they "pine for what is not" (87 [*SPP* 306]).[10]

The "hopeless" epithet not infrequently appended to "romantic" is of more recent vintage, particularly denoting an irrational attachment to "perfect" love, as seemingly unattainable today as in medieval romance. But whether the object with which it is "smit" is sexual or political, the romance mind is characterized by this errant yearning for what is admittedly distant and idealized. The sobriquet "hopeless" marks this romantic as lost to society, often self-confessedly, while also stressing that this terminal condition arises from a hopelessness about the real that gives rise to compensatory – and often illusory – hopes. What the mind cannot "attain," in Hume's words, in the present due to usual "Nature," provokes the romantic's characteristic turns between despair and desire for something "perfectly new." This chapter names as "hopeless romanticism" this generic style of willed maladjustment to reality, which I find exemplified in the life and poetry of Percy Shelley. This romantic disposition derives from the habitual mechanics of hope, which is intrinsically bifurcated, fluctuating between the pain of present dissatisfaction and the joy of future possibility. Characteristically, Shelley's writing often toggles between a dismal account of how things are and optimism for a better tomorrow. Hope's alternating currents of negative and positive affect can be diagnosed psychologically as "maniac" bipolarity (the maid of *The Mask of Anarchy*), philosophically as "skeptical idealism," or formally in the figurative aporias of Shelley's signification.

Of the Romantics, Shelley is perhaps the one most consistently cast as hopelessly naïve for refusing to bound his expectations for world transformation. From his ill-fated foray to Ireland to distribute radical pamphlets to his ambition to publish politically impactful poetry, Shelley stayed recalcitrantly committed to hopes often frustrated, in his lifetime, by unkind reality. Everywhere in his poetry, we find Shelley acknowledging this clash through the play of light and dark, as in *The Revolt of Islam*, where Laon continually strains to promote a vision of future good against the engulfing evils of his age.[11] There is a hint of the hopeless romantic's typical masochism in Shelley's appreciation for "the glorious doom / Of those who sternly struggle to relume / The lamp of Hope o'er man's bewildered lot" (IV.vii.58–60 [*CP* III: 183]). To call the despondency induced by the often dismal "lot" of humanity "glorious" is to find transcendence in the beleaguered battle for reformation. Shelley's predilection for the Enlightenment dialectic of light and dark manifests affectively in his recurring exploration of what it means to dwell in "those dim labyrinths, where / Hope, near imagined chasms, is struggling with despair" (X.xlvi.4205–4206 [294]). Whereas many scholars have wished to find intellectual coherence or programmatic consistency in the antitheses of Shelley's imaginary,[12] I am more inclined to attribute this poetic "struggle" to the temperamental lot of the hopeless romantic, who finds both joy and terror in the "imagined chasms" of an uncertain future (the present being intolerable).

Biography is not irrelevant to Shelley's legacy because appreciation for his poetry has often hinged on opinions on his dogged and disappointed idealism. Political publics and counterpublics come into being not only in reaction to events, issues, and ideology but also in stylistic attunement to the outsized figures who(m they elect to) represent them. Shelley's reception is a case in point. The divisiveness generated by his characteristic drive toward the ideal has everything to do with the way personalities such as his have become partisan objects of avowal and disavowal in mass-mediated democracy. Shelley has thus provoked a number of traditional "critics complaining about [his] effeminacy, or immaturity, or political naivety," from T. S. Eliot's accusation of "adolescence" to F. R. Leavis's critique of his having "a weak grasp on the actual."[13] Both of these accusations (youth, anti-empiricism) are tied to Shelley's insistence that the existence of hope is itself sufficient cause for hope. Shelley's defenders, for their part, work to counter the facile classification of him as a "mere escapist."[14]

From Shelley's time to the present, the sympathy with or antipathy to his hopes has revolved around the predisposition of critics to admit his style of wishful thinking. As one sonneteer wrote in response to the poorly received *The Revolt of Islam*, "The heart that could conceive so bright a day, / Is proof that it may come," concluding, "thou shalt smile and pity, giving thy youth / To glorious hopes, and all-defying Truth."[15] Shelley's hopes – evidenced here by the Spenser-inspired romance he had just published – become "proof" that "so desirable and so necessary an event" as progress may be at hand. Shelley's cultural resonance lies not only in the transmissibility of his verse's feelings (the poet's primary talent as Wordsworth argued) but also in the historical force he incarnates. The stress on Shelley's "youth" here or his fairy-like luminosity in other accounts hints at the way his person condenses an ideological program into a fixed image that can circulate as an icon of either inspiration or naïveté.

Then, as now, the possibility of identifying with Shelley is entwined with a parallel disidentification from the first-generation Romantics who turned their back on democracy, in particular Wordsworth and Southey, who vocally supported anti-revolutionary efforts as well as the Georgian status quo: "Mr. Wordsworth has become hopeless of this world, and therefore would make every body else so; – Mr. Shelley is superior to hopelessness itself; and does not see why all happiness and all strength is to be bounded by what he himself can feel or can effect."[16] This partisan reckoning endures not only for literary-historical reasons but also because it adumbrates the typical stages of political life, from youthful hope and faith in change to adult disappointment, resignation, and "sobriety."[17] Filiation results, as Hunt's words show, from choosing to embrace the personality of Shelley rather than that of Wordsworth. The publicly played-out rivalry of Shelley with the predecessor who inspired him amplifies this ideological rift into a generational dynamic, even as each writer in himself offers ample evidence that this divide between political hope and despair is not only individual and partisan but also internal to all feeling selves capable of evolution, apostasy, and inconsistency.

The centrality of hope to Shelley's biography and poetry manifests in what many critics have recognized as his future orientation. Andrew Franta thus argues that Shelley's poems are addressed to audiences to come while Forest Pyle suggests that "the critical redemption value of Shelley's poetry" lies "in its blank opening onto futurity."[18] Pyle comes to this verdict via the abrupt pivot at the end of "England in 1819." The imbalance between the first twelve lines of evils afflicting Shelley's age and the final couplet's turn to a bright and "blank" future appears unabashedly incongruous. As James Chandler remarks, "when this sort of resolution occurs in comedy we call it 'deus ex machina' and label the work sentimental."[19] Though acutely described, contemporary facts "are" proleptically dispatched to "graves from which a glorious Phantom may / Burst, to illumine our tempestuous day" (13–14 [*SPP* 327]). Given their intractability, these realities can only be interred by conjuring a fantastic light show barely justified by the "glorious" revolutionary precedent 130 years prior. "May" certainly hedges the bet but the sonnet's volta remains scandalously divorced from the quatrains. Even as the poem's title avows historicity, then, it disregards temporal constraint through a supernatural "Phantom" whose nebulousness recalls the present's haunting by the future's shadows in Shelley's *A Defence of Poetry*. That this political deliverance is engineered through the sonnet's form reinforces the sense that the aesthetic is in league with a taste for fantasy and repudiating reality.

No wonder then that this turn has produced robust responses from critics. Much of the interpretation has focused, as Susan Wolfson points out, on which of two meanings of "may" – uncertainty or capability – to privilege and whether the enjambing "burst" of the final line announces Shelley's revolutionary intentions, as Stuart Curran argues.[20] While I agree with Wolfson that this political "question" is "ultimately undecidable," I'm less intent on elaborating the historical and ideological contradictions the sonnet indexes through its formal ambiguity than in emphasizing Shelley's "sentimental" turn.[21] The logic at work here, as elsewhere in his poetry, is less formalist or Whiggish-historical than affective. Leavis forcefully calls out this motive force in decrying "the pathetic weakness" of the final couplet, which makes an "eloquent" contrast with the "unusual strength (for Shelley)" of the preceding lines.[22] Leavis's criticism is chiefly characterological as the parenthetical attack on Shelley's general "weakness" makes clear: "Contemplation of the actual world being unendurable, Shelley devotes himself to the glorious Phantom that may [...] work a sudden miraculous change but is in any case as vague as Demogorgon and as unrelated to actuality."[23] Leavis finds the first twelve lines bracing and the wishful end feeble. This disjuncture typifies Shelley, given to "visionary drift" without "reference to any grasped reality."[24] The final couplet's "pathetic weakness," in the twinned senses of pitiable and pathos-filled, indexes the character of one who finds reality "unendurable" and turns toward the "miraculous agency" of fantasy.[25]

But this weakness also highlights the strength of pathos itself, as hope turns the inherent uncertainty of the future into imagined capability. The hesitation in Shelley's focalized "may" points to hope as the fulcrum feeling to a better "day"; the enjambment registers the way hope can "burst" affectively past present circumstances it wishfully transforms into "graves." If it is apt to classify this mix of struggle and scruple as symptomatic of Shelley's "skeptical idealism," at the same time, this paradoxical label would make into principle what I am arguing is a generic aspect of hope, "an inconstant joy" as Baruch Spinoza called it long ago:

> [T]here is neither hope without fear, nor fear without hope. For he who is suspended in hope and doubts a thing's outcome is supposed to imagine something which excludes the existence of the future thing. And so to that extent he is saddened, and consequently, while he is suspended in hope, he fears that the thing [he imagines] will happen.[26]

In other words, the equivocation that critics have long appreciated in Shelley's verse is not only an intellectual insight but also a result of his hopeless romanticism. Suspension or vacillation within the affective operations of hope at once enables its imaginative movement back and forth between despised present and desired future and gives it the kind of persistence that more univocal feelings rarely achieve. Hopes become socially structuring and saturating insofar as they are amplified in the symbolic oscillation between depressing and uplifting representations of what is and what could be. They thereby achieve an afterlife in the mimetic feelings and psychic investments they produce in publics, whose mass-mediated politics exist in a temporality beyond that of individual feelings.

Here it is apposite to turn to Shelley's depiction of Hope in *The Mask of Anarchy*, which points at once to its social promise, its origins in disappointment, and its unsure power. Hope often arises from a position of weakened agency, made overt in her gendered personification as a "maniac maid" whose "name was Hope, [...] / But she looked more like Despair" (86–88 [*SPP* 319]).[27] As Morton Paley points out, her "maniac" energy echoes that of Martha Ray, from Wordsworth's "The Thorn," who shares Hope's lament, "Misery, oh Misery!"[28] Shelley casts Hope in this especially doleful image, tied to the frustration of love and the supposed loss of a baby, as the gossip in Wordsworth's poem has it. The intertextual echo reinforces Shelley's sociological sense of hope as the recourse of the disenfranchised (or disowned in his own case), those whose autonomy is compromised. The medically pathologizing term "maniac" captures the affective split that shapes the mental landscape of the hopeless romantic, who wavers between an irrational exuberance founded on little more than tantalizing possibility and the depressive background always at the ready to puncture this imaginative effervescence. That the word "despair" etymologically contains hope – from the French negation *dés-espoir* – highlights how much the positive feeling itself is dependent on the misery that gives it occasion. These psychosocial factors give Hope that appearance of "pathetic weakness" common to those of limited sovereignty who yet reject submission to probability's chains.

But, of course, in *The Mask*, Hope's frailty becomes a strength as miraculous as the concluding lunge of "England in 1819." Though Hope cannot fight the overwhelming parade of atrocities riding toward her, she nonetheless manages to block their passage: "Then she lay down in the street, / Right before the horses' feet, / Expecting, with a patient eye, / Murder, Fraud, and Anarchy" (98–101 [*SPP* 319]). Hope's stoppage has often been taken as the earliest representation of nonviolent protest, the action of challenging the status quo by physically declining to let things proceed usually. More generally, though, we might say that hope is an affective version of passive resistance to stifling realities. The refusal to play one's assigned part in the "masque" of the actual is what makes hope agentive but also problematic, because Hope's focus on a distant prospect literally arrests the development in front of her. The invocation of "feet" points at once to the moving train of oppression's apocalyptic horses and to Hope giving up use of her own. Of course, the forward operations of the verse, with its mostly trochaic lines, continue but the poem's plot, in a sense, stops in its tracks here, as yet another ill-defined "Shape" appears climatologically to vanquish reality, succeeded by a spontaneous address describing England's ills and prophesying better times for its people (110).

In doing little but pausing traffic, Hope opens up a space for the force of futurity. This magical transmutation of oppressive reality is the poem's aesthetic legerdemain, a wish fulfillment given an amorphous Shape that reflects hope's capacity to take any form it imagines by jettisoning any facts it wishes.[29] Hope has no reason to believe she will not be crushed but then inexplicably "ankle-deep in blood, / Hope that maiden most serene / Was walking with a quiet mien" (127–129 [*SPP* 320]). Going from "maniac" to "serene," Hope moves past her psychic split as despair's conditions are routed by the Shape, even as the "ankle-deep [...] blood" presents a chilling précis for an actual history of lived struggle. Hope is now "walking" in an echo of the Shape's movement, whose "presence" everyone senses but cannot see "all was empty air": "Thoughts sprung where'er that step did fall" (121, 125 [319]). While the repeated stress on the "footstep" of the

Shape picks up on the locomotion of the poem's personified characters, nonetheless no observable physical reality embodies this *élan vital* beyond Hope's im/mobility (122 [319]). The oppression-defeating "Shape" emerges only with a sequential "When," the same word that introduces Hope (102, 86 [319]). The causal mechanics here rely on a providential temporality or necessity assimilated to the natural cycle, with blustery echoes of Shelley's "Ode to the West Wind." The Shape grows like clouds do; its "steps" pass over human heads "as wind" provoking new "thoughts" (118 [319]). This emergence modeled on meteorological processes suggests that despair must seasonally give way to hope, for "If Winter comes, can Spring be far behind?" (70 [301]).

At the same time, the revolutions (or turns) of cyclical regeneration do not preclude revolutions of rupture and progress. Hope explains her own appearance by invoking her parent, "father Time," whom she describes as

> weak and gray
> With waiting for a better day;
> See how idiot-like he stands,
> Fumbling with his palsied hands!
>
> He has had child after child,
> And the dust of death is piled
> Over every one but me—
> Misery, oh Misery! (90–97 [*SPP* 319])

The characterization of aged Time again puts the stress on weakness, illness, and disability, echoing a feminized Hope's social alterity and physical vulnerability. But if hopes proverbially spring eternal and die as perpetually, Time is also "waiting" for one particular hope to survive, as of course happens when the maniac maid improbably outlasts the poem's tyrannical instruments. Progressive time is imagined in this awaited "better day" that grounds the concluding speech.

The poem's ending vision is more than just spring's seasonal "step" forward "after" winter darkness, as we see in the final address, "as if" spoken by mother nature: "Men of England, heirs of Glory, / Heroes of unwritten story, / Nurslings of one mighty Mother, / Hopes of her, and one another" (147–150 [*SPP* 320]). With this stanza, the only one in the poem entirely in feminine rhyme, Shelley again emphasizes the gendered (perhaps even feminist)[30] agency of hope, which represents, as I have argued, the feeling's endemicity in the experience of the dispossessed. The "weakness" of "waiting," "expecting," and being "patient" is one feature of hopeless romanticism that especially grates those attached to liberal-individualist models of "strong" sovereignty. The "as if" qualification introducing Earth's oration at once emphasizes the speculative nature of these hopes and refuses to locate them in an actual agent, as though they awaited embodiment in the future offspring of the great Mother. If hopes are the individualized "nurslings" of both Time and "one mighty Mother," they are also what bind humans morally in a generational compact with "one another." The poem suggests that while hopes may be frequently buried under "the dust of death," some do produce effects, "unwritten" a "story" as though they may yet be at the time they appear. The introduction of narrative here tilts the procreative impulse away from seasonal hopes eternally born and dying toward the potential for writing a progressive history, in the "better day" that *tellingly* diverges from the story often told, "child after child."

Turning to the flip side of allegory, not abstraction but personage, Hope is also a young woman whose protest, as a number of critics have pointed out, approximates "an image transplanted from contemporary newspaper reports" of Peterloo.[31] Her pose enacts both negation of the present and orientation toward the future. Even if all she seems to be doing in this instance is "expecting, with a patient eye, Murder, Fraud, and Anarchy," the actual threat in front of her does not move her (affectively or physically) because she is eying and animated by another viewpoint (100–101 [*SPP* 319]). The poem's various terms for anticipation here point to the potential power of expectation. As the specific hopes of individuals become a shared structure of feeling, they take on the sort of horizon-resetting force (or "Shape") that can manifest with hindsight as historical inevitability. This temporal gap between the situational emergence of hopes and their possible fulfillment in a "better day" makes it particularly fitting that both Shelley's *The Mask* and "England in 1819" should have been belatedly published in the 1830s, when a number of reformist demands would ultimately, if only partly, be realized. This achievement, along with the eventual dissemination and impact of Shelley's popular radical poems, enacts at the biographical level just the sort of providential trajectory that hope promises.[32]

Looking at the matter historically, Shelley was not wrong to attribute so much power to a feeling rooted in powerlessness. Hope for political reform is what sparked the tens of thousands who demonstrated regularly in the years leading up to Peterloo and even after. How could these disenfranchised protesters conceive of changing things in "probably the most oppressive decade in British history since the Renaissance"?[33] Certainly, the French Revolution gave many the notion that inequitable structures were not fixed forever, but then the restoration of monarchy across Europe after 1814 would seem to have dealt a *coup de grâce* to these dawning ambitions.

But despair itself clears the stage for hope, as shown by the tacit affective logic that drives the "glorious" turns of "England in 1819" and *The Mask*. This is the paradox of hope: it appears unmoored from "the heavy weight of hours" and yet this unmooring is at the same time what – perhaps, eventually – enables alternate realities to emerge, to "quicken a new birth" (55, 64 [*SPP* 300]).[34] Hopes may have no effect in the moment on the way the world works or the unfolding of our personal lives but theirs is "a sense awakening," the verdict of our misery, and attachment to their visions becomes "at once a prophesy and a cause," as Shelley put it in a letter to Hunt (136 [320]).[35]

Because hopes just as often, if not more frequently, die "piled" high, our attachment to them can also be understood as injurious, as Lee Edelman has recently argued in relation to Shelley. Suspension in what Edelman ruefully calls "the romance of temporality" can appear as avoidant of reality, in particular the actual joys available.[36] Hope can sustain the individualizing fantasy that good things will come even as all evidence around us suggests that political and economic structures are made to deny happiness to the mass of humanity. This is a problem more generally with romance, as Lauren Berlant has argued: our optimism about what is around the corner – paradigmatically in the love plot – keeps us attached to systems that do not, on the whole, work for our flourishing.[37] These queer critics insist on the structure of deferral built into this expectant turn to the future, the illusory "promise of happiness" always over the horizon, but their hard-earned wisdom cannot (or has yet to) lessen hope's appeal.[38]

Moreover, this queer scholarship, in its various ways, problematizes the cathecting of political energies onto the figural repository of the child.[39] If critiques of hope as jejune, ineffectual, and self-defeating abound, the feeling appears inevitable because it is tied to the renewal of humanity in "child after child" (94 [*SPP* 319]). It makes sense that the youngest would be associated with hope, for time's passage accumulates "the dust of death" that is "piled" on our dreams. Without the weight of that experience, the young more easily inhabit the perspective of hope. Or, as Shelley puts it in *The Revolt of Islam*, "Hope will make thee young, for Hope and Youth / Are children of one mother" (VIII.xxvii.236–237 [*CP* III: 262]). But the birth of progressive history has also made the hopeless romantic into a subject position available past the years of youth. Indeed, the epithet itself indicates a perverse will to indulge what might be considered infantile wishes well beyond the time of our inexperience. They are "hopeless" not because without hopes – after all, their defining feature is a preference for unrealized futures – but rather because, from the perspective of society, they refuse the only "real" satisfactions to be had. Their attachment to unrealized hopes can thus be taken as an immature refusal to participate in the actually existing. No wonder then that Shelley, whose early death spared us the reactionary later years characteristic of Wordsworth, Southey, and Coleridge, should so often be depicted as naïve and childlike.

At the same time, even as hope may be complicit with passivity and suffering, Berlant acknowledges it as "a scene of negotiated sustenance that makes life bearable."[40] In this regard, then, hope allows one to feel better than one ought to, that is, to live affectively beyond one's means. In Shelley's words, hope "can borrow / For poor to-day, from rich tomorrow."[41] The financial language acknowledges that hope's fancy (imagination's lesser, materialist sibling) gilds meager reality but also the fact that hopes often revolve around yearnings for economic access. Hence, *The Mask*'s emphasis on the precarity of the working classes, whose exploitation is the main evil to be rectified when they "rise like Lions after slumber" (368 [*SPP* 326]). A series of parodic banknotes from the 1810s broadcast this point more explicitly by playing on the controversial replacement of metal currencies by what *The Mask* calls the "forgery" of "paper coin" (180 [321]). Each "promissory" note is framed by paper money's "promise to pay" a sum upon a certain date. But instead of an actual deadline, the banknotes invoke the execution of some political and economic change: sometimes the alteration is wished for and other times it is rebuffed.[42] One note, for instance, attacks the legal system by promising to pay "when the glorious uncertainty of the Law shall have ceased and [...] Attornies [...] shall have gained integrity," signed for "Self, Simple & Pennyless, Simon Lostall." One striking aspect is that this note's grievance (the unfairness of the courts and the law) endures to this day. The dashing of hopes, their failure to come true, does not destroy the ambitions they register, which is part of the reason that "father Time" is incessantly siring them.

The ironic tone of the banknote only heightens the pathos of the "simple" self that has "lost all" except the hope onto which he hangs. The "when" of hope's promise represents the limit point between an impoverished now and a richer, potential future. While these notes rehearse radicals' assorted hopes for progress, they simultaneously pulse with doubts and fears of failure. In parodying the promissory note's legal guarantee, these bills invoke the questionable security of a financial instrument to show the insecurity of hope itself. The only guarantor is the feeling self who imaginatively bridges the divide between an unbearable present and a "better day." This is signaled by another banknote that hopes never to pay its "two pence" because the trifecta of Magna Carta, trial by jury, and Francis Burdett "shall" never "have ceased." The constitutional document is pictured in the corner, "although mutilated, still in existence." This representation points self-referentially to the nature of inscribed paper as a repository of the hopes it records. Founded on an affective compact, partly trust and partly hope, paper promises, much like hopes, cannot be safeguarded by more than affective adherence, as suggested by the mutilated Magna Carta, whose guarantee of habeas corpus, for instance, was suspended twice in the period. These notes' skepticism rehearses the widespread contemporary view of paper currency as the ruse of a government offering "[s]mall slips of thin, silky paper, on which are engraven solemn promises never to be fulfilled."[43] Such "slips" of value symbolized the British state's failure to fulfill its constitutional obligations, calling into question the very future-oriented hopes that reformers communicated in their political messaging.

These "engraven" promises recall the "graves" of "England in 1819," which as Chandler points out may slyly allude to the print technology in which Shelley and his fellow reformers placed so much faith (hence, Shelley published a number of political pamphlets in his lifetime alongside his poetry). When hope inchoate becomes hope articulate, it leaves the domain of an unformed interiority potentially to become the world-shaping words that would lead Shelley to call poets "unacknowledged legislators." In this way, hope's blockade in *The Mask of Anarchy* prompts a speech that would later proliferate in print as a rallying cry for nineteenth-century reformers and beyond. In a similar direction, *Prometheus Unbound* concludes by offering up the "strong words" of Demogorgon, "spells by which to reassume / An empire o'er the disentangled doom" (IV.553 [*SPP* 285]; IV.568–569 [285]). The rhetoric of "spells" in Shelley connects the power of language to magical incantation, arranged in that linguistic form known only to sorcerer-poets. Given the dubious status of witchcraft, though, Shelley's identification of poetic grammar with its etymological cousin, supernatural "glamour," further calls attention to his wishful hopes for language to alter reality through fantastical causation. Can our doom be conquered through this techno-utopian belief in language that "may never pass away" (IV.553 [285])? Perhaps not, but as Berlant points out, "[p]reaching to the choir is always undervalued."[44]

Moreover, whether language will or will not make change happen is beside the point. For this style of hopeless romanticism, as we have seen, does not require empirical support to persist. Rather, hope is an ethical stance, especially when least warranted, as in reactionary times such as those Shelley lived through. The final stanza of *Prometheus Unbound* thus places hope first and last in its "to do" list "to be / Good, great and joyous, beautiful and free" (IV.576–577 [*SPP* 286]):

> To suffer woes which Hope thinks infinite;
> To forgive wrongs darker than death or night;
>   To defy Power, which seems omnipotent;
> To love, and bear; to hope till Hope creates
> From its own wreck the thing it contemplates;
>   Neither to change, nor falter, nor repent; (IV.570–575 [286])

In these closing lines, Hope is offered as the personified counterweight to the similarly capitalized "Power," first tied to the suffering the latter inflicts and second to its defiance. In the first instance, "Hope" arises from the accumulating scale of anguish, much as in *The Mask* Misery presents to us as ever expandingly "infinite" (a word subtly reinforced by the infinitive grammar of the whole stanza), but this perception springs from hope's despairing fancy ("thinks") much as Power "seems" unvanquishable. These "woes" are met with forgiveness, love, and patience, in the same way the maid calmly confronts her ordeal.

In the second instance, the unattributed act – "to hope" – leads to a personification of "Hope," which then "creates" the "thing" it imagined "from its own wreck," a *telos* guaranteed only by the temporally uncertain "till." The couplet rhyme of "creates" and "contemplates" equates the feeling of yearning for some "thing" with the very deed itself, in line with hope's promise. But what exactly is being wrecked by hoping? Shelley is far from clear. One reading is that a hope dies (wrecks itself) once it becomes a real, if undefined, "thing" and no longer just counterfactual feeling. Another possibility is that hope wrecks not itself but the realities it despairs of, turning them into "graves" from which spring forth (à la "Ode to the West Wind") the seeds of what "it contemplates." In this vein, there may be a pun with "recks," whereby the reckoning of hope grounds the emergence of a better day, as the depressing realities it counts up provoke its flight in visionary ideation. The language also suggests the metaphorical slippage by which individuals may be called wrecks, that is, shells of their former selves, hinting yet again at the "pathetic weakness" identified with the self that has lost all but hope.

As we have seen, Shelley repeatedly links hope to a natural cycle of creation and destruction. The wreck thus serves as a fitting, if ambivalent, metaphorical vehicle for hope, especially in its nautical sense as mover of valued goods as well as its failure to attain its intended port.[45] Shelley invokes the well-trodden trope of wrecked hopes in the preface to *The Revolt of Islam*, which aims to rewrite revolutionary disappointments in a more optimistic strain: "There is a reflux in the tide of human things which bears the shipwrecked hopes of men into a secure haven after the storms are past. Methinks, those who now live have survived an age of despair" (*CP* III: 114). The wrecking of hopes does not annihilate them since they find a "secure haven," which can only be their psychological survival within the hearts of "those who now live." Hope's relation to the ship clearly plays upon the uncertainty of ocean travel in an age known for its nautical calamities, returning us to the "may" that does so much work in "England in 1819." These ships filled with hope are clearly sailing toward a terminus of great promise ("may" as capability), but their eventual arrival at their destination always seems in doubt ("may" as perhaps not).[46] Significantly, the ocean here functions as a topos of both promise and peril.

Seascapes are interwoven with hope throughout *The Revolt of Islam*. Indeed, the persistence of hope is modeled on the natural world whose "tides" have yet to stop:

> when Hope's deep source in fullest flow,
> Like earthquake did uplift the stagnant ocean
> Of human thoughts—mine shook beneath the wide emotion.
>
> When first the living blood through all these veins
> Kindled a thought in sense, great France sprang forth,
> And seized, as if to break, the ponderous chains
> Which bind in woe the nations of the earth.
>   (I.xxxviii–xxxix.340–346 [*CP* III: 144])

The linkage of hope with swelling water allows Shelley to connect nature's lifeblood to that which courses through "these veins" of ours. The ocean's "uplifting" motion replicates the "wide emotion" whose "flow" results in a tectonic shift in consciousness. If hope rises like water, the human vessels atop this ocean are at once enabled to move beyond their usual "stagnant" course and possibly endangered by this great commotion. Shelley here connects the historical rupture of the French Revolution to a natural cycle whose flows sometimes "break" with the past.

As is typical in Shelley and *The Revolt of Islam* in particular, natural forces are the model for poetic power:

> as whirlpools draw
> All wrecks of Ocean to their chasm, the sway
> Of thy strong genius, Laon, which foresaw
> This hope, compels all spirits to obey,
> Which round thy secret strength now throng in wide array
>   (IV.xv.131–135 [*CP* III: 186])

The simile here makes "wrecks" into "spirits," suggesting then that the shipwreck ultimately figures not the destruction of hopes but rather the feeling's fundamental division in the "chasm" of psychological depth where darkness struggles with light. In any case, this metaphor shows hope belongs neither entirely to the individual (the wreck) nor to the social (the ocean) but rather to their interplay. Because hope, like all affects, is partly interpersonal and mimetic, it falls and rises like the tides of the sea.

The "throng" and "array" of Laon's contemporaries respond to the "sway" of his "strong genius," the same type of whirlpool personality that "draws" the reader past the verse's turns and "round" the perpetual enjambments of *The Revolt*. For Laon can channel the "secret strength" present within nature, a phrase Shelley later applies to the sublime Mont Blanc. The old man who speaks these truths admits to being a "passive instrument" of Laon, who has "lent, / To me, to all, the power to advance" (IV.xvi.136–139 [*CP* III: 186–187]). If "hope" is also a "lamp" that "time nor chance / Nor change may not extinguish," it requires someone to "rear" it "on high" for all "its gathered beams to bear" (IV.xvi.142–144 [187]). A substance, like water or light, that naturally abounds, hope is guided by the activist poet who "foresaw" its potential course, that is, anticipated and visualized a future that others could only themselves term an "unforeseen deliverance" (IV.xvi.140 [187]).

In their iconic steadfastness, Shelley's hopes are not unlike that giant mountain in the Alps, animated with a "secret strength" that still leaves many of us in awe. Turning back to the end of *Prometheus Unbound*, the final piece in Shelley's ethical catalogue is a refusal to "change," stressed by the further rejection of faltering and repenting. This reiteration performs obstinacy, which is after all the defining trait of the hopeless romantic. For Shelley, this intransigence relies on inscribing his hopes in writing. As Shelley says in "Hymn to Intellectual Beauty" (1817):

> never joy illumed my brow
>   Unlinked with hope that thou wouldst free
>   This world from its dark slavery,
>   That thou—O awful Loveliness,
> Wouldst give whate'er these words cannot express. (68–72 [*CP* III: 77])

Political liberation and aesthetic potency are syntactically parallel: joy arrives simultaneously linked to the lack "that" both hopes disclose. The striving here is typical of Shelley's hope, as beatific illumination pulls the poet from an inadequate present. The otherworldly force "given" to language takes as its endpoint the indeterminate "whate'er" that marks a potentiality not to be delimited. As with hope's speculative effects, language's onward trajectory in the minds of future readers cannot be plotted with certainty.

Of course, such unpredictable futures do not stop Shelley from prophesying, as he does in the final moments of *The Mask*. He anticipates at once a terrible bloodletting (perhaps a vision more realist than romantic) and the counterforce of a popular awakening, anchored by his famous mantra, "Rise like Lions after slumber." As he writes in his penultimate stanza just before these oft-cited lines: "'And these words shall then become / Like Oppression's thundered doom / Ringing through each heart and brain, / Heard again—again—again—" (364–367 [*SPP* 326]). The "unvanquishable number" refers to the people but also alludes to the verse's numbers, whose metrical effects are tied to the linguistic repetition and patterning that beat the drum of hope "again" in an open-ended concatenation onto the future.

In his time, there was certainly more justification in foreseeing dreadful state violence than the democratic rule of the "many" over the "few." And yet, Shelley clung to a hope that his cherished Wordsworth had abandoned, in a year (1819) when doubts were most reasonable. This hopeless romanticism can be parsed in a number of ways. Biographically, it certainly may result from Shelley's early death, which forestalled a later fatalism and conservatism. It may also reflect Shelley's commitment to the sublime power of language to produce effects beyond the intentions of an author and the possibilities of one moment. But I am particularly struck by the fulfilment of Shelley's prophecy in the readership he has accrued since his death. The posthumous vindication of his literary and political ambitions proves the power of hope to run past the limitations of time and place, even as the ongoing scorn of Shelley's detractors enacts at the literary-critical level that political dynamic that all radicals must brave in order to hold on to their visions of as-yet unrealized futures. Hopeless romantics often have a very real understanding of the social obstacles they face, but they nonetheless continue to "rear / That lamp of hope on high [...] the world its gathered beams to bear" (IV.xvi.141–144 [*CP* III: 187]). The many who have found inspiration in Shelley – such as the Chartists, Mahatma Gandhi, Martin Luther King – certainly felt kinship with him in that exquisite balance between hope and despair that he so powerfully described. Likewise, to read Shelley in these times is to feel ourselves like them all on the threshold of a future that some among us have foreseen, to hope that a "better day" will arrive while also fearing that what we imagine may never come to pass.

Notes

1 [Leigh Hunt], "On the Charges Brought against the Reformists," *The Examiner* (July 29, 1810). Italics, here as elsewhere, in the original.
2 On the endurance of romance as realism gained traction, see Srinivas Aravamudan, *Enlightenment Orientalism: Resisting the Rise of the Novel*

(Chicago: University of Chicago Press, 2011). On the legacies of Quixote, see Aaron Hanlon, *A World of Disorderly Notions: Quixote and the Logic of Exceptionalism* (Charlottesville: University of Virginia Press, 2019).
3 Raymond Williams, *Modern Tragedy* (Stanford: Stanford University Press, 1966), 14.
4 Harold Bloom, "The Internalization of Quest-Romance," in Harold Bloom, ed. *Romanticism and Consciousness: Essays in Criticism* (New York: Norton, 1970), 3–24; David Duff, *Romance and Revolution: Shelley and the Politics of a Genre* (Cambridge: Cambridge University Press, 1994); Greg Kucich, *Keats, Shelley, and Romantic Spenserianism* (University Park: Pennsylvania State Press University, 1991).
5 Cited, and roundly rebutted, in Alan Weinberg, "'The Ineffectual Angel': Arnold's Misrepresentation of Shelley," *The Keats-Shelley Review* 23.1 (2009), 82–96, 83.
6 Jane Austen, *Pride and Prejudice* (1813), in *Jane Austen, The Complete Novels* (New York: Penguin, 2006), 280.
7 Of course, romance did formerly have serious political implications (witness Spenser) but nonetheless its allegorical import never quite eclipsed the pleasure-seeking at the heart of its imaginative thrills.
8 Duff, *Romance and Revolution*, 12.
9 David Hume, quoted from Ernest Campbell Mossner, "David Hume's 'An Historical Essay on Chivalry and Modern Honours,'" *Modern Philology* 45.1 (August 1947), 54–60, and cited by Duff, *Romance and Revolution*, 10. The date of composition is of some dispute, ranging from 1725 to 1734. On the question, see John Wright, "Hume on the Origin of 'Modern Honour': A Study in Hume's Philosophical Development," in Ruth Savage, ed. *Philosophy and Religion in Enlightenment Britain: New Case Studies* (Oxford: Oxford University Press, 2012), 187–209.
10 *Don Juan* (XV.xxii) in Lord Byron, *The Complete Poetical Works*, Volume 5, ed. Jerome McGann (Oxford: Clarendon Press, 1986).
11 Throughout this chapter, I use Shelley's revised title of *The Revolt of Islam* rather than the original *Laon and Cythna*, because, as I argue in my book, it best captures a widespread strain of rhetorical and imaginative writing in which the Muslim world served as a setting to argue about political rights in Britain. Gerard Cohen-Vrignaud, *Radical Orientalism: Rights, Reform, and Romanticism* (Cambridge: Cambridge University Press, 2015).
12 Many scholars have examined the Manichean motif of light and dark, often in the context of critically appraising Shelley's "skeptical idealism," including Lloyd Abbey, *Destroyer and Preserver: Shelley's Poetic Skepticism* (Lincoln: University of Nebraska Press, 1979); Stuart Curran, *Shelley's Annus Mirabilis: The Maturing of an Epic Vision* (San Marino: Huntington Library, 1975); and C. E. Pulos, *The Deep Truth: A Study of Shelley's Skepticism* (Lincoln: University of Nebraska Press, 1954).
13 Karen Weisman, "The Lyricist," in Timothy Morton, ed. *The Cambridge Companion to Shelley* (Cambridge: Cambridge University Press, 2006), 45–46.

14 Timothy Webb, *Shelley: A Voice Not Understood* (Manchester: Manchester University Press, 1977), 108.
15 H., "Sonnet. To the Author of 'The Revolt of Islam,'" *The Examiner* (February 8, 1818).
16 [Leigh Hunt], Review of "*Rosalind and Helen, a Modern Eclogue; With Other Poems, by Percy Bysshe Shelley*," *The Examiner* (May 9, 1819).
17 Orrin N. C. Wang, *Romantic Sobriety: Sensation, Revolution, Commodification, History* (Baltimore: Johns Hopkins University Press, 2011).
18 Andrew Franta, "Shelley and the Poetics of Political Indirection," *Poetics Today* 22.4 (Winter 2001), 765–793; Forest Pyle, "'Frail Spells': Shelley and the Ironies of Exile," in Deborah White, ed. *Irony and Clerisy, Romantic Circles Praxis Series* (August 1999), para. 15.
19 James Chandler, *England in 1819: The Politics of Literary Culture and the Case of Romantic Historicism* (Chicago: University of Chicago Press, 1998), 25.
20 Susan Wolfson, "'Romantic Ideology' and the Values of Aesthetic Form," in George Levine, ed. *Aesthetics and Ideology* (New Brunswick: Rutgers University Press, 1994), 188–218, 209–210; Stuart Curran, *Poetic Form and British Romanticism* (Oxford: Oxford University Press, 1986), 55.
21 Wolfson, "Romantic Ideology," 210.
22 F. R. Leavis, *Revaluation: Tradition and Development in English Poetry* (New York: Stewart, 1947), 228.
23 Leavis, *Revaluation*, 228.
24 Leavis, *Revaluation*, 231.
25 Wolfson, "Romantic Ideology," 209.
26 Benedict de Spinoza, *Ethics*, trans. Edwin Curley (New York: Penguin, 1996), 106.
27 Female personifications do not have to connote social alterity or powerlessness, of course, as contemporary images of Britannia or French Liberty prove, but Shelley clearly stresses Hope's vulnerability in his poem.
28 Morton Paley, "Apocapolitics: Allusion and Structure in Shelley's 'Mask of Anarchy,'" *Huntington Library Quarterly* 54.2 (1991), 91–109, 102.
29 As pragmatic critiques of hope tend to point out, this reality-denial can have deleterious effects on agency if those who hope substitute the pleasures of an illusory imagination for the pursuit of happiness through effort and labor.
30 Anne Janowitz, "'A Voice from across the Sea': Communitarianism at the Limits of Romanticism," in Mary Favret and Nicola Watson, eds. *At the Limits of Romanticism: Essays in Cultural, Feminist, and Materialist Criticism* (Bloomington: Indiana University Press, 1994), 83–100.
31 Franta, "Shelley and the Poetics of Political Indirection," 780.
32 On Shelley's influence among working-class activists, see, among many others, Anne Janowitz, *Lyric and Labour in the Romantic Tradition* (Cambridge: Cambridge University Press, 1998).
33 William Keach, "Radical Shelley?" *Raritan* 5.2 (Fall 1985), 120–129, 121.
34 These quotations are taken from "Ode to the West Wind." This is the liberatory kernel in feeling that has so often motivated the field of affect theory,

which is inspired by the "potentiality" in affect's "virtual" reality and its deployment for utopian ends: Brian Massumi, *Parables for the Virtual: Movement, Affect, Sensation* (Durham, NC: Duke University Press, 2002) and José Muñoz, *Cruising Utopia: The Then and There of Queer Futurity* (New York: New York University Press, 2009). On the disconnect between affect theory and Romanticist scholarship, see my own, Gerard Cohen-Vrignaud, "Love Actually: On Affect Theory and Romantic Studies," *The Wordsworth Circle* 51.3 (2020), 300–321.

35 Shelley was referring most specifically to political "faith," but I take this to be part and parcel of hope. Cited in Norman Thurston, "Shelley and the Duty of Hope," *Keats-Shelley Journal* 26 (1977), 22–28, 23.

36 Lee Edelman, "The Pathology of the Future, or the Endless Triumphs of Life," in Jacques Khalip and Forest Pyle, eds. *Constellations of a Contemporary Romanticism* (New York: Fordham University Press, 2016), 35–46, 35.

37 Lauren Berlant, *Cruel Optimism* (Durham, NC: Duke University Press, 2011).

38 Sara Ahmed, *The Promise of Happiness* (Durham, NC: Duke University Press, 2010).

39 Lauren Berlant, *The Queen of America Goes to Washington City: Essays on Sex and Citizenship* (Durham, NC: Duke University Press, 1997) and Lee Edelman, *No Future: Queer Theory and the Death Drive* (Durham, NC: Duke University Press, 2004).

40 Berlant, *Cruel Optimism*, 14.

41 Shelley, "Love, Hope, Desire, and Fear," in Shelley, *Poetical*, 647–648, 37–38.

42 [*A series of twenty-six political squibs under the form of fictitious bank notes.*] (London: S. W. Fores, 1818–1819) 13, 18. Digital images of these banknotes are freely available on the British Library website.

43 [John Wade], *A Political Dictionary* (London: Dolby, 1821), 67.

44 Berlant, *Cruel Optimism*, 238.

45 For more on the nautical implications of Shelley's use of the ocean, see Mandy Swann, "Shelley's Utopian Seascapes," *Studies in Romanticism* 52.3 (Fall 2013), 389–414.

46 This metaphorical strain also bears some relation to the imperial and capitalist history of a mercantile Britain.

CHAPTER 8

Percy Shelley's Sad Exile

Omar F. Miranda

This chapter examines Percy Shelley's *Prometheus Unbound* as a play about exile, including how the condition remains an essential part of everyday life even after tyranny's defeat.[1] This surprising idea first comes into relief in the concluding eight lines of Act I when Panthea informs Prometheus about Asia's "scene of sad exile," an experience that only begins to take place in a remote part of the Indian Caucasus region:

> Asia waits in that far Indian vale,
> The *scene of her sad exile*; rugged once
> And desolate and frozen, like this ravine;
> But now invested with fair flowers and herbs,
> And haunted by sweet airs and sounds, which flow
> Among the woods and waters, from the ether
> Of her transforming presence, which would fade
> If it were mingled not with thine. Farewell!
> (I.824–833 [*SPP* 234–235], emphasis mine)

Contrary to what a reader or auditor might expect, these lines do not describe an exclusively dismal event. While Asia might feel forlorn in an environment that resembles the cold "ravine" where Prometheus is enchained, the scene's frigid setting has subsided in astonishing fashion: Asia's "rugged once / And desolate and frozen" surroundings have turned into a warm and inviting space. The vale's beauty abounds instead with greenery and flowers as well as sweet scents and music. According to the passage, spring's waking landscape is predicated on two phenomena. It corresponds with and reflects Asia's interior changes, while the glow that radiates her inner beauty – the "ether" – "would (also) fade / If it were mingled not with" Prometheus's own "transforming presence," a reference to the Titan's earlier decision to end his hatred and vengeance. Panthea's lines suggest, in other words, that Asia's altered interiority implicates other peoples and places beyond herself and her immediate surroundings. That is, what Shelley calls the "scene of sad exile" is a developing social and affective condition that involves both Asia's and Prometheus's independent and interdependent efforts, a process whose fruits take shape through and beyond the traumas of displacement and dispossession.

This chapter argues that, in addition to treating peaceful revolution, "love against revenge," "transitional justice," "unbinding forgiveness," and "radical suffering" (see James Chandler's chapter in this collection), *Prometheus Unbound* is also fundamentally about the existential and material state of exile, which neither ends nor anticipates a return to a former state or place.[2] Based on this logic, it is no wonder that the drama's major characters, alongside the human community, all evolve together from banished and alienated victims in the first two acts into agents and citizens who are actively ready to expel – to exile – social ill and antagonism as one unified society by the drama's conclusion. I therefore propose that, as a development that brings about the play's dramatic changes from complicity to collaboration, sad exile encompasses the vicissitudes and lessons from both winter and spring throughout and beyond the four acts. This ambivalent condition of literal and metaphorical modes of distancing and re-vision includes the endurance and resistance that Asia and Prometheus employ and Demogorgon ultimately embodies as the play's syncretic exilic spirit. As I show, sad exile is not a one-time removal but rather an invariable function of everyday self-inquiry and critical distancing. It is the necessary recalibration from ongoing withdrawal from Jupiter's system that will continue to ensure the redeemed society's mutually determined rewards and livelihood.

***

Panthea's above-cited description of Asia's "scene" sums up the drama's overall narrative arc because her lines simultaneously recall the early state of pervasive tragedy as much as forecast the liberated condition of the future world. The evolution detailed in this critical passage thus appears to depend heavily on the word "sad," a term whose archaic usages would have permitted Shelley such flexibility.[3] In addition to its traditional meaning of being sorrowful, the adjective "sad" denotes a condition of being "settled, established in purpose [...] steadfast" and "strong, firm, standing fast, esp. in battle."[4] As Panthea suggests, this exilic journey, which extends well beyond the drama's four acts, is bittersweet. Despite the eventual arrival of spring and "fare[ing] well," the final phrase of Act I, the path is neither easy nor effortless. It demands endurance, since Asia must "wait" in the cold and desolated valley.[5] It also requires "investment" and sacrifice, as Panthea informs us. In the end, the "spring" state of things will remain "haunted by sweet airs and sounds," a phrase that, like sad exile, signals its ambivalent registers. To be "haunted" could mean visited habitually, but its more gothic sense, which could include the presence of distracting or troubling ghosts or other disembodied spirits (potentially from times past, present, or future), cannot be dismissed.

To appreciate the protracted evolution and multivalence of sad exile in *Prometheus Unbound*, one must recognize that Shelley opens his mythic retelling in two important ways. The first is through depicting a fallen universe in a conventional state of exile. When the curtain rises, the whole world has already been suffering through the harsh winter under Jupiter's oppressive system, as the major characters have been physically banished, including Demogorgon who resides in isolation in the earth's dark depths. As we already know, Asia has been displaced to a remote, frigid valley of the Indian Caucasus region, presumably near the Hindu Kush mountain range.[6] At center stage in the opening act is Prometheus who has been exiled from heaven and subsequently suffers in chains in a frozen mountainous landscape. As a consequence of a beleaguered world where arbitrary power, rage, revenge, and retribution exist, humans are also sick and hungry. They dwell in deserted islands and dark caves, a representation through which Shelley recalls the state of ignorance from Plato's famous allegory in *The Republic*. We learn that, as Jupiter's "alternating shafts of frost and fire" have made "shelterless [...] pale human tribes [retreat to] mountain caves" (II.iv.53–54 [*SPP* 248]), the natural world's disorder has caused rising ocean tides that have left "foodless men *wrecked* on some oozy isle" (II.iii.46 [244], emphasis mine).

Compounding the experience of these involuntary removals is the spiritual and emotional desolation caused by Jupiter's abandonment of his adherents. In Act II, when Asia memorably details to Demogorgon the history of injustice and oppression, she wonders who or what has caused this forsakenness. "Who made that sense," she ponders (in an echo of Shelley's earlier lyric, "Hymn to Intellectual Beauty"), that "leaves this peopled earth a solitude / when it returns no more?" (II.iv.12, 17–18 [*SPP* 247]). Asia later connects this neglect to exile explicitly, asking Demogorgon how man has become "the *wreck* of his own will, the scorn of the Earth, / The outcast, the abandoned, the alone?" (II.iv.103–105 [249], emphasis mine). At the end of Act I, moreover, we learn that the world's spirits of beauty and harmony have been figuratively sequestered in "homes [that] are the dim caves of human thought" (I.659 [230]). Since humans have been separated from the muses, the mind has also been wrecked under tyranny.

In the tragic world beset by all these literal and metaphorical "wrecks" of exile, such experiences might be agonizing yet not futile. The effects of sorrow's pervasiveness in these first two acts resemble the association that Edward Said later makes between exile and Wallace Stevens's phrase, "a mind of Winter" (from Stevens's "The Snow Man"); despite the characters' misfortune, they have developed "something" out of winter's "nothingness," a contradiction Stevens makes evident through doubling the negatives in his short lyric.[7] For Said, exile is no doubt a "crippling sorrow"; yet, in acknowledging that its "essential *sadness* can never be surmounted," Said appears aware of the experience's double-edged nature, especially since he later dwells in his meditation on exile's recuperative, if difficult, "achievements."[8] Although the rhetoric of nostalgia in *Prometheus Unbound* may, for instance, heighten the collective feeling of suffering, it also stresses the co-extensiveness of time and toleration. In what Stuart Curran has described as the play's "limbo of agony" and "promise not fulfilled but forestalled," the characters yearn for the state of love and wisdom that they once lived, which unexpectedly yields the relief brought about by waiting and longing (I.185; I.252–253 [*SPP* 215, 217]).[9] The Earth (Prometheus's mother) laments its present state of barrenness and error, recalling Prometheus's birth as a hopeful sign to humankind and finding joy in Jupiter's curse.[10] Later, amid the harsh, frozen environment in Act II, Asia desires the warmth of springtime, likening these wishes to "the memory of a dream / Which is now *sad* because it hath been sweet" (II.i.7–9 [235], emphasis mine). Having experienced the sweetness might accentuate the anguish of spring's absence, but it cannot discount the power of the recollection's vividness. The memory is at once painful and productive. As the "King of / sadness" himself, Prometheus may very well set the play's overall ambivalent tone, announcing early in the first act that he has no choice but to "endure" (I.24 [210]). Despite his continued suffering, he is ultimately able to recognize his own errors, including his part in having kept the world in its miserable condition.

These Shelleyan/Saidian mixed understandings, which tie winter's material conditions together with existential endurance, also speak to what I see as Shelley's second intention with the drama's opening. Indeed, the tragic state with which the play begins lays the groundwork for an intentional methodology tied to Shelley's retelling of the Promethean story, one that engages with and adapts several literary sources that are – unsurprisingly – all narratives of exile. These include the classical and "modern" Promethean myths, the history of Demogorgon's portrayal across centuries, the Book of Genesis, Dante Alighieri's *The Divine Comedy*, John Milton's *Paradise Lost*, and Jean-Jacques Rousseau's epistolary novel, *Julie, ou la nouvelle Héloïse* (all discussed later in the chapter).

Through modifying these accounts, Shelley strategically transforms only those particular plot elements that would fruitfully align with a sustainable revolution predicated on a reimagined and redemptive exilic condition, one in which the disenfranchised reclaim and retain their grounding and well-being.

A few years before Shelley wrote *Prometheus Unbound*, he and Lord Byron took a tour of the French-Swiss landscapes made famous by Rousseau's epistolary novel, *Julie*.[11] On July 12, 1816, Shelley wrote a letter to Thomas Love Peacock, reporting on his travels as well as his experience with the book, identifying Meillerie, a French town near Lake Geneva, as the site of the "well-known *scene* of St. Preux's visionary exile" (*Letters* I: 483, emphasis mine).[12] Reading *Julie* for the first time, Shelley developed admiration for what Mary Shelley later characterized as St. Preux's "abnegation of self" and "worship he paid to Love."[13] To recall this moment in Rousseau's adaptation of the medieval legend of the tutor, Peter Abelard, and his pupil and mistress, Héloïse, St. Preux (Julie's former tutor and lover) returns to the French town of Meillerie following ten years of separation from Julie, a period during which she, in honoring her father's wishes and repressing her true love for St. Preux, had instead married someone from her own aristocratic circle (Monsieur de Wolmar). Toward the end of the book, the benefits of St. Preux's sabbatical have become clear. Despite his profound heartache, he managed to resist temptations of suicide, while also suppressing his longings to "penetrate" Julie's bedroom chamber and to "reunite the two halves of [their one] being."[14] Through his decade-long opportunity for self-reflection, St. Preux affirms in the end that his "keen agitations began to take another [more auspicious] course" because his "emotion overcame despair."[15] For him, the span of several years and his deliberate physical removal from his former familiar settings helped him negotiate the codes and expectations of his stratified society, since the difference in his and Julie's classes prevented the lovers from being together. While Shelley's plot will remove such hierarchical injustices altogether, the hard lessons of St. Preux's endurance and self-sacrifice make up some of *Prometheus Unbound*'s fundamental features. In Shelley's hands, the "scene of St. Preux's visionary exile" – one individual's persistence through his lamentable and unjust circumstances – sets the stage for the drama's ambitious "sad scene" of global emancipation.

Shelley's reading of *Paradise Lost* resonates indeed with his ambivalent treatment of Rousseau's novel. In Milton's adaptation of the Book of Genesis, which has divided the cosmos between good and evil, Satan and his minions create their exilic domain in Hell, having revolted against

God's omnipotent power in heaven.[16] In Book V of the epic, Raphael relates the story of Satan's revolt to Adam, describing his personal storytelling as an onerous undertaking, a "sad task and hard."[17] Later, in Book VI, Raphael reemploys the same sense of the adjective as a description for Satan's stubborn and aggressive pursuits. During the second major battle between Heaven and Hell, after Satan and his army of devils have retreated, Zophiel informs his fellow angels that Hell's rebel army has returned to resume its combat:

> Arme, Warriors, Arme for fight, the foe at hand,
> Whom fled we thought, will save us long pursuit
> This day, fear not his flight; so thick a Cloud
> He comes, and settl'd in his face I see
> Sad resolution and secure[18]

Zophiel urges the angels to prepare for battle because Heaven's "foe," Satan, whom they had believed to have fled, has unexpectedly returned ready to fight. In reading Satan's "settl'd" demeanor, the angel detects the determination that the final two lines reinforce with their alliterative patterning. Of course, Zophiel employs "sad" as a double entendre; Satan's unyielding position against Heaven is partly responsible for one of the most famous and tragic banishments of all, the expulsion of humankind from Eden.

Shelley overtly lauds Milton's devil's intransigence in the preface to *Prometheus Unbound* as well as in *A Defence of Poetry*, even as he concedes that Satan's "ambition, envy, revenge, and [...] desire for personal aggrandizement" have tarnished what might have otherwise been hell's redeeming revolution (*SPP* 207). Shelley thus appears to invest his own ambivalence for Satan as a heuristic within the play's recuperative and re-visionary objectives. When the first act opens to a state of oppositional and partisan politics between Jupiter and Prometheus for which the entire world suffers, Shelley has clearly modeled Prometheus's wrath and hatred for Jupiter on Satan's. As Madeleine Callaghan has pointed out, Prometheus is initially a "Satanic double" delivering "Satanic rhetoric," effectively mirroring his source of inspiration (Satan) as much as his enemy (Jupiter).[19] While Jupiter fills "this world of woe" with his antipathy, Prometheus has become complicit; like Satan (and Jupiter), he is "eyeless in hate" (I.283 [*SPP* 218]; I.15 [210]). Defiant, wrathful, and vengeful, he curses Jupiter, while delighting in his foreknowledge that the tyrant will eventually be overthrown. In response, Prometheus becomes Jupiter's victim of "torture and solitude / scorn and despair" through a bipartite structure that keeps the world in its static, frigid, and sorrowful state

(I.14–15 [210]). Nevertheless, despite the suffering, the difficulties have not been altogether vain. As the first act shows, the Titan has mastered the art of being and becoming *steadfast* in the spirit of Milton's devil, even if the ends of Satan's – and Prometheus's – "sad resolution" must be changed.

Behind the Miltonic reimagining of religious and exilic divisiveness is, of course, Dante Alighieri's fourteenth-century epic, *The Divine Comedy*, a narrative from which Shelley also draws in various ways. Perhaps most apparently, Dante's poem has transformed its author's own tragic political exile from Florence into a poetic tale of emancipation. The Italian epic's plotline from exilic victimhood to victory, its reconfiguration of one person's tragedy in banishment into entirely new collective possibilities, is a central feature for Shelley because Dante does not, in fact, track a return to an original (Florentine) homeland. Nevertheless, Shelley took exception to the story of Christian redemption and communion with God in heaven, especially since Dante imagined his epic in part as an expression of vindictiveness. After all, he placed his political opponents throughout the varying layers of hell: in perpetual states of non-redemptive displacement and suffering. In his drama, however, Shelley adapts these key Dantean exilic motifs by conceiving a secularized and inclusive space of difference where living in a liberated state means existing outside the constraints of any one specified doctrinal or denominational order.

Yet, for Shelley, the literary legacy of hate, wrath, and vengeance does not stem exclusively from either *Paradise Lost* or *The Divine Comedy*. The problematic aspects of this archive date much further back to the ancient origins of the Promethean myth itself. According to *Prometheus Unbound*'s preface, Shelley criticized the myth as told by Aeschylus, who based much of his work on Hesiod's earlier version.[20] In Shelley's view, Aeschylus's account of the reconciliation between the "Champion (Prometheus) with the Oppressor of Mankind (Jupiter)" reinforced rather than resolved the problem of tyranny (*SPP* 206). Specifically, Shelley condemned how, in Aeschylus's version, Prometheus's disclosure of Zeus's imminent downfall allows the tyrant to retain his arbitrary power. What Shelley does not explain in his preface, however, is that at the heart of the classical Greek myth's plot lies a cyclical history of overthrows and exiles. In both Hesiod's and Aeschylus's versions, three generations of gods (led by Uranus, Kronos, and Zeus respectively) struggle for power; in each case, the conquered deities end up banished to Tartarus, the lowest and darkest level of the universe (located beneath even Hades). Tartarus becomes the site of exile not only for Uranus and the overthrown Titans but also for Prometheus as a consequence of his disobedience of Zeus.[21] According to this cyclical usurpation of power and sovereignty, exile begets exile through a continual series of downfalls and depositions. The intergenerational trauma of the myth persists, in fact, through Shelley's era with Promethean adaptations produced by many of his contemporaries, including Johann Wolfgang von Goethe, Lord Byron, and his wife, Mary Shelley, all of whom depict the Titan as a defiant rebel against authority.[22] In the end, retellings of the myth across the millennia retained their exilic logic, especially in attending to the destructive partisan divisiveness at each of the narratives' core.

In reconceiving the Promethean accounts of his predecessors and contemporaries, Shelley seems to ask what might be gained when revenge and retribution are dropped from consideration. How do exilic subjectivity and intersubjectivity, in other words, retain their spirit of resistance, defiance, and disavowal without turning to the destructive, violent, and vengeful ends exhibited by Satan and the Titanic and Olympian deities? How might the collective mind of winter, even after experiencing all its sufferings and injustices, redirect the Dantean vindication of victimhood, the visionary endurance and self-sacrifice of St. Preux, and the virtues of Satanic survival and resolve toward achieving a truly common good? According to the drama's reconceptualized plot, moving beyond the impasses of the first two acts must involve thinking critically about the past and the present, as Asia and Prometheus must do in the spirit of their own author reimagining his chosen literary sources. The structure of *Prometheus Unbound* thus relies so fixedly on its reconceptualized "scene of sad exile" because this ongoing act removes the world repeatedly from the deleterious conditions that plague it. This shift from complicity to productive mutuality necessitates various forms of physical and metaphorical removal, resulting from the insightful, if difficult, re-visions of error that accompany the new world's long-term commitments.

***

In keeping with the principles of collaborative withdrawal from Jupiter's tyranny, Prometheus's methodical distancing occurs with the help of those around him. The Earth has permitted him, for instance, to witness a former version of himself when the Phantasm of Jupiter reenacts Prometheus's earlier curse. From both a spatial and a temporal removal, he can finally "recall" his malediction by both remembering as much as retracting his hasty words, as scholars have contended (I.59 [*SPP* 211]).[23] When Prometheus can "see" his blindness, as it were, he is able to acknowledge his errors and his accountability. His *re-vision* leads to his change of heart and desire that "no living thing [...] suffer pain" (I.304–305 [218]).[24] From this literal and figurative distance can Prometheus then shift his attention and effort further away from the tragic impasse with which he has been complicit. Callaghan has described this critical change as the shift from "Satanic rhetoric into Promethean poetry," and, more recently, Merrilees Roberts has theorized it as the disjunction between the "first" Prometheus and "second" Prometheus of the play, who is "both connected to and distanced from his prior self."[25] Through this process, Prometheus retreats far enough to recall/retract his hate but not his "resolution" toward attaining the drama's reformative ends.

Asia's simultaneous transformation, which involves her literal voyage to the depths of the earth and a metaphorically painful journey into the recesses of her psyche, unfolds similarly to Prometheus's.[26] During her introspective and mostly one-sided exchange with Demogorgon, she becomes as wrathful as the Titan does in Act I. When she meditates on the history of the "struggling world" – a "world pining in pain" – she exclaims "curses shall drag [Jupiter] down" (I.577 [SPP 227]; II.iv.29–30 [247]). In her transition out of this rage, Asia must, like Prometheus, directly face her past in a communal and dialogical setting, which includes in her case the immediate physical presence of Panthea and Demogorgon and the distant link to Prometheus and his community of supporters. In this assembly of near and far, she is able to recount what Kate Singer has called "revolutionary trauma," displaying the personal and interpersonal difficulties of working through the past.[27] As Singer has argued, "Asia's affect, her receptivity, and inquisitiveness stand as the inverse of Jupiter's colonizing aggression, and these qualities locate her outside the patriarchal history."[28] Like Prometheus, she will reach outside the Jupiterian system from the outside: her reflections have allowed her, as the allegorical embodiment of love, to rise above "all things [which, in fact,] are subject but eternal Love," a force that has also guided her toward knowledge and freedom (II.iv.120 [250]). Her exile turns from visionary to revisionary – from complicity to collaboration – when her grand exit becomes a joint *uprising* against tyranny, a *rising from* the wintry fallen condition, and a *rising toward* a continually transforming world.

Yet even as Asia and Prometheus withdraw from former selves and systems, these disavowals in the drama do not yield easy narrative shifts to fecundity and bliss. Instead, the work of liberation must persist, as Panthea predicts early on during the "scene of sad exile" passage. Asia's success must be ongoing because it depends on her and her counterpart's "transforming presence[s]," a process reinforced during Shelley's depiction of the avalanche's formation and discharge in Act II. According to this oft-cited passage, the literal route out of winter's stasis and misery, which will bring injustice, oppression, banishment, and desolation to their end, does not leave winter behind:

> Hark! the rushing snow!
> The sun-awakened avalanche! whose mass,
> Thrice sifted by the storm, had gathered there
> Flake after flake, in heaven-defying minds
> As thought by thought is piled, till some great truth
> Is loosened, and the nations echo round,
> Shaken to their roots, as do the mountains now.
> (II.iii.36–42 [*SPP* 244])

In these lines that scholars typically read as metaphor for political revolution, the snowy mountaintop recalls the landscapes of the unredeemed world once inhabited by Asia and Prometheus.[29] A figure for "mass" uprising, the avalanche forms slowly yet steadily, expanding its size physically through "flakes" and figuratively through "thoughts." The three marks of exclamation in the first two lines, along with the numerous enjambments, evoke the momentum of "heaven-defying minds" whose intractable force causes radical change – quite literally as roots are shaken (II.iii.39–40 [244]). Colin Jager has brought this passage into conversation with Shelley's "Mont Blanc," arguing for the social power that is "put into motion through the accretion of bodies that like snowflakes eventually become more than the sum of their parts."[30] Indeed, this onslaught will give way to the triumph of human will over victimhood and oppression. At the same time, the lines emphasize the fact that such "sun-awakened" cooperative action will repurpose rather than dismiss the lessons of winter altogether.

In practical terms, winter in the play becomes associated with the hardships and oppositions that simply will not go away. Prometheus might apologize and remove himself from an oppressive stalemate and system, yet he must still undergo the torment inflicted by the Furies, who, fittingly enough, take advantage of his removed, panoptic perspective that enables him to witness disturbing yet illuminating visions of Christ's crucifixion and the bloody French Revolution. Likewise, Asia's emergence from darkness, which has freed her from her solipsistic self-reflexivity at the volcanic depths, also involves its haunting dimensions. Though she reaches the "Cloud on the Top of a snowy Mountain" on her beautiful chariot, a "ghastly charioteer" accompanies her, as "darkness [...] / Shall wrap in lasting night heaven's kingless throne" (*SPP* 252; II.iv.144, 148–149 [251]). The simultaneity of this representation aligns with the play's broader ambivalent spirit, the "long labours" of repeated resistance that will carry over into the new world (II.iv.173 [252]). Accordingly, the kind of critical self-inquiry and conditioning that Asia and Prometheus have learned and exhibited – those haunting processes that remove us from our own worst selves and our intergenerational traumas – can never go away if breaking with historical cycles remains a priority.

What I am proposing is that Shelley offers a methodology for encountering everyday hardship (even after the play's many transformations) by turning the exilic condition on its head, an inversion that is perhaps best understood through the depiction of Demogorgon across all four acts. Demogorgon is, I suggest, the play's syncretic exilic spirit, and its representation draws, in quintessential Shelleyan fashion, on yet another extensive literary tradition dating back to the classical age. Asia's first encounter with Demogorgon in Act II is consistent with Shelley's myth-making tactics, recalling works by Lucan, Boccaccio, Edmund Spenser, and Milton in which the spirit is typically consigned to the dark depths of an abyss.[31] According to its etymological roots, the "people's monster," Demogorgon initially reflects the alienated and tragic state of the greater populace – the pervasively fallen condition of which Asia's and Prometheus's experiences are also part. Pent in its cave, Demogorgon sits on the "remotest throne" of the earth in the "grey, void Abysm" (II.iii.61; II.iii.72 [*SPP* 245]). As we later learn in Act IV, Shelley describes Demogorgon's separation through the figure of a curtain. "Cover[ing] our being and darken[ing] our birth," the symbolic veil had concealed the light of truth and knowledge (IV.56–60 [271]).[32] Unsurprisingly, Demogorgon's pit of exile becomes associated with a conglomeration of problematic images in the play – dim caves, vacant spaces, precarious abysses – a tropological convergence that brings the world's passive and torpid state, as it were, into relief.[33]

Yet in keeping with Shelley's sequence of re-vision, Demogorgon's position changes alongside Asia's and Prometheus's transformations. Following the flight from its "vacant throne" in the lower depths, the spirit becomes the symbolic gatekeeper of new communal virtues, as exile has changed at last from a passive to an active state (III.i.21 [*SPP* 256]). Indeed, the victims of oppression and misrule have become the new world's victors through the success born out of the principles of methodical change. As Demogorgon informs us, "Gentleness, Virtue, Wisdom, and Endurance" should continuously "seal" or "bar [...] the pit over destruction's strength" (IV.562–564 [285]).[34] The "sceptreless [...] uncircumscribed [...] unclassed, tribeless, and nationless" community that adheres to these values will fend off its counterforces, especially since it can still "fall into imperfection," as Jeffrey Cox has argued, "even into tyranny, the moment we believe we have found an ideal state rather than perpetual reform" (III.iv.194–195 [269]).³⁵ Demogorgon symbolizes this protective force, and, in accordance with such self-preservationist practices, has peacefully removed the former sovereign to a site of metaphorical exile. The metonym for all things harmful and antithetical, Jupiter must be constantly disavowed or, to use Shelley's language, "unregarded," in order to keep at bay those ills associated with the former world, including hatred, vengeance, violence, and, perhaps most importantly, lack of critical self-distance (III.iv.179 [268]).

Alongside Demogorgon's tectonic displacement, which signals the shift toward communal empowerment, Asia and Prometheus transition to an alternative site and state of exile themselves as they withdraw symbolically to their reimagined Platonic cave in Act III. In their removed space, they repeatedly make art and love, producing "Painting, Sculpture, and rapt Poesy, / And arts [...] yet to be" (III.iii.55–56 [*SPP* 260]). They help to generate "the discourses of science, of imaginative wonder, and of social and psychological anatomy" because of the rigor to which they commit, especially since they "search with looks and words of love, / For hidden thoughts each lovelier than the last" (III.iii.55–56 [260]).³⁶ As a result of their efforts, Asia and Prometheus are able to shut out "evil and error" simultaneously (III.iii.62 [260]). To no surprise, "man grows wise and kind" through these activities because "such virtue has the cave and place around" (III.iii.61–63 [262]). What is especially significant about this creative process, which removes things ill through the cultivation of things agreeable, is that the system sustains itself through the insights and protections that the distance of exile has afforded. Through their world-building industry, that is, Asia and Prometheus actively practice what Demogorgon has professed in principle.

By Act IV, then, it becomes evident that the measures and pleasures of the cave now function as the model for the greater world's successes. In symbolic fulfillment of Act I's prophetic "scene of sad exile" on which this chapter has dwelt, Panthea returns by the drama's closing act to offer another signature view of things from afar. Describing the intricacies of the new world – through a re-vision that she meaningfully acquires in a "wood of sweet *sad* thoughts" – she details a society that works together to expunge "evil and error" (IV.201 [*SPP* 275], emphasis mine). Such a collaborative community is, according to Panthea, like "ten thousand orbs" that make up one vast orb of varied colors and sizes – all of which spin, or "whirl," independently and in tandem (IV.241 [276]; IV.246 [277]). This "dynamic and differentiated totality," as William Keach has suggested, creates its ever-whirling motion through what Panthea calls the orbs' "inter-transpicuous" or inter-translucent relationality (IV.246 [277]).[37] The kaleidoscopic social body runs not only by remaining both clear and open but also through a "self-destroying swiftness," which indeed privileges the inclusive communal body above the individual. In the service of the common good, the previous sites of tragic exile (what once existed as dark, vacant caves and abysses where Demogorgon formerly resided) have evolved into active and purposeful spaces.[38] Withdrawing from their own damaging and solipsistic versions, the orbs lay themselves bare through the ongoing process of adjustment: the arduous effort through which the internal and external ultimately reflect one another (IV.249 [277]). As Demogorgon articulates by the final lines, hope is not tied to far-off fantasy but rather to transforming desire into reality continuously: "to hope till Hope creates / From its own *wreck* the thing it contemplates" (IV.573–574 [286], emphasis mine). Hope is directly connected to the play's methodology of action and possibility – linked back to those winters and "wrecks" of exile that are indelibly woven into the new Promethean model of freedom. Panthea's cosmic imaginings thus highlight how the revolution that realizes things like art, love, and justice must persist in the most literal and figurative of senses. Each orb must continue turning (out) by re-turning to those original traumas and wrecks, yet the individual and collective fruits of doing so, of fending off those antithetical forces, make the struggle worthwhile.

***

In *Prometheus Unbound*, Shelley has grounded his play's celebratory outcome on a historically punitive condition that has turned *outside in*, demonstrating how the ever-"revolutionizing" state draws from the records, knowledge, and experiences of the past and the present. As I have suggested, Shelley adapts his predecessors' and contemporaries' narratives of dislocation and loss, thereby putting the play's purported methodology of re-vision into practice firsthand. According to the drama's defamiliarized state of exile, the ever-new society's citizens overcome their tragic conditions through a preservationist dialectical model not unlike the Hegelian understanding of *Aufhebung* or sublation, which links surmounting obstacles and challenges with the willful gains of such empirical knowledges. In the twentieth century, several French philosophers, including Georges Bataille, Jean-Luc Nancy, and Maurice Blanchot, all drew on Hegel's ideas in order to theorize notions of ideal community in defense of Marxist and Communist principles. Even though they disagreed to a large extent about the particulars of such a society, they all explore the germane notion of "ecstasy": the literal idea of standing outside oneself – *ex-stasis* – in the "rapturous" service of privileging and promoting the collective body. That is, a community will form at the convergence of beings who have moved literally and metaphorically toward one common position and purpose. In Nancy's words specifically, community is the "being-ecstatic of Being itself";[39] it is "ecstatic consciousness" where "consciousness *of* self turns out to be outside the self of consciousness."[40] In his later treatise, *Being Singular Plural*, Nancy also argues that the essence of ontology is community: being is "being with"; singularity is plurality in the social state generated through vulnerable exposures and unveilings.[41] I highlight these complex metaphysical notions to suggest that Bataille and his followers might have also done well to draw on Shelley's "ecstatic" ontological framework. This is because, in his drama especially, Shelley elaborates on an evolving exilic condition to theorize how the avalanches of constant change, the "self-destructive" rewards of laying oneself bare, also yield those very privileges of being, as well as becoming, with.

While *Prometheus Unbound* stresses the radical power and privilege of separations created by time and space, those possibilities of seeing things fresh and anew in the world, the play's inspiring visions appear in tension with some of its author's own personal decisions. After all, Shelley lived in an "age of exile" and, despite his egalitarian reconceptualizations of Dante's, Milton's, and Rousseau's ideas, remained surprisingly quiet about one of the saddest and cruelest of exiles that occurred in his lifetime, the African slave trade.[42] Yet, as Amanda Blake Davis has recently and persuasively contended, "*Prometheus Unbound* strives [...] to implicate the reader in its unbinding of hierarchical constructs."[43] Given the drama's engagement with and adaptation of artistic materials across the centuries, the play seemingly passes those same powers of re-vision down the generations. At minimum, then, we ought to acknowledge Shelley's ironic silences in light of the forced mass displacements in his day. At the same time, we might heed many of the drama's insights about attaining meaningful and lasting change, including but not limited to the power of going beyond the ambitions of one visionary exile; navigating our personal traumas with the support of others; acknowledging one's mistakes and complicity; and working tirelessly toward social freedom and equality. As we further interrogate the work that Shelley considered to be his greatest, we might recall that he grounded all these consequential messages on his most sophisticated understanding of a condition that he variously imagined, portrayed, and experienced throughout most of his life.[44] For the glorious evolutions and revolutions of *Prometheus Unbound* ultimately depend on the drama's ever-transformative "scene" through which we conjure the ghosts and wrecks of the past in order to re/turn our contemplations into the reality of the coming world.

Notes

1. I wish to thank Kate Singer for her careful attention to this essay's many iterations. I am also grateful to several others who have given me their suggestions over the years. This chapter has indeed taken shape through the very idea it discusses, especially through the opportunities that temporal and spatial distances have granted.
2. David Bromwich, "Love against Revenge in Shelley's Prometheus," *Philosophy and Literature* 26.2 (2002), 239–259; Colin Jager, "Transitional Justice in *Prometheus Unbound*," *The Workshop* 4 (2016), 26–31; Alexander Freer, "Unbinding Forgiveness: *Prometheus Unbound*," *European Romantic Review* 33.5 (2022), 697–711.
3. Shelley wrote the first act of *Prometheus Unbound* from his exile in Italy shortly following the death of his daughter, Clara. Naturally, while expanding the word's interpretive limits, he also employs the term "sad" in its conventional sense. See Stuart Curran, "Romanticism Displaced and Placeless," *European Romantic Review* 20.5 (2009), 637–650, 647.
4. Definitions two and three are taken from the *Oxford English Dictionary*, 3rd ed. These specific uses of "sad" went obsolete in the sixteenth and seventeenth centuries.
5. For an alternative reading of Asia's more instantaneous and necessary transformation, see Kelvin Everest, "'Mechanism of a Kind Yet Unattempted': The Dramatic Action of *Prometheus Unbound*," *Durham University Journal* 54.2 (1993), 237–245.
6. See Joseph Raben, "Shelley's *Prometheus Unbound*: Why the Indian Caucasus?" *Keats-Shelley Journal* 12 (1963), 95–106.
7. Edward Said, "Reflections on Exile," *Granta* 13 (Autumn 1984), 159–172, 172; Wallace Stevens, *The Collected Poems of Wallace Stevens* (New York: Alfred A. Knopf, 1954), 9–10.
8. Said, "Reflections on Exile," 159. Emphasis mine.
9. Stuart Curran, *Poetic Form and British Romanticism* (Oxford: Oxford University Press, 1986), 199.
10. Mildred Sloan McGill, "The Role of Earth in Shelley's *Prometheus Unbound*," *Studies in Romanticism* 7.2 (1968), 117–128.
11. Jean-Jacques Rousseau, *Julie, or the New Heloise: Letters of Two Lovers Who Live in a Small Town at the Foot of the Alps*, trans. Phillip Stewart and Jean Vaché, in *The Collected Writings of Rousseau*, Volume 6, eds. Roger D. Masters and Christopher Kelly (Hanover: Dartmouth College, 1997).
12. Shelley's visit to the scene is recounted in detail by Mary Shelley's *History of a Six Weeks' Tour* (1817). For further discussion on the subject, see Monika Lee,

Rousseau's Impact on Shelley: Figuring the Written Self (Lewiston: The Edwin Mellen Press, 1999).
13 Mary Shelley, *Notes to the Complete Poetical Work of Percy Bysshe Shelley* (Auckland: The Floating Press, 2010), 83.
14 Rousseau, *Julie*, 75–76.
15 Rousseau, *Julie*, 428.
16 In contrast to the biblical fall, in which mankind brings about its own exile from paradise, humans in *Prometheus Unbound* are victims of the social ill introduced by Saturn. Saturn (Kronos) "refused / the birthright of [human] being, knowledge, and power" (II.iv.38–39 [*SPP* 248]). He also deprived humans of "the skill [...] the thought / Which pierces this dim Universe like light, / Self-empire, and majesty of love" (II.iv.40–42 [248]). By removing human independence (self-empire) and knowledge, Saturn created darkness across minds, which eventually made humans vulnerable to Jupiter's wrath.
17 John Milton, *Paradise Lost*, ed. Gorgon Teskey, Norton Critical Edition, 2nd ed. (New York: W. W. Norton, 2021), V.564.
18 Milton, *Paradise Lost*, VI.537–541.
19 Madeleine Callaghan, "Shelley and Milton," in Michael O'Neill, Anthony Howe, and Madeleine Callaghan, eds. *The Oxford Handbook of Percy Bysshe Shelley* (Oxford: Oxford University Press, 2013), 478–494, 486.
20 Hesiod, *Theogony and Works and Days: A New Translation by M. L. West* (Oxford: Oxford University Press, 2008). The Promethean story's earliest version dates back to Hesiod's *Theogony* (eighth century BCE), which describes the Titan as a trickster deity. Approximately three centuries later, Aeschylus turned the popular story into an elaborate dramatic trilogy, of which only its first part, *Prometheus Bound* (fifth century BCE), survives.
21 Hesiod's *Theogony* describes how Uranus (Heaven), the primordial god of the sky, exiles his children to "misty Tartara" out of fear that they would eventually overthrow him (6). Shortly after this expulsion, Kronos (Saturn), one of Uranus's sons, returns from banishment to overpower his father, castrating and exiling him instead into the darkness. Heaven's children, the Titans (including Prometheus), thereby rise to power, as Kronos becomes the predominant deity of the cosmos. Yet this generation, too, will succumb to the curse of Uranus. In Hesiod's account, Zeus decides to banish the Titans, just as their father Uranus had done, and they are "hidden away down in the misty gloom [...] in a place of decay, at the end of the vast earth" (24–25). A few centuries later, Aeschylus's *Prometheus Bound* describes the exile of the Titans quite similarly, adding how Prometheus plays a significant role in this dramatic event by participating not as an aide to his fellow Titans but to the Olympians. In one address to the Chorus, Prometheus tells how his own "strategy" sent "archaic Kronos and all his allies" to the "black hole of Tartaros," helping Zeus only after the Titans, believing in their power of might over knowledge, refused their brother's help (ll. 325–329). By the end of the play, Prometheus refuses to yield the secret knowledge of Zeus's downfall – information possessed only by him – and is himself cast down to "Tartaros." According to Prometheus's secret knowledge, Zeus's marriage to Thetis will cast the supreme deity "out of His throne and His

tyranny" and he will "end up nowhere" (ll. 1397–1398). Aeschylus. *Prometheus Bound*. Translated by James Scully and C. John Herrington. (Oxford: Oxford University Press, 1975).

22 Goethe's poem, "Prometheus" (1774), portrays a spiteful and vengeful Titan fueling the rigid opposition between him and Zeus. He vows to create "humans in [his own] image, a lineage resembling [him] [Menschen / Nach meinem Bilde, / Ein Geschlecht, das mir gleich sei]" (52–53, my translation). Implied here is that the human race will absorb Prometheus's spite, resentment, and vengeance because Zeus has imposed perpetual "Pain [Schmerzen]" (39) and "Slavery [Sklaverei]" (32). Johann Wolfgang von Goethe, *Selected Poetry of Johann Wolfgang von Goethe*, trans. and ed. David Luke (London: Penguin Books, 2005). Byron's lyric, "Prometheus" (1816), is cast from the same mold, depicting the Titan as a suffering rebel under "inexorable Heaven" (18–19) who endures a "suffocating sense of woe" (10). His "firm will" (55) against Heaven make his deity comparable to Goethe's incontrovertibly "impenetrable" spirit (42). Lord George Gordon Byron, *Byron's Poetry and Prose*, ed. Alice Levine (New York: W. W. Norton, 2010). This retributive structure reappears in Mary Shelley's "modern Prometheus" narrative, *Frankenstein*, through the Faustian drive that leads to Victor's and the creature's individual exiles, despair, and doom. *Frankenstein, or the Modern Prometheus*, Norton Critical Edition, ed. J. Paul Hunter (New York: W. W. Norton, 1996).

23 See David Ferris, "The Time of Judgement: Shelley's *Prometheus Unbound*," in *Silent Urns: Romanticism, Hellenism, Modernity* (Stanford: Stanford University Press, 2000), 134–157.

24 For further discussion on the dramatic action of the drama, see Note 5 as well as John Rieder, "The 'One' in *Prometheus Unbound*," *Studies in English Literature, 1500–1900* 25.4 (1985), 775–800; Richard Isomaki, "Love as Cause in *Prometheus Unbound*," *Studies in English Literature, 1500–1900* 29.4 (1989), 655–673.

25 Callaghan, "Shelley and Milton," 486; Merrilees Roberts, "*Prometheus Unbound*: Reconstitutive Poetics and the Promethean Poet," *The Keats-Shelley Review* 34.2 (2020), 178–193, 181.

26 See, for instance, Barbara Charlesworth Gelpi, "The Source of Desire Seeks the End of Desire (*Prometheus Unbound*, Act II)," in *Shelley's Goddess: Maternity, Language, Subjectivity* (Oxford: Oxford University Press, 1994).

27 Katherine Singer, "Stoned Shelley: Revolutionary Tactics and Women under the Influence," *Studies in Romanticism* 48.4 (2009), 687–707, 698.

28 Singer, "Stoned Shelley," 696.

29 See, for instance, Kim Wheatley, "Paranoid Politics: Shelley and the *Quarterly Review*," in Orrin N. C. Wang, ed. *Romanticism and Conspiracy, Romantic Circles* Praxis Series (July 1997), https://romantic-circles.org/praxis/conspiracy/wheatley/kim2.html.

30 Colin Jager, "Shelley after Atheism," *Studies in Romanticism* 49.4 (2010), 611–631, 626.

31 For classic discussions of Shelley's syncretism, see Harold Bloom, *Shelley's Mythmaking* (New Haven: Yale University Press, 1959); Stuart Curran, "The

Political Prometheus," *Studies in Romanticism* 25.3 (1986), 429–455; Jerrold Hogle, *Shelley's Process: Radical Transference and the Development of His Major Works* (Cambridge: Cambridge University Press, 1998); and Daniel E. White, "'Mysterious Sanctity': Sectarianism and Syncretism from Volney to Hemans," *European Romantic Review* 15.2 (2004), 269–276.

32 Shelley often invokes the figure of the veil. In *A Defence of Poetry*, he describes how poetry "lifts the veil" of the world's hidden beauty (*SPP* 526). In "Mont Blanc," the speaker contemplates if "some unknown omnipotence [has] unfurled / The veil of life and death?" (53–54 [*SPP* 98]). In "On Life," Shelley discusses the "mist of familiarity" that hides us "from the wonder of our being" (*SPP* 476). All these images point to the harmful lack of knowledge associated with the pre-redeemed world of *Prometheus Unbound*.

33 As scholars have noted, Demogorgon resembles Milton's description of Death in *Paradise Lost* who has a "grim" and "dismal" cave (XI.469). While Milton's depiction of Death is shapeless and indistinguishable in "member, joint, or limb" (II.666–673), Demogorgon has "neither limb / nor form – nor outline" (II.iv.4–5 [*SPP* 246]).

34 For recent discussions on the philosophical underpinnings of "vacancy," see Colin Jager, *Unquiet Things: Secularism in the Romantic Age* (Philadelphia: University of Pennsylvania Press, 2015) as well as Kate Singer, *Romantic Vacancy: The Politics of Gender, Affect, and Radical Speculation* (Albany: State University of New York Press, 2019).

35 Jeffrey N. Cox, "The Dramatist," in Timothy Morton, ed. *The Cambridge Companion to Shelley* (Cambridge: Cambridge University Press, 2007), 65–84, 77. Singer also reminds us that "the revolutionaries [...] cannot entirely forget Jupiter's reign but must continually recall that Promethean utopia must be continually recreated at every moment" (701).

36 Curran, *Poetic Form*, 201.

37 William Keach, "The Political Poet," in Morton, ed. *Cambridge Companion to Shelley*, 123–142, 123.

38 For some discussions on Shelley's skeptical philosophy, see Terence Allan Hoagwood, *Skepticism & Ideology: Shelley's Political Prose and Its Philosophical Context from Bacon to Marx* (Iowa City: University of Iowa Press, 1988); Forest Pyle, "'Frail Spells': Shelley and the Ironies of Exile," in Deborah Elise White, ed. *Irony and Clerisy*, Romantic Circles Praxis Series (August 1999), https://romantic-circles.org/praxis/irony/pyle/frail.html; Anthony Howe, "Shelley and Philosophy: 'On a Future State,' 'Speculations on Metaphysics and Morals,' 'On Life,'" in O'Neill, Howe, and Callaghan, eds. *Oxford Handbook of Percy Bysshe Shelley*, 101–116; and Singer, *Romantic Vacancy*.

39 Jean-Luc Nancy, *The Inoperative Community*, ed. Peter Connor, trans. Peter Connor, Lisa Garbus, Michael Holland, and Simona Sawhey, *Theory and History of Literature* 76 (Minneapolis: University of Minnesota Press, 1991), 6.

40 Nancy, *The Inoperative Community*, 19.

41 Jean-Luc Nancy, *Being Singular Plural*, trans. Robert Richardson and Anne O'Byrne (Stanford: Stanford University Press, 2000).

42 See Omar F. Miranda, "The Age of Exile," *Keats-Shelley Journal* 68 (2019), 150–2; JoEllen DeLucia's and Juliet Shields's edited collection, *Migration and Modernities: The State of Being Stateless, 1750–1850* (Edinburgh: Edinburgh University Press, 2019); Curran, "Romanticism Displaced and Placeless"; and Mathelinda Nabugodi's chapter in this volume.

43 Amanda Blake Davis, "Androgyny as Mental Revolution in Act 4 of *Prometheus Unbound*," *The Keats-Shelley Review* 34.2 (2020), 160–177, 163.

44 Many of Shelley's writings consider the divisions created between home and exile such as when he pits Platonic ideals against mundane earthly realities in *Adonais*, his tribute to John Keats, where the eponymous elegized hero has been stellified in the celestial "abode where the Eternal are" (495, [*SPP* 427]). Consider, too, the speaker in "To a Skylark" who arrives at "saddest thought" when contemplating the poem's "blithe" titular creature that exists in some immaterial realm "higher still and higher / From the earth" (6–7 [304]). In *The Sensitive Plant* (1820), the speaker also presents this polarity, distinguishing his mortal life from the immaterial state of beauty and immutability to where both the sensitive plant and the poem's beautiful lady have moved on. Significantly, in "Lines Written among the Euganean Hills" (1818), Shelley begins turning to the collective power of self-separation, imagining a "healing (island) paradise" that is located "far from passion, pain, and guilt" (345, 355 [118]). In the poem, the isle sustains a model community in refuge that nurtures the Earth and makes it "grow young again" (373 [118]).

CHAPTER 9

Shelley in the Overgrowth
Ross Wilson

The idea that climate change might be a good thing is nowadays espoused only by fossil fuel magnates, their propagandists, and dupes.[1] As if the supposed benefits of global heating were the very aim of industrial emissions, lobbyists for capital have sought to portray ballooning amounts of carbon dioxide in the atmosphere as the condition for the resurgence of nature, increased global food production, and the near-elimination of winter deaths. "Carbon dioxide: they call it pollution; we call it life."[2] Really, of course, gesturing to the advantageous side effects of greenhouse gas emissions, all of them spurious, serves as a weak excuse for the pollution that is the necessary corollary of capitalist accumulation: "capitalism, with its industrial body and crown of finance, is sovereign; [...] carbon emissions are the sovereign breathing; [...] there is no survival while the sovereign lives."[3] Our times, from James Hansen's testimony to the US Senate Committee on Energy and Natural Resources in 1988 to the Sixth Assessment Report of the Intergovernmental Panel on Climate Change published in 2022, have been defined by the scientific certainty that industrial emissions cause global heating – and by capital's hucksters continuing to declare that they don't.[4]

It was not always thus with the idea that climate change might be a good thing. As Alan Bewell showed some years ago, Percy Shelley envisaged a "biosocial utopia [...] centred in human beings," predicated in turn on a "republican environmentalism" and "global ecological revolution" that would make "the entire earth serve human needs."[5] I want to rehearse some aspects of Bewell's reading in a moment, not least because Shelley's anthropocentric climatological optimism may at first sight appear drastically unsuited to our times, although it is worth remarking here that there is more to Shelley's image of a fecund, productive earth than mere dismissal of it as hopelessly optimistic would allow. Yet the focus of this chapter is on the image of vegetal overgrowth that returns on a number of occasions in Shelley's later, darker poetry. In particular, as envisaged by Shelley, a resurgent, overgrowing nature often owes its shape to the human ruins it at once conceals and reveals. That concealment and revelation is at once literal – Shelley is interested in how we can see the shapes of the wrecks of past human civilizations beneath the plant life that has overgrown it – and figurative, in the sense that what nature's recolonization of the ruins of civilization suggests is that nature is not merely the basis for history but that history is the basis for nature.[6] I want to suggest that Shelley's fascination with the ways that plants grow over ruins and take their shape enables a set of insights into the relations between nature and civilization, especially when the latter is threatened or has been superseded. Shelley's numerous poetic reflections on the relation between nature and civilization in the wake of the latter's collapse are, of course, especially germane to our times. Reflecting on the changes to the relation between the human and the natural in the two centuries since Shelley beheld the glaciers of Mont Blanc, David Collings concludes his penetrating study of Romantic imaginings of disaster by remarking that "[t]oday, the 'works and ways of man' once threatened by the glaciers threaten them in turn, causing them, as it were, to fly far in dread. It does not follow, of course," Collings usefully reminds us, "that humanity is now the dominant force, that nature is now somehow subjected to human will; on the contrary, the climatological changes we have unleashed function in a complex dynamic well beyond human control."[7] Shelley's poetic responses to the growth of plants over the ruins of civilization also conceive of a dynamic well beyond human control. It is a dynamic in which humanity is by no means the dominant force, as well as one, however, in which nature does not simply exert its domination over humanity either. Rather than erase the traces of a fallen civilization, overgrowing nature perpetuates the remnants of human history in forms that humanity determined but did not, exactly, intend. Shelley's imagination of overgrown ruins is distinct both from the exuberant fantasy of a wholly rewilded nature and also from the sometimes more melancholy vision – deftly elaborated by a range of new materialist, speculative realist, and new pessimist thinkers – of a world without us in it. Shelley envisions a nexus of the human and nonhuman that at once bears the traces of the human in its very lineaments but is nevertheless beyond the reach of further human manipulation.

The image of overgrowth furnished one early biographer of Shelley with a description of Shelley's character and imagination in general. Thomas Jefferson Hogg wrote that Shelley "was a climber, a creeper, an elegant, beautiful, odoriferous parasitical plant; he could not support himself; he must be tied up fast to something of a firmer texture, harder and more rigid than his own, pliant, yielding structure; to some person of a less flexible formation: he always required a prop."[8] Hogg's description is not altogether flattering, to say the least. The first two epithets – "climber," "creeper" – establish Shelley as furtive and self-serving, before the effusion of "elegant, beautiful," and even "odoriferous" strikes a more positive note – only to be negatively qualified again by "parasitical." Hogg certainly viewed himself as having at one point served as the firmer, harder, more rigid structure that, so he alleged, Shelley always needed. I merely register here that I think such a view of Shelley is contestable; my real aim is to suggest, first of all, that we can relate Shelley's interest in and, indeed, affinity for overgrowing vegetation with recent conceptions of rewilding in environmental discourse and activism. Such conceptions have started to have an impact on readings of Romantic writers but they also, in some signal instances, begin from an engagement with Romanticism.[9] However, Shelley can hardly be accounted an advocate for or forerunner of rewilding, intimating instead a vision of a dark rewilding (so to speak) that does not so much restore a healthy balance between nature and humanity but rather overgrows, conceals, and yet perpetuates the wrecks of humanity's imperialistic folly. There are a number of vital – and timely – questions at issue here. Does the colonization of the ruins of one form of human civilization by a resurgent nature represent an improvement on the former? Either way, does human history always end up, insidiously, asserting itself, shaping even as it is covered by vegetal overgrowth? Can we even talk of "nature" in such a circumstance, since, however assertively plants recolonize the ruins of human artifice, they take their shape from and follow the course of just those ruins? Is the ruin of human civilization, in whatever form, the inevitable precondition of the renewal of nature?

Let us work up to these questions by reviewing Shelley's revolutionary climatology, influentially elaborated by Bewell and others. As Michael Verderame has put it with respect to the same early poem that formed the focus of Bewell's discussion, "[t]he imagined paradise of *Queen Mab* is one in which the seasons, and indeed, climate itself, have been eradicated in favor of an evergreen, temperately warm earth."[10] But this "eradication" in fact serves to restore, for Shelley, an earlier, human world. As Bewell's account of the poet's climatological optimism made clear, for instance, Shelley strikingly claimed that, on "yon earth," "Thou canst not find one spot / Whereon no city stood" (II.223–224 [*CP* II: 180]). As Bewell puts it, in contrast to the conventional understanding of the relation between wilderness and cities, for Shelley "cities come first." The persistence of this conviction of the priority of urban civilization is confirmed, for example, by Panthea's visionary deep history of the earth midway through the final act of *Prometheus Unbound*:

> The wrecks beside of many a city vast,
> Whose population which the Earth grew over
> Was mortal but not human; see, they lie,
> Their monstrous works and uncouth skeletons,
> Their statues, homes, and fanes; prodigious shapes
> Huddled in grey annihilation, split,
> Jammed in the hard black deep; and over these
> The anatomies of unknown winged things,
> [...]   —and over these
> The jagged alligator and the might
> Of earth-convulsing behemoth, which once
> Were monarch beasts, and on the slimy shores
> And weed-overgrown continents of Earth
> Increased and multiplied like summer worms
> On an abandoned corpse, till the blue globe
> Wrapt Deluge round it like a cloak (IV.296–315 [*SPP* 278])

The presentation of the history of Earth as being many-layered is emphasized not only with the repetition of "and over these" but also, in the dense verbal sedimentation of these lines, by the largely subterranean repetition (breaking the surface into full appearance, as it were, only twice) of *on* in "c*on*vulsing," "*on*ce," "m*on*arch," "*on*," "c*on*tinents," "On," and "aband*on*ed," a repetition that registers the historical movement of the Earth's history on and on and on and on ....

But if all of the Earth, down, as Shelley had put it in *Queen Mab*, to "the minutest drop of rain," had once been human, why is it no longer (II.212 [*CP* II: 180])? What has happened to dehumanize nature? Panthea's answer – that "Earth grew over" the wrecks of "many of a city vast" – does not really explain how that came to happen or, indeed, how the cities were wrecked in the first place. But as *Prometheus Unbound* itself may be taken to suggest, and as an early work like *Queen Mab* surely did, Shelley conceived of the dehumanization of nature not as a natural process but rather as itself a human one, for which Shelley has a specific name: tyranny. "Tyranny," as Bewell puts it, "*is* ruin"; conversely, "[r]evolution is ecological reclamation, the recovery of nature produced by human labor and love that has been destroyed by social degradation."[11] Bewell shows how Shelley arrived at this vision through adapting the arguments of influential figures such as Montesquieu and Volney; on the particular matter of the ruination effected by tyranny and the restoration effected by revolution, a further parallel with another political writer suggests itself. In the second paragraph of Thomas Paine's 1776 pamphlet, *Common Sense*, Paine eulogizes society – "[s]ociety in every state is a blessing" – and criticizes government – "but government, even in its best state, is but a necessary evil."[12] He goes on: "Government, like dress, is the badge of lost innocence; the palaces of kings are built upon the ruins of the bowers of paradise."[13] Paine's contention that "the palaces of kings are built upon the ruins of the bowers of paradise" operates with a conventional sense of the relation between wilderness ("bowers of paradise") and cities (insofar as palaces belong in cities) and likewise of the fall from an egalitarian into a hierarchical society. Paine's terms, at least, are clearly recognizable in one of the many statements Shelley makes in *A Defence of Poetry* concerning the connections between politics and poetry. Here, specifically, he is describing the effect of the abolition of slavery and the emancipation of women:

> It was as if the statues of Apollo and the Muses had been endowed with life and motion and had walked forth among their worshippers; so that earth became peopled by the inhabitants of a diviner world. The familiar appearance and proceedings of life became wonderful and heavenly; and a paradise was created as out of the wrecks of Eden. And as this creation is itself poetry, so its creators were poets. (*SPP* 525)

The close terminological similarity between Paine and Shelley, however, only serves to highlight a number of differences between them. First and most obvious, Paine's image illustrates the evil – however necessary – of government, while Shelley's illustrates the new, heavenly society that arose after the rectification of historic injustices. And while it is possible that (though he does not specify) wrecker of paradise and builder of palaces are one and the same for Paine, the wider context of the passage in Shelley makes it clear that the creator of the new paradise is only the inheritor of the ruins left by others.

Shelley's vision of a newly built paradise is one in which the earth, instead of being restored to nature, is "peopled." It is worth acknowledging again that Shelley's vision of an earth rendered not only "habitable" but in fact "peopled" and dedicated to serving human ends seems drastically out of step with contemporary environmental thinking. Defrosted poles, cornfields and pastures overspreading the earth, vegetarian predators: such are the features of Shelley's ecological vision and such a vision seems to intimate ecological disaster wrought by agri-industrial fantasy and a world populated by invasive species and the farm-bred lion, as much as it intimates reconciliation between nature and humanity.[14] As Bewell emphasizes, Shelley certainly criticized English society's self-presentation as a garden idyll – though not for any fault in that presentation but rather in England's failure to live up to it. Recent environmental commentators and activists, however, have become rather more circumspect with regard to Romantic conceptions of humanity's place in nature. While paying tribute to Wordsworth's role in the foundation of "the Western conservation movement," for instance, the campaigner and journalist George Monbiot has sought to question the category of "cultural landscape" on the basis of which UNESCO assesses applications for world heritage status. Monbiot cites Wordsworth's celebration of hill-sheep farming in the Lake District as an instance of how we have become acculturated to what is in fact an environmentally damaging practice.[15] Wordsworth stands accused, in Monbiot's account, of fostering "a strange bifurcation in our minds, which sees industrialism as malign and destructive and agriculture as benign and harmonious." It is not that Monbiot wishes to offer a defense of industrialism – far from it – but rather that he thinks we should see agriculture as equally, if not more, to blame for the environmental calamities usually associated with industry instead. "Farming has done more extensive damage to wildlife and habitats than all the factories ever built. Few kinds of farming," he goes on, with particular pertinence to the kind of farming cherished by Wordsworth, but which also affects Shelley's vision of a world covered with "pastures," "have done more harm in proportion to their output than the keeping of sheep in the hills." Monbiot concludes by asking why our aesthetic sensibility ought still to be determined by Wordsworth – a question with which Romanticists have long wrestled – and suggests that "sheepwrecked" landscapes, particularly given their agricultural underproductivity, ought to be restored to nature and rewilded.

There is no need to detain ourselves with the rights and wrongs of Monbiot's reading of Wordsworth, nor with how much Wordsworth's celebration of the Lake District may have in common with Shelley's biosocial utopianism; rather, I want to pause for a moment on the rights and wrongs of rewilding itself. It should be acknowledged straightaway that even in his critique of "cultural landscape," Monbiot allows that it is a potentially useful category, especially because it recognizes the involvement of humans in the natural world – indeed, in *Feral*, Monbiot conceives of rewilding as a process from which humans would benefit as much as anyone or anything else. And he has consistently and trenchantly criticized the tendency of those who might be called establishment environmentalists to blame our environmental crises on "the bogeyman of overpopulation" – a move that Shelley, as we have seen, would likewise have found disgraceful.[16] Yet still, as Irma Allen has suggested in a thorough inquisition of rewilding advocacy, some of that advocacy, including Monbiot's, harbors a series of troubling assumptions. Seizing on Monbiot's observation that in the European Union (EU) an area the size of Poland has come out of agricultural production in recent years and has thus been rendered ripe for rewilding, Allen shows that Poland itself has been the locus of considerable class conflict between small-scale, family farms and large, agri-industrial conglomerates.[17] The reason an area the size of Poland is available for rewilding is that a large number of small-scale farmers and agricultural workers have been sacrificed on the altar of global capital. And the food once grown in the EU continues to have to come from somewhere – often recently de-wilded ecological habitats.

It should be emphasized that Allen's intention is not to stop rewilding in its tracks, nor is it the case that advocates of rewilding like Monbiot, Isabella Tree, and others are content to leave the system of global agriculture, along with the unsustainable levels of Western consumption that it serves, as they are (advocating instead, for example, for plant-based diets, something, again, Shelley would have supported). Yet Allen does usefully bring into the open a number of underexamined assumptions behind rewilding, along with some of its unintended consequences. If there is an overall point to her argument, it is surely that the web of human involvement in nature is much more extensive and fraught than even some of the most sophisticated advocates of rewilding have appeared to allow. Ecological reclamation, whether humans like it or not, involves humans.

Yet however initially dependent upon human intervention the erasure of the marks of human intervention may be, the aim of rewilding is to reproduce a world that exists, so to speak, behind the back and out of the mind of human agents. Chris Washington expands on Shelley's deployment of Milton's Satan's consoling statement that "[t]he mind is its own place" by remarking that "[t]he mind is its own place; the world is another." Washington explains that "[d]espite that 'all things exist as they are perceived, at least to the percipient,' all things also, like Mont Blanc and the eternal power continually walled off from human thought, exist as they are whether or not they are perceived."[18] As Washington shows in his innovative reading of Shelley, a glimpse of that world is all we can manage thanks to the obliterating effect of familiarity (and we may here conceive of "familiarity" as closely akin to humanization). The recognition of the difficulty of achieving and perceiving a world that is not continually shaped by humanity is thus central to Shelley's poetic project – and central to his relevance for our times in which the unintended consequences of the total humanization of nature are rapidly becoming all too apparent.

I alluded earlier in the chapter to Adorno's dismay at the "farm-bred lion." Adorno invoked this unhappy creature in the course of a prescient discussion of the prospects for the reconciliation of humanity with nature.[19] He reflects, as he does with perhaps surprising frequency, on zoos, remarking in particular their involvement with bourgeois class consciousness. Zoos are "laid out on the pattern of Noah's Ark, for since their inception the bourgeois class has been waiting for the flood."[20] Zoos, that is, "are allegories of the specimen or pair who defy the disaster that befalls the species *qua* species." What are undeniably real advances in the humane treatment of captive animals and in the preservation of nature have, Adorno points out, their dialectical underside: "The more purely nature is preserved and transplanted by civilization, the more implacably is it dominated. We can now afford to encompass ever larger natural units, and leave them apparently intact within our grasp, whereas previously the selecting and taming of particular items bore witness to the difficulty we still had in coping with nature." Adorno wishes as little to return to a situation in which humanity struggles to cope with nature as he does to the colonial imperialism of which zoos were an expression or, indeed, to the inhumane treatment of animals. But nor is the enclosure of nature, its division into "units," however large, a salutary prospect for humanity either. "Only in the irrationality of civilization itself," Adorno asserts, "in the nooks and crannies of the cities, to which the walls, towers, and bastions of the zoos wedged among them are merely an addition, can nature be conserved. The rationalization of culture, in opening its doors to nature, thereby completely absorbs it, and eliminates with difference the principle of culture, the possibility of reconciliation." "You'll see more wildlife in Birmingham," Monbiot scoffs at one point in his disparagement of the notion that the "cultural landscape" of the Lake District is a haven for nature. Perhaps he is right – but perhaps that is because it is in Birmingham, rather than the Lake District, that we should rest our hopes for the conservation of nature.[21]

Wherever we should ultimately rest our hopes for the conservation of nature, it is undeniable that the climatological optimism of Shelley's early verse, and the benevolently human (or humanly benevolent) interaction with nature that it betokens, gives way to a more complex, often darker understanding of the involvement of what is (or was) human in what is (or may be) nature.[22] Shelley also anticipates the insight that it is in the "nooks and crannies" – off the main thoroughfares and amongst the ruins (*Gemäuer*, Adorno's somewhat elevated term that Edmund Jephcott translates as "crannies," can also mean both walls and ruins) – of cities that nature's resurgence can be observed.[23] Nature's resurgence, however, need not entail the reconciliation of humanity with nature but rather the mute perpetuation of the traces of humanity in a context drastically beyond humanity's control.

A relatively neutral image of vegetal overgrowth is to be found in the justly celebrated passage of *Epipsychidion* in which the speaker is describing to the addressee, Emily, the home he has chosen for them – an island girded by the blue Aegean (430 [*SPP* 403]). On the island stands a solitary dwelling, "built by whom or how / None of the rustic island-people know," but the building of which the poem's speaker ascribes to "Some wise and tender Ocean-King" (484–485, 488 [404–405]). Notably, he puts the period of the tower's construction "ere crime / Had been invented, in the world's young prime" (488–489 [405]). Donald H. Reiman and Neil Fraistat, the editors of the Norton edition of Shelley's works, helpfully suggest that "[o]ne underlying myth may be that of Nereus, the eldest son of Oceanus," whom Hesiod describes in the *Theogony* as "always right and always gentle" (*SPP* 405, n. 3); whatever the specific mythological precedent, the period invoked is a prelapsarian one and crime is cast as an "invention" rather than (in Hobbesian fashion) as something like the state of nature itself. It is also a period in which ocean-kings (even if not necessarily people) *build*: again, Shelley's sense that cities precede wilderness is in evidence here. This, though, is how the lone dwelling has come to appear by the time of the speaker's description of it:

> It scarce seems now a wreck of human art,
> But, as it were Titanic; in the heart
> Of Earth having assumed its form, then grown
> Out of the mountains, from living stone,
> Lifting itself in caverns light and high:
> For all the antique and learned imagery
> Has been erased, and in the place of it
> The ivy and the wild-vine interknit
> The volumes of their many twining stems;
> Parasite flowers illume with dewy gems
> The lampless halls, and when they fade, the sky
> Peeps through their winter-woof of tracery
> With Moon-light patches, or star atoms keen,
> Or fragments of the day's intense serene;—
> Working mosaic on their Parian floors. (493–507 [405])

Far from consolingly attesting to the survival of the "secret spirit of humanity / […] 'mid the calm oblivious tendencies / Of nature, 'mid her plants, and weeds, and flowers, / And silent overgrowings" in the manner of Wordsworth's wanderer contemplating the devastation of Margaret's "poor Hut" at the conclusion of the first book of *The Excursion*,[24] the above passage from *Epipsychidion* instead presents erasure of the spirit of humanity's works as the precursor, if not precondition, of the artistry wrought by nature's silent overgrowings. The dwelling "*seems* [...] *as it were* Titanic," a conjectural framing that lends a certain – admittedly, appropriate – tentativeness to the following flight of fancy according to which the dwelling emerged "having assumed its form" in the earth. The dwelling "scarce seems now a wreck of human art," but the forming of the dwelling in the earth and the deployment of a sculptural, architectural lexicon in the description of its growth in "living stone, / Lifting itself in caverns light and high" serves to suggest that human art is perhaps not the only kind. To be sure, the suggestion of a Titanic artificer indeed evokes divine – rather than either human or natural – creation, perhaps hinting in turn at a way out of an opposition between human civilization and natural production. But in addition to the fact (already noted) that this suggestion of Titanic construction is only an appearance, the Titans themselves, of course, are a superseded order of divinity, whose creations tend to turn out badly for them. The atmosphere of ambivalence that characterizes this consideration of the dwelling's making thus extends to its putative origins "in the heart / Of Earth" – where "Earth" is at once the material substrate of all nature but also, as a Titan, divine. If the dwelling's origins are not exactly to be found "in human art," that need not mean they are exclusively natural either. A natural artifice is at work elsewhere in these lines – in the volumes of ivy and wild-vine, the winter-woof of the vines that creep over the dwelling, and, above all, in the mosaic that the patches of moonlight form on the Parian floors of the dwelling's halls. Natural elements do not need the support of the wrecked dwelling for their artistry, however. The passage concludes by describing how Earth and Ocean "aloof, from the high towers / And terraces [...] dream / Of waves, flowers, clouds, woods, rocks, and all that we / Read in their smiles, and call reality" (508–511 [405]). We may no longer read "the antique and learned imagery" erased from the dwelling but instead only the smiles of Earth and Ocean as they dream. It is the outward signs of their dreams that are our reality.

In the passage following the one I have just been discussing, the speaker of the poem declares to Emily that he owns the house of which he has been speaking and that Emily will be "lady of the solitude" (he does not ask if she wants to be) (514 [*SPP* 405]). He goes on to say that he has restored human art to it, sending "books and music there, and all / Those instruments with which high spirits call / The future from its cradle, and the past / Out of its grave" – an important restoration of faith in what "high spirits" may be able to evoke (519–522 [405]). In the curtailed sonnet (one of the poem's "Weak Verses," perhaps, lacking the strength to fulfill its length) that concludes *Epipsychidion*, it is just such an ability to evoke the past that the poet ascribes to what he himself has written: "Then call your sisters from Oblivion's cave" (595 [407]). Elsewhere in Shelley's work, the artistry of nature as it grows over the ruins of one formation of humanity is cast as conducive to renewed human artistry. For instance, Shelley gives the following information about the composition of *Prometheus Unbound* in the preface to that poem:

> This Poem was chiefly written upon the mountainous ruins of the Baths of Caracalla, among the flowery glades, and thickets of odoriferous blossoming trees which are extended in ever winding labyrinths upon its immense platforms and dizzy arches suspended in the air. (*SPP* 207)

The site of the poem's composition serves not only as general inspiration for *Prometheus Unbound* but seems to have a specific echo, for example, in the conclusion to Asia's celebrated "enchanted boat" revery at the end of Act II, where she envisages the souls of her and her sister, Panthea, coming "Through Death and Birth, to a diviner day":

> A Paradise of vaulted bowers
> Lit by downward-gazing flowers,
> And watery paths that wind between
> Wildernesses calm and green,
> Peopled by shapes too bright to see (II.v.104–108 [255])

The proximity of "paradise" and "bowers" also echoes Paine's assertion, discussed earlier, that "the palaces of kings are built upon the ruins of the bowers of paradise," and the "watery paths" winding "between / Wildernesses calm and green" – anticipated earlier in Asia's speech, in fact, by the description of her soul floating "ever—forever— / Upon that many winding River, / Between mountains, woods, abysses, / A Paradise of wildernesses!" – evoke the "ever winding labyrinths" of the Baths of Caracalla (II.v.78–81 [254]).

The setting that Shelley describes here gave rise not only to the work of art that is *Prometheus Unbound* itself but also to surely the most widely known image of Shelley, Joseph Severn's *Shelley Composing "Prometheus Unbound" Amidst the Ruins of Rome*, completed in 1845 at the instigation of Shelley's son, Percy Florence Shelley, and some twenty-three years after the poet's death.[25] However well-known it is, it remains a beguiling painting, on which there has been relatively little commentary – apart from Mary's complaint that Severn had got Shelley's nose and mouth all wrong.[26]

Severn's painting bears a resemblance to Joseph Wright of Derby's celebrated 1781 portrait of Sir Brooke Boothby, which shows the landed (and fashionably dressed) gentleman reposing in a pleasingly wooded corner of his estate, addressing the viewer from the canvas and pointing to the name "Rousseau" on the spine of a book on the ground.[27] But where Boothby's romantically unkempt, twilit estate is distinctly in the background of the central figure – except where he props his elbow on a conveniently situated tree – perhaps the most striking feature of the composition of Severn's painting is its stark bifurcation by a twisting tree trunk – a tree that, while it is in leaf, is hardly profuse, and in which it is tempting to see the distorted root for which the visionary of *The Triumph of Life* mistook what was once Rousseau. The tree in Severn's painting, which draws attention up and away from Shelley's gaze (another contrast with the Wright portrait), is the dominating feature of the composition. The tree's roots seem perilously inadequate to its size and habit, giving the impression that it is dizzyingly unsupported by any remnant structure. Something similar is a feature of Shelley's own description of the Baths of Caracalla in the earlier passage: the "dizzy arches" are at once the ruined arches of the baths (on which Severn also dwells) but also the shape of the plants that have subsequently grown over them, which are thus not suspended in the air but rooted, albeit imperceptibly, on the ruins. Moreover, the fact that Shelley's "its" in the final sentence seems to lack a grammatical referent – apart, perhaps, from the poem itself – adds to the sense of finally indeterminable interaction between ruin, thicket, and poem. Add to this the passage's prepositional precocity – "upon," "among," "in," "upon" again – and the relations between what we might envisage as a shaping base and a shaped superstructure are complicated still further. Where Wright of Derby's portrait of Boothby leaning on the helpfully placed tree is meant to celebrate the vision and fortune of its socially elevated subject, Severn's picture of Shelley and the tree that divides the canvas, extending dizzily out into the ether, serve as something like an allegory for the ultimately undecidable relation between historical civilization and vegetal overgrowth, between artifice and nature, authorship and inspiration.

The apparent mystery of the relation of vegetal overgrowth to the ruins of a formation of human civilization underneath it notwithstanding, the inspirational atmosphere of the Baths of Caracalla appears, however, a wholesome air. But overgrowth is often far less than wholesome in Shelley's verse – as in, for instance, the fragment of 1818, "Flourishing vine, whose kindling clusters glow," given the suitably sepulchral title "The Vine Shroud" when it was first published by William Rossetti in 1870:

> Flourishing vine, whose kindling clusters glow
> Beneath the autumnal sun—none taste of thee—
> For thou dost shroud a ruin, and below
> The rotting bones of dead antiquity. (1–4 [*Poems* II: 422])

The Romantic topos of overgrown ruins draws, of course, on a considerable literature dedicated to the wrecks of empire. Felicia Hemans's "The Widow of Crescentius," published in her 1819 volume *Tales, and Historic Scenes, in Verse*, for example, displays its debts to Chateaubriand and Sismondi in its notes and opens "Midst Tivoli's luxuriant glades," where "nature hath resumed her throne / O'er the vast works of ages flown."[28] These are scenes, in Hemans's poem, "where verdure's rich array / Still sheds young beauty o'er decay," but in Shelley's lines, the redemption of decay by youth and beauty appears, to say the least, less assured.[29] The description of the grapes, and of the vine itself, in the opening line is admittedly rather lush, a fact that has caused problems for interpreters of the poem. Kelvin Everest and Geoffrey Matthews, the Longman editors, hit a conundrum when trying to date and to place the composition of this short fragment: "The draft is among material dating from autumn 1818 to spring 1819. Lines 3–4 ["For thou dost shroud a ruin, and below / The rotting bones of dead antiquity"] might suggest Herculaneum or Pompeii, but leaves of the vines were already in decay when S. travelled south from Este on 5 November" (*Poems* II: 422). On the one hand, the fact of the leaves of the vines being (in the editors' resonant phrase) "in decay" would seem to contradict the idea in the poem that the vine itself is flourishing; but on the other hand, that the vine has yielded what initially appears to be a voluptuous, tempting harvest ("kindling clusters") might indeed betoken its flourishing or, at least, evidence that it has flourished. But there is further support in the sole manuscript source of this poem for Everest's and Matthews' implicit sense that the timing and placing of "Flourishing vine, whose kindling clusters glow" is perplexing. Where Shelley eventually writes "none taste of thee" he had initially, incongruously written "sweet violet" – incongruously, both because it is difficult to see how he envisaged "sweet violet" fitting the syntax and meter of the poem, however inchoate they may have been at this stage of drafting, and, moreover, because sweet violet is neither a vine nor does it flower in the autumn. A plausible source for "sweet violet," especially given its natural incongruity in the context of the fragment, may have been Francis Fawkes's translation of Theocritus's tenth *Idyll*: "The letter'd hyacinth's of darksome hue, / And the sweet violet a sable blue."[30] Shelley's rejected – and unseasonal – "sweet Violet" may then have had its roots not in the Italian countryside but in ancient literature. Similarly, the flourishing vine is sustained not by a wholesome, natural hummus but instead by "The rotting bones of dead antiquity." This image of the "bones of antiquity" is familiar from the sequence in *Adonais* where the poet is exhorting the "Fond wretch" who would mourn for Adonais to "go to Rome":

> Go thou to Rome,—at once the Paradise,
> The grave, the city, and the wilderness;
> And where its wrecks like shattered mountains rise,
> And flowering weeds, and fragrant copses dress
> The bones of Desolation's nakedness
> Pass, till the Spirit of the spot shall lead
> Thy footsteps to a slope of green access
> Where, like an infant's smile, over the dead,
> A light of laughing flowers along the grass is spread. (433–441 [*SPP* 425])

The Norton editors offer a consoling gloss to these lines, remarking that Severn, asked by Keats before his death to examine the non-Catholic cemetery in Rome, had expressed pleasure in the violets and daisies amongst the grass there – a circumstance, indeed, that Shelley himself notices in his preface: "The cemetery is an open space among the ruins covered in winter with violets and daisies. It might make one in love with death, to think that one should be buried in so sweet a place" (409–410). The echo of Keats's "I have been half in love with easeful Death" is plain enough, though in the context of the several ambivalences of the above passage from *Adonais*, it may be well to recall that the speaker of "Ode to a Nightingale" was only ever "half in love" and that there may be deaths other than the easeful kind. The "light of laughing flowers," likened to "an infant's smile," is perhaps a conventional enough attempt to counterpose the gloom of death, but the fact that this laughter and smile occur "over the dead" surely introduces a hint of unseemly levity. Though the "flowering weeds" earlier in the stanza may or may not pun on "weeds" as the clothes of mourners, "fragrant copses," in a stanza describing a graveyard, is grimly close to the at once mordant and repulsive image of "fragrant corpses." We are far, here, from the "odoriferous blossoming arches" of the Baths of Caracalla.

In "Flourishing vine," a formation of human civilization frequently credited with having overcome death – namely, antiquity – is shown to have succumbed to death, after all, and is thus drastically opposed to the cycles of natural flourishing and decay that feed upon it (as in the stanza of *Adonais* following the one discussed above: "And grey walls moulder round, on which dull Time / Feeds, like slow fire upon a hoary brand"

[442–443 (*SPP* 425)]). This vegetal growth is starkly not amenable to human uses and pleasures: "none taste of thee." Flourishing, fructifying life turns out to be a perpetuation in life of the death of human civilization itself. In a fragment composed perhaps five months after "Flourishing vine," Shelley does appear to oppose a finally obliterated civilization to an enduring nature: "Rome has fallen, ye see it lying / Heaped in undistinguished ruin / Nature is alone undying" (1–3 [*Poems* II: 453]). As well as the strong verbal echo, the fact that it is Rome – the blame for whose decline and fall Gibbon famously laid at the door of Christianity – that is thus described anticipates the striking assertion in "Ode to Liberty" that "The Galilean serpent forth did creep, / And made thy world an undistinguished heap" (VIII.119–120 [*SPP* 310]). Despite the fact that the assertion that nature is "alone undying" hardly constitutes a celebration of nature's vitality (especially given Shelley's attempts to consider the distinctions between mere perpetuation and actual life), the crucial point to take from both the "Rome has fallen" fragment and the lines from "Ode to Liberty" is that Shelley is willing, at times, to posit a clear distinction between fallen, heaped, undistinguished civilization and the immortality of nature.[31] That this is so, however, makes his insistent return to a more complex, involved relation between civilization and nature all the more compelling. As I have been arguing, the continuity between history and a nature inevitably informed by the historical formations that it succeeds is much more characteristic of Shelley's conception of the relationship between civilization and nature. And as I have suggested, this is a conception that is strikingly apt to our times, in which the human presence in nature is both effectively total and drastically imperiled. Shelley's conception of a world without us that is also a world structured by the traces we leave behind is aimed at mortifying the consolation harbored in the self-annihilating but thereby also self-exculpating fantasy of a world after humans that would somehow be a world wholly without any trace of them. The world without us is also a world without any trace of the damage we have done to it – a world, in other words, that cannot be.

The contrast between a text like "Rome has fallen" and "Flourishing vine" also extends, incidentally, to their different textual statuses. Everest and Matthews describe both "Flourishing vine" and "Rome has fallen" alike as fragments. Yet the grounds for considering the latter as a fragment are much less compelling than in the former case. Both texts are short, to be sure, but in the case of "Rome has fallen," there is no evidence of unresolved – or, indeed, any – attempts at revision; each of the poem's three lines conforms to a standard pattern of eight or (if each syllable of the first line is fully enunciated) nine syllables, and, by means of its starkly stated opposition of civilization and nature, it achieves a certain epigrammatic unity. None of this is the case in "Flourishing vine," which is, so to speak, emphatically fragmentary. The gothic "rotting bones" of the final line are cancelled in the manuscript and, as noted, "none taste of thee" is an acerbic alternative for the initial, literary "sweet violet." "Flourishing vine" is not only a description of the ruin of human civilization and the repulsing of human taste by the fruits of cultivation turned wild but, in its own fragmentary condition, an unflinching enactment of just those processes: as we are starting to roll the sound pattern of the opening line, rung on the Shelleyan keynotes of "kindling clusters glow," the poet reaches for the spittoon: "none taste of them." In their dependence upon the ruins that they colonize, the vines break emphatically free from human needs and purposes. Rather than "The vine, the corn, the olive mild," which prior to the advent of agriculture, the "Ode to Liberty" tells us, "Grew savage yet, to human use unreconciled" (53 [*SPP* 308]) or rather even than the "wild-vine" of the passage from *Epipsychidion* discussed earlier, which interknits the volumes of its stems with those of the ivy where once had been antique and learned imagery, the "flourishing vine" of this fragment has instead turned feral. The wild will return not in accord with human ends and purposes but once those ends and purposes lie in ruins. It is a future that, as numerous fantasies of life after humans and of the world without us in it have entertained, may not be our time but could well be the one that we are preparing. "Go thou to Rome,—" the poet of *Adonais* counselled, "at once the Paradise, / The grave, the city, and the wilderness": the eternal city is Paradise, grave, city, and wilderness neither in sequence nor in carefully demarcated and administered units but all at once (433–434 [425]). It is in the recognition of the irrationality of culture, even as instantiated in its most venerated monuments and achievements, that nature may be conserved and reconciliation with it fulfilled.

Notes

1 Earlier versions of this chapter were presented at the Fifteenth International Conference of the British Association for Romantic Studies, hosted by the University of York, and the conference on Late Romanticism: Past and Present, Katholieke Universiteit Leuven, Belgium. I express my gratitude to the organizers and audiences of those conferences.
2 The quotation is the last line of the voiceover to a short film produced by the Competitive Enterprise Institute in 2006, accessible at: https://unearthed.greenpeace.org/2016/11/18/donald-trump-myron-ebell-cei-climate-change/.

For a catalogue of the supposed benefits of global heating, see Matt Ridley, "Why Climate Change Is Good for the World," *The Spectator*, October 19, 2013, www.spectator.co.uk/article/why-climate-change-is-good-for-the-world.

3   Joshua Clover, "The Rise and Fall of Biopolitics: A Response to Bruno Latour," March 29, 2020, *In the Moment*, https://critinq.wordpress.com/2020/03/29/the-rise-and-fall-of-biopolitics-a-response-to-bruno-latour/.

4   A transcript of Hansen's testimony is available at: https://pulitzercenter.org/sites/default/files/june_23_1988_senate_hearing_1.pdf; the technical summary of the 3,000-page, 2022 Intergovernmental Panel on Climate Change (IPCC) report is available at: www.ipcc.ch/report/ar6/wg2/downloads/report/IPCC_AR6_WGII_TechnicalSummary.pdf. For a recent instance of climate denialism, published after the release of the latest IPCC report, see Melanie Phillips, "Sri Lanka shows the danger of green dogma," *The Times*, July 11, 2022, www.thetimes.co.uk/article/sri-lanka-shows-the-danger-of-green-dogma-sf69m752q.

5   Alan Bewell, *Romanticism and Colonial Disease* (Baltimore: Johns Hopkins University Press, 1999), 211, 216. Compare also the more recent discussions of Shelley that have engaged his conceptions of the relation between humanity and the world, the climate, sustainability, and comparable concerns: Adam R. Rosenthal, "Shelley and the Limits of Sustainability," in Ben R. Robertson, ed. *Romantic Sustainability: Endurance and the Natural World, 1780–1830* (Lanham: Lexington Books, 2015), 233–244; Chris Washington, *Romantic Revelations: Visions of Post-Apocalyptic Life and Hope in the Anthropocene* (Toronto: University of Toronto Press, 2019), especially 28–65; David Collings, *Disastrous Subjectivities: Romanticism, Modernity, and the Real* (Toronto: University of Toronto Press, 2019), 139–69 and 171–180 (on Romanticism and climate change generally); and Michael Verderame, "'We Are As Clouds': Climate and Social Transformation in Shelley," *ISLE: Interdisciplinary Studies in Literature and Environment* 28 (2021), 271–290.

6   In the background here is Theodor W. Adorno's early conception of the idea of natural-history. See "The Idea of Natural-History," trans. by Robert Hullot-Kentor, in *Things beyond Resemblance: Collected Essays on Theodor W. Adorno* (New York: Columbia University Press, 2006), 252–269 and, for commentary, see for instance Deborah Cook, *Adorno on Nature* (Durham: Acumen, 2011), 15–31.

7   Collings, *Disastrous Subjectivities*, 176 (the quotation is from "Mont Blanc" l. 92).

8   Thomas Jefferson Hogg, *The Life of Percy Bysshe Shelley*, 2 volumes (London: Edward Moxon, 1858), II, 46.

9   An instance of the former is Lisa Vargo's "The Rewilding of Dorothy Wordsworth," *The Wordsworth Circle* 52 (2021), 358–367; of the latter, George Monbiot, "Obstinate Questionings," www.monbiot.com/2013/09/02/obstinate-questionings/, first published in *The Guardian*, September 3, 2013. I return briefly to Monbiot, a major popular theorist of and advocate for rewilding, later in the chapter.

10 Verderame, "Climate and Social Transformation in Shelley," 275.

11 Bewell, *Romanticism and Colonial Disease*, 218.

12 Thomas Paine, *Common Sense*, in Bruce Kuklick, ed. *Political Writings* (Cambridge: Cambridge University Press, 1997), 1–45, 3. Though there is evidence that Shelley read *The Rights of Man* (see "Shelley's Reading," in Frederick L. Jones, ed. *The Letters of Percy Bysshe Shelley*, 2 volumes (Oxford: Oxford University Press, 1964), I: 481), there is no positive evidence he read *Common Sense*; hence what I am discussing above is (as I say) a parallel, rather than a source for Shelley in Paine.
13 Paine, *Common Sense*, 3.
14 "The farm-bred lion is as fully tamed as the horse long since subjected to birth control." Theodor W. Adorno, *Minima Moralia: Reflections from Damaged Life*, trans. E. F. N. Jephcott (London: Verso, 1999), 116.
15 Monbiot, "Obstinate Questionings" (from which the ensuing quotations here are also drawn). Monbiot transfers many of these arguments to his book, *Feral: Rewilding the Land, Sea, and Human Life* (London: Penguin, 2014), 153–166, though he excises the critique of Wordsworth in the process.
16 Monbiot, "Population Panic Lets Rich People Off the Hook for the Climate Crisis They Are Fuelling," *The Guardian*, August 26, 2020, www.theguardian.com/commentisfree/2020/aug/26/panic-overpopulation-climate-crisis-consumption-environment. The "bogeyman of overpopulation" is from Robert Fletcher and others, "Barbarian Hordes: The Overpopulation Scapegoat in International Development Discourse," *Third World Quarterly* 35 (2014), 1195–1215, 1196.
17 Irma Allen, "The Trouble with Rewilding," *Undisciplined Environments*, December 14, 2016, https://undisciplinedenvironments.org/2016/12/14/the-trouble-with-rewilding/. Compare Isabella Tree's account of the reasons she and her husband decided to rewild their Knepp Estate in West Sussex: "Small farmers, especially those on marginal land like ours, were increasingly finding it impossible to compete with the new, big industrialized farms," *Wilding: The Return of Nature to a British Farm* (London: Picador, 2018), 32–39 (the quotation is on 33). For a discussion of the rather more complex class politics implicit in the Knepp project itself, see Alex Lee, "Making Rewilding Part of a Socialist Future," *Socialist Resistance*, November 17, 2020, https://socialistresistance.org/making-rewilding-part-of-a-socialist-future/21186.
18 Washington, *Romantic Revelations*, 61, 62.
19 For illuminating commentary on Adorno's conception of reconciliation with nature, a motif central to his thinking, see Cook, *Adorno on Nature*, 55–57, 90.
20 Adorno, *Minima Moralia*, 116. Subsequent quotations from Adorno in this paragraph all appear on the same page.
21 Monbiot, "Obstinate Questionings."
22 Compare Verderame's characterization of the "decisive shift away from the essentially Whiggish narrative of climatic progress in the major work of Shelley's early period, *Queen Mab*" toward an increasingly "negative" portrayal of the relationship between humanity and nature, 274, 275.

23 Compare here Ashton Nichols's conception of "urbanature" developed in his *Beyond Romantic Ecocriticism: Toward Urbanatural Roosting* (New York: Palgrave Macmillan, 2011).
24 William Wordsworth, *The Excursion*, eds. Sally Bushell, James A. Butler, and Michael C. Jaye (Ithaca: Cornell University Press, 2007), 75, Book I, ll. 962–965. For a searching account of this passage, see James K. Chandler, *Wordsworth's Second Nature: A Study of the Poetry and Politics* (Chicago: University of Chicago Press, 1984), 128–130.
25 See Joseph Severn, letter to William E. Gladstone, November 19, 1844, in *Joseph Severn: Letters and Memoirs*, ed. Grant F. Scott (London: Routledge, 2005), 425 and n. 6, for details of Severn's work on the painting. A copy of the picture hangs in the Keats-Shelley Memorial House in Rome, where it is titled *Shelley in the Baths of Caracalla* (the title by which, Scott remarks, it is now more commonly known; the original is in the possession of James Harry Scarlett, 9th Baron Abinger).
26 See Mary Shelley's comments in a letter to Marianne Hunt, quoted by Scott, *Joseph Severn*, 425, n. 6.
27 Oil on canvas, Tate Britain. I was first alerted to this painting by Vargo, 358–359.
28 *Felicia Hemans: Selected Poems, Prose, and Letters*, ed. Gary Kelly (Peterborough, ON: Broadview Press, 2002), 145–172, 146, ll. 1, 17–18.
29 Hemans, *Selected Poems*, ll. 39–40.
30 For Fawkes's translation, see Robert Anderson, ed. *The Works of the British Poets, with Prefaces*, 14 volumes (London: printed for John and Arthur Arch, 1792–1807), 109, Book XIII (1795), ll. 33–34. Compare Jacques Derrida's tracing of the paradigmatically "wild" tulip of Kant's third *Critique* to a textual source: see *The Truth in Painting*, trans. Geoff Bennington and Ian McLeod (Chicago: University of Chicago Press, 1987), 85.
31 On this distinction in Shelley's work, see Ross Wilson, *Shelley and the Apprehension of Life* (Cambridge: Cambridge University Press, 2013), especially 1–20 and 46–65, but compare also Washington, *Romantic Revelations*, 199, n.8.

CHAPTER 10

Creatrix Witches, Nonbinary Creatures, and Shelleyan Transmedia

Kate Singer

However many idealized feminine characters populate Shelley's earlier poems, including *Alastor*'s veiled and Arab maidens, Queen Mab, Ianthe, and Cythna, these figures become even more ethereal in Shelley's last works as they turn less human and, arguably, less gendered.[1] *Prometheus Unbound*'s Asia transmutes into the boat of light akin to *The Triumph of Life*'s "the shape all light," and both spread visionary casts of different varieties over the globe. This worldwide communication has marked resemblances to the Witch of Atlas's "sexless" creation, who first circles the world with her in a pinnace, then flies off while the Witch doses humans with dreams. What has all too often remained unnoticed of the Witch and her creation is the degree to which these figures are increasingly neither real women nor really human.

What if we were to consider the Witch, for example, not simply as a mythical woman who creates a poetic self-reflection in the making of a "Hermaphroditus" but rather as a nonhuman being whose creation of a "sexless thing" interrogates at once binarized sex, gender, and racialized thingliness? Such a reading would take more seriously the nonhuman qualities of the new shape of its being; we could likewise understand the Witch of Atlas as more than an idealized woman but as a posthuman creatrix playing with and undoing forms and substances to offer new instances of being in the world. These figures, as they loosen the shapes of the human, reconsider the ideology of dimorphic biological sex that was arguably just coming into discursive sway at the turn of the nineteenth century.[2] The Witch's creature, with its nonhuman, fluid shape, consequently delinks bodily sex from gender and heteronormative sexuality, even as it offers more fluid bodily performances or social behaviors that verge on what we might call nonbinary genders.

Although scholars have often read a Wollstonecraftian feminism into figures such as Asia and have cited Shelley's forward-thinking polyamory, they also have critiqued the solipsistic masculinity entrenched in his abandonment of Harriet Westbrook, his dalliance with Jane Williams, and his later neglect of Mary Shelley.[3] When it comes to Shelley's relation to gender, sex, and sexuality, it has been difficult to surmount the view of Percy as a veritable Victor Frankenstein – ambitious and idealistic, obsessed with pursuing the hidden secrets of the universe while insensitive or negligent of economic and emotional needs.[4] Shelley may have held a poetic masculine, aristocratic privilege to dodge creditors or to remain distant from his wife's well-documented series of miscarriages, pregnancies, if not the deaths of Clara and William, yet such a feminist Marxist analysis cannot entirely account for Shelley's inventiveness and desire to outthink normative categories of race and gender that were quickly becoming a means of solidifying white bourgeois definitions of the human. *The Witch of Atlas*, with its creatrix figure of the Witch, offers Percy's rewriting of *Frankenstein*'s examination of nonnormative gender, race, and humanity endemic to Victor's creature, and while it may be a privileged one based on an idealism seemingly divorced from the quotidian realities of work and maternity, it offers another model for nonbinary being, one more celebratory of the possibilities of living otherwise.

While it is surprising that Shelley scholars have not put the two works in earnest conversation, it is even more astounding that no scholarly purview has taken seriously Shelley's "Hermaphroditus" figure as a commentary on the thick, derogatory eighteenth-century discourse of "the hermaphrodite," as a critique of Ovid's more violent myth of the genesis of intersex beings, or, more imaginatively, as the dream of an alternative to the period's binary gender-sex systems.[5] For the Witch's creation – whom the Witch only hails as "Hermaphroditus" when it flies off to leave her – exhibits both "gendered" gentleness and strength alongside the morphologies of neither sex. Shelley's poem tries at the very least to move beyond critiques of the multiple ideological models of sex available at the time, "gender relations," or even biopolitical heteronormative sexuality to redraw the very creation of beings whose sex, gender, and human status might likewise be reconfigured in more radical ways.

The poem, as it invents the creation stories of the Witch and then her "sexless thing" as its doubled central narratives, does not see gender or sex as an isolated system; rather, it interrogates an array of intersectional binaristic systems including human/nonhuman, male/female, and racial other/white. While the poem can be read as an allegory of imperial domination,[6] with the Witch's African heritage obviated through Apollo's rape of her mother and the poem's subsequent erasure of Africa, Debbie Lee has argued that the poem's comical veneer presents a parody of the period's simultaneous feminization and colonizing of the African interior. Nahoko Alvey reads the Witch as a hybrid figure of encounter between West and East, created from a union of Apollo and one of the Atlantides (from the Atlas Mountains of Africa), and Jared Hickman has argued for Shelley's use of cosmology as a means of exoticizing Africa even as it offers alternatives forms of love and liberation.[7] Understanding the poem, however, through Valerie Traub's work, which indelibly ties together the Early Modern period's obsession with sexed bodies and the colonial mapping of foreign land, can help us understand the project of reimagining sex and racial categories as necessarily intertwined.[8] Therefore, we might read this poem as an attempt to rewrite several Westernized mythos at once – however much it falls short to our modern ears.

To understand what Shelley might be doing with the myths of gender, race, and the human, we need to look at the host of sources he was reading, including Ovid and Lucian on the Hermaphroditus myth; William Lawrence and John Abernethy on scientific sex and reproduction in Britain and its empire; Erasmus Darwin on nonhuman intersex conditions; and perhaps most importantly Mary Shelley's *Frankenstein* for its thinking about the relations among creation, creation myths (including the Bible and Milton), and gender/sex/sexuality. In his typical syncretic fashion, however, Shelley, does not merely recombine the old stories about gender and sex but rather seeks to rewrite the creation story of Enlightenment Man and his binary others from the very start.[9] To consider how he transmutes this stash of foundational stories, to reimagine Shelley's methodology of (re)creation, I put the Witch's hijinks into conversation with Sylvia Wynter's ideas about the genres of Enlightenment Man and Karen Barad's feminist science studies about materialities recombining within "intra-actions" and new space-times.[10] What I wish to highlight is how the Witch's acts of creation offer a praxis to undo the category of the human (and its gender/racial categories) in ways that are already speaking to our contemporary resistance to anthropocentrism and neoliberal humanism.

In some sense, I do mean "speaking" literally: the Witch's creation – eventually described as an "image" – offers a technology for the communication of new, anti-Enlightenment shapes of being. As a global traveling "image," the creature circulates its new being across time and space, potentially reshaping itself to different constitutions of audiences. This is a Shelley who dreams his idealism past the feminism of Asia's revolution, sister soul mates, or sexual possession.[11] Apposite *Frankenstein*'s melancholy, violent creature who can only see a future alongside a female companion colonizing the South American wilds or a queer exilic "no future" of Arctic proportions, the Witch's creature manifests a labile figure whose posthuman, nonbinary multiplicity of form and communication posits a traveling medium of futural transformation – for us and other generations who will or have already recreated their own genders, relations, and stories of creation.

I The Witch's Genre of Being

One key to Shelley's project to undo creation myths that center (white) Man, and therefore subordinate a whole host of others, is offered to us with the very first, if allegorical, lines of the poem. At the very start of *The Witch of Atlas*, Shelley is at pains to emplot the Witch in a narrative before the instantiation of "Error and Truth."

> Before those cruel Twins, whom at one birth
> Incestuous Change bore to her father Time,
> Error and Truth, had hunted from the earth
> All those bright natures which adorned its prime
> And left us nothing to believe in (49–53 [*SPP* 368])

The poem begins in a time – and space – where the oppositional categories of Error and Truth do not yet exist, in a time before rational or empirical Truth could dispute superstitious Error, in a time before Enlightenment Man had come to deify himself as the exclusive Human. Explaining how modern forms of the Human came to dominate Western thought, Wynter theorizes that the over-representation of biological, rational, political Man as the only "genre" of being human occurred at the behest of a concomitant collapse of the heavenly and earthly realms.[12] Recombining the sublunar and the supralunar into a homogeneity of matter – or what Romanticists have famously called the "natural supernatural" – enabled or forced a new split between the primitive/animalistic/chthonic and rational man, with two forms: "one rationcentric and still hybridly religio-secular, the other purely secular and biocentric."[13] These respective definitions of "Man1" and "Man2" plot the othering of the Global South through two "shifts" that take place first during the Renaissance and then during the development of the physical sciences at the turn of the nineteenth century, a change which reaches its apex with Darwinian evolution and theories of biological race.

By placing the Witch in a timespace before Truth and Error, Shelley locates her before (or after) rational, biocentric time. As the natural/supernatural, feminine focal point of the poem, she rewrites the trajectory to

Man1 and Man2 with an alternative story – of the Witch and her progeny. Her "'being' is a matter of 'becoming,'" to use Neil Fraistat's Shelleyan phrase, into a global, re-mythified world.[14] Her becoming tenders a response to Victor Frankenstein, who could be a quintessential example of Wynter's Men. The dually Enlightenment and alchemical scientist, son of a syndic, collapses life and death's supernatural mystery through his insatiable scientific, biocentric rationality, only to create an abject, Calibanish Other. Percy's poem offers not simply a de- but also a re-mythification needed to remake rational Man (Victor) as magical, alchemical being (the Witch). Rather than creating an abject, primitive other, the Witch creates an even more radically and nonbinaristically defined being – indeed not a Man or Human at all. With her bizarre blend of witchy, mythic pranks and colonial journey through the African continent, the Witch remixes, uninvents, and re-figures a mode of posthuman being that transgresses, however stumblingly, through gendered, racial, and humanistic nineteenth-century boundaries. Such creation does not directly respond to the ills of African colonization or racial capital; it does, in its privileged, whimsical, and utopian way, begin to undo gendered and racial ideologies – the so-called feminine and primitive – to open new spacetimes for other "genres of being," as Wynter terms such alternatives.

The Witch's posthumanism may represent Percy's jocular response to the pessimism of *Frankenstein*'s attitudes toward the fate of those who attempt to reorient the Human. While Percy scholars have made much of his allegedly defensive prologue to the poem and Mary's explanation in the headnote to the poem in her *Posthumous Poems*, we might reread the preliminary six stanzas as his teasing and arguing with her.[15] I want to acknowledge that his comical, lighthearted approach in both the preface and the poem perhaps speaks to his privilege to sideline the material traumas of minoritized being, a position that nevertheless enables him to attempt to dream new dreams about gender.

With the faux imperative "Content thee" with his writing "visionary rhyme," Shelley may not necessarily be exculpating himself from ignoring "human interest" but instead resisting that which is too absorbedly human (8 [*SPP* 367]). The six stanzas of the prologue repeatedly figure animal (nonhuman) metaphors for his poems alongside the question of what constitutes life (or aliveness), perhaps the main topos of *Frankenstein*. He asks whether Mary will condemn his verses "Because they tell no story, false or true" but, likening his verse to a young kitten, further queries, "[m]ay it not leap and play as grown cats do" (4, 6 [367]). This sense of play, of experimentation, may be proleptically resisting our own desire to allegorize Mary's creature or find a clear moral tale in either *Frankenstein* or *The Witch of Atlas*. Yet Percy continues to joke about his sense of life and death: the silken-winged fly "doom to die / When Day shall hide"; his "winged Vision / Whose date should have been longer than a day"; his lament whether "anything of mine is fit to live!" (13–14, 17–18, 24 [367]). All these nonhuman things (cats, flies, poems) manifest a vitality that may die (either at the day's end or the end of their public life), yet their playfulness, their liveliness, become more important than their fated dying. Here, Percy seems to figure a non-allegorical commentary on Mary's creature whose life has lived on through its propositions about who might live and how. Shelley's Witch is not to be unveiled as an allegory for or representation of a particular form of human life; rather, we are to let her live as the not-Human being that she is. Moreover, we are also meant to play across the sub- and supra-lunar, to become posthumans rather than separate ourselves from experimentation (poetic, material, heavenly) through allegory's representation of allegedly hidden truths or identities.

The Witch's Grecian origin/birth story/story of creation would at first seem to reiterate Man1 and Man2 – with its Hellenistic enthusiasm and the Witch's Apollonian patrimony – as god of light, logic, and reason. The Witch comes into being when the Sun "kissed" her mother, one of Atlas's nymphs, "with his beams" (62 [*SPP* 369]). Often read as a Grecian rape, we might also read it as Wynter's fusion of earth and heaven into homogeneous matter. Shelley may be recycling this narrative from Shakespeare's *The Tempest* with its drama of political-rational Western man's colonization and absorption of non-Western magic.[16] This phallic, invasive sexual encounter disappears or destroys the mother, and her African or Titanic heritage, as she births the Witch.

Yet, such transformation may not figure a despoiling as much as an Ovidian shapeshifting, where beings frequently (and violently) change forms through transformations that cannot easily be categorized as death and life and that reorient the relation between rationality and alchemy.[17] During the Witch's creation and gestation scene, her mother "first was changed into a vapour, / And then into a cloud," "then into a meteor," and finally "into one of those mysterious stars / Which hid themselves between the Earth and Mars" (65, 69, 71–72 [*SPP* 369]). The encounter of Apollonian light and the Atlantidean "fair creature" transforms the matrix of materiality four times, a transformation of forms suspended between the heavenly and earthly. As with *Prometheus Unbound*'s Asia, whose metamorphosis into the boat of light re-forms the world, here the mother, when excited by light, changes shape and matter, and endues new, disparate (nonhuman) embodiments. This encounter between god and goddess produces the sublunar mist and cloud but then becomes a "mysterious star," hung between those realms. The suspension between the supra- and sublunar reverses the binarization that Wynter locates as a foundation for rational man and places us in a time and space where linear time and rational truth are likewise suspended. Although it is ten months' time before the Witch comes into being, she "[t]ook shape and motion: with the living form / Of this embodied power," a shape, motion, and power that is "garmented in light" and cannot be accounted for with the rational (Newtonian) motions of Time or the Human codifications of shape (79–80, 81 [369]).

The Witch is already endued, from her very creation, with the changeable qualities of light, which Shelley repeatedly returned to in *Prometheus Unbound* and *The Triumph of Life*. As Mark Lussier, Arkady Plotnitsky, Chris Washington, Richard Sha, and Mary Fairclough have pointed out, Shelley's interest in early physics redraws his understanding of the materiality of light – as both particle and wave – as two forms of materiality at once.[18] Light – and not simply in its abstract form of Enlightenment knowledge – becomes a bringer of posthuman change because its own materiality is multiple and changeable. Barad offers us a seminal feminist scientific account of light's ontological nature, whose particle-wave material status depends upon the apparatus of measurement or observation.[19] Observation alters whether we see light as particles or as waves, and from this principle she derives her notion of "intra-action," where materials are not separate and then put into relation but rather are always already entangled until they are "cut" by apparatuses and discourses into various kinds of things, whether subject and object or other ontologies altogether. For Barad, materialities retain within themselves the possibilities of transformation – of new intra-actions that might alter shape or ontology. Barad leaves the potential for multiple "cuts" that define, iteratively, relations among things and among humans and nonhumans. For Barad, the rational, biocentric human (Wynter's Man1 and Man2) would present only one possible ontological cut of human beings, as Wynter's work undermines allegedly stable and dominant accounts of such ontologies.

The Witch's mom's final materiality as the "mysterious star" evokes both Wynter's collapse of the sub- and supralunar as well as the Baradian potentiality of its light to diffract another ontological future for her daughter. An unknown star hangs in the balance, its thingly nature not jettisoned or forgotten but intrinsic to the Witch's nonhuman status and her interrelations of the human and nonhuman world. This vital shifting of materiality intimates how the collapse of human and nonhuman matter need not automatically validate the binary splitting of rational (white) man and primitive nonwhite other – as it does with Victor and his creature. For both Victor and the Witch entangle science and alchemy to produce creations that redraw the human. Yet Victor notoriously oscillates between his desire, on the one hand, to repatriate himself into his Genevan, human republican family (by finally finishing his degree, returning home, marrying Elizabeth) and his loathed queer orientation to the creature.[20] The Witch, already a being outside the human, embraces her singularity, her own creature, and, consequently, their derangement of European ideologies of race, gender, and the human.

We might further read the purported scene of imperial conception as Shelley's problematic way of thinking past racial binaries along the way to his attempt to deconstruct sex-gender systems. Alvey argues that this moment puts into permanent relation the masculine Western Apollo and a feminine African figure linked to North Africa through the geographic reference to the Atlas Mountains in Morocco and Algeria. The Witch, as their union's "newly born hybrid," marks "something more than an African enchantress or a sensuous female East," a "benevolent queen" who moves well beyond the exploratory imperial penetration of the poem's African landscape through her "power at the margin."[21] We could, alternatively, subsume these varieties of hybridity (posthuman, racial, and, as we shall see, gendered) into Jerrold Hogle's seminal accounts of Shelley's methodology: "this poem seems the supreme example in Shelley's writing of what Wasserman and others have called his 'syncretic mythology', his drawing together of myriad classical and Christian myth figures."[22] Rather than a "fixed reference to a single Truth," Shelley's syncretism offers the "hope of many new interconnections freeing human thought from its most established constructs."[23] Zakiyyah Iman Jackson calls such ideological pliability and violability of racialized bodies a dangerous plasticity, and Shelley's interweaving of myth or the abstraction of hybridity may mark a failed attempt to redraw imperial violence in ways that make invisible the real, material, bodily harm done to African women, black bodies, and the geography of the Global South through the substitution of a pliant figuration of Blackness.[24] Yet the confluence of figuration that alludes to the material but does not relinquish it suggests another – nonbinary – relation between them. The poem attempts to use the seemingly supernatural qualities of pre-Enlightenment and perhaps pre-Platonic materiality to redraw posthuman being to subtend the very categories of gender and race. The Witch's supposed origin may be not so much a feminine, African queen but rather a transmuting matrix who recreates (or intra-acts) her own allegedly representational origins (East and West). The Witch does not spend her time worrying about fixing the human Victors of Man1 and Man2; instead, she concentrates on the alchemy of a new creation who might operate outside the increasingly naturalized categories of race or gender, rationality or biology, science or alchemy.

II Recreating Nonbinary Creations

As with *Frankenstein*, *The Witch of Atlas* is plotted around a series of creations, which together reconsider the Romantic-era twinned births of modern race and binary gender as colonial categories. Mary's modern Prometheus offers a story of posthuman creation, as Washington has argued, that confabulates our understanding of posthuman materiality as intermixing the human and nonhuman.[25] Working with an assemblage of parts, from human and non-human bodies, through a hybrid of alchemical and modern sciences, Victor single-handedly creates a creature that continues to allegorize difference – and abjection – of all kinds, racial, queer, working-class, to name just a few. The Witch's own creation and her early pranks among animals locate her experimentation outside a university laboratory and within the wider world of being and becoming. If she resists Man1's Victoresque rationality, she likewise avoids Man2's biocentric humanism, inherent to his creature's request for a mate. Although critics have reviled what they deem her anti-social nature, her "sad exile," as Omar F. Miranda terms it in this volume, constitutes a safer spacetime away from people for re-visioning the human apart from Man1's and Man2's categorical imperatives.

If her creature's ontology is posthuman, nonbinary, or otherwise indeterminate, its gender and sexuality have, like Victor and his creation, been a hot topic of speculation. Mary's pair are arguably involved in a homosocial/queer tension, which comes to a head in Volume III's master-slave, sado-masochistic globe-trotting.[26] The creature's medicalized creation, which Victor uses to pathologize and deny him humanistic sympathy, has evinced resonances with trans being since Susan Stryker's seminal essay, "My Words to Victor Frankenstein above the Village of Chamonix."[27] Yet the creature's queerness is tempered as much by Victor's obtuse rationality as by their indoctrination by the DeLaceys into the gendered demands of biopolitical reproduction. As much as they learn language from watching "DeLacey TV," they likewise absorb the gendered position of Safie as "treasure" as requisite payment for Felix's revolutionary activities in saving her father from a French *lettre de cachet*. This education in heteronormativity arguably eventuates in the creature's own demands for a female companion – and Victor's imperialist fear of their hideous "new race" of a progeny.

The Witch, however, does not simply allegorize a critique of that novel's Men through a feminine origin point for the creation of new being. She is already born from hybrid human/nonhuman, racial, textual, and geographical sources and thus redoubles her own creation as a Baradian intra-action. This "contexture," what Fraistat terms "a larger whole fabricated from integral parts," extends beyond the textual, as it is woven from texts, bodies, materialities, sexualities, and genders that reconstruct what it means to collaborate in posthuman (re)creation.[28] The Witch's creature comes into being and re-ontologizes being in an intra-action of embodied materials where stories become again written through bodies as recombinant, self-transforming myths.

Unlike the creature in *Frankenstein*, the Witch's creature is not an assemblage or agglomeration of human and animal body parts; she creates her new being with more elemental matter, fire and snow. Initially a "repugnant mass," its elemental matter, though oppositional in temperature, harmonizes through the admixture of "liquid love": "Then by strange art she kneaded fire and snow / Together tempering the repugnant mass / With liquid love – all things together grow / Through which the harmony of love can pass" (321–324 [*SPP* 377]). It is as if Shelley rewrites, in these four lines, one of the essential allegories of creation in *Frankenstein*. Where Victor's creature becomes repugnant to him at the moment of its birth into life, then monstrous when raised without love, sympathy, or human interest, the Witch tempers the ill harmonized elements through liquid love. Such affect is liquid both in its fluidity and in its ability to knead different sorts of matter so that they might "together grow."

As with Victor's creature, much has been made about this creation's gender as a site of precocious creativity. Diane Hoeveler avowed its representation of Romantic androgyny; Amanda Blake Davis has more recently suggested it typifies the opposite of the androgyne.[29] Hogle sees the figure as a representation of Shelley's process of metaphorical transfiguration, channeling Diogenes's four-limbed, ambi-sexed beings in *The Symposium*, Ovid's Hermaphroditus myth, and Pygmalion's pedagogy of gender (also from *The Metamorphoses*).[30] Following a long line of commentators, Karen Swann reads it as a figure for the relationship between artist and creation, though for her this is a creation "impervious to human needs and aims" and thus a form of "radical alterity."³¹ Somewhat ironically, no one has taken the figure – whom the Witch only fleetingly calls out as "Hermaphroditus" when it flies off toward the end of the poem – to refer to the actual and rife period discourse on "hermaphrodites." Nor have scholars taken this narrative as a rewriting of the story of gender and its creation, considering the Greco-Roman source texts as one site of the instantiation of the one-sex model and contemplating Shelley's own age as the murky transition into a two-sex model.³² As Sha has convincingly argued, the Romantic period was one of palpable ambiguity, with these different models of sex and gender circulating in tension.³³ I want to suggest that Shelley's myth of creation and its ties to the myths of sex and gender reveal his interest not simply in what some have read as adolescent polyamory or even more serious pansexuality. Shelley's reading in Roman literature (Ovid and Lucian), in Botany (Darwin), and in medicine (Abernethy, Lawrence, among others) would have offered him medical notions of bodily shape and gender. This archive helped Victoresque men of science construct and medicalize a dimorphic, inherited model of binary sex/gender. Yet it likewise offered alternative and more flexible constructions of body, behavior, and identity still circulating from earlier periods or emerging as a resistance to the growing ideologies of binary sexuation and species on the make.

Shaped from the elements, the Witch's creature may seem, at first, to be a binaristic being made from ice and fire. This combination of icy cold and vital heat resonates with what Thomas Laqueur describes as the Galenic one-sex model, a model endemic in Ovid and Lucian, influenced by Hippocrates and Galen respectively. According to classical Greek medicine, which held sway with the Romans and the British for some time into the eighteenth century, the body's heat determined whether it would manifest male genitalia outside the body or whether, with a more frigid temperament, the penis and testes would retain the homological uterus and ovum inside the body. Even after birth (or puberty), the one-sexed body was labile to friction and overuse: stimulation of the clitoris, particularly in same-sex encounters, could transform bodily morphology.³⁴ Sha's discussion of puberty likewise attests to the prevalence in the Romantic period of understanding all bodies through a one-sex model until they developed secondary sex characteristics.³⁵ As the histories of intersex people became increasingly pathologized through medical accounts of masturbation, puberty, and taxonomies of species, a hefty and abusive discourse circulated in eighteenth- and early nineteenth-century medical literature around those who were termed "hermaphrodites" and who often served as medical or legal test cases to reestablish social gender binaries or biological species (created through heterosexual reproduction).

Returning to the creature's composition of hot fire and cold snow, we might then read the creature as being created from equal parts heat and cold, in a kind of continuous puberty or sexed fluidity. The Witch's tempering, the harmonization of cold and heat with "liquid love," kneads the binary into something not so much unitary as harmonic, having constituent elements arranged in pleasing multiplicity, as varied materials, qualities, or tones are layered, woven, or sounded together. That infamous Shelleyan binding agent – fluid love – itself bespeaks a force and a thing, as Sha has suggested of emotion. Material and discursive, human and nonhuman, nonbinary in myriad ways, "liquid love" figures a metalepsis for nonbinary fluidity itself: at once the harmonization of distinct qualities (heat and cold) and the continuous extension of non-opposing, agglomerated, unsubsumed differences.

Shelley gleaned some part of this fluidity and ambiguity from his Romantic Hellenism, which, as Jonathan Sachs has argued was "skeptical and ambivalent," "complex and ambiguous," and "aggressively political."[36] Sachs is writing about the politics of the Roman Empire – its channeling of Greek democracy, its failures in despotism, and its possible redemption in post-Waterloo Europe. Yet, because Shelley believed in gender equality as a cornerstone of social change, his uses of Ovid's myth likewise triangulate a politics of democratic Hellenism with a play and revivification of other models of gender/sex/sexuality. His commentary on Platonic models of sex and gender filter through his reading of Roman poetry and empire in similarly complex and ambiguous ways, but here it is the Greek binary gender system that fails in its ideas of equality, while Ovid's more trenchant resistance to patriarchal control within *Metamorphoses* reveals an anti-imperial thrust to a re-mythified queer ontology.

In "A Discourse on the Manner of the Ancient Greeks," Shelley repeatedly cites not just gender inequality but binarism as the downfall of Greek manners: "This invidious distinction of humankind as a class of beings [of] intellectual nature into two sexes is a remnant of savage barbarism which we have less excuse than they for not having totally abolished."[37] Tutored in Wollstonecraft's arguments about gender inequality, Shelley ties this problem to the craving after sensation, which likewise results in debauchery (the "habitual libertine"), prostitution, and gay sex.[38] However much Shelley might have attached sexual orientation to gender and however homophobic to anal sex he might have been, that relation does not preclude Shelley's belief in the need to alter the binary sex-gender system, a revolution that he advocates for pretty strenuously.[39] As Alex Gatten argues when historicizing Greek bodily form/shape, Shelley suggests that women were once less beautiful and, in doing so, indicates that the sexed body is not universally stable but would change over time and space.[40] Perhaps despite and due to Shelley's fears of penetrative anal sex and lascivious sexuality, he seemed much more amenable to more radical imaginings of bodily shape that would offer new forms of gender, sex, and sexuality. Shelley's resistance to the sex-gender system in *The Witch of Atlas* repeatedly imagines this shifting of bodily shape – through creation, poetry, dreaming, and traveling.

His many source texts help him recreate this story of labile gender and embodied sex. Roman understandings of sex-gender often tied together bodily and social shiftings, particularly in cases of male effeminacy.[41] Ovid's *Metamorphoses* include numerous stories of shifting sex, from the escape of women into nonhuman bodies (Daphne), prayers that enabled women to become men (Ianthe), unexpected cursed encounters in nature (Tiresias), and of course Hermaphroditus's attempted rape by Salmacis. Such crossings complement Diogenes's account in *The Symposium* of an eight-limbed "third sex," which Shelley translated in 1818, and Shelley's Hermaphroditus might seem to posit a Platonic reversal, as the metamorphosis of Hermes and Aphrodite's son plots a fusing of his masculine body with Salmacis's. The nymph, excited by watching Hermaphroditus bathing, is rebuffed in her seductions. She waits until the youth jumps naked into the pool, wraps herself around him, and prays to the gods never to divide them. Salmacis's violation is not an act of penetration but the denial of Hermaphroditus's consent and the trespass of bodily boundaries, as she forces the two to merge into a single being. Ovid locates this transformation via several metaphors: a snake coiled around its prey, ivy interlacing trees, and a polypus wrapping its tentacles around its prey. The fusion itself is figured as a twig grafted to bark: "So they, by such strict imbracement glew'd / Are now but one, with a double form indew'd"[42] / "two-form fold, so that they could not be called male or female, and seemed neither or either"[43] / "neutrumque, & utrumque videntur," which might read as "neither and both."[44] Hermaphroditus does not, however, remain a singular oddity: he turns and admires himself and then prays to his parents to drug the fountain so that every man that swims in the water will "Return as halfe-woman" ("exeat inde Semivir," or unmanned, effeminate, half a man).

It perhaps cannot be stated too strongly how different a story Ovid tells of the creation of people with intersex conditions than the medicalized othering of "hermaphrodites." Neither does Ovid's merging of sexed bodies create a figure who is shamed for their effeminacy, as many Roman men might be. Rather, Hermaphroditus becomes a site of reproducible, liquid transformation, which then instigates a performative speech to recreate the pool as a space to repeat and transfer that initial bodily and gendered transformation. Unlike the Sapphic sexual encounters that, in eighteenth-century Galenic medical texts, document how mutual masturbation might distend a woman's clitoris into a penis, this Ovidian story leverages female passion as a change that leaves its beings in a sacred and replicable "neither/both" position with regard to sex and gender.

Shelley, in turn, refuses to write his version of Ovid's tale as a gender-sex crossing caused by a violent encounter; neither is this creature simply born this way, as in Plato's account of the third sex or Lucian's account of Hermaphroditus. Rather, the Witch creates her "sexless thing" as a being who does not easily fit into either the one-sex and two-sex humanistic models, sexual dimorphism, or gender binaries.

> A sexless thing it was, and in its growth
> It seemed to have developed no defect
> Of either sex, yet all the grace of both—
> In gentleness and strength its limbs were decked;
> The bosom swelled lightly with its full youth—
> The countenance was such as might select
> Some artist that his skill should never die,
> Imaging forth such perfect purity. (329–336 [*SPP* 377])

Though the Witch calls it "Hermaphroditus" later in the poem, here as "a sexless thing" it lingers in Sha's nonbinary pre-pubescence, defying developing biological and species boundaries. Even if we were to understand "gentleness" and "strength" as feminine and masculine gendering, the two construct a continuum of motion: the softness of action on the one hand and an intensity of agency on the other. Rather than attached to sex organs or to cultural performances, gender becomes a varying intensity of bodily and affective movement. These movements might be modulated without instantiation into specific performances of biological/bodily categories, self-identity, or (social) subjectivity.

We might read this merger or movement of "either" and "both" as a marked resistance to the medicalization of the intersex body, similar to the Sapphic swerve away from the body and into the Neoplatonic metaphysics used by Katherine Philips and her sisterhood when they proclaim love between each other to be one soul in two bodies.[45] Hoeveler argues that the Hermaphroditus idealizes the psychic union of opposing genders, which the poem then parodies when Hermaphroditus disappears into the ether.[46] Rather than a union of the best of both sexes or genders, the term "youth" may extend a Hermes-esque fluidity that offers a body and being before having been gendered through social circulation, medical anatomy, or scientific theories of biological sex. The poetic syntax reinforces the paradox at the heart of Shelley's fluidity of forms that continually turns any Platonic or Ovidian mergers into more restless, multidirectional materialities that continue to move. The line's anaphora of "Of" emphasizes the line's beginning enjambed preposition "Of either" and the end preposition "of both," such that the creature prepositionally possesses "either" gender, "both," or the movement among them. "Either" and "both" would seem to double the binary, to suggest that there is either only one contingent gender present or two. Yet the enjambed double negative "no defect/Of either" also deconstructs the possibility of "either" – that there is no either/or binary. Structuring the line to flow over an open-legged en*jamb*ment, which is then echoed at both the beginning and the end of the line, Shelley suggests that sex is at once "either" and "both" and a series of morphing possibilities. Our minds place both ends of the line together in their parallel syntax, which is then deconstructed by the anaphora of "of," the expression of relationality between two entities as ever-changing and multiple (one-sex, two-sex, both, some, and more). The creature both is sexless and models the possibility of multiple sexes and genders, their "intra-sex," an intra-action of a "sexless thing." In this way, the Witch's creation shares much with what Dana Luciano and Mel Y. Chen describe as the queer inhumanity that transverses the categories of gender and the human and that "has never, in truth, been stable."[47] They write: "the figure of the queer/trans body does not merely unsettle the human as norm; it generates other possibilities – multiple, cyborgian, spectral, transcorporeal, transmaterial – for living."[48]

As we reorient our readings of Shelleyan gender around the notion of the "sexless," we need also attend to the use of "thing" as no simple, celebratory nod to the mythic and nonhuman. Coupled with the passage's remark on "perfect purity," the creature's thingliness resounds with contemporary debates that tied sexual dimorphism (and the alleged gender binary that arose from genital difference) to racial and species difference being mapped out in Western discourse upon the backs of enslaved women. Shelley's one-time doctor and associate William Lawrence's 1819 *Lectures on Physiology, Zoology, and the Natural History of Man* gives just one example of the turn in medical discourse from the one-sex to the two-sex model constructed from examples of African women. Lawrence, in early chapters, dwells solely on the biological basis of binaristic genital difference found in all mammals across humans and animals, partially in response to Darwin's poetic glorification of ambi-sexed plant species.[49] In his later extensive remarks on the climatological enlargement of African women's labia, nymphae, and buttocks, he asserts, "[t]here are no essential differences in the organs of generation; their construction and functions are the same in the various races of mankind."[50] As Jennifer Morgan has argued about earlier British texts of colonial encounter, "[g]ender did not operate as a more profound category of difference than race; instead, racialist discourse was deeply imbued with ideas about gender and sexual difference that, indeed, became manifest only in contact with each other."[51] The dimorphic binarization of sexed bodies underwrites the idea that multiple races nevertheless constituted the same species, even as the comparative distention of black women's bodies becomes a limit case of humanity. Shelley's "sexless thing" therefore might be seen as a blunt tool of resistance to the ideologies of sexual dimorphism as well as the racial gendering that contributed to that model. His attempt to re-ontologize a posthuman, nonbinary being poses a poetic if idealistic critique of humanistic, racial bioreproduction, including what Wynter would call the myth of Man2.

With such texts in mind, the youth's "lack of defect" and its "perfect purity" may echo to us with Aryan overtones that would then paint any resistance to bodily difference as white (ableist) privilege. Here we might see Shelley's double radicalism and complicity. Such a creature could be said to defy contemporaneous gender or racial (biological) identification while also verging into a post-racial/post-gender future. This strong, gentle "youth" might erase the violent histories of racialized and hermaphroditic discourse in the very attempts to route those signifying and ideological systems away from the medicalized, empirical reification of race.

Shelley's refusal to call the Witch's creature a "hermaphrodite" – or even a refusal to label it as the Greek "Hermaphroditus" – until the moment it flies off into the world is perhaps most suggestive of his evasion of deterministic discourses or historical poetics and his venture into new forms of embodiment, being, and signification. My choice to avoid calling the Witch's creature "Hermaphroditus" is meant to enact this skepticism. To repeat that naming would cement this creature as only Greco-Roman in its mythological provenance, rather than a recreation of Greek, Roman, and colonial sources that is likewise seeking to flee from them. Moreover, using that name would instantiate the creature within the violent and problematic discourse on eighteenth-century intersex people, whose empirical fixity Shelley challenges with a necessarily changeable, iterative myth. As with *Frankenstein*, the creature is only called "monster" or "wretch" by those who would abject its otherness (including the creature himself). The Witch only calls her creation "Hermaphroditus!" as it leaves her – perhaps as a poem in the world, perhaps as a child into adulthood, but perhaps as a being that will escape whatever exclamatory identifications a creator might belatedly try to give it. Its body – ungendered and unraced but now ready to unfurl its wings, made iteratively moveable – becomes a medium, a being and its own mediated transmission of that being. As the Witch and her creation take their riverine boat trip through time and space, so the creature eventually flies from the river into more nebulous ether, becoming part of the world beyond the Witch's ken. Shelley in this way links gender as fluid movement to a medium that might transverse bodily and material boundaries – and all those stifling conventionally imposed categories.

III The Creature's New Media

For the Witch, Shelley tells us, has fashioned her creature as a "shape" and "image": "And a fair Shape out of her hands did flow— / A living Image, which did far surpass / In beauty that bright shape of vital stone / Which drew the heart out of Pygmalion" (323–328 [*SPP* 377]). Numerous commentators have read the allusion to Pygmalion as the Witch's solipsistic enrapture with her own creation, which she places facing her in the Apollonian pinnace, to bask at during the first part of her river journey.[52] Rather than assume the "living Image" represents the Witch's self-image, we might envision the creature with the power to embody a shape and image that is a living enactment of a being beyond binaries. As an "image," this creature could be the simulation of an unreal person or a mental picture or representation of an idea. As a "Shape" that has flowed from the Witch, it constitutes a moving embodiment of nonbinary gender and/or sex. This figure – a bodily shape and a figure of speech – offers a metalepsis for a fluid, vital, and moving being that is not one life but a liv*ing* in the world.

Made from the elements, it embodies and transmits a moving image of its multidirectional, fluctuating materiality that does not become beholden to gender or sexed reproduction of life. Unlike the creature and Victor's queer panicked chase around the world in Volume III of *Frankenstein*, the Witch as a posthuman creatrix unbinds herself and her creature from the biopolitical tyranny of the heteronormative family romance when she creates another sort of shape with its own ontology. Even when she might desire to keep it close or identify it as "Hermaphroditus," it necessarily absconds from her grasp – and graduates into the world to intra-act with other bodies and (re)create them. Equally as important, the transversal potentiality of the creature as sexless movement itself transforms how we understand embodied communication – or how we might come to know and understand nonbinary being.

As a material "image" of fluidity, the creature becomes a sort of incipient media for labile being – a living form of communication for about nonbinary being. As text and body, material and discourse, raced and unraced, this creature is a living transcoding of cultural categories through shifting, transitive movements of its moving embodiment. While the Witch and her creation move down river, "the Image lay / With folded wings and unawakened eyes, / And o'er its countenance did play / The busy dreams" (362–364 [*SPP* 378]). As a dreaming image, the creature continues to shape and spread the image of new being even while dreaming it. Through its dreams, the Witch's creation does not simply store or process the "information" of nonbinary sex; rather, in its circulation and transmission of its body amid a global world, it intra-acts and transfigures that very "information" about sex as itself fluid, material, and transmissible.[53] Her creature revises Shelleyan idealism as a medium and means, a non-static apparatus, to bend and cross realities, rather than simply or suddenly "recut" them, as Barad theorizes one intra-action to the next. Shelley's "transreal" recreation of reality entails a transmission – the "in" and "through" of media – that reinvents reality through new media.[54] This is the creature's radical potential: its traveling as an image of fluidity that, in its transreality, potentially (re)circulates and (re)communicates Witch2 and Creation2, and on and on.

Her creation may implicitly figure those abstractions especially available to the white imagination, with idealism that routes the hard reality of the many gender-nonconforming people attempting to live in the first decades of the nineteenth century. That plasticity of the living "Image" may depend upon an "unraced" and therefore invisible whiteness that enables the circulation, transmission, and amplification, inadvertent or not, of the colonizing imagination. Lee's and Hoeveler's readings, however, both suggest that we might see such circulation as a parody of white cartography and communication. Yet, because the poem works within a logic "[o]f either [...] of both," it suggests that the creature's new media employs either, both, and neither white indoctrination and radical communication via living image, always potentially shifting into one another, no matter the radicality of the message.

Shelley is ultimately concerned with a creatrix – likened at the poem's end to a "sexless bee," who transmits confabulatory media that might recreate the very distinctions among human and nonhuman materialities (589 [*SPP* 385]). Not the dream of a universal medium but a transmedia that can move across difference without evanishing it, the Witch's creature circulates in a restive world that cannot be cordoned off by binary gender, by impending racialization, by life and death, or by clear demarcations of reality and myth. Such worldwide mediation may be too fantastical for quotidian gendered and racial violence, and it certainly bequeaths a heavily ethereal burden on people such as Anne Lister, Mary Diana Dods/David Lyndsay, or the Public Universal Friend, all writing and dreaming new forms of gendered living. If not an everyday means of gender revolution, Shelley nonetheless offers dreams of queerness for bodies that may "wake to weep" but also must live by the performative exhortation "Dream thou," as he writes in "The Flower That Smiles Today" (21, 20 [469]).[55] Rather than simply understanding gender as a nonbinary resistance to a binary, the Witch and her creation urge us to remythify being as reorienting movements, as bodies that will change and signify over time and space. Even so, they ask us to consider how we might recreate the nonbinary as our bodies intra-act with the body of Shelley's nonhuman poems and his dreams of ever-moving creations.

Notes

1. Much initial thinking for this chapter was done in intra-action with Chris Washington for a paper titled "Intersex Posthumanism? Wollstonecraft, Shelley, and Romantic Politics in the Anthropocene" given at the Seattle Modern Language Association conference in 2020. I need to extend so many thanks to my coeditor Omar F. Miranda, who graciously and expertly edited multiple versions of this essay, to Lily Gurton-Wachter and Amelia Worsley for always helping me organize and figure out the work's real being, as well as to the University of San Francisco students of "Percy Shelley's Life and Works" Spring 2022 and Mount Holyoke College's "Nonbinary Romanticism" Fall 2022, who braved tangling with the poem alongside me.
2. See, for starters, Thomas Laqueur, *The Making of Sex: Body and Gender from Greeks to Freud* (Cambridge, MA: Harvard University Press, 1990); Valerie Traub, *Thinking Sex with the Early Moderns* (Philadelphia: University of Pennsylvania Press, 2015); and Richard Sha, *Perverse Romanticism: Aesthetics and Sexuality in Britain, 1750–1832* (Baltimore: Johns Hopkins University Press, 2009).
3. For discussions of Wollstonecraft and Shelley, see Jillian Heydt-Stevenson and Kurtis Hessel "*Queen Mab*, Wollstonecraft, and Spinoza: Teaching 'Nature's Primal Modesty'," *European Romantic Review* 27.3 (2016), 351–363 and Charlotte

Gordon, *Romantic Outlaws: The Extraordinary Lives of Mary Wollstonecraft and Her Daughter Mary Shelley* (New York: Random House Publishing, 2015).

4 See Christopher Small, *Ariel Like a Harpy: Shelley, Mary and Frankenstein* (London: Gollancz, 1972), 101; and Mary K. Patterson Thornburg, *The Monster in the Mirror: Gender and the Sentimental/Gothic Myth in Frankenstein* (Ann Arbor: UMI Research Press, 1987), 8.

5 Colin Carman's chapter on *The Witch of Atlas* and *The Sensitive Plant* offers an exception as it considers Ovid's myth as a part of Shelley's Platonism and reads the Witch's creature through Foucauldian, Freudian, and botanic hermaphroditism as a "precursor to the homosexual role and to the androgyny ascribed to his (and her) mysterious subjectivity." My account takes different historicist and theoretical tacks that necessarily understand eighteenth-century discourses of anatomy and racial science as entwined in Shelley's reading and as provoking Shelley to imagine something outside either "homosexuality" or "androgyny." See Carman, *The Radical Ecology of the Shelleys: Eros and Environment* (New York: Routledge, 2018), 77–117, 102. For other accounts of the Witch's creature and gender, see Harold Bloom, *Shelley's Mythmaking* (New Haven: Yale University Press, 1959), 165–204; Diane Hoeveler, *Romantic Androgyny: The Women Within* (Philadelphia: University of Pennsylvania Press, 1990); and Karen Swann, "Shelley's Pod People," in Forest Pyle and Marc Redfield, eds. *Romanticism and the Insistence of the Aesthetic*, *Romantic Circles* Praxis Series (February 2005), https://romantic-circles.org/praxis/aesthetic/index.html.

6 See Frederic S. Colwell, "Shelley's 'Witch of Atlas' and the Mythic Geography of the Nile," *ELH* 45.1 (1978), 69–92.

7 See Debbie Lee, "Mapping the Interior: African Cartography and Shelley's *The Witch of Atlas*," *European Romantic Review* 8.2 (Spring 1997), 169–184; Nahoko Alvey, *Strange Truths in Undiscovered Lands: Shelley's Poetic Development and Romantic Geography* (Toronto: Toronto University Press, 2009), 145–180; and Jared Hickman, *Black Prometheus: Race and Radicalism in the Age of Atlantic Slavery* (New York: Oxford University Press, 2017), 217–264.

8 Valerie Traub, "The Psychomorphology of the Clitoris, or The Reemergence of the Tribade in English Culture," in Valeria Finucci and Kevin Brownlee, eds. *Tropes of Reproduction in Literature from Antiquity through Early Modern Europe* (Chapel Hill: Duke University Press, 2001), 153–186.

9 See the Introduction to this volume, Note 25, for sources on syncretism.

10 See Karen Barad, *Meeting the Universe Halfway: Quantum Physics and the Entanglement of Matter and Meaning* (Durham, NC: Duke University Press, 2007) and Sylvia Wynter, "Unsettling the Coloniality of Being/Power/Truth/Freedom: Towards the Human, after Man, Its Overrepresentation – An Argument," *Centennial Review* 3.3 (1993), 257–337.

11 See especially Teddi Chichester Bonca, *Shelley's Mirrors of Love: Narcissism, Sacrifice, and Sorority* (Albany: SUNY Press, 1999); Barbara Gelpi, *Shelley's Goddess: Maternity, Language, Subjectivity* (New York: Oxford University Press, 1992); and Nathanial Brown, *Sexuality and Feminism in Shelley* (Cambridge, MA: Harvard University Press, 1979).

12 Wynter, "Unsettling the Coloniality of Being/Power/Truth/Freedom."
13 Wynter, "Unsettling the Coloniality of Being/Power/Truth/Freedom," 282.
14 Neil Fraistat, *The Poem and the Book* (Chapel Hill: University of North Carolina Press, 1987), 176.
15 Although she first publishes this poem without the introductory stanzas in 1824, she does publish it as the second poem in the volume, and eventually includes those stanzas in the 1839/40 edition. Many thanks to Madeleine Callaghan for her reminding me of these complexities – and for the Zoom conversation she indulged on the poem.
16 As Prospero had enchained the ambi-gendered Ariel and learned bookish arts to steal Sycorax's birthright, Apollo rapes a nymph to create a hybridly raced Witch, stealing magic from indigenous beings through reproduction (and miscegenation). Percy read *The Tempest* in 1818, and Mary read it in 1820, according to "Mary Shelley's Reading List" on *Romantic Circles*, https://romantic-circles.org/editions/frankenstein/MShelley/readalph.
17 Mary and Percy read Ovid's *Metamorphoses* together twice, in 1815 and 1820, according to "Mary Shelley's Reading List" on *Romantic Circles*, https://romantic-circles.org/editions/frankenstein/MShelley/readalph.
18 See Mark Lussier, *Romantic Dynamics: The Physicality of Matter* (New York: Palgrave Macmillan, 1999); Arkady Plotnitsky, "All Shapes of Light: The Quantum Mechanical Shelley," in Betty T. Bennett and Stuart Curran, eds. *Shelley: Poet and Legislator of the World* (Baltimore: Johns Hopkins University Press, 1996), 263–273; Chris Washington, "The Dark Side of the Light: Triumph of Love in Shelley's *The Triumph of Life*," in Joel Faflak, ed. *The Futures of Shelley's Triumph*; *Romantic Circles* Praxis Series (October 2019), https://romantic-circles.org/praxis/triumph; and Richard Sha, *Imagination and Science in Romanticism* (Baltimore: Johns Hopkins University Press, 2018).
19 Barad, *Meeting the Universe Halfway*.
20 See, for example, James Holt McGavaran, "'Insurmountable Barriers to Our Union': Homosocial Male Bonding, Homosexual Panic, and Death on the Ice in *Frankenstein*," *European Romantic Review* 11.1 (2000), 46–67.
21 Alvey, 158, 159, 180. See also Lee's reading of the Witch as a satire of masculine penetration of the mysterious African continent.
22 Jerrold E. Hogle, "Visionary Rhyme: The Sensitive Plant and The Witch of Atlas," in Michael O'Neill, Anthony Howe, and Madeleine Callaghan, eds. *The Oxford Handbook of Percy Bysshe Shelley* (New York: Oxford University Press, 2013), 360–374, 367.
23 Hogle, "Visionary," 370.
24 Zakiyyah Iman Jackson, *Becoming Human: Matter and Meaning in an Antiblack World* (New York: New York University Press, 2020).
25 See Chris Washington, "Non-binary *Frankenstein*?" in Orrin N. C. Wang, ed. *Frankenstein in Theory: A Critical Anatomy* (New York: Bloomsbury, 2021), 65–83, as well as Kate Singer, Ashley J. Cross, and Suzanne L. Barnett, *Frankenstein in Material Transgressions: Beyond Romantic Bodies, Genders, Things* (Liverpool: Liverpool University Press, 2020), 1–3.

26 For a discussion of the intersections (and misalignments) of Eve Sedgwick's notions of the homosocial and homophobic and Mary's novel, see Andrew Parker "The Age of *Frankenstein*," in Lauren Berlant, ed. *Reading Sedgwick* (Chapel Hill: Duke University Press, 2019), 178–188.
27 See also Jack Halberstam, *Skin Shows: Gothic Horror and the Technology of Monsters* (Chapel Hill: Duke University Press, 1995); Anson Koch-Rein, "Trans-lating the Monster: Transgender Affect and *Frankenstein*," *Lit: Literature Interpretation Theory* 30.1 (2019), 44–61; Jolene Zigarovich, "The Trans Legacy of *Frankenstein*," *Science Fiction Studies* 45.2 (July 2018), 260–72; and Harlan Weaver, "Monster Trans: Diffracting Affect, Reading Rage," *Somatechnics* 3.2 (2013), 287–306.
28 Fraistat, *The Poem and the Book*, 4.
29 See Hoeveler, *Romantic Androgyny*, and Amanda Blake Davis, "Androgyny as Mental Revolution in Act 4 of *Prometheus Unbound*," *The Keats-Shelley Review* 34.2 (2020), 160–177.
30 Hogle, "Visionary."
31 Karen Swann, *Lives of the Dead Poets: Keats, Shelley, Coleridge* (New York: Fordham University Press, 2019), 87.
32 See Lacquer's account in *Making Sex*.
33 Sha, *Perverse Romanticism*, 78–140.
34 See Valerie Traub, "The Psychomorphology of the Clitoris," *Gay and Lesbian Quarterly* 2.1–2 (1995), 81–113.
35 According to Richard Sha, "The Uses and Abuses of Historicism: Halperin and Shelley on the Otherness of Ancient Greek Sexuality," in Richard Sha, ed. *Historicizing Romantic Sexuality*, *Romantic Circles* Praxis Series (January 2006), para. 41.

> Unlike us, Romantic medical writers tended to think of puberty as the moment in which two essentially feminine sexes became fully differentiated into male and female. The surgeon William Lawrence and friend of the Shelleys referred to pre-pubescent children as 'equivocal beings.' Unlike us, who tend to see the primacy of genital difference, the Romantics saw puberty as the moment in which secondary differentiation made feminized males become real men.

36 Jonathan Sachs, "'Yet the Capital of the World': Rome, Repetition, and History in Shelley's Later Writings," *Nineteenth-Century Contexts* 28.2 (June 2006), 105–126, 124.
37 Timothy Clark, *Shelley's Prose or The Trumpet of Prophecy* (Albuquerque: University of New Mexico Press, 1966), 277.
38 Clark, *Shelley's Prose*, 221.
39 Sha has persuasively argued in "The Uses and Abuses of Historicism" that Shelley others Greek "homosexuality" for, to his mind, its violent and nonconsensual pederasty, even as he identifies the inequality of the sexes that he argues led Greek men to invest in intellectual, emotional, and sexual relations among themselves.
40 Alex Gatten, "Formal Perversions: Queer Poetics and the Turn in Romantic Verse," PhD diss. (University of Connecticut, 2020).

41 See, for example, Maud W. Gleason, "Elite Male Identity in the Roman Empire," in David Stone Potter and David J. Mattingly, eds. *Life, Death, and Entertainment in the Roman Empire* (Ann Arbor: University of Michigan Press, 2010), 67–84.

42 I have quoted from George Sandys' 1632 English translation of Ovid, which was popular with Keats, and which seems to bear resonance to *The Witch of Atlas*. George Sandys, *Ovid's Metamorphosis (1632: An Online Edition)*, ed. Daniel Kinney (University of Virginia E-text Center, n.d.), https://ovid.lib.virginia.edu/sandys/4.htm.

43 This rendering is taken from the more recent Kline translation. Ovid, *Metamorphoses*, trans. Anthony S. Kline (University of Virginia E-Text Center, 2000), IV.346–388, https://ovid.lib.virginia.edu/trans/Metamorph.htm.

44 Shelley would have of course read Ovid in the original. The 1727 Burmann edition of Latin text reads: "Sic ubi complexu coierunt membra tenaci, / Nec duo funt, & forma duplex, nec femina dici, / Nec puer ut poflint; neutrumque, & utrumque videnturr." A rough translation follows: "Thus, when members are joined together, Neither are there two nor the form doubled, nor can it be called female, / Neither a child to be desired; neither and both are seen" (translation mine). Peter Burmann, *Ovidii Nasonis, Metamorphosen* (Amsterdam: R. & J. Westenios, & G. Smith), 1727, https://archive.org/details/publiiovidiinaso020ovid/page/n7/mode/2up.

45 See, for example, Katherine Philips's "Friendship an Emblem, or the Seal. To My Dearest Lucasia":

> The hearts thus intermixed speak
> A Love that no bold shock can break;
> For Joyn'd and growing, both in one,
> Neither can be disturb'd alone. (1–4)

The Collected Works of Katherine Philips: Volume One: The Poems, ed. Patrick Thomas (Essex: Stump Cross Books, 1990), 106.

46 Hoeveler, *Romantic Androgyny*, 249–255.

47 Mel Y. Chen and Dana Luciano, "Queer Inhumanisms," *GLQ* 25.1 (2019), 113–117, 113.

48 Chen and Luciano, "Has the Queer Ever Been Human?" *GLQ* 21.2-3 (2015), 183–207, 187.

49 See Myra J. Hird, "Animal Trans," in *Queering the Non/Human*, ed. Noreen Giffney (New York: Routledge, 2008), 227–247.

50 William Lawrence, *Lectures on Physiology, Zoology, and the Natural History of Man* (London: J. Callow, 1819), 419.

51 Jennifer Morgan, *Laboring Women: Reproduction and Gender in New World Slavery* (Philadelphia: University of Pennsylvania Press, 2004), 15.

52 See Michael O'Neill, "Fictions, Visionary Rhyme and Human Interest: A Reading of Shelley's 'The Witch of Atlas'," *The Keats-Shelley Review* 2 (1987), 103–133 and Richard Cronin, "Shelley's Witch of Atlas," *The Keats-Shelley Review* 26 (1977), 88–100.

53 I am influenced by Micha Cárdenas's notion of the transreal: "Building on the notion of 'trans' from 'transgender,' I propose that transreal aesthetics cross

the boundaries of realities created by a fragmentation of reality that occurred as a result of postmodern theory and emerging technologies." They elaborate: "To say that I am transreal is a strategy for embracing a gender that exceeds daily reality on Planet Earth and that says back to all the people who have tried to make me choose between man or woman that I choose to be a shape-shifter, a dragon and a light wave." Cárdenas, *The Transreal: Political Aesthetics of Crossing Realities* (New York: Atropos Press, 2012), 23, 30.

54 As Orrin N. C. Wang suggests in his recent book *Techno-Magism: Media, Mediation, and the Cut of Romanticism* (New York: Fordham University Press, 2022), the "'in' and 'between' prepositioning of media" manifest "as not phenomenal quandaries, but more exactly as tropes – not hopelessly beholden to such categories as time and space but aboriginally inciting them," 11.

55 Percy Bysshe Shelley, *The Complete Poetical Works*, ed. Mary Wollstonecraft Shelley (Philadelphia: Chrissy and Markley, 1852), 320.

CHAPTER 11

Action at a Distance
Communication and Material Entanglement in Queen Mab *and* The Mask of Anarchy

Mary Fairclough

Throughout his life, Percy Bysshe Shelley reflected on the theory and practice of communication across distances of space and time. This essay argues that Shelley offers a unique account of the way that poetry mediates or overcomes distance. In doing so, it contributes to a rich scholarly discussion of communications media and mediation in the Romantic period, but it argues that for Shelley the creative power of poetry overcomes spatial and temporal distance, and even negates mediation itself. Shelley's account of poetic creation and communication coalesces both with the material sciences of his own age and with much more recent investigations of quantum physics. For Shelley, communication at a distance always has powerful political implications. In the two poems under discussion here, *Queen Mab* and *The Mask of Anarchy*, Shelley first establishes and tests his account of unmediated communication and then attempts to put it to work in the repressive political atmosphere of 1819.

At the start of his career, Shelley focuses on the physical media of such distant communication. Two sonnets of August 1812, "To a Balloon Laden with Knowledge" and "On Launching Some Bottles Filled with Knowledge into the Bristol Channel," celebrate his actual practices for disseminating his pamphlet *Declaration of Rights*, with its claims that "A man has a right to unrestricted liberty of discussion" and "A man has not only a right to express his thoughts, but it is his duty to do so" (*Prose* 58). Such expression and discussion are made possible by what we would call communications media, Shelley suggests.[1] Each sonnet apostrophizes its vehicle, praising the balloon's "Bright ball" and the bottles' "dark green forms" (1 [*CP* II: 65]; 2 [66]). But each also switches from the medium to the "knowledge" it bears, which seems to act with more than material power. In "To a Balloon," the "spark" that the balloon bears, "gleaming on a hovel's hearth," becomes a bright "beacon in the darkness of the Earth"; in "On Launching some Bottles," their "freight" in turn kindles a "radiance [that] gleams from pole to pole" (10, 12 [*CP* II: 65]; 10, 12 [*CP* II: 66]). Shelley suggests a distinction between the material qualities of these vessels and the more evanescent vital qualities of "knowledge."

Later in his career, especially in exile in Italy, the practices of long-distance communication became even more practically important. In 1819 in particular, Shelley felt the spatial and temporal distance from political events at home. He continued to sustain his communication at a distance with both readers and collaborators; as Nikki Hessell has discussed, Shelley, with Leigh Hunt and Lord Byron, established the project of the journal *The Liberal* across distances of space and time, and his collaborators continued to do so after his death.[2] And many of Shelley's later poetic works, as Omar F. Miranda has recently shown, interrogate questions of communication across time and space to the extent that they might meet the description of a "global lyric": "an open and convocative poetic form of personal voice seeking 'farthest horizons' whose resulting dilated sphere traverses boundaries of race, culture, time, and/or space."[3] In this essay, I take up this rich model of Shelley's open, space-traversing poetics but focus on the problem of mediation.

Important analyses of Romantic media and mediations by Andrew Burkett, Yohei Igarashi, and Celeste Langan and Maureen N. McLane have tended to begin their discussions with a focus on the material media of Romantic art and literature, from print, to lithography, to telegraphy, to theater. Shelley, as we have seen, is interested in physical forms of mediation, but his developing account of matter renders mediation itself unnecessary. As Langan and McLane note, like balloons and bottles, a medium connotes "a middle layer; a means; an intermediary; a transmitting conduit; an impeding conduit; a solution or solvent; a physico-technical apparatus; a route; a conductor; an instrument; a means of communication; a physical object for the storage of data."[4] What these diverse phenomena share is the quality of in-betweenness, standing between the "knowledge" of Shelley's sonnets and their audience. Likewise, mediation for Clifford Siskin and William Warner is "the work done by tools, by what we would now call 'media' of every kind – everything that intervenes, enables, supplements, or is simply in between."[5] Shelley is fascinated by questions of communication, but I argue that he makes the case for specifically poetic "knowledge" as resisting or negating these forms of mediation. Poetic knowledge is not transmitted by an intermediary but rather makes its interventions through an alternate process, which we can term "action at a distance."

I argue that, after 1812, Shelley's work orients itself to the vital, dynamic qualities of poetic knowledge itself, rather than the media that form and bear it, to the extent that his vision for poetry becomes a form of action at a distance. According to the *Oxford English Dictionary*, action at a distance is "the action of one object on another regardless of the presence or absence of an intervening medium [...] influence without a physical intermediary."[6] Shelley's action at a distance thus does away with the in-between qualities of mediation. In *The Connected Condition*, Yohei Igarashi posits such a model of unmediated "influence" in what he terms the Romantic "dream of communication": "The fantasy [...] of a transfer of thoughts, feelings, and information between individuals made as efficient as possible [...] the wish for mediated forms of communication made more effective so as to feel like unmediated contact."[7] However, while Igarashi makes a strong case for the Romantic period as a networked age, the gap between such fantasies of communication and their manifestations in material technologies means that poets like Shelley have to imagine new means of communicating across distance. Shelley's creative attempt to complicate, even annihilate mediation undoes distances of space and time, promising to reach and generate new audiences and even, as I suggest in what follows, to create new worlds.

Shelley displayed intent interest and investment in systems of communication and transport that mediated his work.[8] But much of his writing seems to aspire to the condition of powerful, instantaneous communication without a communicating medium.[9] Such visions of unmediated communication are vitally important for the exiled poet with aspirations to cultural and political influence at home. Shelley's account of unmediated communication at a distance is not a mere flight of unrealized fancy; it is rooted in his scientific and affective understandings of matter. Shelley abandons the opposition we see in his early sonnets between material medium and evanescent subject and instead produces an account of dynamic matter that reconstitutes models of time and space and promises to do away with mediation altogether. In doing so, his work offers an account of time that differs from Jonathan Sachs's account of both the fast time enabled by Romantic media systems and the slow time of newly understood environmental, media, and social evolution.[10] Shelley offers a vision of matter that "cuts" distances of time as well as space to offer newly formed phenomena outside of temporal and spatial systems.

Shelley's investigation of mediation and matter chimes with accounts of materiality that are still being unraveled. As Richard C. Sha has shown, Shelley is among a number of Romantic writers who engage with contemporary physical sciences to understand matter as dynamic, as constituted by forces rather than individualized atoms or corpuscles.[11] This dynamic model of matter, Sha suggests, informs both Shelley's understanding of mediation and of action at a distance. "Shelley's theory of dynamic matter has neither need of an ether nor of a God behind it because there is only continuous interaction of matter."[12] A dynamic material universe does away with intervening media of all kind, and, Sha notes, it thus enables action at a distance: "Because atomism requires direct contact between corpuscles – there can be no action at a distance [...] [But with the] turn to force [...] action no longer requires direct contact."[13] Shelley's engagement with contemporary science provides him with a crucial foundation for his conception of unmediated communication and action as well as the importance of poetry for investigating and articulating such action.

As Sha notes, Romantic engagements with dynamic matter are phenomenological; in the absence of empirical proof of the operation of matter, the Romantic physical sciences showed that "one could think about matter but not know it."[14] And such Romantic thought experiments resonate with more recent investigations of matter, which reveal a still more radical aspect of Shelley's action at a distance. These are the quantum "thought experiments" produced by physicists like Niels Bohr, Werner Heisenberg, Albert Einstein, and Erwin Schrödinger in the 1920s and experimentally proved a century later. Shelley's account of matter and mediation strikingly coalesces with Karen Barad's treatment of quantum physics. Barad presents an "agential realist understanding of matter as a dynamic and shifting entanglement of relations, rather than a property of things."[15] She argues that matter's radical dynamism complicates our very categories of time and space: "Matter is a dynamic intra-active becoming that never sits still – an ongoing reconfiguring that exceeds any linear conception of dynamics in which effect follows cause end-on-end, and in which the global is a straightforward emanation outward of the local."[16] Barad's account of matter, I suggest, is a crucial tool for reading Shelley's treatment of action at a distance.

Commentators have noted such connections between Shelley's poetics and twentieth- and twenty-first-century quantum physics. Mark Lussier and Arkady Plotnitsky both argue for a "quantum mechanical Shelley," noting how his work resonates with quantum physics' dislocation of "the causal dynamics by means of which the behavior of physical objects is determined and that allows one to know with certainty their positions and motion."[17] And more recently, both Chris Washington and Kate

Singer have specifically argued for the importance of Barad's work for reading Shelley, Washington making the case for love in the *Triumph of Life* as Baradian "intra-action" and Singer showing how Barad's account of matter informs our understanding of Shelley's "materialist literary methodology that intertwines relational, moving matter with language's own dynamism."[18] I build on these studies to argue that Shelley's account of dynamic matter performs Baradian "reconfiguring" of space and time. I argue that, for Shelley, poetry in particular enables a radical interrogation of matter and mediation, not merely because, as Sha notes, it prioritizes the play of the imagination but also because it produces distinct relations to space and time. In Barad's terms, we might read Shelley's poetics as an apparatus, a tool that cuts space-time in a distinct way and produces new possibilities for not only understanding but also remaking the world.

Shelley's poetry presents a developing account of matter that enables unmediated action at a distance through its reworking of space and time. In *Queen Mab*, Mab herself declares her command of "the wonders of the human world [...] / Space, matter, time, and mind" (VIII. 49–50 [*CP* II: 224]). *Queen Mab*'s account of material forces overcoming distance has incipient political power, as Shelley makes the case for the significance of the operation of the smallest atom and its effects on the grandest cosmological and societal systems. But Shelley articulates the urgent political power of such accounts of action at a distance most explicitly in *The Mask of Anarchy*. In the aftermath of the Peterloo Massacre of 1819, Shelley is determined that distances of time and space must be overcome in order to produce a unified response to the outrage. In contrast to the explicitly mediated political communications of his sonnets of 1812, in *The Mask of Anarchy* the voice of protest and reform is heard "over the Sea" and across the nation, apparently producing action at a distance (2 [*SPP* 316]). I read *The Mask of Anarchy* as a political test of the radical theorizing of *Queen Mab*, a test that meets sharp challenges in the repressive political environment of 1819. Commentators tend to note the future-oriented qualities of both *Queen Mab* and *The Mask of Anarchy*, connecting such orientation to utopian arguments in both poems.[19] But a quantum reading of Shelley's work radically unsettles such gestures to futurity and to improvement. The material entanglements of *Queen Mab* and *The Mask of Anarchy* disrupt progressive models of time and space and instead suggest that unmediated action and communication might repeatedly remake the world in new forms.

I Baradian Entanglements

Quantum physics demonstrates that, in a quantum state, particles and indeed systems become "entangled." Doug Jackson defines such entanglement as:

> a condition in which pairs of particles are created whose quantum states cannot be described independently of one another, regardless of their physical and temporal separation. Entanglement therefore describes an uncanny form of causality across time and space so that any action upon one has an instantaneous effect on the other, irrespective of distance.[20]

Though this particle behavior was experimentally demonstrated in the 1920s, there was much debate over the cause of such quantum entanglement. As Barad notes, for Niels Bohr, the apparently "uncanny" effects of entanglement were clearly a property of matter: "the so-called instantaneous communication between spatially separated systems is explained by the fact that these allegedly separated states are not really separate at all, but rather 'parts' of one phenomenon."[21] Albert Einstein did not share this view and expressed skepticism that what he termed *spukhafte Fernwirkung*, or "spooky action at a distance," might be a property of matter itself, as he refused to believe that any information could travel faster than the speed of light.[22] Einstein argued instead for "hidden variables," phenomena as yet undetected that might mediate and explain quantum entanglement. But more recent experimental work has gradually ruled out the possibility of hidden variables. As Barad notes, "nature is not correctly described by a local hidden-variables theory [...] This is no mere philosophical prejudice but an empirical fact."[23] Bohr's thought experiments have been experimentally proved to show that in a state of quantum entanglement particles mutually affect one another despite apparent separation by distance.

The understanding of matter established by quantum physics challenges received models of both space and time. Summarizing recent empirical work on entangled states, George Greenstein and Arthur Zajonc note: "we must think in terms of nonlocality, and/or we must renounce the very idea that individual objects possess discrete attributes."[24] Barad develops this account of nonlocality to unsettle any idea of "individual objects." She challenges the notion of discrete objects in space, as experimental apparatus and human observation are inseparable from the object of study. A recent quantum eraser experiment confirms:

> [T]he atom is not a separate object but rather an inseparable part of the phenomenon [...] [W]e see evidence for the ontological priority of phenomena over objects. If one focuses on abstract individual entities the result is an utter mystery, we cannot account for the seemingly impossible behavior of the atoms.[25]

For Barad, the apparent "impossible" action at a distance produced by entanglement is a result of the reconceptualization of materiality from "object" to "phenomenon." In this reworking, "[t]here is not this knowing from a distance. Instead of there being a separation of subject and object, there is an entanglement of subject and object, which is called the 'phenomenon.'"[26] Barad's use of "phenomenon" retains the uncertainty Sha identifies at the heart of Romantic engagement with dynamic matter. And yet, Barad notes, it is possible to achieve objectivity without denaturing the "intra-active" "entanglement of subject and object" in phenomena. Barad refers to this means of knowing as an agential "cut," enabled by experimental apparatus: "knowing is a direct material engagement, a cutting together-apart, where cuts do violence but also open up and rework the agential conditions of possibility."[27] Such knowing is not a result of distance: "objectivity is premised on [...] an individuation-within-and-as-part-of-the-phenomenon enacted in the placement of the cut [...] rather than an absolute notion of externality."[28] And Barad stresses that it is also "contingent"; as Washington notes, "each new intra-action manifests a new relation between the discursive and the material, the subject and object," revealed by a new cut.[29] Thinking of quantum behavior as "intra-actions" within a continuous phenomenal system rather than between distinct objects separated by space is the means, Barad notes, to overcome the apparent "utter mystery" of entanglement.[30] But in order to do so, we must undo received notions of space, time, and matter.

Barad thus proposes an "understanding of matter as a dynamic and shifting entanglement of relations, rather than a property of things."[31] This emphasis on "relations" is fundamental to her account: "relata do not pre-exist relations; rather, relata-within-phenomena emerge through specific intra-actions."[32] Relations cannot be understood according to received spatial models because they manifest within continuous phenomena and thus disrupt and reform our account of time and space:

> Matter's dynamism is generative not merely in the sense of bringing new things into the world but in the sense of [...] engaging in an ongoing reconfiguring of the world. Bodies do not simply take their places in the world [...] Rather, "environments" and "bodies" are intra-actively co-constituted.[33]

Barad's account of matter in terms of mutually constitutive phenomena rather than discrete objects decenters the primacy of human experience. It gives material processes a creative force in which time and space are repeatedly remade: "Such a dynamics is not marked by an exterior parameter called time, nor does it take place in a container called space. Rather, *iterative intra-actions are the dynamics through which temporality and spatiality are produced and iteratively reconfigured*."[34] As we have seen, objective "cuts" reveal new entanglements, and this process is potentially endlessly reproduced; the cut "is an act that occurs iteratively every time we see or understand matter into being."[35] Washington accounts for the "astonishing" consequences of Barad's work as follows:

> [Q]uantum entanglement alters the very ways in which we understand ontology for humans: the world only exists in a non-fixed [...] space and time repeatedly created by the production of new spacetime worlds that are, in turn, created simultaneously by newly created subjects and objects. And since entanglement instantiates space and time new worlds are made with each entanglement.[36]

For Washington, Barad's emphasis on the creative force of entanglement is crucial for our reading of Shelley. Her "reconceptualization of quantum matter as entangling the subject and object in a space and time of their own making in an act of creative simultaneity, reveals a [...] [bold] and politically radical Shelley."[37] Like Washington, I suggest that Shelley's work does not merely represent but aims to reform the world creatively, and his account of matter produces a model of action at a distance that does away with cause and effect, however instantaneous, and instead suggests a form of poetic creativity in which mediation is replaced by intra-actions that continually recreate the world.

Though they seem at times to touch the metaphysical, Barad's claims are founded in experimental physics. Commenting on the quantum eraser experiment, she returns to Einstein's work, to declare:

> There is no spooky-action-at-a-distance co-ordination between individual particles separated in space or individual events separated in time. Space and time are phenomenal, that is, they are intra-actively produced in the making of phenomena; neither space nor time exist as determinate givens outside of phenomena.[38]

Barad's work helps us to move past Einstein's account of mediating "hidden variables" and the logic of cause and effect on which they rely. In phenomenal systems, time and space are iteratively remade rather than instantaneously communicated across, or mediated. Indeed Vicki Kirby draws attention to a key Baradian statement in the notes to *Meeting the Universe Halfway*:

> Rather blasphemously, agential realism denies the suggestion that our access to the world is mediated, whether by consciousness, experience, language, or any other alleged medium [...] [A]gential realism calls into question the presumption that a medium [...] is even necessary.[39]

For Barad, dynamic models of matter undo mediation entirely and thus approach the fantasy of unmediated communication and action posited by accounts of action at a distance. Such action is manifested in Shelley's poetics. Shelley makes action at a distance a political goal, and he suggests that poetry is the means through which this goal might be identified and enacted. I argue that we might treat poetry, in Shelley's scheme, as a form of Baradian apparatus with the facility to offer "agential cuts," to provide moments of insight within intra-active, unmediated, material, phenomenal systems.

II *Queen Mab*'s Dynamic Matter

Shelley's engagement with matter in *Queen Mab* demonstrates his informed interest in the contemporary physical sciences and their potential to enact new understandings of the social and political world as well as the physical environment.[40] In the poem, matter is a dynamic and elastic phenomenon, intimately connected with human experiences and institutions. Mab notes in Canto V that "Matter, with all its transitory shapes" is subject to the will of mankind (V.134, *CP* II: 201). And in Canto VIII "every shape and mode of matter lends / Its force to the omnipotence of mind" (VIII. 235–236 [229]). As Sha notes, "shape" is "an important descriptor within Romantic physics," which Michael Faraday among others uses to connote "a provisional materiality."[41] Shelley's use of the term in relation to matter in *Queen Mab* fits Sha's claim that "shape" emphasizes "the phenomenality of matter."[42] Shelley's accompanying notes engage further with contemporary physics and establish the principles on which matter's various "shape and mode" are built.

From the outset, Shelley presents matter, space, and time as mutually constitutive and makes poetry the means of intuiting and even creating such entanglements.[43] Canto I narrates the journey of the spirit of Ianthe and Queen Mab from earth to the regions of space and the fairy's celestial palace. But from her first interactions with Ianthe, Mab connects this spatial flight with her control of time: "The secrets of the immeasurable past [...] / The future, from the causes which arise / In each event, I gather" (I.169–173 [*CP* II: 170]). Canto I's journey from earth to space emphasizes the cosmological scale of Shelley's narrative and the contemporary physical sciences on which he draws. Shelley stresses the vast scale and endless activity of this cosmological theatre, as

> the chariot's way
> Lay through the midst of an immense concave
> Radiant with million constellations, tinged
> With shades of infinite colour,
> And semicircled with a belt
> Flashing incessant meteors. (I.231–236 [172])

Shelley's account of the light of such "radiant" constellations and "sun's unclouded orb" draw on up-to-the-minute accounts of the operation of light (I.233, 242 [172]). Shelley's note to these lines cites Thomas Young's 1801 "double slit" experiment on light, to ponder the question, as Lussier puts it, "is light a wave or a particle?"[44] Shelley entertains both accounts, noting: "Light consists either of vibrations propagated through a subtle medium, or of numerous minute particles repelled in all directions from the luminous body" (*CP* II: 239). For Washington, Shelley's even-handedness "demonstrates a mind determined to speculate on the hither side of known reality," and he notes the connection between Young's thought experiment cited by Shelley and the work of Bohr and then Barad.[45] I suggest, too, that Shelley's engagement with light in his notes prompts him to interrogate other forms of materiality and to develop the possibility of unmediated connection even across vast cosmological schemes.

At the close of Canto I, Shelley appeals to a "Spirit of Nature." At first, this spirit is situated in the grand cosmological phenomena of Mab and Ianthe's journey:

> Spirit of Nature! Here—
> In this interminable wilderness
> Of worlds, at whose immensity
> Even soaring fancy staggers,
> Here is thy fitting temple! (I.264–268 [*CP* II: 173])

But Shelley switches from the vast and sublime to a very different scale and type of phenomena in the succeeding lines:

> Yet not the lightest leaf
> That quivers to the passing breeze
> Is less instinct with thee;

> Yet not the meanest worm
> That lurks in graves and fattens on the dead,
> Less shares thy eternal breath! (I.269–274 [173])

Shelley's "Spirit of Nature" is common to both vast meteorological and cosmological systems and the "lightest" and "meanest" life forms on earth. Shelley does not quite descend to the microscopic scale of particle physics, but he nonetheless suggests that systems at macroscopic and microscopic scales are continuous phenomena rather than separate states and that they are "instinct," "imbued or charged with [...] a moving or animating force or principle."[46] As Shelley develops his account of matter over the course of the poem, he builds on this vision of material life as "instinct" with dynamic forces.

In Canto II of *Queen Mab*, Shelley shifts from hints of interconnected phenomena at varied scales to an account of Mab's and Ianthe's privileged vision of such interconnections, moving to the poem's most explicit gesture to a form of Baradian entanglement. Mab and Ianthe look down upon the earth from Mab's palace, and the narrator declares:

> None but a spirit's eye,
> And in no other place
> But that celestial dwelling, might behold
> Each action of this earth's inhabitants. (II.87–90 [*CP* II: 176])

This privileged vision is granted because Mab's palace seems distinct from the regular physical laws of the universe. This, combined with the bravery required for radical inquiry, produces a new form of insight:

> matter, space, and time,
> In those aërial mansions cease to act;
> And all-prevailing wisdom, [...]
>   o'erbounds
> Those obstacles of which an earthly soul
>   Fears to attempt the conquest. (II.91–96 [176])

Equipped with a new "intellectual eye," Ianthe's spirit is able to use her insights into "matter, space, and time." Her eye provides a form of Baradian cut, enabling her to perceive the connections, indeed the entanglement, of apparently separate human and natural events, creating a new vision of one phenomenal system:

> How wonderful! [...] the weak touch
> That moves the finest nerve
> And in one human brain
> Causes the faintest thought, becomes a link
> In the great chain of nature. (II.102–108 [176])

Canto II articulates *Queen Mab*'s central claims that spatial and temporal events are always in relation, that human concerns are intimately entangled with those of material "nature," and that the insights of poetry, Ianthe's intellectual eye, can define and make visible such entanglement.

Shelley shifts from spatial to temporal exploration, as Mab presents a succession of visions of past empires. But as her survey concludes, Mab demonstrates that the decline and fall of human empires is precipitated by humans' lack of awareness of their material form and connection with their environment. "Virtue and wisdom, truth and liberty" are "Fled" (II.206, 207 [*CP* II: 179–180]). The return of such principles Shelley suggests, should be predicated on a reminder of humankind's material nature:

> There's not one atom of yon earth
>   But once was living man;
> Nor the minutest drop of rain,
>   That hangeth in its thinnest cloud,
>   But flowed in human veins: (II.211–215 [180])

In Shelley's account of mutable and enduring matter, questions of causality are destabilized, and human experience radically decentered. For Shelley as for Barad, here "'environments' and 'bodies' are intra-actively co-constituted." Only "human pride," Mab declares, prevents the cut that makes visible such entanglements. Shelley ends Canto II by restating how such forces demand new conceptions of "matter, space, and time":

> those viewless beings,
> Whose mansion is the smallest particle
>   Of the impassive atmosphere,
>   Think, feel and live like man;
> [...]
>   And the minutest throb
>   That through their frame diffuses
>   The slightest, faintest motion,
>   Is fixed and indispensable
>   As the majestic laws
>   That rule yon rolling orbs. (II.231–243 [180–181])

As Lussier notes, Shelley maps the universe "from macrocosmic to microcosmic dimensions," making the case for the dynamic "intra-action" of material forces even at vast scales and great cosmological distances.[47] There is no distinction between human and environment in this play of dynamic material phenomena and no need for mediation within such continuous systems.

Canto II thus establishes a model of matter that Shelley sustains in *Queen Mab*'s surveys of time, space, and human society. In the visions of an ideal state with which Shelley ends the poem, he imagines these material entanglements across spatial scales and temporal epochs cut, made explicit, understood, and celebrated. In both Canto VI and Canto VIII, Shelley makes earthly existence "Symphonious" to or with "the planetary spheres," and, as we have seen, Mab brings her vision and guardianship of "Space, matter, time and mind" together as, in another objective cut, "Futurity / Exposes […] its treasure" (VI.41 [*CP* II: 207]; VIII.18 [223]; VIII.50–51 [224]). In Canto IX, as in Canto I, Mab surveys time and space to declare:

> O happy Earth, reality of Heaven!
> To which those restless souls that ceaselessly
> Throng through the human universe, aspire!
> Thou consummation of all mortal hope!
> Thou glorious prize of blindly working will,
> Whose rays, diffused throughout all space and time,
> Verge to one point and blend forever there! (IX.1–7 [230])

Shelley's "human universe" is a material universe. The "will" is conceived as "rays" that, like light, underpin the foundations of "space and time" but which are "forever" in motion, defying containment and explanation. Connection through space and time are a function of the dynamic materialities of Shelley's universe; they are not mediated by "hidden variables" but are entanglements generated by the functions of matter itself. Shelley's account of the moments of insight, of cut, generated by Mab herself and by Ianthe's intellectual eye, present poetic knowledge not as contained within a medium but rather as the cut that reveals material intra-actions. It also reworks questions of communication across distance. Shelley moves away from a model of transmission mediated from point to spatial or temporal point and instead proposes a phenomenal system in which bodies and forms are always already entangled, and which the cut of poetry can reveal and create in potentially endless new forms. Such an understanding of the material universe, time, and space forms the source of Shelley's urgent response to political contingencies, distance, and belatedness in *The Mask of Anarchy*.

III *The Mask of Anarchy*'s Political Intra-actions

The material conditions of Shelley's *The Mask of Anarchy* point to the difficulties, even impossibilities, of unmediated communication at a distance in 1819 and thus pose a sharp challenge to the theoretical visions of *Queen Mab*. In contrast to the earlier poem's historical sweep and visions of futurity, *The Mask of Anarchy* addresses an urgent contemporary crisis. On August 16, 1819, yeomanry and horse guards attacked an unarmed crowd at a meeting for parliamentary reform in St. Peter's Fields, Manchester, trampling and stabbing at least eighteen people to death.[48] On that day, Percy and Mary Shelley were near Livorno in Italy, in mourning for the recent death of their son, William. This distance of thousands of miles delayed Shelley's receipt of news from home. His first report of what became known as the Peterloo Massacre arrived in a letter from his publisher on September 5, nearly three weeks later. Shelley's own response was immediate; he noted in a letter of September 6 that the "torrent of my indignation has not yet done boiling in my veins," and by September 21, with the aid of newspapers sent by friends, he had completed a draft of *The Mask of Anarchy* (*Letters* II: 116–117). He sent the poem to Leigh Hunt for publication in *The Examiner* newspaper on September 23, five weeks after Peterloo; Hunt declined to publish.[49]

The Mask of Anarchy is, then, a response to Peterloo that is markedly belated and highly mediated by the postal system and newspaper press. And yet, in the poem, Shelley presents a vision of unmediated communication across time and distance, a communication that catalyzes political justice. The nature and effectiveness of Shelley's political intervention in *The Mask of Anarchy* have been much discussed, but here I am most interested in the ways in which Shelley's poem complicates notions of distance, causality, and mediation. Shelley's vision of political action at a distance in *The Mask of Anarchy* is informed by his account of the material universe in *Queen Mab*, and as in the earlier poem, Shelley's treatment of matter and mediation resonates with the insights of quantum physics. But in *The Mask of Anarchy*, Shelley puts his treatment of matter, space, and time to political work. The violent power of the state can be overcome, Shelley suggests, by a form of action at a distance in which the cut of poetry creates a vision of resistance, of a people united across time and space against forces of tyranny. *The Mask of Anarchy* is a poem for our times, not so much because of its much-discussed gestures to futurity but rather because it destabilizes temporal distinctions of all kinds.[50]

In *The Mask of Anarchy*, distances of time and space are repeatedly overcome, be they distances between the poet-speaker and the events he describes or distances between human and natural elements and constituents of the poem's "nation." Whereas *Queen Mab* centered on the dynamic qualities of light, in *The Mask of Anarchy* Shelley considers the medium of sound.[51] But the operation of sound across impossible distances seems to negate its mediating function, as communication in the poem shifts instead to something akin to the material intra-actions described by Barad. The opening stanza depicts the speaker as exiled and distant:

> As I lay asleep in Italy
> There came a voice from over the Sea,
> And with great power it forth led me
> To walk in the visions of Poesy. (1–4 [*SPP* 316])

The otherworldliness of the "visions of Poesy" and the ludic play of the "Mask," for Andrew Franta, constitute "a mode of address that necessarily distances [Shelley] from an audience."[52] I suggest that at the start of the poem an unearthly "vision" is required to undo the distance between the speaker and events at home. But as *The Mask of Anarchy* progresses, Shelley presents an account of both human activity and natural forms as parts of a phenomenal system in which distances of time and space can be overcome through unmediated material processes.

In both the nightmarish spectacle of Anarchy's triumph and its defeat through the power of hope, *The Mask of Anarchy* unsettles distances of time and space and deprioritizes human activities in its account of the operation of material forces in the human and natural environment. Anarchy and his crew make an impossibly broad and swift tour of the nation:

> With a pace stately and fast,
> Over English land he passed
> [...]
>
> And with glorious triumph, they
> Rode through England proud and gay
> [...]
>
> O'er fields and towns, from sea to sea,
> Passed the Pageant swift and free,
> Tearing up, and trampling down;
> Till they came to London town. (38–53 [*SPP* 317–318])

"From sea to sea" the simultaneously "stately and fast" pageant advances, "tearing up" all in its path (50 [317]; 38 [317]; 52 [318]). The vibrations of the procession affect an even wider area, as "their trampling shook the ground" and their "tempestuous cry" serves to "sicken" the heart of auditors (43 [317]; 55 [318]). But their destructive power is counteracted by the apparently fragile female figure of Hope.

Hope is a human "maid," but she is quickly associated with an evanescent "Shape," "A mist, a light, an image" (86, 110, 103 [*SPP* 319]). Like the "shape" of Faraday's physics, and "every shape and mode of matter" in

Queen Mab, this Shape's properties are phenomenal, disrupting laws of matter and scale.[53] It is "small at first and weak," but, like "vapour," shifts

> Till as clouds grow on the blast,
> Like tower-crowned giants striding fast
> And glare with lightnings as they fly,
> And speak in thunder to the sky,
>
> It grew—a Shape arrayed in mail
> Brighter than the Viper's scale
> [...]
>
> On its helm, seen far away,
> A planet, like the Morning's, lay; (104, 105, 106–115 [319])

Hope's "Shape" shifts not only its form but also its scale, through meteorological to cosmological phenomena, with potent associated material forces like lightning. This shifting shape has the power to destroy the corruptions and depredations of Anarchy, Shelley suggests, by uniting material forces against usurpation. As in *Queen Mab*, poetry seems to conduct an agential cut, providing knowledge of, indeed creating, material phenomena operating intra-actively at multiple scales and forms. The "Shape" shifts once more into an articulation, the speech that comprises the rest of the poem. This voice, too, and its "words of joy and fear," challenge conceptions of time and space (138 [320]). It has no clear location or source; as Marc Redfield notes, "[t]he more closely one attends to the poem, the more difficult it becomes to say who or what this voice is."[54] It appears to arise out of the Shape's material meteorological and cosmological phenomena:

> A rushing light of clouds and splendour,
> A sense awakening and yet tender
> Was heard and felt— (135–137 [320])

The "Men of England" speech that follows can thus be read as an example of communication at impossible distance, arising not from a locatable source mediated through time and space but rather from a continuous phenomenal system comprising the entangled forces of human and environment and cut, re-created, and made visible through poetic utterance.

The Mask of Anarchy's central speech comprises a hymn, offering detailed analysis of and protest against political things as they are in Britain. But Shelley puts its disruption of received models of time and space to polemical use at two moments in particular. The voice responds to the violence of political authorities by calling for and describing two distinct "assemblies" of the people. The second of these, "a vast assembly," has recognizable features of the Manchester crowd on August 16, as the voice calls for that crowd to be "calm and resolute" even as they are attacked (295, 319 [*SPP* 324–325]). But the first "great Assembly" is much more difficult to locate in time and space. The voice declares:

> Let a great Assembly be
> Of the fearless and the free
> On some spot of English ground
> Where the plains stretch wide around.
>
> Let the blue sky overhead,
> The green earth on which ye tread,
> All that must eternal be
> Witness the solemnity. (262–269 [323])

At first glance, this seems a physical gathering of reformers, on a particular "spot of English ground" at a particular time. Yet this is "some spot," not particularized, surrounded by unnamed plains. Human activity is framed and given significance by the environmental forms of sky and earth, which impart "eternal," not temporal, meaning to the gathering. And, as the voice continues, the "Assembly" shifts further from a particularized location and time:

> From the corners uttermost
> Of the bonds of English coast,
> From every hut, village and town
> Where those who live and suffer moan
> For others' misery or their own, (270–274 [323])

As the voice describes the human participants of this "Assembly," the physical impossibility of the gathering becomes clearer. The crowd is gathered from the "uttermost" corners of England and from "every" dwelling place subject to suffering, so by implication, the whole nation. I have written elsewhere about this assembly as a virtual meeting, noting the parallels with actual simultaneous meetings of 1819, events orchestrated and highly mediated by the newspaper press.[55] But informed by the models of material entanglements and unmediated communication at a distance established in *Queen Mab* and given political significance here, we can read the material and political energies forming this assembly as a kind of entanglement, for a moment located in time and space by the cut of poetic articulation but potentially endlessly recreated. Such a vision has enormous polemical power, which might mitigate the chilling powers of distance, repression, and censorship. Shelley undoes the distinction between local assembly and political nation; both might be considered as one phenomenal system, in which bonds of solidarity and fellow feeling are not transmitted across distance but rather instantaneously created anew with every poetic cut.

The celebrated conclusion to *The Mask of Anarchy* repeats and builds upon this conception of materialized political forces enacted across space and time. The voice declares:

> And that slaughter to the Nation
> Shall steam up like inspiration,
> Eloquent, oracular;
> A volcano heard afar.
>
> And these words shall then become
> Like oppression's thundered doom
> Ringing through each heart and brain,
> Heard again—again—again—(360–367 [*SPP* 326])

News of the "slaughter" of political tyranny is sublimated to the meteorological and geological phenomena of "steam" and volcanic vapor. The sound of such phenomena is not mediated but impossibly "heard afar," across the nation, and, the poem implies, by the speaker thousands of miles away, as each repeated poetic cut reveals new entanglements. The suggestion that this is an effect of materialized intra-action grows stronger as, like the "Men of England" speech "heard and felt," these words ring "again—again—again—" through both "the heart and brain" of "each" auditor, wherever their location. As Lussier notes, "Shelley's best poetry describes a universal cohesion created through waves, a vast network of matter woven from energy."[56] This materialized "network" or phenomenal system negates the spatial distances that threaten to isolate both the protesting inhabitants of England and the exiled speaker. They are united to form a political force of unplaceable location and "unvanquishable number" in the poem's closing lines (369 [326]).

The future-oriented gestures of Shelley's poetry are often explicit and much discussed; on the one hand, then, this quality makes him an obvious poet "for our times." But the impact of Shelley's vision of a materialized phenomenal universe is, I suggest, more interesting. Shelley's vision of unmediated communication through space and time enables a different understanding of his hopes and fears for the transmission of poetry, especially its reception by a future audience. Franta notes that "[i]n emphasizing poetic transmission, even to the extent of identifying poetry's power with its reception, Shelley acknowledges a dependence on the technology of writing."[57] A Baradian account of the entangled materialities of Shelley's work negates such anxieties in two ways. First, the visions of communication that we see in *Queen Mab* and *The Mask of Anarchy* do away with the mediating form of the written word, which becomes a kind of "hidden variable," an unnecessary explanatory step for a quantum communication that comprises "intra-actions" within a phenomenal system rather than mediated transmission between distinct objects and spaces. And second, such entangled materialities profoundly disrupt our notion of temporal distance and dislocation. For Barad, "neither space nor time exist as determinate givens." In *The Mask of Anarchy*'s two assemblies, Shelley takes into account the suffering material bodies of those who resist state violence, but he also offers an alternate vision of their materiality, in which assembly and nation become one phenomenal system revealed through poetic cut, not temporalized in 1819 but reenacted across time and space. Shelley is for our times because he is of our time.

Notes

1 As John Guillory notes, "The term *mediation* and the problem of communication do not seem to have been brought together in any systematic way until the later nineteenth century," but Shelley connects physical media with acts of communication here. John Guillory "Enlightening Mediation," in Clifford Siskin and Michael Warner, eds. *This Is Enlightenment* (Chicago: University of Chicago Press, 2010), 37–63, 53.
2 Nikki Hessell, "Elegiac Wonder and Intertextuality in the *Liberal*," *Romanticism*, 18.3 (2012), 239–249.
3 Omar F. Miranda, "The Global Romantic Lyric," *The Wordsworth Circle*, 52.2 (2021), 308–327, 322.
4 Celeste Langan and Maureen N. McLane, "The Medium of Romantic Poetry," in James Chandler and Maureen N. McLane, eds. *The Cambridge Companion to Romantic Poetry* (Cambridge: Cambridge University Press, 2008), 239–262, 242. See also Andrew Burkett, *Romantic Mediations: Media Theory and British Romanticism* (Albany: State University of New York Press, 2016).
5 Clifford Siskin and William Warner, "Introduction," in Siskin and Warner, eds. *This Is Enlightenment*, 5.
6 "action at a distance, n." *Oxford English Dictionary* (*OED*) *Online*, March 2022, www-oed-com.libproxy.york.ac.uk/view/Entry/1938?redirectedFrom=action+at+a+distance.
7 Yohei Igarashi, *The Connected Condition: Romanticism and the Dream of Communication* (Stanford: Stanford University Press, 2019), 4, 6.
8 John Gardner, "Shelley's Steamship," *Keats-Shelley Journal*, 71 (2022), 87–113; Richard C. Sha, *Imagination and Science in Romanticism* (Baltimore: Johns Hopkins University Press 2018), 68–69.
9 At times Orrin N. C. Wang's latest account of mediation comes close to this possibility of unmediated communication. He uses "the image or figure of a cut that realizes the in, through, and off of media and mediation, the intractable inbetween, that (de-)structures the articulatory practice of media as mediation." The "cut" is important for my account of Shelley too, though it is derived from a different tradition. Orrin N. C. Wang, *Techno-Magism: Media, Mediation, and the Cut of Romanticism* (New York: Fordham University Press, 2022), 19.

10 Jonathan Sachs "Eighteenth-Century Slow Time: Seven Propositions," *The Eighteenth Century* 60.2 (2019), 185–205.
11 Sha, *Imagination and Science*, 31.
12 Sha, *Imagination and Science*, 70.
13 Sha, *Imagination and Science*, 33.
14 Sha, *Imagination and Science*, 33.
15 Karen Barad, *Meeting the Universe Halfway: Quantum Physics and the Entanglement of Matter and Meaning* (Durham, NC: Duke University Press, 2007), 224.
16 Barad, *Meeting the Universe*, 170.
17 Mark S. Lussier, *Romantic Dynamics: The Poetics of Physicality* (Macmillan, 2000), 44; Arkady Plotnitsky, "All Shapes of Light: The Quantum Mechanical Shelley," in Betty T. Bennett and Stuart Curran, eds. *Shelley: Poet and Legislator of the World* (Baltimore: Johns Hopkins University Press, 1996), 263–310, 264.
18 Chris Washington, "The Dark Side of the Light: The Triumph of Love in Shelley's *The Triumph of Life*," in Joel Faflak, ed. *The Futures of Shelley's Triumph*, *Romantic Circles* Praxis Series (October 2019), https://romantic-circles.org/praxis/triumph/praxis.2019.triumph.washington.html; Kate Singer, *Romantic Vacancy: The Poetics of Gender, Affect, and Radical Speculation* (Albany: State University of New York Press, 2019), 83.
19 Greg Ellerman reads "a utopian future, in which humans will reconcile themselves to nature" in *Queen Mab*. Greg Ellerman, "A Poetics of Ether," *European Romantic Review* 29.3 (2018), 389–398, 393. On utopianism in *Queen Mab* and *Mask of Anarchy*, see Seth T. Reno, "The Violence of Form in Shelley's *Mask of Anarchy*," *Keats-Shelley Journal* 62 (2013), 80–98; Michael Scrivener, *Radical Shelley: The Philosophical Anarchism and Utopian Thought of Percy Bysshe Shelley* (Princeton: Princeton University Press, 1982).
20 Doug Jackson, "Environmental Entanglement," *Journal of Architectural Education* 71.2 (2017), 137–140, 137. See also Barad on "simultaneity," *Meeting the Universe*, 272.
21 Barad, *Meeting the Universe*, 174.
22 Albert Einstein to Max Born, March 3, 1947, in *The Born-Einstein Letters: Correspondence between Albert Einstein and Max and Hedwig Born from 1916 to 1955* (New York: Walker, 1971), 158. See also Barad, *Meeting the Universe*, 272–273 and D. J. P., "What Is Spooky Action at a Distance? Why Some Things Are Neither Here nor There," *The Economist*, March 16, 2017.
23 Barad, *Meeting the Universe*, 291–292. See also *The Born-Einstein Letters*, 273, 318.
24 George Greenstein and Arthur G. Zajonc, *The Quantum Challenge: Modern Research on the Foundations of Quantum Mechanics* (Burlington: Jones and Bartlett, 1997), 144, cited in Barad, *Meeting the Universe*, 292.
25 Barad, *Meeting the Universe*, 315.
26 Karen Barad, "Matter Feels, Converses, Suffers, Desires, Yearns and Remembers," in Rick Dolphijn and Iris van der Tuin, eds. *New Materialism: Interviews and Cartographies* (London: Open Humanities Press, 2012), 48–70, 52.

27 Barad, *Meeting the Universe*, 55.
28 Barad, *Meeting the Universe*, 321.
29 Barad, *Meeting the Universe*, 348; Washington, "Dark Side of the Light."
30 Barad, *Meeting the Universe*, 234, 338.
31 Barad, *Meeting the Universe*, 224.
32 Barad, *Meeting the Universe*, 140. See Washington, "Dark Side of the Light."
33 Barad, *Meeting the Universe*, 170.
34 Barad, *Meeting the Universe*, 179, emphasis original. See also page 223 and 234 for Barad's debt to Donna Haraway's conception of the container model of space.
35 Kate Singer, Ashley Cross, and Suzanne L. Barnett, "Introduction: Living in a New Material World," in Singer, Cross, and Barnett, eds. *Material Transgressions: Beyond Romantic Bodies, Genders, Things* (Liverpool: Liverpool University Press, 2020), 1–28, 18.
36 Washington, "Dark Side of the Light."
37 Washington, "Dark Side of the Light."
38 Barad, *Meeting the Universe*, 315.
39 Barad, *Meeting the Universe*, 409, cited in Vicki Kirby "Matter Out of Place: 'New Materialism' in Review," in Vicki Kirby, ed. *What If Culture Was Nature All Along?* (Edinburgh: Edinburgh University Press, 2017), 1–25, 17.
40 Ellerman argues that in *Queen Mab* ether is a material medium, a "vehicle of a utopian natural history" in the poem: "Poetics of Ether," 390. As I have suggested, my account of Shelleyan mediation informed by Barad complicates such visions of a utopian future.
41 Sha, *Imagination and Science*, 84, 62.
42 Sha, *Imagination and Science*, 84.
43 For Alan Weinberg, "the poem is not confined to a representation of linear or sequential temporality: it repeatedly shifts focus from one aspect of time to another." Alan Weinberg, "Freedom from the Stranglehold of Time: Shelley's Visionary Conception in *Queen Mab*," *Romanticism* 22.1 (2016), 90–106, 91. Weinberg investigates the connections between *Queen* Mab's representation of space and time and Lucretius and Spinoza, rather than quantum physics.
44 Lussier, *Romantic Dynamics*, 141.
45 Washington, "Dark Side of the Light," par. 3.
46 "instinct, adj." *OED Online*. March 2022, www-oed-com.libproxy.york.ac .uk/view/Entry/97086?rskey=gzmqYK&result=2&isAdvanced=false.
47 Lussier, *Romantic Dynamics*, 147. Shelley connects macro- and microscopic scales again at the end of Canto III, 226–232, in *CP* II: 188–189.
48 Robert Poole, *Peterloo: The English Uprising* (Oxford: Oxford University Press, 2019), 1.
49 Richard Holmes, *Shelley: The Pursuit*, 2nd ed. (New York: Harper Perennial, 2005), 532.
50 Andrew Franta, "Shelley and the Poetics of Political Indirection," *Poetics Today* 22.4 (2001), 765–793; Marc Redfield, *The Politics of Aesthetics: Nationalism, Gender, Romanticism* (Stanford: Stanford University Press, 2003); Susan Wolfson, "'Romantic Ideology' and the Values of Aesthetic Form," in George

Levine, ed. *Aesthetics and Ideology* (New Brunswick: Rutgers University Press, 1994), 188–218; Susan Wolfson, *Romantic Shades and Shadows* (Baltimore: Johns Hopkins University Press, 2018), 114.
51 Ian Haywood analyzes the soundscape of Shelley's poem in "The Sounds of Peterloo," in Michael Demson and Regina Hewitt, eds. *Commemorating Peterloo: Violence, Resilience and Claim-Making during the Romantic Era* (Edinburgh: Edinburgh University Press, 2019), 57–83, 58.
52 Franta, "Political Indirection," 777. See also Wolfson, "Romantic Ideology," 206, and *Formal Charges: The Shaping of Poetry in British Romanticism* (Stanford: Stanford University Press, 1997), 196.
53 For Washington, Shelley's "Shape" in *The Triumph of Life* is another "exemplar of discursive-material quantum entanglement." Washington, "Dark Side of the Light," par. 14.
54 Redfield, *Politics of Aesthetics*, 157.
55 Mary Fairclough, "Peterloo at 200: The Radical Press, Simultaneous Meetings and *The Mask of Anarchy*," *The Keats-Shelley Review* 33.2 (2019), 171–173.
56 Lussier, *Romantic Dynamics*, 143.
57 Franta, "Political Indirection," 791.

CHAPTER 12

Educating the Imagination/ Defending Shelley Defending

Joel Faflak

I

Shelley wrote *A Defence of Poetry* in 1821 as a response to Thomas Love Peacock's "The Four Ages of Poetry" (1820), which appeared in the first and only issue of *Ollier's Literary Miscellany*.[1] Charles Ollier, also Shelley's publisher, discontinued the periodical before the *Defence* could appear, and Shelley died before he could publish his essay as a pamphlet. Mary Shelley intended to publish the *Defence* in *The Liberal*, but that periodical also folded. The essay finally appeared as the opening work in Mary's edition of her husband's *Essays, Letters from Abroad, Translations and Fragments* (1840), the year after her 1839 edition of *The Poetical Works of Percy Bysshe Shelley*. Yet, despite these obstacles, what other factors explain the essay's delayed publication? The prophetic conclusion of Shelley's essay offers one answer:

> Poets are the hierophants of an unapprehended inspiration, the mirrors of the gigantic shadows which futurity casts upon the present, the words which express what they understand not, the trumpets which sing to battle and feel not what they inspire: the influence which is moved not, but moves. Poets are the unacknowledged legislators of the World. (*SPP* 535)

Shelley's poets capture through the vitality of their metaphors the future's dark shadows, yet without knowing their eventual impact. That is to say, poetry announces a world that *will have come*, as if the present already apprehends the future, but without any idea what it might mean ("words which express what they understand not"). Moreover, that this "influence" "moves" but "is moved not" suggests a potentially dangerous enthusiasm, a source of action and agency that also needs to be curbed. Evoking a preternatural feeling about the future, then, Shelley's *Defence* states its case as if by refusing, or not knowing how, to do so, like the narrator's thoughts "which must remain untold" in Shelley's last, unfinished poem, *The Triumph of Life*, even as he goes on to describe the scene of their cognition

(21 [*SPP* 484]). Not telling also tells a different story and offers a different way of knowing the world, the sign of a malleable, adaptive mind built to deal with crisis. That certain forces would instrumentalize this creative capacity, however, makes such a mind all the more prone to influence.

The visionary ending of the *Defence* evokes the strange temporality Maurice Blanchot associates with prophetic speech, in which "it is not the future that is given, but the present that is taken away."[2] This "impossible future" is one we "would not know how to live and that must upset all the sure givens of existence."[3] The "thought of impossibility" draws us away "from the space in which we exercise power" to indicate a "reserve in thought itself, a thought not allowing itself to be thought in the mode of appropriative comprehension."[4] In Shelley's *The Triumph of Life*, this impossibility defines how the disaster of history shapes the mind, its thoughts perpetually generated and trampled by a "shape all light" (*SPP* 352). In this chapter, I want to align this impossibility with a mind liberated in order to find itself yet unable to find its bearings, and thus prone to uselessness. I associate this uselessness with an ongoing crisis in the humanities and the teaching of literature. Shelley's essay reads within a history indifferent to poetry the imagination's animating response to the deadening effects of utility, like the leaves of Shelley's West Wind scattered to announce a new birth. The humanities find themselves facing a similar struggle against the time's demand for relevance. While the outcome remains to be seen, let us at least consider what options Shelley's essay suggests. If an uncertain mind is the quality of any attempt to live in and with the present, thus making it vulnerable to appropriation, perhaps uncertainty nonetheless remains the mind's greatest capacity for change.

II

History has suspected the imagination at least since Socrates cautioned Ion about infecting his audience with the divine madness of Homer's inspiration. Socrates succumbed to his own warning when charged with corrupting the minds of Athenian youth, to which danger Plato replied by exiling poets from his ideal republic for taking fictions as truths, what Sir Phillip Sidney then taught as poetry's primary function. Caught in this conflict of sensations between rejecting and embracing poetry's utility, the *Defence* distinguishes between poetry as verbal art, anchored in its everyday practice and teaching or its evolution throughout literary history, and poetry as a transhistorical force for change. Shelley directs his rage against an emergent information age that threatens to bury us in facts, like Gradgrind in Charles Dickens's *Hard Times* or the law's grinding entropy in *Bleak House*:[5]

> We have more moral, political and historical wisdom, than we know how to reduce into practise; we have more scientific and economical knowledge than can be accommodated to the just distribution of the produce which it multiplies. The poetry in these systems of thought, is concealed by the accumulation of facts and calculating processes [...] The cultivation of poetry is never more to be desired than at periods when, from an excess of the selfish and calculating principle, the accumulation of the materials of external life exceed the quantity of the power of assimilating them to the internal laws of human nature. The body has then become too unwieldy for that which animates it. (*SPP* 530–531)

Amidst the relentless formation of "systems of thought" that inform and sustain culture, Shelley appeals to their original articulation as phantasy. If society forgets *this* "poetry," knowledge becomes the dead weight of the endless viscera archived by the "promoters of utility" in the "book of common life" (529). The only solution to such an "unmitigated exercise of the calculating faculty" is transformation through perpetual acts of imagination: "We want the creative faculty to imagine that which we know; we want the generous impulse to act that which we imagine; we want the poetry of life: our calculations have outrun conception; we have eaten more than we can digest" (529, 530).

While poetry's "vitally metaphorical" function contests "utility," however, the poetry Shelley describes is also a self-consuming artifact, in which "want" signifies a privation to be satisfied but also a desire for something evermore about to be that can't (*SPP* 512). Poetry seems caught between feeding the imagination's hunger for figuration and curtailing its gluttony. As both "centre and circumference of knowledge," at once the form and process of its own unfolding, poetry exposes the difference within our relation with the real and thus the profound absence of reality from itself (531). An earlier criticism surmised "two planes of thought in Shelley's aesthetics – one Platonistic and mimetic, the other psychological and expressive."[6] Waged between the desire for art's completion by the Ideal and the need to understand the desire itself, however, the *Defence* offers a kind of negative Platonism not unlike deconstruction's version of Shelley, in which language compensates for the absence of the things it represents. By negating reality, language exposes us to the unfathomable nature of our being that can never be filled except by creative acts that never satisfy the yearning. Indeed, there is something voracious and atavistic about poetry's drive to find new lands for the imagination to explore: "Poetry enlarges the circumference of the imagination by replenishing it with thoughts of ever new delight, which have the power of attracting and assimilating to their own nature all other thoughts, and which form new intervals and interstices *whose void for ever craves fresh food*" (*SPP* 517, emphasis mine). Rather than "imagine that which we know," poetry generates its own creative energy as if *ex nihilo*, the primal energy of a black hole whose impact exceeds representation, almost as if to feed on its own burnout.

If this relentless creativity is how poetry delights, what does it teach us, especially when the circumference drawn, then exceeded, by imagination is both within and beyond the poet's grasp? For Tilottama Rajan, the "self-displacing energy" of Shelley's poetry "insists on the imagination as dynamic and vital but thereby unable to fix meaning."[7] Addressing "episodes to that great poem, which all poets, like the co-operating thoughts of one great mind, have built up since the beginning of the world" (*SPP* 522), the *Defence* assumes "that the work is to be found in unassimilated portions of the text, in revolutionary sparks that a later reader develops, often in opposition to what the major portion of the text seems to say."[8] Thought "is precisely the site of a paradox: dissemination as the scattering and unfixing of unitary meaning, dissemination as communication."[9] Yet by suspending enlightenment as an alternate form of illumination, this indeterminacy invites other determinations.[10] For Shelley, the "true utility" of poetry "[renders the mind] the receptacle of a thousand unapprehended combinations of thought," by which pleasure the "imagination is enlarged by a sympathy with pains and passions" of others (*SPP* 529, 517, 520).[11] But such revelation exposes poetry to the distortion of its educative potential, to making the energy of thought a sensation that requires policing, even condemnation. The "vitally metaphorical" labor of interpretation that is the hallmark of the humanities also exposes this pleasure to ideological capture. In short, if our critical, affective, and transformational task is never to make up our minds in order to resist the status quo, the status quo can just as easily make up our minds for us. The rhetorical urgency of Shelley's response is very much to defend against this foreboding, which he senses in Peacock's essay. In doing so, however, does Shelley play into the hands of a crisis about which Peacock was only half kidding (if he was) or does it foment that crisis (especially if he wasn't)?

Against Peacock, Shelley insists that "the literature of England [...] has arisen as it were from a new birth" (*SPP* 535). But "as it were" suggests an uncertainty about the future that resonates to the present in the humanities. Retrofitting Shelley's reputation was one focus of the emergence of Romantic studies since the mid-twentieth century.

Subsequent criticisms – feminism, poststructuralism, postcolonialism, new historicism, queer studies, to name a few – have rethought Romanticism as a process of "restless self-examination" compelling our repeated analysis.[12] One might think that the new university, craving the "fresh food" of innovation for innovation's sake, would welcome this explosion of approaches, especially its informed social response. But this restlessness also marks our field as rather faceless. We might recall Arthur O. Lovejoy's discrimination of Romanticism as a multiple personality T. E. Hulme diagnosed by separating a healthy classicism from an unwieldy and morbid Romanticism. This fate has since become Romanticism's imaginative asset, the aesthetic incitement to robust and diverse political response. Yet has this protean nature come back to haunt us, urging us to make up our mind while preying on the fact that we can't?

Shelley's vision of poetry as the evolution of unanticipated mutations is a potent model for our field's ongoing revitalization, exemplified by this volume's editors and contributors. But the imagination's malleability makes it ripe for manipulation, the danger of which Shelley seems equally aware. His essay's vacillating nature doesn't help. The "vitally metaphorical" language of poets, which includes the writing of Dante, Homer, and Shakespeare, but also Plato, Bacon, and "the authors of revolutions" (*SPP* 515),

> marks the before unapprehended relations of things, and perpetuates their apprehension, until the words which represent them, become through time signs for portions or classes of thoughts instead of pictures of integral thoughts; and then if no new poets should arise to create afresh the associations which have been thus disorganized, language will be dead to all the nobler purposes of human intercourse. (512)

Later, Shelley goes from saying that poetry "lifts the veil from the hidden beauty of the world, and makes familiar objects be as if they were not familiar" (517) to suggesting that the "universe" eventually becomes "annihilated in our minds by the recurrence of impressions blunted by reiteration," requiring poetry to "create afresh the associations which have been thus disorganized" (533). Between the limits of language, which confront us with the finitude of existence, and the potential for endless recombination within that finitude, Shelley emphasizes the transformative power of an "unapprehended inspiration." Yet is this recombination the symptom of the mind at work on itself or of a mind ready-made for brainwashing by the modes of ceaseless production capitalism has imposed on the modern university?

Shelley's emphasis on the "unapprehended" should by now make us, well, a little apprehensive.[13] Thought's endless synergy also suggests an imagination stretched to absurdity, like the Grecian urn that teases Keats out of thought. Two of the more gothic moments in the *Defence* signal an endlessly deferred, missed, even pointless encounter with the very thing imagination means to attain. Shelley refers to "the mind in creation" as a "fading coal which some invisible influence, like an inconstant wind, awakens to transitory brightness," a force that can never be "durable in its original purity and force" (*SPP* 531). For "when composition begins, inspiration is already on the decline, and the most glorious poetry that has ever been communicated to the world is probably a feeble shadow of the original conception of the poet" (531). Earlier he refers to the poet as a "nightingale who sits in darkness, and sings to cheer its own solitude with sweet sounds; his auditors are as men entranced by the melody of an unseen musician, who feel that they are moved and softened, yet know not whence or why" (516). If poetry's transformational potential is proleptic, it arrives stillborn, in need of reanimation, like Mary Shelley's scientist obsessed with revivifying what in *Adonais* her husband calls "corpses in a charnel" (349). Yet it also marks an anxiety about alternative views post-1789. Such dangers threatened Edmund Burke but would not have threatened the man who wrote *The Necessity of Atheism*, and whose *Queen Mab* or *Laon and Cythna* were the target of censorship. Yet by 1821 such dangers surely inform *A Defence of Poetry*. What, then, should we do with Shelley's injunction to use the imagination to legislate a better world? Paul de Man's deconstructive Shelley posits a meaningless positing of meaning.[14] But what about the Shelley who still imagines the world can be changed, Shelley as patron saint of the Chartist movement, for instance?

III

Peacock's stadial theory of English verse ends in the brass age of his contemporaries, among whom the poet is a "semi-barbarian in a civilized community," the opposite of the "useful or rational man" and "cannot claim the slightest share in any one of the comforts and utilities of life of which we have witnessed so many and so rapid advance."[15] Peacock urges "intelligent men" to "stop wasting their time writing poetry and apply themselves to the new sciences, including economics and political theory, that could improve the world" (*SPP* 509).[16] But Peacock's satire, if it is satire, suggests a dangerous paradox about the advent of political economy informing progress in Shelley's time. For instance, Shelley's essay doesn't mention Adam Smith, whose invisible hand of the marketplace, articulated in *The Wealth of Nations* (1776), haunts Shelley's text as the phantom menace of social change not entirely dissimilar to the power of the invisible mind forming itself within Shelley's conception of poetry. Either figure evokes a kind of gothic prosthesis governing two versions of progress uncannily related by assuming a social consensus or *sensus communis*. Shelley's poetry seems toothless for its evocation of a future *avenir* that may or may not materialize, whereas Smith's designation insists upon its eventuality as a way of "inevitably plotting the economic process toward a final state of equilibrium," a fiscal balance not unlike the impartial assurances of human sympathy in his earlier *The Theory of Moral Sentiments* (1759).[17] Conversely, Shelley's displacing energy of poetry has more to do with revolutionary upset than with establishing equilibrium, just as the forces of economic progress, like those of affective exchange, have the potential to go awry, albeit not in a manner Smith would have advocated.[18]

What, then, does Shelley's *A Defence of Poetry* tell us about the current state of crisis within the humanities? Paul Reitter and Chad Wellmon argue that "*the self-understanding of the modern humanities didn't merely take shape in response to a perceived crisis; it also made crisis a core part of the project of the humanities.*"[19] Different from the "disordered desires, unruly passions, or the presence of evil" that were the object of an earlier *studia humanitatis*, the modern humanities are tasked with addressing "historical changes: industrialization, new technologies, natural science, and capitalism," not to mention climate change and the constant threat of geopolitical chaos, a "permanent relationship to the present [that] links the modern humanities to the temporality of crisis."[20] Because the humanities "*both depended on and played a crucial part in the rise of the modern research university*" in nineteenth-century Germany and then in the United States, the demands of instrumental rationality in providing "practical moral succour for a new age" immediately put them at odds with Max Weber's call for the humanities to "be conducted value free, without moral presuppositions."[21] This "'polytheism of values'"[22] aligns with Shelley's defense of imagination as the "great instrument of moral good" (*SPP* 517). Yet it traps the humanities between naming its singular purpose, its "world-historical mission," and the ongoing critique of its common ground, which is fundamental to this purpose but which makes proving our relevance that much more difficult.[23]

Perhaps, then, the crisis of the humanities stems from the assumption that they have "intrinsic value."[24] Shelley's *Defence* speaks to a historical continuity not unlike T. S. Eliot's tradition but rewrites its creative catalyst as the free radical of change, what *Prometheus Unbound* calls a "voice to be accomplished" (III.iii.67 [*SPP* 261]). At the end of Shelley's lyrical drama, Demogorgon, a placeholder for the impossibility of identity if ever there was one, urges us "to hope, till Hope creates / From its own wreck the thing it contemplates," not unlike Walter Benjamin's angel moving onward fueled by the toxic waste of catastrophe as, paradoxically, its constitutive possibility (IV.573–574 [286]).[25] But it is easy to overlook the fact that something has to or will inevitably *get wrecked* in the process. Which begs the question: might Shelley, if he saw how the humanities have evolved, contemplate their ruin as a necessary gesture to clear space for some future incarnation, if such an incarnation is even possible? We might ask the same question of Romantic studies itself.

IV

The title of my essay paraphrases Northrop Frye, for whom, as for the New Critics or Leavis's Great Tradition, the teaching of literature offers a bulwark of culture against the anarchy of one's historical moment, programmatically laid out in Frye's *Anatomy of Criticism*.[26] Frye wrote *The Educated Imagination* as a work of public intellectualism in Canada as we anticipated our centennial in 1967.[27] That is to say, the stakes were not just academic but patriotic, indicative of "a great and free development of the national will." But Frye also shares Shelley's anxiety: "Is it possible that literature, especially poetry, is something that a scientific civilization like ours will eventually outgrow?"[28] He continues: "Shelley's essay is a wonderful piece of writing, but it's not likely to convince anyone who needs convincing."[29] Frye's groundbreaking study of William Blake, of course, was another sign of a resurgence of interest in Romanticism that continues to this day.[30] He defends literature as secular scripture, an autonomous imaginative realm that expresses Weber's "polytheism of values." Literature needed to reach beyond the history that produced it in order to outmaneuver the "promoters of utility" who "follow in the footsteps of poets, and copy the sketches of their creations into the book of common life" (*SPP* 529). Frye thus asks what it means to be educated in the first place, although he assumes a certain kind of education. As Deanne Bogdan argues, Frye avoids the politics of race, class, or gender that necessarily shape how teachers teach and readers read and have become essential to our understanding of the field. The *Defence* is especially attuned to these experiences because, for Shelley, poetry is "the only one [of the arts] that dictates the actual material of its expression," which means that "poetry alone actually produces the material of its own ontology" and thus actively expresses the shifting means of an unavoidable yet necessary confrontation with the political.³¹

Shelley uses the word "common" nine times in the *Defence*, which suggests an alliance with the status quo but also a countervailing response that itself risks being universalist. And there is the paradoxical situation in which poetry finds itself. Poetry expresses a continuous historical force, what in *Adonais* Shelley calls the "loveliness" of which each poem is a "portion" (*SPP* 379). Yet in the *Defence*, poems form the "unassimilated portions" (515) that do not necessarily add up to a "whole," avatars of history whose uncertain unfolding heralds an "unapprehended" future. This makes their protean nature one of the more transformative and disruptive aspects of Shelley's *Defence*. Poetry's defamiliarizing affects and effects confront us with the feeling of consciousness, and consciousness *as* feeling, that contemporary neuroscience is only beginning to understand.³² That a poem might literally generate, impact, and shape in turn how we embody ourselves makes poetry – its making but especially its reading – a startling *existential* force that embeds us within the evolving process of discovering the new as the unknown. Yet this revolutionary urge chafes against the pedagogic demands of learning about the world in order to be its productive citizens. If the root of education is *educatio* (reading, breeding, bringing up) or *educare* (to train, bring forth, lead forward, raise up), then Shelley's *Defence* leaves maddeningly, even dangerously unstated what one is being led toward, trained for, a breeding that might even produce oppressive social forms. Even a universalist like Frye realized that a lack of common purpose might prove the Achilles' heel of the struggle of the humanities to justify themselves.

Ben Lerner begins his brief but brilliant *The Hatred of Poetry* by quoting Marianne Moore's aptly titled "Poetry":

> I, too, dislike it.
> Reading it, however, with a perfect contempt for it, one discovers in it, after all, a place for the genuine.³³

The title names the poem's subject, but the real tension is between "I" and "it," as if to insist on an anonymity that engenders "perfect contempt," yet at the same time to name this diasporic site as a "place for the genuine" in which the "I" might find itself. With a nod to Shelley, Lerner writes that, as a rebuttal to the "'calculative' avarice of a materialistic society, [...] the use of poetry is therefore entwined with its uselessness [...] its lack of practical utility."³⁴ Yet "[i]t's precisely because of the contradictory nature of the poetic vocation – it is both more and less than work" – "that we are embarrassed by and disdainful of the poet's labor."[35] Put another way, that poetry is always already arcane and inscrutable is the power of its impotence, a counterintuitive gesture to be sure. Shelley himself said that *Prometheus Unbound*, one of Romanticism's most challenging texts largely untouched by critics until seminal readings by Earl Wasserman or Harold Bloom, "was never intended for more than five or six persons" (*Letters* II: 388).[36] We also need to remember that in place of the promised second part of his essay, which was to "have for its object an application of these principles [explored in the first part] to the present state of the cultivation of Poetry," Shelley instead wrote *Adonais*, an elegy that struggles almost literally to bring Keats back to life (*SPP* 535). This missing supplement suggests the failure to apply theory by turning interpretation to practical use – a melancholic response to that failure, a failed mourning for poetry's missed encounter with its own potentiality. And yet this failure of theory is at the same time the triumph of poetry.

Isn't such a *méconnaissance* precisely Shelley's point? The "true utility" of poetry can and should be *more poetry*, the feedback loop of imagination as the eternal recurrence of its creative potential to transform the world. This is Shelley's space of a revolutionary potential by which, as he states in "Ode to a West Wind," we "Drive [our] dead thoughts over the universe / Like withered leaves to quicken a new birth," and "by [our] incantation of [Shelley's] verse / Scatter, as from an unextinguished hearth / Ashes and sparks, [his] words among mankind!" to herald the "trumpet of a prophecy" (63–69 [*SPP* 300–301]). We understand the value of educating the imagination to be the fulfilment of this potential. For Frye, this signified the cultivation of a learned civil society, which in the midst of the Vietnam War and civil unrest was at the very least a quaint notion. But something of his argument for the imagination's autonomy compels me here, by which I mean its radically disseminative energy among and between subjects, and thus as a challenge to the very notion of the subject. For we now exist on the fault line between a literature that tells the truth otherwise and one that can or should be put to use so that we don't accept the trap of the given. A poetry that never lies because it never affirms has morphed into fake news and alternative facts as we sift through what perpetual interpretation looks like when relayed to us by social media. Add to this the existential threat of a pandemic and we have Shelley's West Wind as a perfect storm: a neoliberal academy in which the humanities, always resistant to instrumentalization, a threat to be deactivated, need to be instrumentalized to maximum capacity or perish altogether. Shelley poses a terrifying prospect: poetry needs to solve the same problem it created in the first place. Writing an elegy in place of the second half of the *Defence* might be Shelley's yearning to opt out altogether before his final poem traps him in a world of "untold" thoughts.[37] Yet the silence of that final gesture, left in the wake of Shelley's drowning, leaves a "void that craves fresh food," leaves us to ask what hope might be created from the wreck it contemplates to educate our imaginations in perilous times.

In a recent collection of essays, Judith Butler, addressing the tension between universality and difference, argues "for critically re-evaluating [...] what cannot be measured by the metrics by which the humanities are increasingly judged."[38] She continues that "instrumentality" cannot be "the only way of thinking about what it means to make a difference."[39] Yet "instrumentality" now seems a foregone conclusion, so that we can only measure resistance in terms of what we desire to transform, if not overthrow. Even more ominously, such a compromise risks eliding forces that distinguish grievable from non-grievable life,[40] which in turn risks missing voices otherwise "blunted by reiteration." In the same volume, Paul W. Kahn locates the humanities in the "gap between what we know and what we create [...] One interpretation can only be met by another interpretation. What I have called 'thinking with' is what the humanities have always taught."[41] As a lawyer, Kahn understands the fungibility of truth: one person's interpretation might mean liberty while another's might lead to incarceration. Yet poetry has a different legislative impact, one that demands "humility before the power of creation that is revealed through the subject, but is not possessed by the subject."[42] Kahn goes one better than Butler: "This experience of free creativity, which goes to the heart of who we are but remains a mystery, is as close to the sacred as many of us are likely to get."[43]

What else could we be or should we ask for in the midst of the essentially migratory process of historical change? The question isn't a new one, even if the conditions for asking it exert a particular contemporary urgency. Charles Darwin, like his grandfather before him, made such observations unavoidable, however much the fallout regalvanized conservative forces through whose prescriptive view we are all, increasingly, being viewed.[44] But that is itself to invoke a language of crisis on which the humanities thrive, a crisis that materialized Shelley's response to Peacock in the first place. In *Suspiria de Profundis*, Thomas De Quincey writes: "Among the powers in man which suffer by this too intense life of the *social* instinct none suffers more than the power of dreaming."[45] "Habitually to dream magnificently," we "must have a constitutional determination to reverie."[46] One of De Quincey's solutions, besides opium, is solitude, a pulling away from social engagement – a rather dangerous thing to ask of those of us who are feeling the long-term effects of isolation.[47] If Shelley retreats from didactic literature, however, it is only to embrace the vitality of metaphor. My concern here is addressing the "usefulness" of the humanities at a time when wasting time with speculation and contemplation seems more than ever a necessity in stepping back from the world of things as they are in order to see their "obviousness" otherwise.

In the opening section of "In Memory of W. B. Yeats," W. H. Auden apostrophizes Yeats's passing as a moment of what Schopenhauer would call "deadening languor,"[48] of a boredom that barely registers an awareness of its creative potential: "O all the instruments agree / The day of his death was a dark cold day."[49] In the second section, boredom becomes the point:

> For poetry makes nothing happen: it survives
> In the valley of its saying where executives
> Would never want to tamper; it flows south
> From ranches of isolation and the busy griefs,
> Raw towns that we believe and die in; it survives,
> A way of happening, a mouth.[50]

Jonathan Culler says of apostrophe that it makes nothing happen in reality but it *does* make something happen in the poem, which is to indicate a different form of survival: "Nothing need happen because the poem itself is to be the happening."[51] Auden risks giving into boredom, for only then might we make ourselves still enough to hear and feel other stirrings. That is to say, apostrophe makes nothing happen although prosopopoeia animates objects to register the affect of a grievable life. Anticipating the survival of the spirit of poetry itself in the second section, this maneuver figuratively – which is to say within the ontology of the poem, literally – breathes life into the final panegyric of the third. Moving from pleasure to utility to meaning, Shelley's essay ends up with the idea of the poem as "happening," of figuration itself *as* happening. As a form of *un*acknowledged legislation, such an event remains radically indeterminate except to register the happening itself, although at the same time the experience is all too real. Shelley understood this when it came to mourning the grievable life of poets and their works: "O, weep for Adonais!" (2, 19, 73 [*SPP* 411, 412, 413]). It may be his only option was to turn Keats into a star, as if to forestall the struggle of mourning altogether. Yet by indicating "stages in a drama of mind" and thus the poem itself as a mode of consciousness, apostrophe, however painful, is able to sing, maybe even to redeem and silence the pain.[52] If relevance is what we are after, it may be necessary for us to avoid singing quite so stridently as Shelley does in the *Defence*, and yet at the same time to avoid getting trapped in the present in order to see beyond. But then again, regardless of whether or not things have always been thus, we may no longer have the luxury of not being defensive.

Notes

1. I thank Kate Singer and Omar F. Miranda for the invitation to contribute to this volume and for their incisive and generous commentary, which has made for a much better essay. I also thank the Department of English at Dalhousie University, where I gave an earlier version of this essay and from whom I received wonderful feedback.
2. Maurice Blanchot, "Prophetic Speech," in *The Book to Come*, trans. Charlotte Mandell (Stanford: Stanford University Press, 2003), 79.
3. Blanchot, "Prophetic Speech," 79.
4. Blanchot, *The Infinite Conversation*, trans. Susan Hanson (Minneapolis: University of Minnesota Press, 1993), 43.
5. For a recent account of the media ecology of Shelley's writing, see Yohei Igarashi, "Shelley amid the Age of Separations: Romantic Sociology and Romantic Media Theory," in Andrew Burkett, ed. *Multi-Media Romanticisms*, Romantic Circles Praxis Series (November 2016), https://romantic-circles.org/praxis/multi-media/praxis.2016.multi-media.igarashi.html.
6. M. H. Abrams, *The Mirror and the Lamp: Romantic Theory and the Critical Tradition* (New York: Oxford University Press, 1956), 126.
7. Tilottama Rajan, *The Supplement of Reading: Figures of Understanding in Romantic Theory and Practice* (Ithaca: Cornell University Press, 1990), 293, 292.
8. Rajan, *The Supplement of Reading*, 286.
9. Rajan, *The Supplement of Reading*, 296. See Jerrold Hogle's account of transference as the nomadic principle of Shelley's aesthetics. *Shelley's Process: Radical Transference and the Development of His Major Works* (New York: Oxford University Press, 1988), 15.
10. See Joel Faflak, "The Difficult Education of Shelley's *The Triumph of Life*," *Keats-Shelley Journal* 58 (2009), 53–78. See also "Dancing in the Dark with Shelley," in Jacques Khalip and Forrest Pyle, eds. *Constellations of a Contemporary Romanticism* (New York: Fordham University Press, 2016), 166–185.
11. See Julie A. Carlson, "Like Love: The Feel of Shelley's Similes," in Joel Faflak and Richard C. Sha, eds. *Romanticism and the Emotions* (Cambridge: Cambridge University Press, 2014), 76–97. See also Chris Washington, "The Dark Side of the Light: The Triumph of Love in Shelley's *The Triumph of Life*," in Joel Faflak, ed. *The Future of Shelley's Triumph, Romantic Circles* Praxis Series (October 2019), https://romantic-circles.org/praxis/triumph/praxis.2019.triumph.washington.html.

12 Tilottama Rajan, *Dark Interpreter: The Discourse of Romanticism* (Ithaca: Cornell University Press, 1980), 25.
13 Timothy Webb argues that Shelley's use of negatives like "unapprehended" "insists on the difficulty of definition, the problems of communication, the cramping boundaries of language." "The Unascended Heaven: Negatives in Prometheus Unbound," in Kelvin Everest, ed. *Shelley Revalued: Essays from the Gregynog Conference* (Leicester: Leicester University Press, 1983), 37–62, excerpted in *SPP* 708.
14 See Paul de Man, "Shelley Disfigured," in *The Rhetoric of Romanticism* (New York: Columbia University Press, 1984), 93–123.
15 Thomas Love Peacock, "Four Ages of Poetry," in Russell Noyes, ed. *English Romantic Poetry and Prose* (New York: Oxford University Press, 1956), 1249, 1250.
16 The editors continue that Peacock's urging of "intelligent men" to abandon poetry comes in light of his own "failing as a poet [who] had recently begun work at the East India Company" (*SPP* 509).
17 Stefan Andriopoulos, "The Invisible Hand: Supernatural Agency in Political Economy and the Gothic Novel," *ELH* 66 (1999), 739–758, 739. See also Julia M. Wright, "The Gothic Frontier of Modernity: The 'Invisible Hand' of State-Formation in Deadwood," in Jennifer Greiman and Paul Stasi, eds. *The Last Western: Deadwood and the End of American Empire* (New York: Continuum, 2012), 42–61.
18 As Anahid Nersessian notes, "[i]t seems (or so Shelley implies) that the robust intellectual climate of the Enlightenment did not see economics coming. Its dreams of music combined with optics, or physics combined with sculpture, has fallen by the wayside of a march of progress that takes the *oikonomia* of human civilization as its most distinctive priority." *Utopia, Limited: Romanticism and Adjustment* (Cambridge, MA: Harvard University Press, 2015), 181.
19 Paul Reitter and Chad Wellmon, *Permanent Crisis: The Humanities in a Disenchanted Age* (Chicago: University of Chicago Press, 2021), 3, emphasis in original.
20 Reitter and Wellmon, *Permanent Crisis*, 6.
21 Reitter and Wellmon, *Permanent Crisis*, 19, 18, emphasis in original.
22 Reitter and Wellmon, *Permanent Crisis*, 16.
23 Reitter and Wellmon, *Permanent Crisis*, 19.
24 Judith Butler, "Ordinary, Incredulous," in Peter Brooks and Hilary Jewett, eds. *The Humanities and Public Life* (New York: Fordham University Press, 2014), 15–40, 27.
25 Speaking of the "state of emergency" in which he lives as "rule" rather than "exception," Benjamin describes the "angel of history" blown towards the future by the storm of progress fueled by the accumulating debris – "one single catastrophe" – of the past. Walter Benjamin, "On the Concept of History," in Howard Eiland and Michael W. Jennings, eds. *Selected Writings, Volume 4, 1938–1940*, trans. Edmund Jephcott and Others (Cambridge, MA: Harvard University Press, 2003), 392.
26 Northrop Frye, *Anatomy of Criticism: Four Essays* (Princeton: Princeton University Press, 1957).

27 Northrop Frye, *The Educated Imagination* (Toronto: Canadian Broadcasting Corporation, 1963).
28 Frye, *The Educated Imagination*, 8.
29 Frye, *The Educated Imagination*.
30 Frye, *Fearful Symmetry: A Study of William Blake* (Princeton: Princeton University Press, 1947).
31 Deanne Bogdan, *Re-educating the Imagination: Towards a Poetics, Politics, and Pedagogy of Literary Engagement* (Toronto: Irwin, 1992), 39, 41.
32 See most recently Michael Solms, *The Hidden Spring: A Journey to the Source of Consciousness* (New York: W. W. Norton, 2021).
33 Cited in Ben Lerner, *The Hatred of Poetry* (London: Fitzcarraldo Editions, 2016), 7.
34 Lerner, *The Hatred of Poetry*, 71–72.
35 Lerner, *The Hatred of Poetry*.
36 Percy Shelley to John Gisborne, January 26, 1822. As a countervailing argument to Shelley's concern, see Omar F. Miranda, "Between Page and Stage: The Happy Medium of Romantic Drama," in Omar F. Miranda, ed. *On the 200th Anniversary of Lord Byron's* "Manfred," *Romantic Circles* Praxis Series (June 2019), https://romantic-circles.org/praxis/manfred/praxis.2019.manfred.miranda.html. Miranda makes the compelling argument that Shelley's play offers a kind of prototypical technological imaginary that anticipates the use of spectacle in Broadway and West End productions, thus offering what he calls a "happy medium" between the stageable and the purportedly unstageable elements of Shelley's lyrical drama.
37 In *The Apocalyptic Vision in the Poetry of Shelley* (Toronto: University of Toronto Press, 1964), Ross Woodman calls *Adonais* "a metaphysical defence of self-murder," 172. See also Jacques Khalip's *Last Things: Disastrous Form from Kant to Hujar* (New York: Fordham University Press, 2018), which proposes the apparent dead end of lastness as a different attunement to survival.
38 Butler, "Ordinary, Incredulous," 33.
39 Butler, "Ordinary, Incredulous," 29.
40 See Butler's account of the precarity of life in *Frames of War: When Is Life Grievable?* (London: Verso, 2016).
41 Paul W. Kahn, "On Humanities and Human Rights," in Brooks and Jewett, eds. *The Humanities and Public Life*, 116–122, 120, 117.
42 Kahn, "On Humanities and Human Rights," 120.
43 Kahn, "On Humanities and Human Rights."
44 See the essays in Joel Faflak, ed. *Marking Time: Romanticism and Evolution* (Toronto: University of Toronto Press, 2018).
45 Thomas De Quincey, *Suspiria de Profundis*, in Thomas De Quincy, ed. *Confessions of an English Opium-Eater and Related Writings*, ed. Joel Faflak (Peterborough, ON: Broadview Press, 2008), 135.
46 Thomas De Quincey, *Suspiria de Profundis*, 134.
47 See Michael Pollan, *How to Change Your Mind: What the New Science of Psychedelics Teaches Us about Consciousness, Dying, Addiction, Depression, and Transcendence* (New York: Penguin, 2019), for an updated vision of how the

same expansion of consciousness De Quincey advocates requires a momentary departure from the present.
48 Arthur Schopenhauer, *The World as Will and Representation*, 2 volumes, trans. E. F. J. Payne (New York: Dover Publications, 1969), I, 164.
49 W. H. Auden, "In Memory of W. B. Yeats," in Stephen Greenblatt, Carol T. Christ, Alfred David et al., eds. *The Norton Anthology of English Literature*, Volume 2, 9th ed. (New York: W. W. Norton, 2013), ll. 5–6 or ll. 30–31.
50 Auden, "In Memory of W. B. Yeats," ll. 36–41.
51 Jonathan Culler, "Apostrophe," in *The Pursuit of Signs: Semiotics, Literature, Deconstruction* (Ithaca: Cornell University Press, 1981), 149.
52 Culler, "Apostrophe," 148.

Further Reading

Abbey, Lloyd. *Destroyer and Preserver: Shelley's Poetic Skepticism.* Lincoln: University of Nebraska Press, 1979.
Abdel-Hai, M. "Shelley and the Arabs: An Essay in Comparative Literature." *Journal of Arabic Literature* 3 (1972), 72–89.
Abrams, M. H. *The Mirror and the Lamp: Romantic Theory and the Critical Tradition.* New York: Oxford University Press, 1956.
Abrams, M. H. *Natural Supernaturalism: Tradition and Revolution in Romantic Literature.* New York: W. W. Norton and Company, 1973.
Alexander, Meena. "Shelley's India: Territory and Text, Some Problems of Decolonization." In *Shelley: Poet and Legislator of the World*, eds. Betty T. Bennett and Stuart Curran, 169–178. Baltimore: Johns Hopkins University Press, 1996.
An, Young-Ok. "Beatrice's Gaze Revisited: Anatomizing 'The Cenci.'" *Criticism* 38.1 (1996), 27–68.
Aveling, Edward B. and Eleanor Marx Aveling. *Shelley's Socialism.* Journeyman Chapbook: No. 3. London: Journeyman Press, 1979.
Barnett, Suzanne L. *Romantic Paganism: The Politics of Ecstasy in the Shelley Circle.* New York: Palgrave, 2017.
Behrendt, Stephen C. "Beatrice Cenci and the Tragic Myth of History." In *History and Myth: Essays on English Romantic Literature*, ed. Stephen C. Behrendt, 214–234. Detroit: Wayne State University Press, 1990.
Bennett, Betty T. and Stuart Curran, eds. *Shelley: Poet and Legislator of the World.* Baltimore: Johns Hopkins University Press, 1996.
Bewell, Alan. *Romanticism and Colonial Disease.* Baltimore: Johns Hopkins University Press, 1999.
Bieri, James. *Percy Bysshe Shelley: A Biography: Youth's Unextinguished Fire, 1792–1816.* Danvers: Rosemont Publishing, 2004.
Binfield, Kevin. "'May They Be Divided Never': Ethics, History, and the Rhetorical Imagination in Shelley's 'The Coliseum'." *Keats-Shelley Journal* 46 (1997), 124–147.
Bloom, Harold. *Shelley's Mythmaking.* New Haven: Yale University Press, 1959.
Bloom, Harold. *Poets and Poems.* New York: Chelsea House Publishers, 2005.
Bonca, Teddi Chichester, *Shelley's Mirrors of Love: Narcissism, Sacrifice, and Sorority.* Albany: State University of New York Press, 1999.

Borushko, Matthew, "Violence and Nonviolence in Shelley's 'Mask of Anarchy.'" *Keats-Shelley Journal* 59 (2010), 96–113.
Borushko, Matthew, ed. *The Politics of Shelley: History, Theory, Form. Romantic Circles* Praxis Series (October 2015). https://romantic-circles.org/praxis/shelley_politics.
Bowers, Will and Mathelinda Nabogodi, eds. *Reading Shelley on the Bicentenary of his Death. European Romantic Review* 33.5 (2022), 609–757.
Brigham, Linda. "The Postmodern Semiotics of *Prometheus Unbound.*" *Studies in Romanticism* 33.1 (1994), 31–56.
Brookshire, David, ed. *Percy Shelley and the Delimitation of the Gothic. Romantic Circles* Praxis Series (October 2015). https://romantic-circles.org/praxis/gothic_shelley.
Brown, Nathaniel. *Sexuality and Feminism in Shelley*. Cambridge, MA: Harvard University Press, 1979.
Bundock, Chris. "Historicism, Temporalization, and Romantic Prophecy in Percy Shelley's *Hellas.*" In *Rethinking British Romantic History, 1770–1845*, eds. Porscha Fermanis and John Regan, 144–164. Oxford: Oxford University Press, 2014.
Callaghan, Madeleine. *Eternity in British Romantic Poetry*. Liverpool: Liverpool University Press, 2022.
Callaghan, Madeleine. *Shelley's Living Artistry: Letters, Poems, Plays*. Liverpool: Liverpool University Press, 2017.
Callaghan, Madeleine. *The Poet-Hero in the Work of Byron and Shelley*. London: Anthem Press, 2019.
Cameron, Kenneth Neil. *The Young Shelley: Genesis of a Radical*. New York: Macmillan, 1950.
Camoglu, Arif. "White Revolutionary Subjecthood in Percy B. Shelley's *Laon and Cythna.*" *Essays in Romanticism* 30.2 (October 2023), 187–199.
Carlson, Julie A. *England's First Family of Writers: Mary Wollstonecraft, William Godwin, Mary Shelley*. Baltimore: Johns Hopkins University Press, 2007.
Carlson, Julie A. "Like Love: The Feel of Shelley's Similes." In *Romanticism and the Emotions*, eds. Joel Faflak and Richard C. Sha, 76–97. Cambridge: Cambridge University Press, 2014.
Carman, Colin. "'Freedom Leads It Forth': Queering the Epithalamium in *Prometheus Unbound.*" *European Romantic Review* 24.5 (2013), 579–602.
Carman, Colin. *The Radical Ecology of the Shelleys: Eros and Environment*. New York: Routledge, 2019.
Chander, Harish. "Thematic Affinities in Shelley and Tagore." *South Asian Review* 27.2 (2006), 48–71.
Chander, Manu Samriti. "Framing Difference: The Orientalist Aesthetics of David Roberts and Percy Shelley." *Keats-Shelley Journal* 60 (2011), 77–94.
Chandler, James. *England in 1819: The Politics of Literary Culture and the Case of Romantic Historicism*. Chicago: University of Chicago Press, 1998.
Clark, Timothy. *Embodying Revolution: The Figure of the Poet in Shelley*. Oxford: Clarendon Press, 1989.
Clark, Timothy and Jerrold E. Hogle, eds. *Evaluating Shelley*. Edinburgh: Edinburgh University Press, 1996.

Coffey, Bysshe Inigo. *Shelley's Broken World: Fractured Materiality and Intermitted Song*. Liverpool: Liverpool University Press, 2021.
Cohen-Vrignaud, Gerard. *Radical Orientalism: Rights, Reform, and Romanticism*. Cambridge: Cambridge University Press, 2015.
Colbert, Benjamin. "Romantic Palingenesis, or History from the Ashes." *European Romantic Review* 28.3 (2017), 369–378.
Collings, David. *Disastrous Subjectivities: Romanticism, Modernity, and the Real*. Toronto: University of Toronto Press, 2019.
Cox, Jeffrey. *Romanticism in the Shadow of War: Literary Culture in the Napoleonic Wars Years*. Cambridge: Cambridge University Press, 2014.
Crompton, Louis. *Byron and Greek Love: Homophobia in Nineteenth Century England*. Los Angeles: University of California Press, 1985.
Crook, Nora and Derek Guiton. *Shelley's Venomed Melody*. Cambridge: Cambridge University Press, 1986.
Curran, Stuart. *Poetic Form and British Romanticism*. Oxford: Oxford University Press, 1986.
Curran, Stuart. "Romanticism Displaced and Placeless." *European Romantic Review* 20.5 (2009), 637–650.
Curran, Stuart. *Shelley's Annus Mirabilis: The Maturing of an Epic Vision*. San Marino: Huntington Library, 1975.
Curran, Stuart. *Shelley's Cenci: Scorpions Ringed with Fire*. Princeton: Princeton University Press, 1970.
Curran, Stuart. "The Political Prometheus." *Studies in Romanticism* 25.3 (1986), 429–455.
Davis, Amanda Blake. "Androgyny as Mental Revolution in Act 4 of *Prometheus Unbound*." *The Keats-Shelley Review* 34.2 (2020), 160–177.
Dawson, P. M. S. *The Unacknowledged Legislator: Shelley and Politics*. Oxford: Clarendon Press, 1980.
De Man, Paul. *The Rhetoric of Romanticism*. New York: Columbia University Press, 1984.
Demson, Michael. "'Let a Great Assembly Be': Percy Shelley's 'The Mask of Anarchy' and the Organization of Labor in New York City, 1910–30." *European Romantic Review* 22.5 (2011), 641–655.
Demson, Michael. *Masks of Anarchy: The History of a Radical Poem from Percy Shelley to the Triangle Factory Fire*. Brooklyn: Verso, 2013.
Dick, Alex J. "'The Ghost of Gold': Forgery Trials and the Standard of Value in Shelley's *The Mask of Anarchy*." *European Romantic Review* 18.3 (2007), 381–400.
Donohue, Joseph W., Jr. "Shelley's Beatrice and the Romantic Concept of Tragic Character." *Keats-Shelley Journal* 17 (1968), 53–73.
Drew, John. *India and the Romantic Imagination*. Delhi: Oxford University Press, 1987.
Duff, David. *Romance and Revolution: Shelley and the Politics of a Genre*. Cambridge: Cambridge University Press, 1994.
Duffy, Cian. *Shelley and the Revolutionary Sublime*. Cambridge: Cambridge University Press, 2005.
Eeckhout, Bart. "Roaming through World Literature: Shelley's Wind, Stevens's Blackbird, Coetzee's Hugo Claus, and the Desire for Poetic Transformation." *Wallace Stevens Journal* 46.2 (2022), 215–234.

Ellermann, Greg. "Red Shelley, Once Again." *Keats-Shelley Journal* 68 (2019), 104–105.
Endo, Paul. "The Cenci: Recognizing the Shelleyan Sublime." *Texas Studies in Literature and Language* 38.3/4 (1996), 379–397.
Erkelenz, Michael. "Inspecting the Tragedy of Empire: Shelley's *Hellas* and Aeschylus' *Persians*." *Philological Quarterly* 76.3 (1997), 313–337.
Everest, Kelvin. *Keats and Shelley: Winds of Light*. Oxford: Oxford University Press, 2022.
Everest, Kevin, ed. *Shelley Revalued: Essays from the Gregynog Conference*. Leicester: Leicester University Press, 1983.
Faflak, Joel. "Dancing in the Dark with Shelley." In *Constellations of a Contemporary Romanticism*, eds. Jacques Khalip and Forest Pyle, 167–185. New York: Fordham University Press, 2016.
Faflak, Joel. "The Difficult Education of Shelley's *The Triumph of Life*." *Keats-Shelley Journal* 58 (2009), 53–78.
Faflak, Joel, ed. *The Futures of Shelley's Triumph of Life*. *Romantic Circles* Praxis Series (October 2019). https://romantic-circles.org/praxis/triumph.
Fairclough, Mary. "Peterloo at 200: The Radical Press, Simultaneous Meetings and *The Mask of Anarchy*." *The Keats-Shelley Review* 33.2 (2019), 159–174.
Ferriss, Suzanne. "Percy Bysshe Shelley's *The Cenci* and the Rhetoric of Tyranny." In *British Romantic Drama: Historical and Critical Essays*, eds. Terence Allan Hoagwood and Daniel P. Watkins, 208–228. London: Associated University Presses, 1998.
Foot, Paul. *Red Shelley*. London: Sidgwick and Johnson with Michael Dempsey, 1980.
Foot, Paul. *Shelley's Revolutionary Year*. London: Redwords, 1990.
Fraistat, Neil. "Illegitimate Shelley: Radical Piracy and the Textual Edition as Cultural Performance." *PMLA* 109.3 (1994), 409–423.
Fraistat, Neil. *The Poem and the Book: Interpreting Collections of Romantic Poetry*. Chapel Hill: University of North Carolina Press, 1987.
Franta, Andrew. "Shelley and the Poetics of Political Indirection." *Poetics Today* 22.4 (Winter 2001), 765–793.
Freer, Alexander. "A Genealogy of Narcissism." *Nineteenth-Century Literature* 74.1 (June 2019), 1–29.
Goldstein, Amanda Jo. *Sweet Science: Romantic Materialism and the New Logics of Life*. Chicago: University of Chicago Press, 2017.
Goslee, Nancy. "Shelley's Greek 'Discourse': Ancient Manners and Modern Liberty." *The Wordsworth Circle* 36.1 (Winter 2005), 2–5.
Hamilton, Paul. *Percy Bysshe Shelley*. Liverpool: Liverpool University Press, 2000.
Haywood, Ian. "The Sounds of Peterloo." In *Commemorating Peterloo: Violence, Resilience and Claim-Making during the Romantic Era*, eds. Michael Demson and Regina Hewitt, 57–83. Edinburgh: Edinburgh University Press, 2019.
Henderson, Graham. *The Real Percy Bysshe Shelley*. December 15, 2023. www.grahamhenderson.ca.
Hickman, Jared. *Black Prometheus: Race and Radicalism in the Age of Atlantic Slavery*. Oxford: Oxford University Press, 2017.
Hoagwood, Terence Alan. *Skepticism & Ideology: Shelley's Political Prose and Its Philosophical Context from Bacon to Marx*. Iowa City: University of Iowa Press, 1988.

Hodgson, John A. "The World's Mysterious Doom: Shelley's *The Triumph of Life*." *ELH* 42.4 (1975), 595–622.

Hogle, Jerrold E. *Shelley's Process: Radical Transference and the Development of His Major Works.* New York: Oxford University Press, 1988.

Holmes, Richard. *Shelley: The Pursuit,* 2nd ed. New York: Harper Perennial, 2005.

Igarashi, Yohei. *The Connected Condition: Romanticism and the Dream of Communication.* Stanford: Stanford University Press, 2019.

Igarashi, Yohei. "Shelley Amid the Age of Separations: Romantic Sociology and Romantic Media Theory." In *Multi-Media Romanticisms,* ed. Andrew Burkett. *Romantic Circles* Praxis Series (November 2016). https://romantic-circles.org/praxis/multi-media/praxis.2016.multi-media.igarashi.html.

Jager, Colin. "Shelley After Atheism." *Studies in Romanticism* 49.4 (2010), 611–631.

Jager, Colin. "Transitional Justice in *Prometheus Unbound.*" *The Workshop* 4 (2016), 26–31.

Jager, Colin. *Unquiet Things: Secularism in the Romantic Age.* Philadelphia: University of Pennsylvania Press, 2015.

Jones, Michael Owen. "In Pursuit of Percy Shelley, 'The First Celebrity Vegan': An Essay on Meat, Sex, and Broccoli." *Journal of Folklore Research* 53.2 (2016), 1–30.

Kalim, M. Siddiq. *The Social Orpheus: Shelley and the Owenites.* Lahore: Government College, 1983.

Kantor, Jamison. "Percy Shelley, Political Machines, and the Prehistory of the Postliberal." In *British Literature and Technology, 1600–1830,* eds. Kristin M. Girten, Aaron R. Halon, and Joseph Drury, 139–163. Lewisburg: Bucknell University Press, 2023.

Keach, William. "Radical Shelley?" *Raritan* 5.2 (Fall 1985), 120–129.

Keach, William. "Rise Like Lions? Shelley and the Revolutionary Left." *International Socialism* 2.75 (1997). www.marxists.org/history/etol/newspape/isj2/1997/isj2-075/keach.htm.

Keach, William. *Shelley's Style.* London and New York: Methuen, 1984.

Kim, Joey S. "Disorienting 'Shapes' in Shelley's *The Revolt of Islam.*" *The Keats-Shelley Review* 32.2 (2018), 134–147.

Kipperman, Mark. "History and Ideality: The Politics of Shelley's *Hellas.*" *Studies in Romanticism* 30.2 (1991), 147–168.

Kohler, Michael. "Shelley in Chancery: The Reimagination of the Paternalist State in 'The Cenci.'" *Studies in Romanticism* 37.4 (1998), 545–589.

Kucich, Greg. *Keats, Shelley, and Romantic Spenserianism.* University Park: Pennsylvania State Press University, 1991.

Kuiken, Kir. *Imagined Sovereignties: Toward a New Political Romanticism.* New York: Fordham University Press, 2014.

Langan, Celeste and Maureen N. McLane. "The Medium of Romantic Poetry." In *The Cambridge Companion to British Romantic Poetry,* eds. James Chandler and Maureen N. McLane, 239–262. Cambridge: Cambridge University Press, 2008.

Leask, Nigel. *British Romantic Writers and the East: Anxieties of Empire.* Cambridge: Cambridge University Press, 1992.

Lee, Debbie. *Slavery and the Romantic Imagination.* Philadelphia: University of Pennsylvania Press, 2004.

Lindstrom, Eric. "Poetry Is Not a Luxury: Audre Lorde and Shelleyan Poetics." In *Romantic Poetics of Public Freedom*, eds. Lily Gurton-Wachter and Tristram Wolff. *Romantic Circles* Praxis Series (December 2021). http://romantic-circles.org/praxis/publicfeeling/praxis.2021.publicfeeling.lindstrom.html.

Lussier, Mark S. *Romantic Dharma: The Emergence of Buddhism into Nineteenth-Century Europe*. New York: Palgrave Macmillan, 2011.

Lussier, Mark S. *Romantic Dynamics: The Poetics of Physicality*. New York: Palgrave Macmillan, 2000.

Makdisi, Saree. *Romantic Imperialism: Universal Empire and the Culture of Modernity*. Cambridge: Cambridge University Press, 1998.

Matthew, Patricia A., ed. *Race, Blackness, and Romanticism*. Studies in Romanticism 61.1 (2022), 1–181.

McGrath, Brian. "Shelley, among Other Things." *MLN* 133.5 (December 2018), 1188–1205.

Mercer, Anna. *The Collaborative Literary Relationship of Percy Bysshe Shelley and Mary Wollstonecraft Shelley*. London: Routledge, 2021.

Michael, Timothy. *British Romanticism and the Critique of Political Reason*. Baltimore: Johns Hopkins University Press, 2016.

Miranda, Omar F. "Between Page and Stage: The Happy Medium of Romantic Drama." In *On the 200th Anniversary of Lord Byron's Manfred*, ed. Omar F. Miranda. *Romantic Circles* Praxis Series (June 2019). https://romantic-circles.org/praxis/manfred/praxis.2019.manfred.miranda.html.

Miranda, Omar F. "On Phoenix Wings: Lucille Clifton's Romantic Renewals." In *Race, Blackness, and Romanticism*, ed. Patricia Matthew. *Studies in Romanticism* 61.1 (2022), 125–135.

Miranda, Omar F. "*Prometeo Desencadenado*: The Afterlife of Percy Shelley's *Prometheus Unbound* in the Americas." In *Latin American Afterlives*, eds. Olivia Loksing Moy and Marco Ramírez Rojas. *Romantic Circles* Praxis Series (July 2020). https://romantic-circles.org/praxis/latinam/praxis.2020.latinam.miranda.html.

Miranda, Omar F. "The Global Romantic Lyric," *The Wordsworth Circle* 52.2 (June 2021), 308–327.

Mole, Tom. *What the Victorians Made of Romanticism: Material Artifacts, Cultural Practices, and Reception History*. Princeton: Princeton University.

Morgan, Jen. "Uses of Shelley in Working-Class Culture: Approximations and Substitutions." *Key Words: A Journal of Cultural Materialism* 13 (2015), 117–137.

Morton, Timothy. *Shelley and the Revolution in Taste: The Body and the Natural World*. Cambridge: Cambridge University Press, 2009.

Morton, Timothy, ed. *The Cambridge Companion to Shelley*. Cambridge: Cambridge University Press, 2007.

Mushakavanhu, Tinashe. "Anarchies of the Mind: An Imagined Conversation Between Two Writers." *Wasafiri* 27.4 (2012), 82–88.

Mulhallen, Jacqueline. *Percy Bysshe Shelley: Poet and Revolutionary*. London: Pluto Press, 2015.

Nabugodi, Mathelinda. *Shelley with Benjamin: A Critical Mosaic*. London: UCL Press, 2023.

Nabugodi, Mathelinda. "A Triumph of Black Life?" *Keats-Shelley Journal* 70 (2021), 133–141.
Nersessian, Anahid, ed. *Laon and Cythna; Or, the Revolution of the Golden City*. Peterborough, ON: Broadview Press, 2016.
Nersessian, Anahid. *Utopia, Limited: Romanticism and Adjustment*. Cambridge, MA: Harvard University Press, 2015.
O'Neill, Michael. *The Human Mind's Imaginings: Conflict and Achievement in Shelley's Poetry*. New York: Oxford University Press, 1989.
O'Neill, Michael. *Shelleyan Reimaginings and Influence: New Relations*. Oxford: Oxford University Press, 2019.
O'Neill, Michael, Anthony Howe, and Madeleine Callaghan, eds. *The Oxford Handbook of Percy Bysshe Shelley*. New York: Oxford University Press, 2013.
Paley, Morton D. "Apocapolitics: Allusion and Structure in Shelley's 'Mask of Anarchy'." *Huntington Library Quarterly* 54.2 (1991), 91–109.
Peterfreund, Stuart. *Shelley among Others: The Play of The Intertext and The Idea of Language*. Baltimore: Johns Hopkins University Press, 2001.
Pulos, C. E. *The Deep Truth: A Study of Shelley's Skepticism*. Lincoln: University of Nebraska Press, 1954.
Pyle, Forest. *Art's Undoing: In the Wake of a Radical Aestheticism*. New York: Fordham University Press, 2013.
Pyle, Forest. "'Frail Spells': Shelley and the Ironies of Exile." In *Irony and Clerisy*, ed. Deborah Elise White. *Romantic Circles* Praxis Series (August 1999). https://romanticcircles.org/praxis/irony/pyle/frail.html.
Pyle, Forest. "Kindling and Ash: Radical Aestheticism in Keats and Shelley." *Studies in Romanticism* 42.4 (December 2003), 427–459.
Pyle, Kai. "Ningaabii'an Negamotawag: Translating Shelley into Ojibwe." *Studies in Romanticism* 61.4 (Winter 2002), 491–502.
Quillin, Jessica K. *Shelley and the Musico-Poetics of Romanticism*. Surrey and Burlington: Ashgate, 2012.
Rajan, Tilottama. *Dark Interpreter: The Discourse of Romanticism*. Ithaca: Cornell University Press, 1980.
Rajan, Tilottama. *The Supplement of Reading: Figures of Understanding in Romantic Theory and Practice*. Ithaca: Cornell University Press, 1990.
Redfield, Marc. *The Politics of Aesthetics: Nationalism, Gender, Romanticism*. Stanford: Stanford University Press, 2003.
Reno, Seth T. *Amorous Aesthetics: Intellectual Love in Romantic Poetry and Poetics, 1788–1853*. Liverpool: Liverpool University Press, 2019.
Reno, Seth T. "The Violence of Form in Shelley's 'Mask of Anarchy'." *Keats-Shelley Journal* 62 (2013), 80–98.
Richardson, Alan. *A Mental Theater: Poetic Drama and Consciousness in the Romantic Age*. University Park: Pennsylvania State University Press, 1988.
Rieger, James. *The Mutiny Within: The Heresies of Percy Bysshe Shelley*. New York: George Braziller, 1967.
Roberts, Hugh. *Shelley and the Chaos of History: A New Politics of Poetry*. University Park: Pennsylvania State University Press, 1997.
Roberts, Merrilees. "*Prometheus Unbound*: Reconstitutive Poetics and the Promethean Poet." *Keats-Shelley Review* 34.2 (2020), 178–193.

Roberts, Merrilees. *Shelley's Poetics of Reticence: Shelley's Shame.* New York/London: Routledge, 2020.
Rohrbach, Emily. *Modernity's Mist: British Romanticism and the Poetics of Anticipation.* New York: Fordham University Press, 2016.
"Romanticism and Pop Culture." *Romantic Circles.* https://romantic-circles.org/lab/pop-culture.
Rosenthal, Adam R. "Shelley and the Limits of Sustainability." In *Romantic Sustainability: Endurance and the Natural World, 1780–1830*, ed. Ben R. Robertson, 233–244. Lanham: Lexington Books, 2015.
Rossington, Michael. "Theorizing a Republican Poetics: P. B. Shelley and Alfieri." *European Romantic Review* 20.5 (2009), 619–628.
Rossington, Michael. "William Michael Rossetti and the Organization of P. B. Shelley in the Later Nineteenth Century." *European Romantic Review* 26.3 (2015), 387–393.
Ruston, Sharon. *Shelley and Vitality.* Houndmills: Palgrave Macmillan, 2005.
Sachs, Jonathan. "'Yet the Capital of the World': Rome, Repetition, and History in Shelley's Later Writings." *Nineteenth-Century Contexts* 28.2 (June 2006), 105–126.
Schacht, Benjamin. "Freedom Songs: Socialist Multiculturalism and the Protest Lyric from Percy Shelley to Chaim Zhitlovsky." *The Gotham Center for New York City History* (2021). www.gothamcenter.org/blog/freedom-songs-socialist-multiculturalism-and-the-protest-lyric-from-percy-shelley-to-chaim-zhitlovsky.
Schmid, Susanne and Michael Rossington, eds. *The Reception of P.B. Shelley in Europe.* London: Bloomsbury, 2008.
Scott, Heidi. *Chaos and Cosmos: Literary Roots of Modern Ecology in the British Nineteenth Century.* University Park: The Pennsylvania State University Press, 2014.
Scrivener, Michael. *Radical Shelley: The Philosophical Anarchism and Utopian Thought of Percy Bysshe Shelley.* Princeton: Princeton University Press, 1982.
Sha, Richard. *Imagination and Science in Romanticism.* Baltimore: Johns Hopkins University Press, 2018.
Sha, Richard. "The Uses and Abuses of Historicism: Halperin and Shelley on the Otherness of Ancient Greek Sexuality." In *Historicizing Romantic Sexuality*, ed. Richard Sha. *Romantic Circles* Praxis Series (January 2006). https://romantic-circles.org/praxis/sexuality/sha/sha.html.
Shaaban, Bouthaina. "Shelley in the Chartist Press." *Keats-Shelley Memorial Bulletin* 34 (1983), 41–60.
Shelley, Mary. "Preface and Notes to *The Poetical Works of Percy Bysshe Shelley* (1839)." In *The Novels and Selected Works of Mary Shelley*, Volume 2, eds. Nora Crook, Pamela Clemit, and Betty T. Bennett, 253–330. London: Pickering & Chatto, 1996.
Shelley, Percy Bysshe. *The Complete Poetry of Percy Bysshe Shelley*, eds. Donald H. Reiman, Neil Fraistat, Nora Crook, et al. 4 volumes to date. Baltimore: Johns Hopkins University Press, 2000–.
Shelley, Percy Bysshe. *The Letters of Percy Bysshe Shelley*, ed. Frederick L. Jones. 2 volumes. Oxford: Clarendon Press, 1964.
Shelley, Percy Bysshe. *The Poems of Shelley*, eds. Geoffrey Matthews, Kelvin Everest, Cian Duffy, Michael Rossington, et al. 4 volumes to date. New York/London: Routledge, 1989–.
Shelley, Percy Bysshe. *The Prose Works of Percy Bysshe Shelley*, ed. E. B. Murray. Oxford: Clarendon Press, 1993.

Shelley, Percy Bysshe. *Shelley's Poetry and Prose*, Norton Critical Edition, 2nd Edition, eds. Donald H. Reiman and Neil Fraistat. New York: W. W. Norton and Company, 2002.

Shelley, Percy Bysshe. *Popular Songs: The Political Poems of 1819–1820*. Seattle: Entre Ríos Books, 2016.

Shih, Terence H. W. "The Romantic Revival in Early China and Taiwan: Hsu Chih-Mo's Poetics of Liberty." In *English Romanticism in East Asia*, ed. Suh-Reen Han. *Romantic Circles* Praxis Series (December 2016). https://romantic-circles.org/praxis/eastasia.

Shih, Terence H. W. "The Romantic Skylark in Taiwanese Literature: Shelleyan Religious Skepticism in Xu Zhimo and Yang Mu." In *British Romanticism in Asia: The Reception, Translation, and Transformation of Romantic Literature in India and East Asia*, eds. Alex Watson and Laurence Williams, 319–339. Singapore: Palgrave, 2019.

Singer, Kate. *Romantic Vacancy: The Poetics of Gender, Affect, and Radical Speculation*. Albany: State University of New York Press, 2019.

Singer, Kate. "Stoned Shelley: Revolutionary Tactics and Women under the Influence." *Studies in Romanticism* 48.4 (2009), 686–707.

Solomonescu, Yasmin. "Percy Shelley's Revolutionary Periods." *ELH* 83.4 (2016), 1105–1133.

Sperry, Stuart M. *Shelley's Major Verse: The Narrative and Dramatic Poetry*. Cambridge, MA: Harvard University Press, 1988.

Stabler, Jane. *The Artistry of Exile: Romantic and Victorian Writers in Italy*. Oxford: Oxford University Press, 2013.

Steffan, Truman Guy. "Seven Accounts of the Cenci and Shelley's Drama." *Studies in English Literature* 9.4 (1969), 601–618.

Sun, Emily. *On the Horizon of World Literature: Forms of Modernity in Romantic England and Republican China*. New York: Fordham University Press, 2021.

Sun, Emily. "Shelley's Voice: Poetry, Internationalism, and Solidarity." *European Romantic Review* 30.3 (2019), 239–247.

Suzuki, Rieko. *The Shelleys and the Brownings: Textual Re-Imaginings and the Question of Influence*. Liverpool: Liverpool University Press, 2022.

Swann, Karen. *The Lives of the Dead Poets: Keats, Shelley, Coleridge*. New York: Fordham University Press, 2019.

Swann, Karen. "Shelley's Pod People." In *Romanticism and the Insistence of the Aesthetic*, eds. Forest Pyle and Marc Redfield. *Romantic Circles* Praxis Series (February 2005). https://romantic-circles.org/praxis/aesthetic/swann/swann.html.

Swann, Mandy. "Shelley's Utopian Seascapes." *Studies in Romanticism* 52.3 (Fall 2013), 389–414.

Tetreault, Ronald. *The Poetry of Life: Shelley and Literary Form*. Toronto: Toronto University Press, 1987.

Thurston, Norman. "Shelley and the Duty of Hope." *Keats-Shelley Journal* 26 (1977), 22–28.

Ulmer, William. *Shelleyan Eros: The Rhetoric of Romantic Love*. Princeton: Princeton University Press, 1990.

Verderame, Michael. "'We Are as Clouds': Climate and Social Transformation in Shelley." *ISLE: Interdisciplinary Studies in Literature and Environment* 28.1 (2021), 271–290.
Wang, Orrin N. C. *Fantastic Modernity: Dialectical Readings in Romanticism and Theory*. Baltimore: Johns Hopkins University Press, 1996.
Wang, Orrin N. C. *Romantic Sobriety: Sensation, Revolution, Commodification, History*. Baltimore: Johns Hopkins University Press, 2011.
Wang, Orrin N. C. *Techno-Magism: Media, Mediation, and the Cut of Romanticism*. New York: Fordham University Press, 2022.
Warren, Andrew B. *The Orient and the Young Romantics*. Cambridge: Cambridge University Press, 2014.
Warren, Andrew B. "'Unentangled Intermixture': Love and Materialism in Shelley's 'Epipsychidion'." *Keats-Shelley Journal* 59 (2010), 78–95.
Washington, Chris. *Romantic Revelations: Visions of Post-Apocalyptic Life and Hope in the Anthropocene*. Toronto: University of Toronto Press, 2019.
Wasserman, Earl R. *Shelley: A Critical Reading*. Baltimore: Johns Hopkins Press, 1971.
Wasserman, Earl R. *Shelley's Prometheus Unbound: A Critical Reading*. Baltimore: Johns Hopkins Press, 1965.
Webb, Timothy. *Shelley: A Voice Not Understood*. Manchester: Manchester University Press, 1977.
Weinberg, Alan. "Freedom from the Stranglehold of Time: Shelley's Visionary Conception in *Queen Mab*." *Romanticism* 22.1 (2016), 90–106.
Weinberg, Alan. "'The Ineffectual Angel': Arnold's Misrepresentation of Shelley." *The Keats-Shelley Review* 23.1 (2009), 82–96.
Weinberg, Alan M. and Timothy Webb, eds. *The Neglected Shelley*. Burlington: Routledge, 2016, 95–116.
Weisman, Karen A. *Imageless Truths: Shelley's Poetic Fiction*. Philadelphia: University of Pennsylvania Press, 1994.
Wilson, Ross, ed. *Percy Shelley in Context*. Cambridge: Cambridge University Press, in press.
Wilson, Ross. *Shelley and the Apprehension of Life*. Cambridge: Cambridge University Press, 2013.
Wolfson, Susan J. *Formal Charges: The Shaping of Poetry in British Romanticism*. Stanford: Stanford University Press, 1997.
Wolfson, Susan J. *Romantic Shades and Shadows*. Baltimore: Johns Hopkins University Press, 2018.
Wolfson, Susan. "'Something must be done': Shelley, Hemans, and the Flash of Revolutionary Female Violence." In *Fellow Romantics: Male and Female British Writers, 1790–1835*, ed. Beth Lau, 99–122. London: Routledge, 2016.
Woodman, Ross. *The Apocalyptic Vision in the Poetry of Shelley*. Toronto: University of Toronto Press, 1964.
Wroe, Ann. *Being Shelley: The Poet's Search for Himself*. New York: Vintage Books, 2007.
Young, Art. *Shelley and Nonviolence*. The Hague: Mouton, 1975.
Zephaniah, Benjamin. *The Life and Rhymes of Benjamin Zephaniah: The Autobiography*. London: Scribner, 2019.
Zephaniah, Benjamin. *Too Black, Too Strong*. Hexham: Bloodaxe Books, 2001.

Index

1830 Removal Act, 24, 28

Abernethy, John, 216, 224
abolition, 10, 63–82, 93, 199
Adorno, Theodor, 1, 202
Aeschylus, 67, 119, 182
   The Persians, 76, 77
Africa/Africans, 1, 63, 65, 66, 71, 72, 75, 78, 80, 81, 90, 99, 110, 111, 113, 128, 189, 215, 216, 218, 219, 221, 222, 228, 229, 233
ageism, 2, 11, 43–59
Alighieri, Dante, 50, 65, 179, 182, 183, 189, 264
Allen, Irma, 200–201
Alvey, Nahoko, 216, 221
anti-racism, 11, 85–101
Arendt, Hannah, 73
Arnold, Matthew, 2, 43, 44, 126, 157
Auden, W. H., "In Memory of W. B. Yeats," 271

Bacon, Sir Francis, 67, 117, 264
Barad, Karen, 14, 216, 220, 223, 231, 241–249, 252, 255
Bataille, Georges, 188, 189
Bell, Charles, *Anatomy and Philosophy of Expression*, 144
Benjamin, Walter, 1, 267
Bentham, Jeremy, 118–119, 127
Berlant, Lauren, 166–168
Bewell, Alan, 46–48, 52, 195, 197–199
Binfield, Kevin, 58
Black Lives Matter, 69, 94, 113
Black Power movement, 128
Blackness, 10–12, 89, 92–101, 221
Blake, William, 267
Blanchot, Maurice, 188, 261
Bloom, Harold, 269
Bloom, Paul, *Against Empathy*, 143, 149, 150
Boccaccio, Giovanni, 186
Bogdan, Deanne, 267
Bohr, Niels, 241, 243, 247
Bowers, Will, 5
Bradley, Arthur, 9

Brand, Dionne, 82
Breithaupt, Fritz, 149
Buddhism, 150, 151
Burke, Edmund, 124, 148, 265
   Philosophical Enquiry, 139–141
Burkett, Andrew, 239
Butler, Judith, 111, 115, 270
Byron, George Gordon, Lord, 6, 47, 67, 70, 125–127, 180, 183, 239

Callaghan, Madeleine, 181, 184
Carlson, Julie A., 5, 8, 11, 12
Carman, Colin, 8
Chakrabarty, Dipesh, *The Climate of History in a Planetary Age*, 150
Chandler, James, 11, 12, 161, 168, 177
Chartists, 1, 90, 172, 265
Chen, Mel Y., 228
Cherokee, 10, 24, 25, 28, 29, 31, 33–35, 37, 38
Chickasaws, 24, 31
Choctaw, 24, 31, 37
civil disobedience, 111, 115
civil rights movement, American, 12, 108, 110–112, 115, 128
civil rights movement, Irish, 128
Clairmont, Claire, 67
climate change, 58, 149, 150, 195, 196, 266. *See also* sustainability
Cobbett, William, 114, 115
cognitive historicism, 133–134
Cohen-Vrignaud, Gerard, 12, 13
Coleridge, Samuel Taylor, 167
   Biographia Literaria, 70
   "The Rime of the Ancient Mariner," 34
Collings, David, 196
colonialism, 7, 11, 69, 77, 218
Cooper, Ivan, 128
Cox, Jeffrey, 186
Csengei, Ildiko, 141, 142
Culler, Jonathan, 271
Curran, Stuart, 39, 161, 179
Curtis Act, 31, 34. *See also* treaties

Darwin, Charles, 134, 270
Darwin, Erasmus, 216, 224, 229
Davis, Amanda Blake, 189, 223
de Man, Paul, 9, 47, 54, 265
De Quincey, Thomas, 124
    Suspiria de Profundis, 270
deconstruction, 9, 54, 95, 99, 262, 265
Dickens, Charles, 262
disability, 10, 11, 43–59, 164
Dods, Mary Diana, 232
Duffy, Cian, 59

Edelman, Lee, 166
Einstein, Albert, 241, 243, 245
Eliot, T. S., 2, 43, 44, 57, 58, 159, 266
Ellerman, Greg, 9
empathy, 10, 12, 14, 133–151
    dark, 4
Engels, Friedrich, 1
environmental justice, 1, 13, 46–49, 95, 134, 149, 150, 197, 200, 246
equality, 1, 7, 118, 124, 158, 189, 225
Erkelenz, Michael, 77
Everest, Kelvin, 207, 209
The Examiner, 156, 251
exile, 3, 4, 10, 12, 13, 91, 176–190, 222, 239, 240, 252, 255

Faflak, Joel, 14
Fairclough, Mary, 14, 220
Faraday, Michael, 246, 252
Fawkes, Francis, *Idyll*, 207
feminism, 1, 14, 52, 68, 70, 91, 164, 214–216, 220, 264
Ferris, David, 79
Foot, Paul, 48, 90, 92
Foucault, Michel, 55
Fraistat, Neil, 203, 218, 223
Franta, Andrew, 160, 252, 255
French Revolution, 71, 72, 76, 165, 170, 185
Frye, Northrop, 127, 267–269
    The Educated Imagination, 267

Galen, 224, 227
Gandhi, Mohandas, also Mahatma, 1, 12, 110–115, 120, 127–129, 172
Garland-Thomson, Rosemarie, 55
Gatten, Alex, 226
gender, 1, 2, 7, 10, 13, 14, 43, 74, 98, 162, 164, 214–232, 267
Global South, 217, 221
Godwin, William, 57, 58, 129
    "Of an Early Taste for Reading," 65–66
    Political Justice, 110
    St. Leon, 58

Goethe, Johann Wolfgang von, 64, 183
Greek War of Independence, 7, 67, 76, 77
Greenstein, George, 243
Gregory, James Roane, 10, 24, 29–34, 37–39

Hansen, James, 195
Harjo, Joy, 10, 38, 39
Hartman, Saidiya, 69, 73
Hegel, Georg Wilhelm Friedrich, 188
    Phenomenology, 133
Hein, Grit, 143
Heisenberg, Werner, 241
Hemans, Felicia, "The Widow of Crescentius," 207
Henderson, Graham, 10, 90
Hermaphroditus, 99, 214–216, 223–231
Hesiod, 182, 203
    Theogony, 203
Hessell, Nikki, 10, 239
Hickman, Jared, 216
Hippocrates, 224
historicism, 5, 47, 133–134, 264
Hoagwood, Terence, 9
Hodgson, John A., 45, 54
Hoeveler, Diane, 223, 227, 231
Hogg, James, *Private Memoirs and Confessions of a Justified Sinner*, 140
Hogg, Thomas Jefferson, 91, 196–197
Hogle, Jerrold, 48, 221, 223
Holmes, Richard, 6
Homer, 261, 264
homosexuality, 80, 222, 225
hope, 4, 8, 10–13, 29, 32, 44, 47, 57, 64, 66, 68, 71, 72, 79, 98, 108, 120, 129, 156–172, 188, 202, 252, 255, 267, 270
Hulme, T. E., 264
humanities, 6, 14, 150, 260–272
Hume, David, 67, 136–141, 143–144, 146–147, 150, 158
    Treatise of Human Nature, 137–138
Hunt, Leigh, 89, 112, 114, 119, 156–158, 160, 166, 239
    The Examiner, 156, 251

Iacoboni, Marco, 135–136, 140, 149
Igarashi, Yohei, 239–240
    The Connected Condition, 240
Indian freedom movement, 12
Indigenous peoples, 2, 10, 23–39, 70
intergenerational, 2, 3, 10, 11, 23, 26–28, 38, 39, 43–59, 165, 182, 183, 186, 189, 217
intersex, 215, 216, 224, 226, 227, 229
Ireland, 25, 93, 108, 128, 159

Jackson, Andrew, 28
Jackson, Doug, 243
Jackson, Zakiyyah Iman, 221

Jager, Colin, 185
Justice, Daniel Heath, 38

Kahn, Paul K., 270
Kant, Immanuel, 95, 139
Keach, William, 91, 187
Keats, John, 51, 64–67, 112, 208, 265, 269, 271
  "Ode on a Grecian Urn," 51
  "Ode to a Nightingale," 208
King, Martin Luther Jr., 1, 12, 115, 128, 172
kinship, 3, 10, 11, 15, 26, 28, 31, 34, 35, 172
Kipperman, Mark, 76
Kirby, Vicki, 245
Kuiken, Kir, 37

Langan, Celeste, 239
Laqueur, Thomas, 224
Lawrence, William, 216, 224
  Lectures on Physiology, Zoology, and the Natural History of Man, 228
Lawson, James, 108, 110–113, 115, 120, 121, 127, 128
Leask, Nigel, 142
Leavis, F. R., 159, 161, 267
Lee, Debbie, 215, 231
Lerner, Ben, *The Hatred of Poetry*, 268
Lewis, John, 108, 111–113, 115, 121, 127, 128
Lister, Anne, 232
Lorenz, Taylor, 58
Lovejoy, Arthur O., 264
Lucan (Marcus Annaeus Lucanus), 186
Lucian (Lucian of Samosata), 216, 224, 227
Luciano, Dana, 228
Lucretius, Titus Lucretius Carus, 48, 67
Lussier, Mark, 8, 220, 241, 247, 249, 255
Lyndsay, David. *See* Dods, Mary Diana

Marx, Karl, 1
Marxism, 9, 91, 188, 215
Matthews, Geoffrey, 207, 209
Mbembe, Achille, 81
McGann, Jerome, 65
McLane, Maureen N., 239
media and communication, 3, 14, 43, 70, 100, 230–232, 238–256, 269
Mills, Aaron, 26
Milton, John, 3, 64–66, 117, 120, 179–182, 186, 189, 201, 216
  Paradise Lost, 179–182
Miranda, Omar F., 13, 222, 239
mirror neurons, 133–151
Monbiot, George, 200, 201, 202
Moore, Marianne, "Poetry," 268
Morgan, Jennifer, 229
Morton, Timothy, 8

Moten, Fred, 11, 92–95, 97–99
  "barbara lee," 11, 85–89, 93, 101
Muscogee Nation, 28, 31
Mvskoke Creek, 10, 24, 28–33, 38, 39

Nabugodi, Mathelinda, 5, 7, 11
Nancy, Jean-Luc, 188, 189
  Being Singular Plural, 189
Neoplatonism, 142, 227
New Criticism, 267
new historicism, 9, 264
nonbinarism, 2, 3, 10, 14, 214–232
nonhuman, 4, 8, 10, 13, 150, 196, 214, 232
nonviolence, 1, 12, 48, 71, 90, 108–129, 163

O'Brien, Sharon, 28
Ocasio-Cortez, Alexandria, 44, 46
O-ge-maw-ke-ke-to, 27, 28
Oliveira, Camila, 10, 96
Ollier, Charles, 67, 76, 112, 114, 260
O'Neill, Eliza, 148
O'Neill, Michael, 48
Ovid, 215, 216, 219, 223–225
  Metamorphoses, 225–228

Paine, Thomas, 199, 205
  Common Sense, 199
Paley, Morton, 162
Parker, Robert Dale, 30, 31
Parker, William, 88–89, 94
Patterson, Orlando, 73
Peacock, Thomas Love, 180, 270
  "The Four Ages of Poetry," 260, 263, 265
Pelosi, Nancy, 44, 46
Peterloo Massacre, 5, 32, 34, 90, 110, 114, 116, 117, 127, 165, 242, 251, 254
Philip, M. NourbeSe, *Zong!*, 75–76, 99
Philips, Katherine, 227
Plato, 4, 9, 64, 88, 142, 187, 221, 225, 227, 228, 261, 262, 264
  The Republic, 178
  The Symposium, 63, 80, 223, 226
Plotnitsky, Arkady, 220, 241
Poe, Edgar Allan, "The Purloined Letter," 140
polyamory, 9, 214, 224
postcolonialism, 264
posthumanism, 3, 95, 214–232
poststructuralism, 9, 264
Prinz, Jesse, "Against Empathy," 150
protest, 1, 2, 7, 9, 69, 89, 90, 96, 100, 108, 110, 116, 118, 163, 165, 242, 253, 255
Public Universal Friend, 232
Pushmataha, 37
Pyle, Forest, 9, 160
Pyle, Kai, 9

Quarterly Review, 67
queer, 8, 14, 70, 166, 217, 221, 222, 225, 228, 230, 232

race, 10, 11, 13, 23, 28, 63–82, 98, 214–232, 239, 267
racism, 35, 58, 85, 88, 92, 95
  anti-Black, 63–65, 69, 72, 85
Rajan, Tilottama, 263
Ramachandran, V. S., 134, 149
Redfield, Marc, 253
Reiman, Donald H., 203
Reitter, Paul, 266
relationality, 1–15, 25–28, 30–38, 47, 54, 63–68, 71, 77–79, 101, 111, 117, 122, 124, 126, 127, 133–134, 136–137, 139, 145–148, 150–151, 170, 188, 196–199, 206, 209, 215–223, 225, 228, 241–242, 245–246, 249, 262, 264, 266
Reno, Seth, 53
rewilding, 2, 13, 195–210
Richards, I. A., 126
Richardson, Alan, 12
Rideau Purchase. *See* treaties
Ridge, John Rollin, 10, 24, 29, 35–39
  "Mount Shasta," 36, 37
  "To a Mockingbird Singing in a Tree," 35
Roberts, Hugh, 48
Roberts, Merrilees, 184
Rossetti, William Michael, 206
Rousseau, Jean-Jacques, 11, 67, 136, 189
  Emile, or Treatise on Education, 136, 141
  Julie, ou la novelle Héloïse, 179–180

Sachs, Jonathan, 225, 240
Said, Edward
  "Reflections on Exile," 179
Salt, Henry, 1, 12, 113–116, 119, 127–129
Schopenhauer, Arthur, 271
Schrödinger, Erwin, 241
Seminole, 24, 31
sensibility, 115, 122, 124–126
Severn, Joseph, 205, 206, 208
Sexton, Jared, 81
Sha, Richard, 8, 220, 224, 225, 227, 240, 241, 242, 244, 246
Shakespeare, William, 264
  The Tempest, 219
Sharpe, Christina, 81
Sheldrake, Merlin, *Entangled Life*, 150
Shelley, Mary, 9, 57, 147, 148, 180, 183, 205, 215, 218, 251, 260, 265
  as editor of *Posthumous Poems*, 23, 44, 218
  Frankenstein, 1, 14, 58, 90, 215, 216, 218, 221–223, 230
Shelley, Percy Bysshe
  and bicentenary, 2, 5–6, 43, 90

Shelley, Percy Bysshe works
  Adonais, 2, 13, 63, 64, 67, 68, 208, 210, 265, 268, 269, 271
  Alastor, or the Spirit of Solitude, 122, 214
  "To a Balloon Laden with Knowledge," 238
  The Cenci, 12, 63, 67, 73–76, 119, 133–151
  "The Coliseum," 11, 58, 59
  Declaration of Rights, 238
  A Defence of Poetry, 6, 7, 14, 39, 64, 67, 70, 77, 86, 115, 136, 142, 161, 181, 199, 260–272
  "A Discourse on the Manners of the Ancient Greeks Relative to the Subject of Love," 63, 79–80, 225
  "England in 1819," 12, 23–34, 37, 39, 44, 90, 160, 163, 165, 166, 168, 170
  Epipsychidion, 13, 43, 203–205, 210
  Hellas, 63, 67, 68, 76–81
  "Hymn to Intellectual Beauty," 171, 178
  "Julian and Maddalo," 67
  Laon and Cythna, 63, 71, 214, 265
  The Mask of Anarchy, 1, 12, 23–25, 33, 37, 39, 51, 88, 90, 92, 93, 96, 110, 111, 114, 159, 162–169, 171, 238, 242, 250–256
  "Mont Blanc," 3, 24, 36, 119, 185, 201
  The Necessity of Atheism, 16, 91, 265
  "Ode to Liberty," 90, 209, 210
  "Ode to the West Wind," 44, 90, 164, 169, 269
  "On Launching Some Bottles filled with Knowledge into the Bristol Channel," 238
  "On Life," 44
  "Ozymandias," 1, 10, 96
  Peter Bell the Third, 100, 119, 125, 126
  A Philosophical View of Reform, 110–120
  "Poetical Essay on the Existing State of Things," 90
  Prometheus Unbound, 3, 5, 7, 12, 13, 43–46, 49, 58, 67, 68, 112, 114, 116, 119–122, 124–125, 127–128, 133, 146, 148, 151, 168–169, 171, 176–190, 198, 205–206, 214, 219, 220, 267, 269
  Queen Mab, 1, 3, 5, 44–46, 52, 58, 67, 68, 197, 198, 214, 238, 242, 246–250, 251, 253, 254, 255, 265
  The Revolt of Islam, 12, 119, 159, 160, 166, 169–171
  "Song to the Men of England," 90, 114, 128
  "Stanzas Written in Dejection Near Naples," 119
  The Triumph of Life, 5, 9, 11, 43–59, 116, 206, 214, 220, 242, 260, 261
  "The Vine Shroud," 206–210
  The Witch of Atlas, 5, 14, 214–232
  "To a Skylark," 35
  "To Wordsworth," 122
Sidney, Sir Phillip, 261

Singer, Kate, 13–14, 184, 242
Singer, Tania, 143
Singh, Julietta, 68
Siskin, Clifford, 239
Six Acts, 117
slavery, 7, 10–12, 35, 63–82, 93, 171, 199
Smith, Adam, 121, 138–139, 141, 147
   The Theory of Moral Sentiments, 136, 142, 266
   The Wealth of Nations, 266
Socrates, 45, 50–51, 56, 261
Sophocles, *Oedipus at Colonus*, 59
Southey, Robert, 67, 129, 160, 167
   The Curse of Kehama, 129
Spenser, Edmund, 64, 160, 186
Sperry, Stuart, 48
Spinoza, Baruch, 67, 117, 120, 162
Spolsky, Ellen, 134
Stevens, Wallace, "The Snow Man," 179
Stryker, Susan, "My Words to Victor Frankenstein above the Village of Chamonix," 222
sustainability, 47
Swann, Karen, 223
sympathy, 4, 9, 12, 121, 125, 133–151, 160, 222, 223, 263, 266

temporality, 2–9, 39, 52, 67, 76, 121, 161–166, 169, 183, 238–256, 261, 266
Thomson, James, 65
   "Rule, Britannia!," 78, 79
Too-qua-stee, 10, 24, 29, 33–34, 37–39
   "The Dead Nation: An Elegy at the Tomb of the Cherokee Nation, by One of Her Own Sons," 33, 34
   "A Vision of the End," 34
Trail of Tears, 24, 29, 33. *See also* Indigenous peoples
Traub, Valerie, 216
treaties, 2, 10, 23–39
Tree, Isabella, 201
Tutu, Desmond, 128

vegetarianism, 1, 52, 91, 93, 113–115, 199
vegetation, 195–210
Verderame, Michael, 197
Voltaire, 45, 48, 129
   Candide, 129

Wang, Fuson, 11
Wang, Orrin N. C., 9
Warner, William, 239
Warren, Andrew, 9
Washington, Chris, 201, 220, 222, 241, 242, 244, 245, 247
Wasserman, Earl, 221, 269
Webb, Timothy, 39, 77
Weber, Max, 266, 267
Wellmon, Chad, 266
Wendell, Susan, 52, 53
Westbrook, Harriet, 215
Wilberforce, William, 72, 75
Williams, Jane, 215
Williams, Raymond, 126, 156–157
Wilson, Ross, 13
Wolfson, Susan, 39, 161
Wollstonecraft, Mary, 71, 214, 225
Womack, Craig, 24
Wordsworth, William, 43, 53–54, 70, 122–127, 160, 167, 172, 200, 203
   The Excursion, 204
   "Ode: Intimations of Immortality" from Recollections of Early Childhood, 53–54
   Poems (1815), 122–124
   "The Thorn," 162
workers' movements, 1, 90, 127
Wynter, Sylvia, 216–220, 229

Young, Thomas, 247

Zajonc, Arthur, 243
Zephaniah, Benjamin Obadiah Iqbal, 92–94, 96
Zunshine, Lisa, 134, 144
Zuroski, Eugenia, 70

For EU product safety concerns, contact us at Calle de José Abascal, 56–1°, 28003 Madrid, Spain or eugpsr@cambridge.org.

www.ingramcontent.com/pod-product-compliance
Ingram Content Group UK Ltd.
Pitfield, Milton Keynes, MK11 3LW, UK
UKHW022111260226
468464UK00019B/412